OSF DISTRIBUTED COMPUTING ENVIRONMENT

Guide to Writing

DCE

Applications

OSF DISTRIBUTED COMPUTING ENVIRONMENT

Guide to Writing

DCE

Applications

JOHN SHIRLEY
WEI HU
DAVID MAGID
Digital Equipment Corporation

O'Reilly & Associates, Inc.
103 Morris Street, Suite A
Sebastopol, CA 95472

Guide to Writing DCE Applications
by John Shirley, Wei Hu, and David Magid

Cover design by Edie Freedman
Cover illustration by Chris Reilley

Editor: Andy Oram

Printing History:

June 1992:	First Edition.
March 1993:	Minor corrections.
May 1994:	Second Edition.
November 1994:	Minor corrections.

This book is printed on acid-free paper with 50% recycled content, 10-15% post-consumer waste. O'Reilly & Associates is committed to using paper with the highest recycled content available consistent with high quality.

ISBN: 1-56592-045-7

Table of Contents

Chapter 2: Using a DCE RPC Interface 25

Chapter 3: How to Write Clients 47

Chapter 7: Using Object UUIDs   *135*

Chapter 8: Using Authenticated RPC   *193*

Chapter 9: Writing a Server that Uses Authenticated RPC   *211*

Chapter 10: Context Handles   *235*

Figures

Examples

Tables

Preface

In this book we describe how to develop application programs that use Distributed Computing Environment Remote Procedure Call (DCE RPC) software. DCE RPC enables programs to call procedures that execute in other processes on a network. We do not describe how to migrate applications from earlier versions of RPC to this version. We developed the examples in this book on OSF/1 and MIPS ULTRIX systems. The Grade Server example was also tested on SGI systems running IRIX (SVR4).

Audience

To successfully use this book you need to know the C programming language, be experienced with common programming techniques, and understand some basic networking concepts. We designed this book for two levels of DCE application developers:

- The developer of a client for an application that has an existing interface and server.

- The developer of an interface and server.

Related Documentation

We designed this book to be used with the DCE documentation set. Especially relevant is the documentation set reference material explaining the Interface Definition Language (IDL), attribute configuration files (ACF), and DCE RPC runtime routines. The material explaining threads is also useful to the developer of multi-threaded DCE applications.

Another book in this series, *Understanding DCE*, describes how all the DCE components work together. If you want to use DCE together with systems that run Microsoft RPC, you should also read the O'Reilly book *Distributing Applications Across DCE and Windows NT*.

Utilities used in DCE application development include *uuidgen*, *idl*, and *rpccp*. Reference material on these utilities is also in the DCE documentation set.

Conventions

Throughout the book we use the following typographic conventions:

Constant width

indicates a language construct such as an IDL keyword, a code example, system output, or user input. Words in constant width also represent application-specific variables and procedures.

Bold introduces new terms or concepts.

Italic words or characters in command syntax or examples indicate variables for which the user supplies a value. Italicized words in the text represent system elements such as commands, filenames, directory names, and user functions or RPC-specific routines.

[] enclose attributes in interface definitions and Attribute Configuration Files (ACFs) and are part of the syntax. Note that this is different from the common convention in which brackets enclose optional items in format and syntax descriptions.

% represents system prompts.

S> represents a server system prompt to distinguish it from a client system prompt.

C> represents a client system prompt to distinguish it from a server system prompt.

To execute commands, you must press the Return key. The Return key is assumed (not shown) in examples.

Book Organization

This book is divided into the following eleven chapters and nine appendices:

Chapter 1, *Overview of an RPC Application*, shows how a simple DCE application works.

Chapter 2, *Using a DCE RPC Interface*, shows how to read a DCE RPC interface definition (a file ending in *.idl*), which is a file that declares the remote procedures of an interface.

Chapter 3, *How to Write Clients*, discusses how to develop client programs for DCE RPC interfaces. Topics include binding methods, finding servers, customizing binding handles, handling errors or exceptions, and compiling clients.

Chapter 4, *Pointers and Arrays*, shows how pointers and arrays are defined in an interface and how to develop applications to use them.

Chapter 5, *How to Write a Server*, discusses how to develop a server program for a DCE RPC interface. Topics include initializing a server, writing remote procedures, and compiling servers.

Chapter 6, *Using a Name Service*, describes a name service database and how to use it with distributed applications.

Chapter 7, *Using Object UUIDs*, shows how to use object UUIDs so that clients can choose servers on the basis of resources at the server site.

Chapter 8, *Using Authenticated RPC*, introduces DCE security and shows how to write a client that uses authentication.

Chapter 9, *Writing a Server that Uses Authenticated RPC*, continues the discussion of security and shows how to write a server that uses authentication.

Chapter 10, *Context Handles*, shows how to maintain a state (such as a file handle) on a specific server between remote procedure calls from a specific client.

Chapter 11, *Using Pipes for Large Quantities of Data*, shows how to write DCE programs that efficiently transmit data.

Appendix A, *IDL and ACF Attributes Quick Reference*, shows all the attributes in the interface definition language (IDL) and attribute configuration file (ACF).

Appendix B, *DCE RPC Runtime Routines Quick Reference*, shows all the RPC runtime routines organized into convenient categories.

Appendix C, *The Arithmetic Application*, is a small application that shows the basics of remote procedure calls.

Appendix D, *The Inventory Application*, is a somewhat richer application than *The Arithmetic Application*, showing different IDL data types, how to use attribute configuration files (ACFs), and how to find servers by importing information from a name service database.

Appendix E, *The OK Banking Application*, shows a basic use of Object UUIDs.

Appendix F, *The Better Banking Application*, takes the Appendix G application several steps further and shows a recommended use of Object UUIDs.

Appendix G, *The Grade Server Application*, shows how to implement simple security in an RPC application.

Appendix H, *The Remote_file Application*, shows how to use context handles and how to find servers using strings of network location information.

Appendix I, *The Transfer_data Application*, shows how to use advanced RPC features including pipes and customized binding handles.

How to Use this Book

If you are just developing a client for an existing DCE RPC interface and server, read the following chapters first:

- Chapter 1, *Overview of an RPC Application*
- Chapter 2, *Using a DCE RPC Interface*
- Chapter 3, *How to Write Clients*

Read other chapters as needed to learn how to develop applications that use more features of interface definitions.

If you are developing a network interface with accompanying server, read the following:

- Chapter 1, *Overview of an RPC Application*
- Chapter 2, *Using a DCE RPC Interface*
- Chapter 3, *How to Write Clients*
- Chapter 4, *Pointers and Arrays*
- Chapter 5, *How to Write a Server*

Obtaining the Example Programs

The example programs in this book are available electronically in a number of ways: by FTP, FTPMAIL, BITFTP, and UUCP. The cheapest, fastest, and easiest ways are listed first. If you read from the top down, the first one that works for you is probably the best. Use FTP if you are directly on the

Internet. Use ftpmail if you are not on the Internet, but can send and receive electronic mail to internet sites (this includes CompuServe users). Use BITFTP if you send electronic mail via BITNET. Use UUCP if none of the above work.

FTP

To use FTP, you need a machine with direct access to the Internet. A sample session is shown, with what you should type in boldface.

```
% ftp ftp.uu.net
Connected to ftp.uu.net.
220 ftp.UU.NET FTP server (Version 6.34 Thu Oct 22 14:32:01 EDT 1992) ready.
Name (ftp.uu.net:andyo): anonymous
331 Guest login ok, send e-mail address as password.
Password: andyo@ora.com (use your user name and host here)
230 Guest login ok, access restrictions apply.
ftp> cd /published/oreilly/dce/applic_guide
250 CWD command successful.
ftp> binary (Very important! You must specify binary transfer for compressed files.)
200 Type set to I.
ftp> prompt (Convenient, so you are not queried for every file transferred)
Interactive mode off.
ftp> mget *
200 PORT command successful.
        .
        .
        .
ftp> quit
221 Goodbye.
%
```

Each *.Z* archive contains all the source code and configuration information required for building one example. Extract each example through a command like:

```
% zcat arithmetic.apr94.tar.Z | tar xf -
```

System V systems require the following *tar* command instead:

```
% zcat arithmetic.apr94.tar.Z | tar xof -
```

If *zcat* is not available on your system, use separate *uncompress* and *tar* commands.

The *tar* command creates a subdirectory that holds all the files from its archive. The *README.apr94* file in this subdirectory describes the goals of the example and how to build and run it; the text is an ASCII version of the introductory material from the corresponding appendix in this book.

FTPMAIL

FTPMAIL is a mail server available to anyone who can send and receive electronic mail to and from Internet sites. This includes most workstations that have an e-mail connection to the outside world, and CompuServe users. You do not need to be directly on the Internet. Here's how to use FTPMAIL.

Send mail to *ftpmail@decwrl.dec.com.* In the message body, give the name of the anonymous *ftp* host and the *ftp* commands you want to run. The server will run anonymous *ftp* for you and mail the files back to you. To get a complete help file, send a message with no subject and the single word "help" in the body. The following is an example mail session that should get you the examples. This command sends you a listing of the files in the selected directory, and the requested example files. The listing is useful in case there's a later version of the examples you're interested in.

```
% mail ftpmail@decwrl.dec.com
Subject:
reply andyo@ora.com              (where you want files mailed)
connect ftp.uu.net
chdir /published/oreilly/dce/applic_guide
dir
get README.apr94
binary
uuencode                          (or btoa if you have it)
get arithmetic.apr94.tar.Z
get inventory.apr94.tar.Z
get ok_banking.apr94.tar.Z
get better_banking.apr94.tar.Z
get grade_server.apr94.tar.Z
get remote_file.apr94.tar.Z
get transfer_data.apr94.tar.Z
quit
%
```

A signature at the end of the message is acceptable as long as it appears after "quit."

All retrieved files will be split into 60KB chunks and mailed to you. You then remove the mail headers and concatenate them into one file, and then *uudecode* or *atob* it. Once you've got the desired *.Z* files, follow the directions under FTP to extract the files from the archive.

VMS, DOS, and Apple Macintosh versions of *uudecode, atob, uncompress,* and *tar* are available. The VMS versions are on *gatekeeper.dec.com in /archive/pub/VMS.*

BITFTP

BITFTP is a mail server for BITNET users. You send it electronic mail messages requesting files, and it sends the files back to you by electronic mail. BITFTP currently serves only users who send it mail from nodes that are directly on BITNET, EARN, or NetNorth. BITFTP is a public service of Princeton University. Here's how it works:

To use BITFTP, send mail containing your ftp commands to *BITFTP@PUCC*. For a complete help file, send HELP as the message body.

The following is the message body you should send to BITFTP:

```
FTP  ftp.uu.net  NETDATA
USER  anonymous
PASS your Internet e-mail address (not your bitnet address)
CD  /published/oreilly/dce/applic_guide
DIR
GET README.apr94
BINARY
GET arithmetic.apr94.tar.Z
GET inventory.apr94.tar.Z
GET ok_banking.apr94.tar.Z
GET better_banking.apr94.tar.Z
GET grade_server.apr94.tar.Z
GET remote_file.apr94.tar.Z
GET transfer_data.apr94.tar.Z
QUIT
```

Once you've got the desired *.Z* files, follow the directions under FTP to extract the files from the archive. Since you are probably not on a UNIX system, you may need to get versions of *uudecode, uncompress, atob*, and *tar* for your system. VMS, DOS, and Apple Macintosh versions are available. The VMS versions are on *gatekeeper.dec.com* in */archive/pub/VMS*.

Questions about BITFTP can be directed to Melinda Varian, *MAINT@PUCC* on BITNET.

UUCP

UUCP is standard on virtually all UNIX systems, and is available for IBM-compatible PCs and Apple Macintoshes. The examples are available by UUCP via modem from UUNET; UUNET's connect-time charges apply.

You can get the examples from UUNET whether you have an account or not. If you or your company has an account with UUNET, you will have a system with a direct UUCP connection to UUNET. Find that system, and type:

```
uucp uunet\!~/published/oreilly/dce/applic_guide/  yourhost\!~/yourname/
```

The backslashes can be omitted if you use the Bourne shell (*sh*) instead of *csh*. The files should appear some time later (up to a day or more) in the directory */usr/spool/uucppublic/yourname*. If you don't have an account but would like one so that you can get electronic mail, then contact UUNET at 703-204-8000.

If you don't have a UUNET account, you can set up a UUCP connection to UUNET using the phone number 1-900-468-7727. As of this writing, the cost is 50 cents per minute. The charges will appear on your next telephone bill. The login name is "uucp" with no password. For example, an *L.sys/Systems* entry might look like:

```
uunet Any ACU 19200 1-900-468-7727 ogin:--ogin: uucp
```

Your entry may vary depending on your UUCP configuration. If you have a PEP-capable modem, make sure s50=255s111=30 is set before calling.

It's a good idea to get the file */published/oreilly/dce/applic_guide/ls-lR.Z* as a short test file containing the filenames and sizes of all the files in the directory.

Once you've got the desired *.Z* files, follow the directions under FTP to extract the files from the archives.

PC-DCE Examples

Gradient Technologies, Inc. has released a version of DCE called PC-DCE, which runs on Microsoft Windows and has been licensed by several vendors. While the techniques in this book were developed on UNIX systems, they apply equally well to PC-DCE. The examples, however, require some changes to adapt to a different operating system.

Ray Costello at Gradient has written Windows versions of the seven examples in this book, and that company has kindly offered to make them available to the public. We have placed them online in the directory */published/oreilly/dce/applic_guide/pc-dce*. Look there for the files:

```
arithmet.apr94.tar.Z
inventry.apr94.tar.Z
ok.apr94.tar.Z
better.apr94.tar.Z
grade.apr94.tar.Z
remote_f.apr94.tar.Z
xferdata.apr94.tar.Z
```

Acknowledgments

This book originated as a companion to Digital Equipment Corporation's DCE documentation set. We are in debt to Tonie Franz and Frank Willison, then managers at Digital, both of whom contracted John to write the first edition of this book. Their confidence in John gave him an opportunity that he found exceptionally rewarding. We especially thank the architects and developers of the IDL compiler at Digital, including Jerry Harrow, Tony Hinxman, Dick Annicchiarico, and Al Simons. Numerous reviews and good advice were also received from developers, writers, and editors at Digital, including Margie Showman, Ken Ouellette, Mary Orcutt, and Marll McDonald.

After several drafts were complete, some people thought this book should be published on its own. This required significant additions of material to explain portions of DCE. Andrew Oram and Steve Talbott were the driving force coaxing us to find the important explanatory information to accompany the programming examples. Some of the people at O'Reilly & Associates who put great efforts into this book include Eileen Kramer, Jeff Robbins, and Edie Freedman. Engineers at Locus Computing Corporation who reviewed portions of this book include Mark Heroux, Clem Cole, and Marty Port. We are indebted to the management at Locus for making Clem available to us in a general advisory role.

Additional help and support came from Ram Sudama, Diane Sherman, Susan Scott, David Strohmeyer, Karol McIntyre, Wei Hu, Susan Hunziker, Andy Ferris, Vicki Janicki, Beth Martin, Dan Cobb, Lois Frampton, Steve Miller, Madeline Cormier, Jim Teague, Eric Jendrock, Gary Schmitt, Ellen Vliet, Judy Davies, Judy Egan, Ward Rosenberry, Collis Jackson, David Kenney, Suzanne Lipsky, Darrell Icenogle, Terry Tvrdik, Howard Mayberry, and of course John's wife, Linda McClary.

The second edition of this book benefitted particularly from the comments of Gerald Cantor, Choong Y. Chew, Ray Costello, Irene Hu, Ken Ouellette, and Ram Sudama. Gerald Cantor generously offered source code to illustrate some security-related techniques. Leslie Chalmers copyedited and produced the second edition.

Thanks go to Ray Costello at Gradient Technologies, Inc., for providing the Windows versions of examples in this book, and to David Kenney there for coordinating the sharing of examples between O'Reilly and Gradient.

Joint Venture

This book was produced as a cooperative effort between Digital Equipment Corporation and O'Reilly & Associates. We wish in particular to thank Tonie Franz, a former Publications Supervisor at Digital, and Frank Willison, former Publications Manager. Tonie's intelligent and energetic oversight of the writing process was key to the book's successful completion, while Frank's surpassing skill and delicacy in clearing a path through corporate formalities was essential both to get the project under way and to keep it moving smoothly.

While we at O'Reilly & Associates frequently work closely with vendors of hardware and software, this book gave us an opportunity for much more extensive cooperation and mutual support than is customary. It is a model we like, and we believe the end result testifies to the value of sharing one's resources in this way.

1

Overview of an RPC Application

A traditional application is a single program running on a single computer system, where a procedure and its caller execute in the same address space. In contrast, the **client-server model** for distributed applications embodies a client program (client) and a server program (server), usually running on different systems of a network. The client makes a request to the server, which is usually a continuously running daemon process, and the server sends a response back to the client (see Figure 1-1).

The **remote procedure call** mechanism is the simplest way to implement client-server applications because it keeps the details of network communications out of your application code. The idea is that each side behaves as much as possible the way it would within a traditional application: the programmer on the client side issues a call, and the programmer on the server side writes a procedure to carry out the desired function. To convey the illusion that you are working in a single address space, some hidden code has to handle all the networking. Many related issues are also involved, such as converting data between formats for different systems, and detecting communication errors.

Figure 1-2 shows the relationship between your application code and the RPC mechanism during a remote procedure call. In client application code, a remote procedure call looks like a local procedure call, because it is actually a call to a client stub. (A **stub** is surrogate code that supports remote procedure calls. Later in this chapter we'll discuss how stubs are created and what they do.) The **client stub** communicates with the **server stub** using the **RPC runtime library**, which is a set of standard runtime routines that supports all DCE RPC applications.)

The server's RPC runtime library receives the remote procedure call and hands the client information to the server stub. The server stub invokes the remote procedure in the server application.

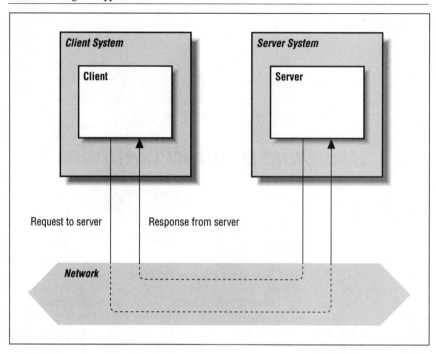

Figure 1-1: Client-server model

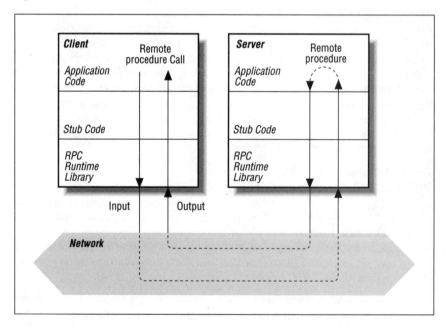

Figure 1-2: RPC mechanism

When the server finishes executing the remote procedure, its stub communicates output to the client stub, again by using the RPC runtime library. Finally, the client stub returns to the client application code.

Figure 1-3 shows the three phases required to develop a distributed application. An essential part of the RPC mechanism is an **interface**, which is a set of remote procedure declarations. Given the same interface, client and server development of an application can occur in parallel and on separate systems of the network.

In this chapter we will create an entire RPC application from scratch. Naturally, we'll use every shortcut and simplification the system offers to accomplish this feat. But when you get done with the chapter, you will know the place of all the major RPC features, and how an application is developed.

You may not need to develop an entire application as shown in this chapter. If the interface and server already exist, your development may require only the client.

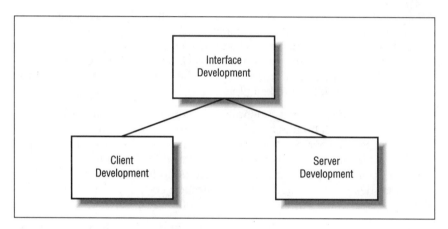

Figure 1-3: Application development

The arithmetic application

The arithmetic example in this chapter demonstrates a very simple one-client/one-server RPC application. Suppose a remote server system uses special hardware, such as an array processor. In our example, the client performs an arithmetic operation on arrays by calling a remote procedure that uses the array processor. The remote procedure executes on the server system, taking two arrays as arguments and adding together the elements of the arrays. The remote procedure returns the results to the client in a third array argument. Finally, the results of the remote procedure are displayed on the client system.

The arithmetic example is deliberately limited in order to demonstrate the basics of a distributed application implemented with RPC. We describe each portion of the application in this chapter, and Appendix C shows the complete code. The preface tells you how to obtain source code online for this example, and other examples in the book. Windows versions for PC-DCE, the Gradient Technologies product, are also available online.

A Simple Interface

When writing a local application, should you start by deciding exactly what functions you'll call and what arguments they take? Well, if you were dividing the work among multiple programmers and needed to clarify the interfaces between their work, you probably would proceed that way. The same reasoning applies to a distributed program: the client and server are being developed separately. Since the boundary or interface between them is the procedure call itself, you have to specify its attributes at the start.

So an interface consists of what the client and the server have to agree on; it contains some identifying information and a few facts about the remote procedures. Each **procedure declaration** includes the name of the procedure, the data type of the value it returns (if any), and the order and data types of its parameters (if any). An **interface definition** contains a set of procedure declarations and data types.

Just as programmers select functions from libraries, client application writers use interface definitions to determine how to call remote procedures. Server application writers use interface definitions to determine the data type of the remote procedure's return value, and the number, order, and data types of the arguments. The interface definition is like a design document that ties the client and server application code together. It is a formal definition describing the set of procedures offered by the interface.

You write the interface definition in the **Interface Definition Language** (IDL). The IDL closely resembles the declaration syntax and semantics of C. But attributes have been added, and these allow information to be sent over a network.

You may think that we have introduced an unnecessary level of complexity here, but you will see that keeping the salient features of a distributed application in one file—the interface definition—makes it easier to scale up development to multiple servers and many clients for those servers.

Figure 1-4 shows the utilities used and the files produced when developing the arithmetic interface. The *uuidgen* utility generates a **universal unique identifier** (UUID) used in the interface definition to distinguish this interface from any other interface on the network. You use a text editor to write the rest of the interface definition, *arithmetic.idl*. When the interface definition is complete, compile it with the IDL compiler (*idl*) to generate stubs and a C header file that you use to develop the client and server programs.

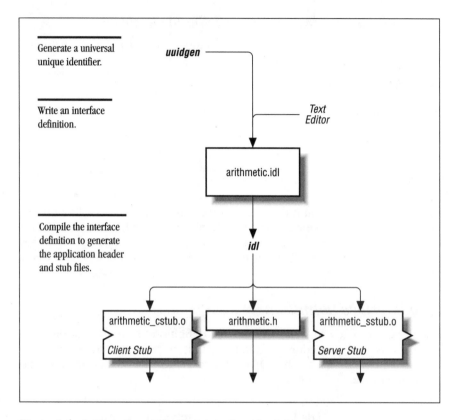

Figure 1-4: Arithmetic application: interface development

Universal Unique Identifiers

When you write a new interface, you must first generate a universal unique identifier (UUID) with *uuidgen*. A UUID is simply a number that the *uuidgen* utility generates using time and network address information so that no matter when or where it is generated, it is guaranteed to be unique. A UUID is like a fingerprint that uniquely identifies something—such as an interface—across all network configurations.

An interface UUID is an excellent example of how you tie a client and server together through the IDL file. When a client makes a remote procedure call, its UUID has to match that of the server. The RPC runtime library performs this check; this way you don't get unexpected results.

More complicated applications use UUIDs for other reasons besides identifying an interface. These uses are discussed in Chapter 7, *Object UUIDs*.

Generating a UUID in an interface definition template

To generate and display a UUID in a template for an interface definition, type the following command:

```
% uuidgen -i
[
uuid(A0DF7780-4C89-11C9-BD65-08002B0ECEF1),
version(1.0)
]
interface INTERFACENAME
{

}
```

In this example, the output appears at the terminal, but generally you save it in a file with the extension *.idl*. Replace the template name INTER-FACENAME with a name you choose for the new interface. In the next section, we use a template like this to develop the arithmetic interface definition.

The Interface Definition

Now we are ready to write an interface definition. Here we put data type definitions and procedure declarations that need to be shared between server and client. Later, the IDL compiler creates the header file and stubs from the interface definition, for use in your application.

The interface definition includes syntax elements called **attributes**, which specify features needed for distributed applications. Attributes convey information about the whole interface or items in the interface, including data types, arrays, pointers, structure members, union cases, procedures, and procedure parameters. For example, the in attribute specifies an input parameter for a remote procedure. You can pick out attributes in the file because they're enclosed in square brackets.

Example 1-1 shows a simple interface definition. The text consists of a **header** and **body**. The header contains a uuid attribute and the name assigned to the interface. The body specifies all procedures for the interface; it contains the procedure declarations with the data types and constants that are used in the procedure declarations. There is only one procedure declared in our example, and that procedure adds two input arrays and returns the results in a third array.

Example 1-1: A Simple Interface Definition

```
/* FILE NAME: arithmetic.idl */
/* This Interface Definition Language file represents a basic arithmetic */
/* procedure that a remote procedure call application can use.          */
[
uuid(C985A380-255B-11C9-A50B-08002B0ECEF1)          /* Universal Unique ID ❶*/
]
interface arithmetic                      /* interface name is arithmetic❷*/
{
    const unsigned short ARRAY_SIZE = 10; /* unsigned integer constant  ❸*/
    typedef long long_array[ARRAY_SIZE];  /* array type of long integers❹*/

    void sum_arrays (    /* sum_arrays procedure does not return a value ❺*/
        [in] long_array a,              /* 1st parameter is passed in  */
        [in] long_array b,              /* 2nd parameter is passed in  */
        [out] long_array c              /* 3rd parameter is passed out */
    );
}
```

❶ The uuid attribute specifies the interface UUID. The interface definition header for any distributed application requires a uuid attribute.

❷ The last part of the interface definition header contains the keyword interface followed by the name chosen for the interface (arithmetic).

❸ You can define constants for type definitions and application code. In this example, we define ARRAY_SIZE to set the bounds of arrays.

❹ You can define data types for use in other type definitions and procedure declarations. In this example, we define a data type that is an array of ten long integers. The indexes of arrays begin at 0, so the index values for this array range from 0 to 9.

❺ The remainder of this interface definition is a procedure declaration. A procedure of type void does not return a value. The in and out parameter attributes are necessary so the IDL compiler knows which direction the data needs to be sent over the network.

> [in]: A value is passed in to the remote procedure when it is called from the client.
>
> [out]: A value is passed back from the server to the calling procedure on the client when the procedure returns. A parameter with the out directional attribute must be a pointer or array so that the parameter can be passed to the client stub by reference.

Stub and Header Generation Using the IDL Compiler

When the interface definition is complete, you compile it with the IDL compiler, which creates the following:

- A C language header file that contains definitions needed by the stubs and your application code. You can now include the header file in client and server application code.

- A client stub file, which you will link with the client portion of the application. During a remote procedure call, the client stub code is intermediate between your client application code and the RPC runtime library.

- A server stub file, which you will link with the server portion of the application. During a remote procedure call, the server stub code is intermediate between your server application code and the RPC runtime library.

When you invoke the IDL compiler, the interface definition goes through two phases: a preprocessing phase that generates the header file and intermediate C language stub files, and a compilation phase that generates stub object code.

To invoke the IDL compiler and create the header and stub files for the arithmetic interface, type the following:

```
% idl arithmetic.idl
```

In this example, we generate the header file and the object stub files of the client and server in one compilation. The IDL compiler generates object stub files by default, but you may retain intermediate C language stub files by using appropriate IDL compiler options.

If you develop the client and server on different systems, copies of the interface definition and the IDL compiler must reside on both the client and server systems. To generate object code correctly for different kinds of systems, compile the interface definition for the client stub on the client system, and for the server stub on the server system.

A Simple Client

We'll start our coding with the client because it's so simple. In fact, you will not be able to detect any difference between our client and a traditional, single-system program! That's one of the beauties about DCE—it hides most of the networking complexity from the client developer.

To develop a client, you have to be able to read and interpret the interface definition. To use all the capabilities of RPC, you must also know the RPC runtime routines. The client example here, however, requires no RPC runtime routines.

Figure 1-5 shows the files and utilities needed to produce a client. You write the client application code (*client.c*) in C. Currently, DCE provides libraries only for C. Remote procedure calls in a client look like local procedure calls. (The server portion of the application implements the remote procedures themselves.) You must include the header file (*arithmetic.h*) produced by the IDL compiler, so that its type and constant definitions are available.

After compiling *client.c* with the C compiler, you can create the executable client by linking the client stub (*arithmetic_cstub.o*), which is produced by the IDL compiler, with the client object file and the DCE library. Example 1-2 shows a simple client.

Example 1-2: A Simple Client

```
/* FILE NAME: client.c */
/* This is the client module of the arithmetic example. */
#include <stdio.h>
#include "arithmetic.h"    /* header file created by IDL compiler ❶*/

long_array a ={100,200,345,23,67,65,0,0,0,0};
long_array b ={4,0,2,3,1,7,5,9,6,8};

main ()
{
    long_array result;
    int       i;

    sum_arrays(a, b, result);          /* A Remote Procedure Call ❷*/
    puts("sums:");
    for(i = 0; i < ARRAY_SIZE; i++)
      printf("%ld\n", result[i]);
}
```

❶ The client code includes the header file produced by the IDL compiler.

❷ The client calls the remote procedure **sum_arrays** using the two initialized arrays as input. It then displays the elements of the resulting array.

The following section shows how to write the server for the arithmetic application.

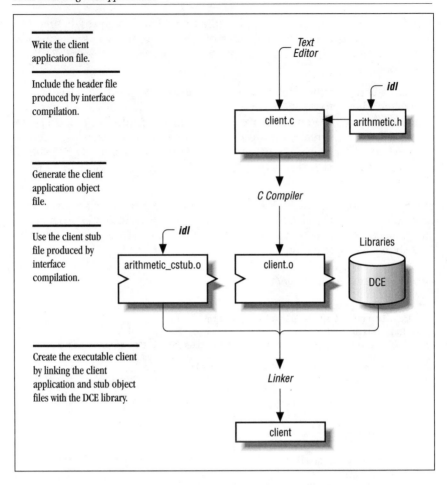

Figure 1-5: Arithmetic application: client development

A Minimal Server

Developing a server requires you to know the interface definition and some RPC runtime routines. You write two distinct portions of code:

- The actual remote procedures—this is sometimes called the **manager**

- Code to initialize the server

You make calls to the RPC runtime routines mainly in the server initialization, which prepares the server to listen for remote procedure calls. For our arithmetic application, server initialization is the only code that requires the use of runtime routines.

Figure 1-6 shows the files and utilities needed to produce a server. You must write the remote procedures (*procedure.c*) and server initialization code (*server.c*) in C. You need the header file (*arithmetic.h*) produced by the IDL compiler because it contains definitions required by the remote procedures and runtime calls.

After compiling the server application with the C compiler, you create the executable server by linking the server stub (*arithmetic_sstub.o*), which is produced by the IDL compiler, with the server application object files and the DCE library.

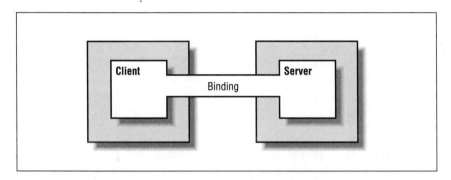

Figure 1-6: Arithmetic application: server development

Remote Procedure Implementation

The programmer who writes a server must develop all procedures that are declared in the interface definition. Refer to the interface definition (*arithmetic.idl*) and the header file generated by the IDL compilation (*arithmetic.h*) for the procedure's parameters and data types. Example 1-3 shows the code for the remote procedure of the arithmetic application.

Example 1-3: A Remote Procedure Implementation

```
/* FILE NAME: procedure.c */
/* Implementation of procedure defined in the arithmetic interface. */
#include <stdio.h>
#include "arithmetic.h"          /* header file produced by IDL compiler ❶*/

void sum_arrays(a, b, c)         /* implementation of sum_arrays procedure ❷*/
    long_array a;
    long_array b;
    long_array c;
    {
    int i;
```

Example 1-3: A Remote Procedure Implementation (continued)

```
for(i = 0; i < ARRAY_SIZE; i++)
    c[i] = a[i] + b[i];      /* array elements are each added together ❸*/
}
```

❶ The server code includes the header file produced by the IDL compiler.

❷ The procedure definition matches its corresponding declaration in the interface definition.

❸ The procedure implementation is completed.

So far, the client and server application code has been much like any other application. In fact, you can compile and link the client and remote procedures, and run the resulting program as a local test.

Before going on to write the server initialization code, we found it useful to discuss how the arithmetic application works in a distributed environment.

A Distributed Application Environment

When a client makes a remote procedure call, a **binding** relationship is established with a server (see Figure 1-7). **Binding information** is network communication and location information for a particular server. Conveniently, in the arithmetic application, the client stub and the RPC runtime library automatically find the server for you during the remote procedure call. Figure 1-8 illustrates that binding information acts like a set of keys to a series of gates in the path a remote procedure call takes toward execution.

Binding information includes the following:

1. **Protocol Sequence**

   A protocol sequence is an RPC-specific name containing a combination of communication protocols that describe the network communication used between a client and server. For example, ncacn_ip_tcp represents the protocol sequence for a Network Computing Architecture connection-oriented protocol, over a network with the Internet Protocol and the Transmission Control Protocol for transport.

2. **Server Host**

   The client needs to identify the server system. The server host is the name or network address of the host on which the server resides.

3. **Endpoint**

   The client needs to identify a server process on the server host. An endpoint is a number representing a specific server process running on a system. It is typically a port number for TCP or UDP.

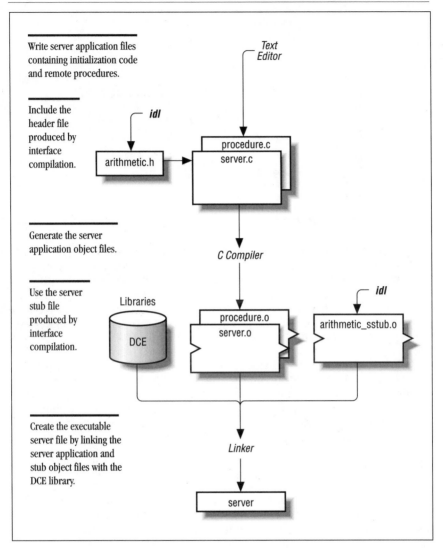

Figure 1-7: Binding

To help clients find servers in a flexible and portable manner, DCE provides a name service to store binding information. **Name service** is a general term for a database service that stores information for distributed applications—that is, a service that offers the same information to applications running on different systems. Using the name service, a server can store binding information that a client on another system can retrieve later. The particular name service offered with DCE is called the Cell Directory Service (CDS). (The terms "name service" and "directory service" are equivalent.)

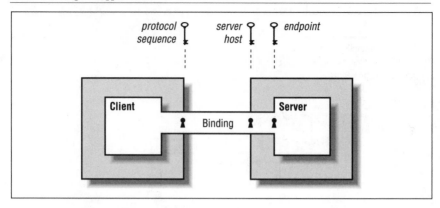

Figure 1-8: Binding information

The RPC runtime library contains a general set of functions called **name service independent** (NSI) routines. Thus, to store binding information, your server calls an NSI routine. This routine internally communicates with CDS in order to put information into the database. NSI routines are a level of abstraction above the particular name service on a system. So they could theoretically be used to access another name service, in case your system didn't have CDS (but all DCE systems do).

Distributed applications do not require the name service database, but we recommend that you use it. Alternatives to using the name service are to manage binding information directly in client and server code, or to create your own application-specific method of advertising and searching for servers. These alternatives present more maintenance problems than if you use the name service routines.

Figures 1-9, 1-10, and 1-11 show how the arithmetic application uses binding information, and how the remote procedure call completes.

A server must make certain information available to clients. Figure 1-9 shows the typical steps needed each time a server starts executing. A server first registers the interface with the RPC runtime library, so that clients later know whether they are compatible with the server. The runtime library creates binding information to identify this server process. The server places the binding information in appropriate databases so that clients can find it. The server places communication and host information in the name service database. The server also places process information (endpoints) in a special database on the server system called the **local endpoint map**, which is a database used to store endpoints for servers running on a given system. In the final initialization step, a server waits while listening for remote procedure calls from clients.

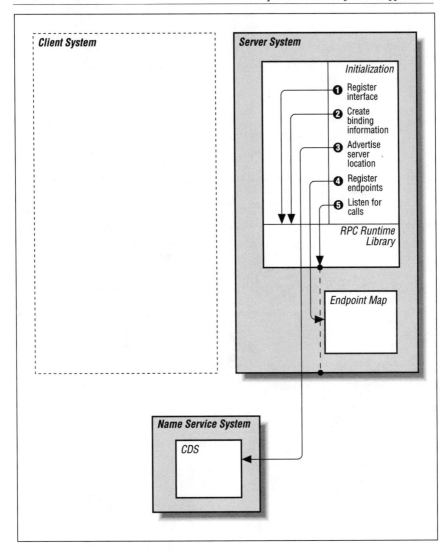

Figure 1-9: Server initializing

When the server has completed initialization, a client can find it by obtaining its binding information, as illustrated in Figure 1-10. A remote procedure call in the client application code transfers execution to the client stub. The client stub looks up the information in the name service database to find the server system. The RPC runtime library finds the server process endpoint by looking up the information in the server system's endpoint map. The RPC runtime library uses the binding information to complete the binding of the client to the server. Chapter 3, *How to Write Clients*, discusses variations on how to obtain server binding information.

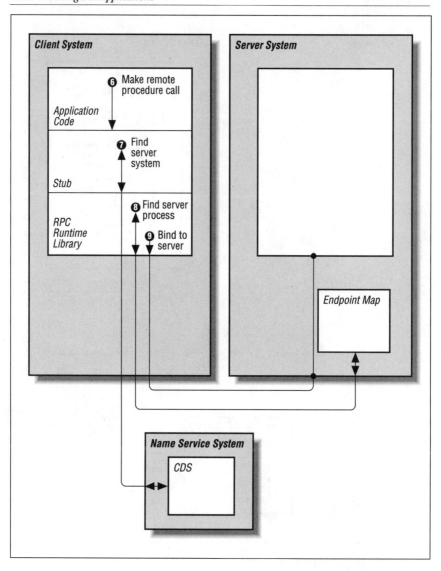

Figure 1-10: Client finding a server

As shown in Figure 1-11, the remote procedure executes after the client finds the server. The client stub puts arguments and other calling information into an internal RPC format that the runtime library transmits over the network. The server runtime library receives the data and transfers it to the stub, which converts it back to a format the application can use. When the remote procedure completes, the conversion process is reversed. The server stub puts the return arguments into the internal RPC format, and the server runtime library transmits the data back to the client over the network. The client runtime library receives the data and gives it to the client stub, which converts the data back for use by the application.

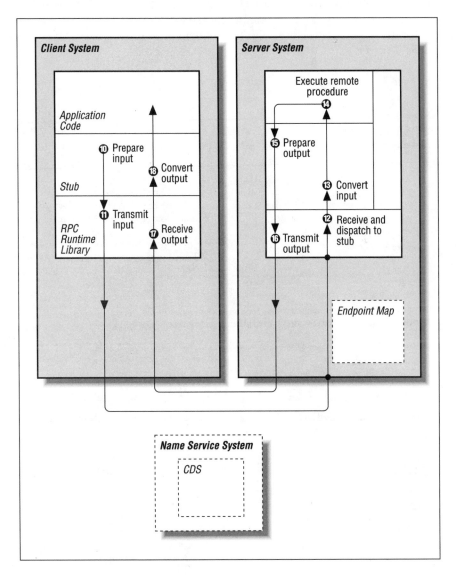

Figure 1-11: Completing a remote procedure call

Server Initialization

As illustrated in Figure 1-9, a server must make certain information available to the RPC runtime library and clients, before it can accept remote procedure calls. Example 1-4 contains the server initialization code for the arithmetic application, illustrating the sequence of steps to initialize a typical RPC server.

Example 1-4: A Minimal Server Initialization

```
/* FILE NAME: server.c */
#include <stdio.h>
#include "arithmetic.h"              /* header created by the IDL compiler */
#include "check_status.h"            /* header with the CHECK_STATUS macro */

main ()
{
    unsigned32          status;            /* error status (nbase.h)        */
    rpc_binding_vector_t *binding_vector; /*set of binding handles(rpcbase.h)*/
    unsigned_char_t     *entry_name; /*entry name for name service (lbase.h)*/
    char *getenv();
    rpc_server_register_if(     /* register interface with the RPC runtime ❶*/
        arithmetic_v0_0_s_ifspec,   /* interface specification (arithmetic.h) */
        NULL,
        NULL,
        &status                                            /* error status */
    );
    CHECK_STATUS(status, "Can't register interface\n", ABORT);

    rpc_server_use_all_protseqs(            /* create binding information ❷*/
        rpc_c_protseq_max_reqs_default,  /* queue size for calls    (rpcbase.h)*/
        &status
    );
    CHECK_STATUS(status, "Can't create binding information\n", ABORT);

    rpc_server_inq_bindings(    /* obtain this server's binding information ❸*/
        &binding_vector,
        &status
    );
    CHECK_STATUS(status, "Can't get binding information\n", ABORT);

    entry_name = (unsigned_char_t *)getenv("ARITHMETIC_SERVER_ENTRY");
    rpc_ns_binding_export(      /* export entry to name service database ❹*/
        rpc_c_ns_syntax_default,     /* syntax of the entry name   (rpcbase.h) */
        entry_name,                  /* entry name for name service        */
        arithmetic_v0_0_s_ifspec,    /* interface specification (arithmetic.h)*/
        binding_vector,              /* the set of server binding handles  */
        NULL,
        &status
    );
    CHECK_STATUS(status, "Can't export to name service database\n", ABORT);
```

Example 1-4: A Minimal Server Initialization (continued)

```
rpc_ep_register(              /* register endpoints in local endpoint map ❺*/
    arithmetic_v0_0_s_ifspec,  /* interface specification (arithmetic.h) */
    binding_vector,            /* the set of server binding handles      */
    NULL,
    NULL,
    &status
);
CHECK_STATUS(status, "Can't add address to the endpoint map\n", ABORT);

rpc_binding_vector_free(      /* free set of server binding handles ❻*/
    &binding_vector,
    &status
);
CHECK_STATUS(status, "Can't free binding handles and vector\n", ABORT);

puts("Listening for remote procedure calls...");
rpc_server_listen(            /* listen for remote calls            ❼*/
    rpc_c_listen_max_calls_default,/*concurrent calls serviced (rpcbase.h)*/
    &status
);
CHECK_STATUS(status, "rpc listen failed\n", ABORT);
}
```

❶ **Register the interface.** Register the interface with the RPC runtime library by using the *rpc_server_register_if* routine. The arithmetic_v0_0_s_ifspec variable is called an **interface handle**. It is produced by the IDL compiler and refers to information that applications need, such as the UUID. We describe the NULL arguments in Chapter 5, *How to Write a Server*.

The CHECK_STATUS macro is defined in the *check_status.h* header file for the applications in this book. It is used to interpret status codes from runtime calls (see Example 3-12). Figure 1-9, step 1 is now complete.

❷ **Create binding information.** To create binding information, you must choose one or more network protocol sequences. This application, like most, calls *rpc_server_use_all_protseqs* so that clients can use all available protocols. During this call, the RPC runtime library gathers together information about available protocols, your host, and endpoints to create binding information. The system allocates a buffer for each endpoint, to hold incoming call information. DCE sets the buffer size when you use the *rpc_c_protseq_max_calls_default* argument.

❸ **Obtain the binding information.** When creating binding information, the RPC runtime library stores binding information for each protocol sequence. A **binding handle** is a reference in application code to the information for one possible binding. A set of server binding handles is called a **binding vector.** You must obtain this information through the *rpc_server_inq_bindings* routine to pass the information to other DCE services with other runtime routines. Figure 1-9, step 2 is now complete.

❹ **Advertise the server location in the name service database.** In this example, the server places (exports) all its binding information in the name service database using the *rpc_ns_binding_export* runtime routine.

The *rpc_c_ns_syntax_default* argument tells the routine how to interpret an entry name. (The current version of DCE has only one syntax.) The `entry_name` is a string obtained in this example from an environment variable set by the user specifically for this application, ARITHMETIC_SERVER_ENTRY (discussed at the end of this chapter when the appliction is run). The interface handle, `arithmetic_v0_0_s_ifspec`, associates interface information with the entry name in the name service database. The client later uses name service routines to obtain binding information by comparing the interface information in the name service database with information about its own interface. Figure 1-9, step 3 is now complete.

❺ **Register the endpoints in the local endpoint map.** The RPC runtime library assigns endpoints to the server as part of creating binding information. The *rpc_ep_register* runtime routine lets the endpoint map on the local host know that the process running at these endpoints is associated with this interface. Figure 1-9, step 4 is now complete.

❻ **Free the set of binding handles.** Memory for the binding handles was allocated with a call to the *rpc_server_inq_bindings* routine. When you have finished passing binding information to other parts of DCE, release the memory using the *rpc_binding_vector_free* routine.

❼ **Listen for remote calls.** Finally, the server must wait for calls to arrive. Each system has a default for the maximum number of calls that a server can accept at one time. DCE sets this maximum when you use the *rpc_c_listen_max_calls_default* argument. Figure 1-9, step 5 is now complete.

All of the server code is now complete. The compilation of the application is shown in the next section.

Producing the Application

So far we have written the interface definition, produced the stubs and header file from the interface definition with the IDL compiler, and written the client and server portions of the application. To produce the application, compile and link the client and server separately, each on the system where you want its executable to run.

DCE Libraries

DCE-distributed applications must be linked with the DCE libraries, which may vary depending on your system and vendor. This book uses the following options for a link on an OSF/1 system:

```
-ldce -lcma
```

The **-lcma** option (Concert Multithreaded Architecture library) is required because DCE RPC uses threads internally. To use the makefiles shown in the appendices of this book, you may need to modify the list of libraries; check your DCE vendor's documentation.

The following sections assume that your client and server files are available to the respective client and server systems.

Compile and Link the Client Code

Recall that Figure 1-5 shows the utilities used and files produced when developing a client. The compilation and final link of the client are shown here:

1. Compile the client C language source file on the client system (represented by the shell prompt, **C>**) to generate the client object file.

   ```
   C> cc -c client.c
   ```

2. Link the client object file and client stub file with the DCE library to create the executable client file.

   ```
   C>  cc -o client client.o arithmetic_cstub.o -ldce -lcma
   ```

Compile and Link the Server Code

Recall that Figure 1-6 shows the utilities used and files produced when developing a server. The compilation and final link of the server are shown here:

1. Compile the server C language source files on the server system (represented by the shell prompt, **S>**), including the remote procedure implementation and the server initialization, to create the server object files.

   ```
   S> cc -c server.c procedure.c
   ```

2. Link the server object files and server stub file with the DCE library to create the executable server file.

```
S>  cc -o server server.o procedure.o arithmetic_sstub.o \
    -ldce -lcma
```

Running the Application

We designed the arithmetic application for simplicity. One of our shortcuts was to let the client automatically find the server by using the name service to retrieve server binding information. The client stub obtains the binding information exported by the server to the name service database, and the client RPC runtime library completes the remote procedure call. This automatic binding method requires you to set the RPC-specific environment variable, RPC_DEFAULT_ENTRY, on the client system, so the client stub has an entry name with which to begin looking for the binding information. More advanced applications can use binding methods not dependent on the login environment.

For this example, we use a simplistic approach by assigning to RPC_DEFAULT_ENTRY the same entry name used in the server initialization when exporting the binding information to the name service database. Chapter 6 describes details of naming entries and searching in a name service database.

To run the distributed arithmetic application, follow these steps:

1. This server exports binding information to a name service database. Exporting requires read and write access permission to the name service. Use a system at your site established for testing distributed applications or see your name service administrator to establish permission.

2. Execute the server. For this example, the application-specific environment variable, ARITHMETIC_SERVER_ENTRY, is set prior to running the server. This variable represents a name for the entry that this server uses when exporting the binding information to the name service database. The usual convention for entry names is to concatenate the interface and host names. We use an environment variable here because the name can vary depending on which host you use to invoke the server. If you do not supply a valid name, the binding information will not be placed in the name service database, and the program will fail. The prefix /.:/ is required to represent the global portion of a name in the hierarchy of a name service database. For this example, assume that the server resides on the system **moxie**.

```
moxie>  setenv ARITHMETIC_SERVER_ENTRY /.:/arithmetic_moxie
moxie>  server
```

3. For the client system (represented by the C> prompt), set the RPC environment variable RPC_DEFAULT_ENTRY to the name of the server's entry name in the name service database. The client stub can then automatically begin its search to find the server.

```
C> setenv RPC_DEFAULT_ENTRY /.:/arithmetic_moxie
```

4. After the server is running, execute the client on the client system.

```
C> client
sums:
104
200
347
26
68
72
5
9
6
8
```

5. The server is still running and should be terminated with a *kill* command or by typing ^C (Ctrl/C).

Figure 1-12 summarizes the development of the arithmetic application.

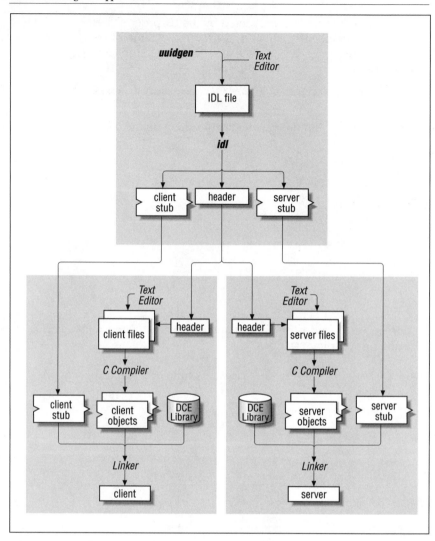

Figure 1-12: Arithmetic application: complete development

2

Using a DCE RPC Interface

As we discussed in Chapter 1, the first step in creating a distributed application is to write an **interface definition**. This is also known as an IDL file because it is written in the DCE Interface Definition Language and ends in the suffix *.idl*. This file contains definitions that the client and server share, and a list of all the procedures offered by the server. This chapter explains what interface definitions need to contain.

An interface definition is usually written by the person developing the server because it describes the procedures offered by that server. Client developers need to read and interpret the definition. All servers that support the interface must implement the remote procedures using the same data types and parameters. All clients must call the remote procedures consistently.

A **procedure declaration** in an interface definition specifies the procedure name, the data type of the value it returns (if any), and the number, order, and data types of its parameters (if any).

Interface definitions are compiled with the IDL compiler (*idl*) to create the header and stub files. You use the header file with your application C code, and link the stub files with your application object code and the RPC runtime library to create a distributed application. If you make a mistake when writing an interface definition, the IDL compiler gives useful messages to help you correct what is wrong.

Interface Definition Language (IDL)

Use the Interface Definition Language (IDL) to define the necessary data types and declare the remote procedures for an interface. Declarations in IDL are similar to declarations in C,* with the addition of attributes.

Attributes

Interface definition **attributes** are special keywords that offer information to help distribute an application. They are enclosed in square brackets in the IDL file. All of them facilitate network use in one way or another:

* Some attributes distinguish one interface from another on a network. They guarantee that a client finds the servers that implement the proper remote procedures. For example, the uuid attribute declares the UUID for the interface.

* Some attributes explicitly describe data transmitted over a network. Some aspects of data in C that you take for granted must be described explicitly for a distributed application. For example, a union is a data structure that allows different data types in the same area of memory. Your application uses another variable to keep track of which data type is valid. In a distributed program, this additional variable must be specified in IDL so it is transmitted with a union parameter.

* Some attributes make data transmission more efficient. In a local application, procedures have access to both parameters and global variables so that any amount of data can be accessed efficiently. In a distributed application, all data used by the client and the remote procedure must be passed as parameters and transmitted over the network. Since most parameters are passed in only one direction, you use attributes to specify whether each parameter is used for input, output, or both.

Tables A-1 through A-8 in Appendix A show all IDL attributes with brief descriptions of each. In this chapter, we discuss the IDL attributes so you know how to write an interface definition. But to really understand how those attributes reflect your use of data in an application, you have to see them along with the application's C code—and that will appear in later chapters.

---

*IDL is currently designed to work with C for programming DCE applications. However, IDL has features such as boolean and byte data types, so that it will work in future versions for languages other than C.

Structure of an Interface Definition

An interface definition includes some or all of the following:

- The interface header
  - Interface header attributes
  - Interface name

- The interface body
  - Import statements
  - Constant definitions
  - Data type definitions
  - Procedure declarations

Interface Header Attributes

These specify RPC features that apply to an entire interface. One is the name that you have chosen, such as `arithmetic` in the application shown in Chapter 1. But choosing a name is not enough because someone could easily create another application called `arithmetic`, and a client would be confused about which to use. That is where the interface UUID and the version number come in.

As we saw in Chapter 1, you generate a UUID through *uuidgen*. This distinguishes your `arithmetic` even when someone else steals your name to create a different interface. But the creators of DCE and Microsoft RPC recognized that an interface does not stay the same forever; you are likely to update it regularly. So they also allow for a **version number** in the interface header. A complete version number consists of a major and minor version number. For example, if a version number is 2.1, the major version is 2 and the minor version is 1.

During a remote procedure call, the following rules determine whether a client can use an interface that a server supports:

- The UUID of the client and server must match.
- The major version number of the client and server must match.
- The minor version number for the client must be less than or equal to the minor version number for the server. A client minor version number that is less than the server minor version number indicates an upwardly compatible change to the interface on the server.

When you create new versions of an interface by adding new declarations and definitions, increase the minor version number. Any other changes to an interface require a major version number change, essentially creating a different interface.

The Inventory Application

The application we use in this chapter is a simple inventory: a product database is stored on the server system, and a client makes inquiries based on a part number. The complete application is shown in Appendix D.

Example 2-1 shows the header in the interface definition of the inventory application.

Example 2-1: Interface Header Attributes

```
/* FILE NAME: inventory.idl */
[                                        /* brackets enclose attributes❶*/
uuid(008B3C84-93A5-11C9-85B0-08002B147A61),/* universal unique identifier❷*/
version(1.0),                            /* version of this interface❸*/
pointer_default(ptr)                     /* pointer default          ❹*/
] interface  inventory                   /* interface name           ❺*/

{
/* The body of an interface definition consists of import statements,     */
/* constant definitions, data type definitions, and procedure declarations. */
  .
  .
  .
}
```

❶ Brackets enclose attributes in interface definitions.

❷ The uuid is a required attribute that uniquely identifies an interface. All copies of this interface definition contain the same UUID.

❸ The version is an optional attribute used to identify different versions of an interface. In this example, the major version number is 1 and the minor version number is 0.

❹ The pointer_default is an optional attribute needed by some interface definitions so that pointer data is efficiently transmitted.

❺ The keyword interface and a name are required to identify the interface. The IDL compiler uses this name to construct data structure names. Client and server code use these data structures to access information about the interface.

Table A-1 lists and describes all interface header attributes.

Type Definitions, Data Attributes, and Constants

In C, a data type can map to different sizes on different systems. For example, a long data type in C may be 16, 32, or 64 bits, depending on the system. The size of an IDL data type, however, must be the same on all systems so that DCE applications can exchange data.

When you compile the interface definition, the IDL compiler generates C code data types that begin with idl_, and places them in the header file. For example, a typedef in an interface definition uses the IDL data type long as follows:

```
typedef long part_num;
```

The IDL compiler generates the data type idl_long_int, corresponding to the long IDL type, and places it in the header file as follows:

```
typedef idl_long_int part_num;
```

You use the new data type, part_num, in your application code. Although the size of a particular IDL data type is always the same, it may map to different standard C data types on different systems. The idl_ data types are defined in a DCE RPC-supplied header file to map to the proper sized C data types for the system on which the compile took place. For example, the idl_long_int data type on 32-bit systems corresponds to the long C type, but on a 64-bit system, its corresponding C type might be int. The IDL compiler takes care of the proper mapping between the generated idl_ data types and your local system's C data types.

Table 2-1 shows the basic IDL data types, the size of each in bits, and the corresponding idl_ data types. Use the IDL data types in interface definitions for type definitions, constant declarations, and procedure declarations. Use the idl_ data types in your RPC application code for all return values and parameters in remote procedure calls.

Table 2-1: IDL Basic Data Types

IDL Data Type	Size	C Code Data Type
boolean	8 bits	idl_boolean
byte	8 bits	idl_byte
char	8 bits	idl_char
void	-	void
void *	opaque	application specific
handle_t	opaque	rpc_binding_handle_t, handle_t
error_status_t	32 bits	unsigned32, unsigned long, error_status_t

Table 2-1: IDL Basic Data Types (continued)

IDL Data Type	Size	C Code Data Type
	Integers	
small	8 bits	idl_small_int
short	16 bits	idl_short_int
long	32 bits	idl_long_int
hyper	64 bits	idl_hyper_int
unsigned small	8 bits	idl_usmall_int
unsigned short	16 bits	idl_ushort_int
unsigned long	32 bits	idl_ulong_int
unsigned hyper	64 bits	idl_uhyper_int
	Floating Point	
float	32 bits	idl_short_float
double	64 bits	idl_long_float
	International Characters	
ISO_LATIN_1	8 bits	ISO_LATIN_1
ISO_UCS	32 bits in a structure	ISO_UCS
ISO_MULTI_LINGUAL	16 bits in a structure	ISO_MULTI_LINGUAL

For 32-bit systems, you can use the standard C data types (long, float, and so on) for remote procedure return values and parameters, because most of the IDL data types map to the comparable C data type. For example, the long IDL type maps to idl_long_int, which maps to a long C type on a 32-bit system. However, to assure that your DCE application code will port to other systems, use the C code data types from Table 2-1 in your application code.

Table 2-2 contains notes about some of the IDL data types.

Table 2-2: Notes on IDL Data Types

IDL_Type	Notes
boolean	Data that is either idl_true or idl_false.
byte	Data is not automatically converted when transmitted over the network to a system with a different data format. Use this type to transmit data that is untyped or opaque so that no conversion is performed on it.

Table 2-2: Notes on IDL Data Types (continued)

IDL_Type	Notes
char	An unsigned, 8-bit character. C uses the char data type to represent 8-bit integers as well as characters, and it interprets them as signed on some systems and unsigned on others. Use the IDL char data type for true character data and use small or unsigned small to represent 8-bit integers in interface definitions.
void	Indicates that a procedure does not return a value.
void *	Used with the context_handle attribute to define context handles. It refers to opaque data, the details of which are hidden from you. See Chapter 10, *Context Handles*.
handle_t	Data that denotes a binding handle. Section 3.1.3 describes how to use this data type to define binding handles in an interface definition.
error_status_t	Data that denotes an RPC communication status
ISO_LATIN_1	The Latin character set defined by the International Standards Organization
ISO_UCS	The universal character set defined by the International Standards Organization
ISO_MULTI_LINGUAL	A subset of the characters of type ISO_UCS that can be represented in two bytes

How do the IDL data types help to distribute an application? The explanation lies in how the client and server stubs handle data that might need to change as it moves from one computer system to another.

During a remote procedure call, the client stub prepares input parameters for transmission, and the server stub converts the data for use by the server application. When the remote procedure completes execution on the server system, the server stub prepares the output parameters for transmission and the client stub converts the data for the client application.

Marshalling is the process during a remote procedure call that prepares data for transmission across the network. Marshalling converts data into a byte-stream format and packages it for transmission using a **Network Data Representation** (**NDR**). NDR allows successful data sharing between systems with different data formats. It handles differences like big-endian versus little-endian (byte order), ASCII characters versus EBCDIC characters, and other incompatibilities.

Data transmitted across the network undergoes a process called **unmarshalling**. If the data format of sender and receiver is different, the receiver's stub converts the data to the correct format for that system, and passes the data to the application.

Example 2-2 shows a constant and two type definitions for the inventory interface.

Example 2-2: IDL Type Definitions

```
[
/* The header of an interface definition consists of interface header  */
/* attributes and the name of the interface.                           */
  .
  .
  .
] interface inventory
{
    const long MAX_STRING = 30;                 /* constant for string size❶*/

    typedef long     part_num;                  /* inventory part number❷*/

    typedef [string] char part_name[MAX_STRING+1];      /* name of part❸*/
    .
    .
    .
/* The remainder of the interface definition consists of other data    */
/* type definitions and the procedure declarations.                    */
}
```

❶ Use the keyword const followed by a data type to declare a constant to use in type definitions and application code.

❷ Use the keyword typedef followed by a data type to define a new data type.

❸ A data type is not sufficient to completely describe some kinds of data. Attributes provide the necessary extra information. In this example, the string attribute enclosed in brackets applies to the character array part_name, so that it becomes a null-terminated string.

Table A-4 lists and describes all the data type attributes. So far we have seen only basic IDL data types. Now we will explain how to construct more complex data types in an interface definition.

Pointers

In a distributed application, a pointer doesn't provide the same convenience and efficiency that it does in a local application because there is stub overhead such as memory allocation, copying, and transmitting all the data the pointer refers to. IDL contains two kinds of pointers to balance efficiency with maximum pointer capabilities.

A **full pointer** has all of the capabilities usually associated with pointers. These capabilities require additional stub overhead during a remote procedure call to identify the data the pointer refers to, to determine whether the pointer value is NULL, and to determine whether two pointers point to the same data.

A **reference pointer** is a simpler pointer that refers to existing data. A reference pointer has a performance advantage, but limited capabilities compared to a full pointer. No new memory can be allocated for the client during the remote procedure call, so memory for the data must exist in the client before the call is made.

The `ptr` attribute represents a full pointer and the `ref` attribute represents a reference pointer. Chapter 4, *Pointers and Arrays*, discusses how to use pointers.

Arrays

Array index values begin at 0 in IDL, as in C. For example, the array `arr[10]` defined in an interface definition has elements `arr[0]`, `arr[1]`, `...`, `arr[9]` when you use it in the client or server code.

Arrays are expensive to transmit, so IDL provides some sophisticated ways to keep down the amount of data actually sent over the network. Here are the kinds of arrays provided:

Fixed array
: A fixed array has constant index values for its dimensions. This is like a standard C array.

Varying array
: A varying array has a maximum size determined at compile time, just like a fixed array. But it also has subset bounds represented by variables. Only the portion of the array you need is transmitted in a remote procedure call.

Conformant array
: The size of a conformant array is represented by a dimension variable so that the actual size is determined when the application is running.

Chapter 4 discusses arrays in more detail.

Strings

In C code it is convenient to use strings to manipulate character data. C library routines, such as *strcpy*, recognize a null character as the end of a string in the character array. In IDL, all characters in an array are transmitted, including null characters. Therefore, you must explicitly define strings with the `string` attribute, so that only the characters up to a null character are transmitted. Example 2-3 shows some string definitions.

Example 2-3: Defining Strings in IDL

```
const long MAX_STRING = 30;              /* a constant for string size */
.
.
.

typedef [string] char part_name[MAX_STRING+1];       /* name of part ❶*/
typedef [string, ptr] char *paragraph;       /* description of part ❷*/
```

❶ To specify a string, apply the `string` attribute to a character or byte array. In this example, the string size is 31 to accommodate the terminating null byte, but the maximum string length is 30. The data type of the array elements must be a `char` or `byte`, or defined with a type definition that resolve to a `char` or `byte`. The data type can also be a structure whose fields all resolve to a `char` or `byte`.

❷ This example specifies a **conformant string** by applying the `string` attribute to a pointer to a `char` or `byte` data type.

A conformant string has the maximum length allocated in the application code. You can also specify a conformant string using array syntax. For example, the following is another way to define the conformant string `paragraph`:

```
typedef [string] char paragraph[];
```

When you use a conformant string as an input parameter to a remote procedure, the amount of data that is transmitted is determined from the current string length. If the string parameter is both input and output, however, apply an array attribute `size_is` or `max_is` to the string so the length can increase when the remote procedure completes. Chapter 4 discusses array attributes in greater detail.

Enumerated types

IDL provides an enumerated type, just as modern versions of the C language do. The idea is to provide a set of symbolic names to make source code more self-documenting. These names are associated by the compiler to a set of integer values, but the values usually have no more significance than to distinguish one name from another. In Example 2-4, the keyword `enum`, followed by a list of identifiers, maps the identifiers to consecutive integers starting with 0. For this example, we use enumeration to specify more than one kind of measurement unit for parts in the inventory. Some parts are counted as whole items, while other parts are measured by weight.

Example 2-4: Defining an Enumerated Type in IDL

```
typedef enum {
    ITEM, GRAM, KILOGRAM
} part_units;                               /* units of measurement */
```

Structures

You define structures in IDL the same way you do in C. In Example 2-5 the struct keyword is followed by a list of typed members that define a structure. For this example, two structures are shown. The structure part_price contains a units-of-measurement member and a price-per-unit member. The part_units data type is an enumerated type. The structure part_record represents all the data for a particular part number. As in C, any user-defined types such as part_num must be defined before they are used.

Example 2-5: Defining Structures in IDL

```
typedef struct part_price {                 /* price of part */
    part_units units;
    double     per_unit;
} part_price;

      .
      .
      .

typedef struct part_record {                /* data for each part */
    part_num      number;
    part_name     name;
    paragraph     description;
    part_price    price;
    part_quantity quantity;
    part_list     subparts;
} part_record;
```

Discriminated unions

In C a union is a data structure that stores different types and sizes of data in the same area of memory. For example, this union stores a long integer or a double precision floating-point number:

```
typedef union {
    long int number;
    double   weight;
} quantity_t;
```

To keep track of what type is stored in the union, the application must use a discriminator variable that is separate from the union data structure. This creates a special requirement for a distributed application. If a remote procedure call includes a union parameter, the remote procedure has no way of knowing which member of the union is valid unless it receives the discriminator along with the union.

In IDL, a **discriminated union** includes a discriminator as part of the data structure itself, so that the currently valid data type is transmitted with the union. When you define a discriminated union, it looks like a combination of a C union and switch statement. The switch defines the discriminator, and each case of the switch defines a valid data type and member name for the union.

Example 2-6 shows how to define a discriminated union.

Example 2-6: Defining a Discriminated Union in IDL

```
typedef enum {
    ITEM, GRAM, KILOGRAM
} part_units;                                    /* units of measurement */
    .
    .
    .

         ❶               ❷              ❸
typedef union switch(part_units units) total {   /* quantity of part */
    case ITEM:      long int number;
    case GRAM:                            ❹
    case KILOGRAM: double   weight;
} part_quantity;                         ❺
```

❶ You begin the definition of a discriminated union data type with the keywords typedef union.

❷ Use the keyword switch to specify the data type and name of the discriminator variable, units. The data type part_units is a previously defined enumerated type. A discriminator can be Boolean, character, integer, or an enumerated type.

❸ Define the name of the union, total, prior to listing the union cases.

❹ Use the keyword case followed by a value to specify the data type and name of each union member. The case value is the same type as the discriminator variable. In this example, a union defines the quantity of a part in an inventory. Some parts are counted as whole items while other parts are weighed. This union offers a choice between defining the quantity as a long integer or as a double precision floating-point number. The union case GRAM has the same data type and name as the case KILOGRAM.

❺ The name of the new data type is part_quantity, which you use in application code to allocate a discriminated union variable.

In application code, the discriminated union is a C structure. The IDL compiler generates a C structure with the discriminator as one member and a C union as another member. Example 2-7 shows the structure in the generated header file for the corresponding discriminated union in Example 2-6.

Example 2-7: A Discriminated Union Generated by the IDL Compiler

```
typedef struct {
  part_units units;
  union {
    /* case(s): 0 */
    idl_long_int number;
    /* case(s): 1, 2 */
    idl_long_float weight;
  } total;
} part_quantity;
```

You must set the union discriminator in the application code to control which union case is valid at any time in the application. Example 2-8 shows how you can use the discriminated union in application code.

Example 2-8: Using a Discriminated Union in Application Code

```
part_record part;              /* structure for all data about a part */❶
.
.
.
result = order_part(part.number, &(part.quantity), account);          ❷
if(result > 0) {
    if(part.quantity.units == ITEM)                                   ❸
        printf("ordered %ld items\n", part.quantity.total.number);    ❹
    else if(part.quantity.units == GRAM)
        printf("ordered %10.2f grams\n", part.quantity.total.weight);
    else if(part.quantity.units == KILOGRAM)
        printf("ordered %10.2f kilos\n", part.quantity.total.weight);
}
```

❶ In the inventory application, the **part_quantity** discriminated union is a member of the **part_record** structure shown in Example 2-5.

❷ The **part.quantity** structure member is the discriminated union. In this example, you request a quantity of a part to order, and the remote procedure returns the actual quantity ordered.

❸ The **part.quantity.units** member is the discriminator for the union.

❹ The **part.quantity.total** member is the union, which contains number and weight cases.

If you omit the union name (`total` in Example 2-6), then the IDL compiler generates the name `tagged_union` for you. You can access the structure members in application code as follows:

```
part.quantity.units = ITEM;
part.quantity.tagged_union.number = 1;
```

Pipes

Pipes can make data transmission much more efficient than regular remote procedure calls in the following cases:

- Large amounts of data must be transmitted at one time.

- The total amount of data is unknown until the application is running, such as when processing files.

- The data is incrementally produced and consumed, such as with instrument data collection.

Our inventory application does not use pipes. See Chapter 11, *Using Pipes for Large Quantities of Data*, for a discussion of pipes.

Procedure Declarations and Parameter Attributes

At the heart of an interface definition are the procedures that a server offers. The inventory application contains several remote procedures; you can find them in the interface definition in Appendix D.

Each parameter of a remote procedure is declared with its own attributes. The most important ones are the directional attributes in and out.

In the C language, parameters of procedure calls are passed by value, which means a copy of each parameter is supplied to the called procedure. The variable passed is an input-only parameter because any manipulation of the procedure's copy of the variable does not alter the original variable. In order for a variable to be an parameter, a pointer to the variable is passed.

With a remote procedure call, we must be concerned with whether a parameter is input, output, or both. It is more efficient if the RPC runtime library can transmit data only in the relevant direction. The attributes in and out are used in an interface definition to distinguish data transmission direction for a parameter. All parameters must have at least one directional attribute. An output parameter must be a pointer or an array, as it must be in C.

Example 2-9 shows procedure declarations and some associated parameter attributes.

Example 2-9: Procedure Declarations and Parameter Attributes

```
.
.
.
.
] interface inventory
{
/* The beginning of the interface definition body usually contains   */
/* constant and type definitions (and sometimes import declarations).*/
.
.
.

    /*********************** Procedure Declarations ***********************/
    boolean is_part_available(           /* return true if in inventory   ❶*/
        [in] part_num number             /* input part number */
    );

    void whatis_part_name(               /* get part name from inventory  ❷*/
        [in]  part_num  number,          /* input part number */
        [out] part_name name             /* output part name   */
    );

    paragraph get_part_description(      /* return a pointer to a string  ❸*/
        [in]  part_num  number
    );

    void whatis_part_price(              /* get part price from inventory   */
        [in]  part_num  number,
        [out] part_price *price
    );

    void whatis_part_quantity(           /* get part quantity from inventory */
        [in]  part_num      number,
        [out] part_quantity *quantity
    );

    void whatare_subparts(               /* get list of subpart numbers    */
        [in]  part_num number,
        [out] part_list **subparts       /* structure containing the array ❹*/
    );

    /* Order part from inventory with part number, quantity desired, and   */
    /* account number.  If inventory does not have enough, output lesser    */
    /* quantity ordered.  Return values: 1=ordered OK,                      */
    /* -1=invalid part, -2=invalid quantity, -3=invalid account.            */

    long order_part(  /* order part from inventory, return OK or error code */
        [in]      part_num      number,
        [in,out]  part_quantity *quantity,           /* quantity ordered ❺*/
        [in]      account_num   account
    );
} /* end of interface definition */
```

❶ As in C, an IDL procedure can return a value. In the above example, the `is_part_available` procedure returns a Boolean value of `idl_true` if the part number is available in the inventory.

❷ Procedures defined with the void type do not return a value. Input parameters have the `in` directional attribute and output parameters have the `out` directional attribute. As in C, arrays and strings are implicitly passed by reference, so the string name does not need a pointer operator.

❸ Some procedures return a data structure or a pointer to a data structure. In this example, the data type `paragraph` has been defined in the interface definition as a `char *` type. It is a full pointer to a string representing the description of the part. This remote procedure allocates new memory on the client side.

❹ Output parameters require pointers to pointers when new memory is allocated. Pointers to pointers are discussed in Chapter 4.

❺ Parameters that are changed by the remote procedure call use both `in` and `out`. In this example, a part is ordered with the part number, the quantity, and an account number. If the input quantity units are wrong or the quantity requested is more than the inventory can supply, the remote procedure changes the quantity on output.

Due to communication errors and disruptions that can occur, sometimes remote procedures will not complete or execute at all. If communication is disrupted, it is useful if some procedures automatically retry execution. A procedure is **idempotent** if it can execute more than once with the same arguments to produce identical results without any undesirable side-effects. If you want an idempotent procedure to automatically retry execution, use the `idempotent` attribute.

Table A-7 shows all parameter attributes and Table A-8 shows all procedure attributes.

Using the IDL Compiler

The IDL compiler generates the header and stub files needed to incorporate the interface in a client or server. The input for an IDL compilation is an interface definition file, ending in *.idl*. Figure 2-1 shows the utilities used and files produced during interface production.

An attribute configuration file (ACF) is an optional file, ending in *.acf*. It contains information that changes how the IDL compiler interprets the interface definition. We'll look at the ACF file later in this chapter.

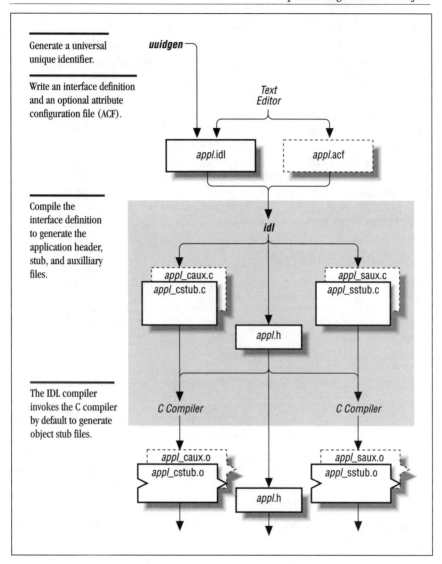

Figure 2-1: Producing an interface

Depending on which compiler options you use, the IDL compiler produces the client stub, server stub, or both sets of stub files. The stub file names contain the *_cstub* suffix for clients and the *_sstub* suffix for servers. By default, the IDL compiler produces the header file (ending in *.h*) and object stub files (ending in *.o*) for both the client and server. The IDL compiler generates intermediate C stub code and invokes the C compiler to generate object stub files. When the IDL compiler generates object code, you can control which output and intermediate files it produces, and what options it uses.

The IDL compiler produces auxiliary files automatically when certain features are used. Auxiliary file names contain the _caux_ suffix for clients and the _saux_ suffix for servers.

Auxiliary files contain special routines required for certain data types to prepare the data for transmission. You have to link the auxiliary object files with your application when these data types are used. The routines are placed in auxiliary files rather than in the stub, so that you can use the data types in other interface definitions without linking in the entire stub. Features in interface definitions that require auxiliary files include self-referential pointers and pipes. The `out_of_line` attribute in an ACF also requires auxiliary files.

Generating Client Files

To generate the interface header file and client stub file for the inventory interface, type the following command:

```
C> idl inventory.idl -v -server none -Iexplicit -out explicit
```

Here is an explanation of the options:

-v   The verbose option displays what the IDL compiler is doing.

-server none This option suppresses the generation of stub none and auxiliary files for the server.

-Iexplicit   The -I option causes the IDL compiler to use the additional directory when it searches for files. For one of the clients of the inventory application, an ACF in the *explicit* directory is needed.

-out explicit This option places the output files in the chosen directory, *explicit*.

Generating Server Files

To generate the interface header file and server stub file for the inventory interface, type the following command:

```
S> idl inventory.idl -v -client none
```

Here is an explanation of the options:

-v   The verbose option displays what the IDL compiler is doing.

-client none   This option suppresses the generation of stub and auxiliary
                 files for the client.

Using an ACF To Customize Interface Usage

You can control some aspects of RPC on the client side without affecting
the server. The opposite is also true. These aspects should not be in the
interface definition because we do not want to force them on all clients and
servers. A client or server developer can use an optional attribute configuration file (ACF) to modify the way the IDL compiler creates stubs, without changing the way the stubs interact across the network. This assures
that all copies of an interface behave the same when clients and servers
interact.

The most significant effect an ACF has on your application code can be the
addition of parameters to remote procedure calls not declared in the interface definition. For example, the `explicit_handle` attribute adds a binding
handle as the first parameter to some or all procedures. Also, the
`comm_status` and `fault_status` attributes can add status parameters to
the end of a procedure's parameter list. See Table A-9 for a complete list of
ACF attributes.

If you develop both clients and servers for an interface, you can use different ACFs (or no ACF) for the client and server. Since this can cause differences between the header files generated for the client and server, it is
good development practice to separate the client and server output when
using ACFs.

You do not specify an ACF when you compile an interface; instead, the IDL
compiler automatically uses an ACF if one is available in the search directories. The name of an ACF must match the name of the IDL file it is associated with. The file extension must be *.acf*.

An ACF is useful for a number of situations: selecting binding methods,
controlling errors, excluding procedures, and controlling marshalling.

Selecting a Binding Method

As will be explained in Chapter 3, *How to Write Clients*, three different
binding methods exist. You can choose how much to let the stub do for
you and how much to control binding within your own code.

The `auto_handle` ACF attribute selects the automatic binding method,
which causes the client stub to automatically select the server for your client. In the arithmetic application in Chapter 1, for instance, any server
found by the client stub would be sufficient. An additional advantage
offered by automatic binding is error recovery: if server communication is

disrupted, the client stub can sometimes find another server, one transparent to the application code.

The `implicit_handle` ACF attribute selects the implicit binding method, which allows you to select a specific server for your remote procedure calls. For example, if many inventory servers representing different warehouses are available on the network, you may want your client to select a specific one.

The `explicit_handle` ACF attribute selects the explicit binding method, which lets you select a specific server for each remote procedure call. For example, if your client needs data from many servers simultaneously, you need a way to control which remote procedure call uses which server.

Example 2-10 is an ACF used by the IDL compiler to produce the header and stub files for the implicit client example of the inventory application.

Example 2-10: An Attribute Configuration File (ACF)

```
/* FILE NAME: inventory.acf (implicit version)*/
/* This Attribute Configuration File is used in conjunction with the    */
/* associated IDL file (inventory.idl) when the IDL compiler is invoked. */
[
implicit_handle(handle_t global_binding_h)   /* implicit binding method ❶*/
]
interface  inventory    /* The interface name must match the IDL file. ❷*/
{
}
```

❶ The `implicit_handle` attribute applies to the entire interface. A global binding handle of type `handle_t` is established in the client stub to refer to binding information a client uses to find a server.

❷ The interface name (`inventory`) must match the interface name in the corresponding IDL file.

Controlling Errors and Exceptions

An **exception** is a software state or condition that forces the application to go outside its normal flow of control. Such an event may be produced by hardware (such as memory access violations) or software (such as array subscript range checking). DCE applications cause communication and server errors to be raised as exceptions. Unless you design your program to handle the exceptions, the program will exit.

An ACF can save you the trouble of writing extra layers of exception handling code. The `comm_status` and `fault_status` attributes apply to procedure parameters or procedure return results. If these attributes are present, communication and server errors are communicated to the client as values in the named parameters rather than raised as exceptions. Chapter 3 discusses error and exception control in greater detail.

Excluding Unused Procedures

The code and nocode ACF attributes allow you to define which proce-dures the client stub supports. For example, if a client uses only four out of twenty remote procedures declared in the interface, the client stub code does not need the overhead of the other procedures. However, all the pro-cedures of an interface definition must be implemented by the server.

Controlling Marshalling and Unmarshalling

The out_of_line ACF attribute causes constructed data types such as unions, pipes, or large structures to be marshalled or unmarshalled by aux-iliary routines, thus reducing stub size. The out_of_line attribute directs the IDL compiler to place marshalling and unmarshalling code in IDL auxili-ary stub files, rather than in the direct flow of stub code. If stub size is a concern, use out_of_line on constructed data types that are used in more than one remote procedure.

The in_line ACF attribute causes data types to be marshalled or unmarshalled as fast as possible. The in_line attribute directs the IDL compiler to place marshalling and unmarshalling code for constructed data types in the direct flow of stub code, rather than as a separate IDL com-piler-generated auxiliary routine. This is the default for an interface.

The in_line and out_of_line attributes affect only the stub code. They require no change to application code.

3

How to Write Clients

In this chapter we discuss how to develop client programs for DCE RPC interfaces. It is a good idea to read Chapter 1 for a complete overview of a distributed application, and Chapter 2 to familiarize yourself with features of interface definitions.

We discuss client development before server development because you may develop a client for an existing interface and server. We describe server development in Chapter 5. The code for all applications is shown in Appendices C through I.

Binding

The first question that probably comes to mind when you begin to develop a client is: How does a remote procedure call find the server it needs? Essentially, the client must create a binding, as described in Chapter 1, and load it with information that lets the RPC runtime library find the server.

Binding information mainly includes a communication protocol sequence, a host name or address, and a server process address on the host (endpoint). If you are familiar with Internet Protocols, these are similar to a protocol family, an Internet address, and a port assignment.

Binding information can be obtained automatically and be completely invisible to your client application code. To the other extreme, you can obtain binding information by calling RPC runtime routines and using a **binding handle** as a parameter in a remote procedure call. The level of control you need depends on the needs of your client program.

A binding handle is the data structure that manages binding in applications. The handle is a reference (pointer) to information for one possible binding.

DCE supplies the Cell Directory Service (CDS) as a convenient, distributed name service database to store names and locations of network services. Servers use RPC runtime routines to store binding information in the name service database. Clients use other RPC runtime routines to retrieve binding information from the name service database and create binding handles for remote procedure calls.

A server's binding information can also be stored in an application-specific database or supplied to client programs by some other means, for example, as arguments when the client is invoked. If your client would not benefit from a name service (or your client system does not have a running name service), you can use RPC runtime routines in applications to convert strings of binding information to binding handles used by remote procedure calls.

Implementing a Binding Method

For each remote procedure call, the binding handle is managed in one of the following ways.

Automatic method

The client stub automatically manages bindings after the application calls a remote procedure. The client stub obtains binding information from a name service database and passes the binding handle to the RPC runtime library. If the connection is disrupted, new binding information can sometimes be automatically obtained and the call is tried again.

Implicit method

A binding handle is held in a global area of the client stub. After the application calls a remote procedure, the stub passes the binding handle to the RPC runtime library. You write application code to obtain the binding information and set the global binding handle with RPC runtime routine calls.

Explicit method

An individual remote procedure call in the application passes a binding handle explicitly as its first parameter. You write application code to obtain the binding information and set the binding handle with RPC runtime routine calls.

Figure 3-1 shows a comparison of binding methods in relation to the client code. For each method, the top portion of the box represents the client application code you write. The bottom portion of each box represents the client stub code that the IDL compiler generates. The shading represents the portion of the client where binding handles are managed.

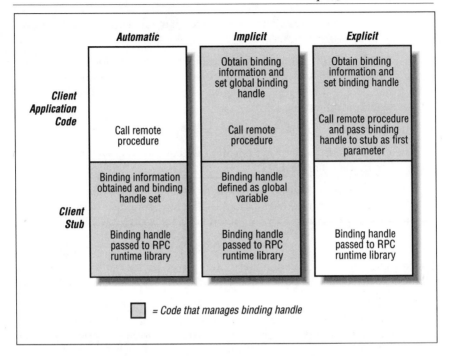

Figure 3-1: A comparison of binding management methods

For any given client instance, different methods may be employed for different remote procedure calls. For example, one remote procedure call can use the automatic method and another remote procedure call can use the explicit method.

Automatic binding is convenient for learning and test purposes. But it is not useful for most production applications because you cannot use security, as discussed in Chapter 9.

The automatic and implicit methods apply to an entire interface. If you use either the automatic or implicit method for an interface, you can also use the explicit method for some or all remote procedure calls to that interface. The explicit method takes precedence over the automatic and implicit methods because the binding handle is visible as the first parameter in the procedure.

If a client uses more than one interface, you can use the automatic method for all remote procedure calls to one interface and the implicit method for all remote procedure calls to the other interface. However, a client cannot use the automatic and implicit methods simultaneously, for remote procedure calls to the same interface.

The implicit and explicit methods require that your application code obtain binding information and manage the binding handles. Binding handles need to be obtained and managed in the client application code under the following circumstances:

- The client uses a specific server.

- The client needs to set authentication and authorization information for specific binding handles.

- The server has more than one implementation of the same remote procedure. An application uses object UUIDs to distinguish between different remote procedure implementations. This is discussed in Chapter 7, *Object UUIDs*.

Use an attribute configuration file (ACF) in order to establish a binding method with the attributes `auto_handle`, `implicit_handle`, or `explicit_handle`.

A **context handle** is a special remote procedure parameter defined in an interface definition with the `context_handle` attribute. Applications use a context handle in a sequence of remote procedure calls to refer to a context (state) on a specific server. We mention context handles briefly here with binding methods because they carry with them binding information and thus can act as a binding handle for remote procedure calls. When the context handle is active, it carries with it the binding information necessary to find the same server as it did before, and the server maintains the context for that particular client. (Chapter 10 describes context handle use.)

Deciding on binding methods

In some cases, you do not have to choose a binding method for procedures if you do not want to. When the interface definition is compiled, the automatic binding method is used by default except in the following cases:

- The first parameter of a procedure declaration is a binding handle.

- The procedure declaration has an input context handle.

- An ACF establishes a different binding method.

Suppose the first parameter of a procedure declaration is a binding handle. This procedure must use the explicit method. You cannot take away a parameter declared in the interface definition, so this remote procedure cannot use either the automatic or implicit methods.

The next decision you may make is whether to use the automatic or implicit method for all procedures without binding or context handle parameters. If you just want any valid server for your remote procedure calls, the automatic method should be adequate. The automatic method works fine if the network is relatively small. However, you have no control over which server you get, so applications that use servers scattered over a wide area may be inefficient. If most of your remote procedure calls need to use a specific server chosen in your application code, the implicit method is appropriate.

Suppose you have determined that individual remote procedure calls need control over which server each uses. For example, if you use a print server application, one call may request a server near you to print a file. Your next call may request a server in a different location to print another copy for your department manager. If you have determined that you need this kind of binding control for individual remote procedure calls, use the explicit method.

The explicit method is necessary for clients that make multithreaded remote procedure calls. For example, a commodity trade application may request a commodity price with remote procedure calls to many locations at the same time. This server selection control also lets you balance network load in your application. Most of the applications in this book are single-threaded.

Automatic Binding Management

The automatic binding management method is the simplest because you don't have to manipulate the binding handle in your interface definition, ACF, or application code. The binding handle is hidden from you in the client stub. After you set an RPC-specific environment variable, the complexity of binding management is done entirely by the client stub code and the RPC runtime library. If you lose a server connection, the automatic method will try to rebind for you. With this method there is a relatively short learning curve to get a distributed application running.

Many applications do not require that you control binding, so it is easier to let the underlying RPC mechanism find a server. The server is selected from a set of servers that support the interface. If the particular server makes no difference, use the automatic method. For example, for a mathematics interface, the first server that supports it is probably sufficient.

The automatic method is demonstrated in the arithmetic application and shown in detail in Chapter 1. For this chapter, however, we use one of the clients for the inventory application, so you can compare client development between different methods for the same application. The application is shown in detail in Appendix D.

Interface development for automatic binding

There are no special requirements in the interface for automatic binding. If you wish, you can use the `auto_handle` attribute in an ACF for documentation.

Client development for automatic binding

The client requires you to:

1. Include the IDL-generated header file with the **#include** compiler directive in the client application code:

    ```
    /* FILE NAME: i_client.c */
    /****** Client of the inventory application ******/
    #include <stdio.h>
    #include <stdlib.h>
    #include "inventory.h" /* header file created by the IDL compiler */
         .
         .
         .
    ```

2. Link the client application object code with the client stub, client stub auxiliary file (if available), and the DCE libraries:

    ```
    C>  cc -o i_client.exe i_client.o inventory_cstub.o -ldce -lcma
    ```

3. Set the environment variable `RPC_DEFAULT_ENTRY` to a valid name service entry so the client stub can automatically begin a name service database search:

    ```
    C> setenv RPC_DEFAULT_ENTRY /.:/inventory_group
    ```

The client system must have access to a name service database on the network. Your system administrator can tell you if you have access to a name service.

The remote procedure call looks just like a local procedure call. The procedure returns a Boolean value of `idl_true` if the part number is in the inventory or `idl_false` if it is not:

```
case 'a': if (is_part_available(part.number)) /* Remote Procedure Call */
            puts("available: Yes");
```

```
else
    puts("available: No");
break;
```

If your client uses the automatic method for an interface, you can override it for specific procedures using the **explicit_handle** attribute on the procedures in an ACF.

See Chapter 6 for more information on the name service.

Server development for automatic binding

For clients to use the automatic method, a server must advertise binding information to a name service entry with the *rpc_ns_binding_export* runtime routine in the server initialization code. Alternatively, an administrator can insert the information from the shell using the DCE RPC control program (*rpccp*).

Implicit Binding Management

Implicit binding gives you the control of binding management in the client application without a visible binding handle parameter in a remote procedure call. Use the implicit method for applications that need the same server for all or most remote procedure calls of an interface. An ACF defines the binding handle, and the IDL compiler generates it as a client-global variable in the client stub. The client application code sets the binding handle before any remote procedure calls. During a remote procedure call, the client stub uses the global binding handle to complete the call to the RPC runtime library.

In this part of the chapter, we'll develop a client for the inventory application that uses the implicit method. The rationale is that, in this application, you may need to choose a specific server in order to access the right data base. Once a server is found, the rest of the remote procedure calls can use the same one.

Interface development for implicit binding

Use the **implicit_handle** attribute in an ACF to declare the global binding handle for the client, as shown in Example 3-1. When you compile the interface definition with the ACF available, a global binding handle is defined in the client stub. The stub uses the handle every time the client calls a remote procedure for this interface.

Example 3-1: An ACF for the Implicit Binding Method

```
/* FILE NAME: inventory.acf (implicit version)*/
/* This Attribute Configuration File is used in conjunction with the    */
/* associated IDL file (inventory.idl) when the IDL compiler is invoked.*/
[
implicit_handle(handle_t global_binding_h)    /* implicit binding method */
]
interface  inventory    /* The interface name must match the IDL file. */
{
}
```

The `handle_t` type is an IDL data type used to define a binding handle
named `global_binding_h`.

Client development for implicit binding

The client code includes the IDL-generated header file, obtains a binding
handle, and assigns the binding handle to the global binding handle (see
Example 3-2).

Example 3-2: A Client with the Implicit Binding Method

```
/* FILE NAME: implicit_client.c */
/***** Client of the inventory application with implicit method *****/
#include <stdio.h>
#include <stdlib.h>
#include "inventory.h"  /* header file created by the IDL compiler  ❶*/
.
.
.
  do_import_binding("/.:/inventory_group", &global_binding_h);  /* ❷*/
.
.
.
    case 'a': if (is_part_available(part.number))              /* ❸*/
       puts("available: Yes");
    else
       puts("available: No");
    break;
```

❶ The IDL-generated header file must be included with the **#include** compiler directive.

❷ The client must obtain binding information and assign its handle to the
   global binding handle. The binding information can be obtained from
   the name service database as in this example, or it can be constructed

from strings of binding information. The `do_import_binding` procedure is developed later in this chapter.

❸ A remote procedure call looks just like a local procedure call.

If your client uses the implicit method for an interface, you can override it
for specific procedures using the `explicit_handle` attribute on the procedures in an ACF.

Server development for implicit binding

Although there are no special requirements in server development, a server
must export to a name service database if the clients use a name service to
find servers. As an alternative, the server binding information can be
exported to the name service database with the DCE RPC control program
(*rpccp*). The server for the inventory application exports binding information.

Explicit Binding Management

Explicit binding manages each remote procedure call separately. The first
parameter of the remote procedure call is a binding handle. Use the explicit
method when your application needs to make remote procedure calls to
more than one server. This method is the most visible in an application
because a binding handle is passed as the first parameter of the remote procedure. You completely control the binding management in the client
application code.

If the procedure declaration in the interface definition has a binding handle
as the first parameter, you must use the explicit method. However, if the
procedure declaration does not have a binding handle parameter, you can
add one by using an ACF. In this case, after you compile the interface definition, the remote procedure is defined in the header file with an additional
binding handle as the first parameter.

We'll use another client from the inventory application to demonstrate the
explicit method.

Interface development for explicit binding

An interface definition or an ACF uses the `handle_t` data type to define
binding handle parameters. Application code uses the `rpc_bind-
ing_handle_t` data type to represent and manipulate binding informa-
tion.*

---

*The `handle_t` and `rpc_binding_handle_t` data types are equivalent. The `handle_t`
data type exists for compatibility with earlier RPC versions. The `rpc_binding_handle_t`
data type exists for consistency in data type naming for the RPC runtime routines.

Suppose we want to use the explicit method for a remote procedure that has no explicit binding handle as the first parameter. We use an ACF with the explicit_handle attribute, making the IDL compiler add a binding handle as the first parameter. The is_part_available procedure is defined in the interface as follows:

```
boolean is_part_available(   /* return true if in inventory */
    [in] part_num number      /* input part number */
);
```

An ACF that adds a binding handle parameter is shown in Example 3-3.

Example 3-3: Adding Binding Handles with an ACF

```
/* FILE NAME: inventory.acf (explicit version)*/
/* This Attribute Configuration File is used in conjunction with the    */
/* associated IDL file (inventory.idl) when the IDL compiler is invoked. */
[
explicit_handle            /* explicit binding method */
]
interface  inventory       /* The interface name must match the idl file. */
{
}
```

When the IDL compiler uses this ACF, all procedure declarations in the header file have a binding handle of type handle_t, named IDL_handle, added as the first parameter. If you use the explicit_handle attribute this way, none of the remote procedure calls to this interface can use the automatic or implicit method for this client instance. The header file generated by the IDL compiler contains the following:

```
extern idl_boolean is_part_available(
#ifdef IDL_PROTOTYPES
        /* [in] */ handle_t IDL_handle,
        /* [in] */ part_num number
#endif
);
```

You can also use the explicit_handle attribute on a specific procedure in the ACF to add a binding handle as the first parameter. For example, this

ACF associates a binding handle parameter only with the is_part_available procedure:

```
interface inventory
{
    [explicit_handle] is_part_available();
}
```

Example 3-4 defines a binding handle explicitly in the interface definition. An interface is more restrictive when a binding handle is defined this way because clients cannot use the automatic or implicit binding methods for the procedure. (The is_part_available procedure is not declared this way for the inventory interface.)

Example 3-4: Defining a Binding Handle in the Interface Definition

```
boolean is_part_available(     /* return true if in inventory */
    [in] handle_t binding_h,   /* explicit, binding handle */
    [in] part_num number       /* input part number       */
);
```

Use the remote procedure in your application code the same way whether the binding handle is declared with an ACF as in Example 3-3, or in the original interface definition as in Example 3-4. Later in this chapter we'll show how to create an application-specific, customized binding handle in the interface definition through the handle attribute.

Client development for explicit binding

Before making the remote procedure call, the client must obtain binding information and set the binding handle. The methods of obtaining binding information for the explicit method are almost the same as for the implicit method. For the explicit method you use a specific binding handle instead of assigning the binding information to the implicit global binding handle.

Example 3-5: A Client with the Explicit Binding Method

```
/* FILE NAME: explicit_client.c */
/***** Client of the inventory application with explicit method ********/
#include <stdio.h>
#include <stdlib.h>
#include "inventory.h"          /* header file created by the IDL compiler❶*/
    .
    .
    .
    rpc_binding_handle_t binding_h;        /* declare a binding handle ❷*/
    .
    .
    .
```

Example 3-5: A Client with the Explicit Binding Method (continued)

```
do_import_binding("/.:/inventory_group", &binding_h);  /* find server ❸*/
  .
  .
  .

    case 'a': if (is_part_available(binding_h, part.number))          /*❹*/
       puts("available: Yes");
    else
       puts("available: No");
    break;
```

❶ Include the IDL-generated header file with the **#include** compiler directive.

❷ Declare binding handles of type `rpc_binding_handle_t` in the application.

❸ The client must obtain binding information from the name service database, or it can be constructed from strings of binding information. Example 3-7 shows how the application-specific procedure `do_import_binding` uses the name service database.

❹ Notice that the first parameter is the binding handle. The call to `is_part_available` in client application code is the same whether the code in Example 3-4 or 3-3 is used to define the explicit handle.

Server development for explicit binding

If the interface definition does not have a binding handle parameter for the remote procedure, and you want the remote procedure to obtain client binding information (such as for authentication and authorization, discussed in Chapter 9), you must use an ACF with the `explicit_handle` attribute to create the binding handle parameter.

If clients use a name service to find servers, the server must export to a name service database. As an alternative, the server binding information can be exported to the name service database with the DCE RPC control program (*rpccp*).

Steps in Finding Servers

Recall that Figure 1-10 shows one way to find a server. In this figure, the client stub and the RPC runtime library handle all binding management outside of the application code. The client stub automatically finds the server system binding information in a name service database. The binding handle is set and passed to the RPC runtime library, which finds the server process binding information (endpoint) in the server system's endpoint map. The RPC runtime library uses the complete binding information to bind to the server.

The key to finding a server is to obtain a protocol sequence, a server host name or address, and an endpoint. A binding handle for the remote procedure call is set to point to this binding information.

The following discussion is a generalization of what happens during the server finding process. It includes the choices you (or the RPC runtime library) have about where to obtain the necessary binding information. Where these steps are executed (client application, client stub, or RPC runtime library) depends on the kind of binding handle and binding method used.

Finding a Protocol Sequence

A client and server can communicate over a network if they both use the same network communication protocols. A protocol sequence is found in one of two ways:

- The preferred method is to use a name service database to import or look up both a host address and protocol sequence at the same time. To set the binding handle, use the RPC runtime routines that begin with *rpc_ns_binding_import_* or *rpc_ns_binding_lookup_*. If your application uses the automatic method, the client stub does this for you.

- The other method is to use a protocol sequence string obtained from your application or from a call to the *rpc_network_inq_protseqs* routine. Use the RPC runtime routines *rpc_string_binding_compose* and *rpc_binding_from_string_binding* to set the binding handle.

A **protocol sequence** is a character string containing three items that correspond to options for network communications protocols. RPC represents each valid combination of these protocols as a protocol sequence. The protocol sequence consists of a string of the options separated by underscores. The only current, valid option combinations are shown in Table 3-1.

Table 3-1: Valid Protocol Sequences

Protocol Sequence	Common Name	Description
ncacn_ip_tcp	Connection protocol sequence	Network Computing Architecture connection over an Internet Protocol with a Transmission Control Protocol for transport.

Table 3-1: Valid Protocol Sequences (continued)

Protocol Sequence	Common Name	Description
ncadg_ip_udp	Datagram protocol sequence	Network Computing Architecture datagram over an Internet Protocol with a User Datagram Protocol for transport.
ip	Datagram protocol sequence	A short version of the protocol sequence ncadg_ip_udp.

The three protocols of a protocol sequence are for RPC communication, network host addressing, and network transport.

1. The RPC protocol for communications has two options:

   - Network Computing Architecture connection-oriented protocol (ncacn)

   - Network Computing Architecture datagram protocol (ncadg)

2. The network address format used as part of the binding information is the Internet Protocol (ip).

3. The transport protocol for communications has two options:

   - Transmission control protocol (tcp)

   - User datagram protocol (udp)

Most servers should use all available protocol sequences so clients using the interface will have every opportunity to find and use a server.

The connection protocol sequence is good for establishing and maintaining a binding, so use it for clients that use one or a few servers. The tcp transport is considered reliable because the protocol guarantees message delivery.

Timeouts work differently for different protocol sequences. To find out about the availability of a specific server, ncacn_ip_tcp is the better protocol sequence because if the server is unavailable, you receive the error quickly. Use ncacn_ip_tcp for debugging your client during remote procedure calls. Otherwise, the process will timeout when the debugger stops it. The connection protocol sequence works better for a wide area network (WAN) because the datagram protocol sequence will probably have timeout problems. Clients can control timeouts using the RPC runtime routines *rpc_mgmt_set_com_timeout* and *rpc_mgmt_inq_com_timeout*.

The datagram protocol sequence has low operating system overhead, so use it for clients that need to bind to many servers. If a remote procedure broadcasts its call to all hosts on the local network, it must use `ncadg_ip_udp`. The `broadcast` attribute on a procedure declaration in the interface definition declares the broadcast capability.

Finding a Server Host

You can find a server host name or network address in two different ways:

- Use a name service database to import or look up a host address and at the same time get a protocol sequence. Use the RPC runtime routines that begin with *rpc_ns_binding_import_* or *rpc_ns_binding_lookup_* to set the binding handle. If your application uses the automatic method, the client stub does this for you.

- Use a host name or host network address string obtained from your application. Use the RPC runtime routines *rpc_string_binding_compose* and *rpc_binding_from_string_binding* to set the binding handle.

A **partially bound binding handle** is one that contains a protocol sequence and server host, but not an endpoint. This handle is what you get from CDS. It means you have identified the server's system, but not the server process on that system. The binding to a server cannot complete until an endpoint is found.

When a partially bound binding handle is passed to the RPC runtime library, an endpoint is automatically obtained for you from the interface or the endpoint map on the server's system.

Finding an Endpoint

A binding handle that has an endpoint as part of its binding information is called a **fully bound binding handle**. Endpoints can be well-known or dynamic. A **well-known endpoint** is a preassigned system address that a server process uses every time it runs. Usually a well-known endpoint is assigned by the authority responsible for a transport protocol. A **dynamic endpoint** is a system address of a server process that is requested and assigned by the RPC runtime library when a server is initialized. Most applications should use dynamic endpoints to avoid the network management needed for well-known endpoints.

You can use your application code to obtain an endpoint, but it is best to let the RPC runtime library find an endpoint for you. An endpoint is found in one of four ways:

- If the binding information obtained during an import or lookup of the protocol sequence and host in the name service database includes an endpoint, the binding handle is fully bound in one step. The name service database can be used to store well-known endpoints. But dynamic endpoints are never stored in the name service database because their temporary nature requires significant management of the database, which degrades name service performance.

- A well-known endpoint is found that was established in the interface definition with the `endpoint` attribute. The RPC runtime library (or your application) finds the endpoint from an interface-specific data structure.

- An endpoint is found from the endpoint map on the server system. These endpoints can be well-known or dynamic. The RPC runtime library first looks for an endpoint from the interface specification. If one is not found, the RPC runtime library looks in the server's endpoint map. When an endpoint is found, the binding to the server process completes. To obtain an endpoint from a server's endpoint map, use the *rpc_ep_resolve_binding* routine or routines beginning with *rpc_mgmt_ep_elt_inq_* in your application.

- You can use a string from your application that represents an endpoint, and then use the RPC runtime routines *rpc_string_binding_compose* and *rpc_binding_from_string_binding* to set the binding handle. These endpoints can be well-known or dynamic.

Interpreting Binding Information

This section reveals what goes on in the `do_import_binding` procedure shown earlier in the chapter. When you use implicit or explicit binding, you need to interpret the binding information. To take a simple case, suppose you want to use a server on a particular host—this means you need to extract the host from the binding handles you get from CDS and isolate the host name in each handle.

You may interpret the binding information of a binding handle to control which server a remote procedure call will use or which binding handles a server will offer. Binding handles refer to the following binding information:

- Object UUID

- Protocol sequence

- Network address or host name

- Endpoint

- Network options

Object UUIDs are part of an advanced topic discussed in Chapter 7. Network options are specific to a protocol sequence and not relevant to the connection-oriented or datagram protocol sequences.

Example 3-6 shows how to use RPC runtime routines to interpret binding information. You use these routines in either a server or client. The do_interpret_binding procedure is called in the do_import_binding procedure (see Example 3-7).

Example 3-6: Interpreting Binding Information

```
/* FILE NAME: do_interpret_binding.c */
/* Interpret binding information and return the protocol sequence. */
#include <stdio.h>
#include <dce/rpc.h>
#include "check_status.h"

void do_interpret_binding(binding, protocol_seq)
rpc_binding_handle_t binding;   /* binding handle to interpret (rpcbase.h) */
char            *protocol_seq;      /* protocol sequence to obtain */
{
    unsigned32      status;                          /* error status */
    unsigned_char_t *string_binding;  /* string of binding info. (lbase.h) */
    unsigned_char_t *protseq;          /* binding component of interest */

    rpc_binding_to_string_binding(          /* convert binding information */
                                            /* to string ❶*/
        binding,                            /* the binding handle to convert */
        &string_binding,                    /* the string of binding data */
        &status
    );
    CHECK_STATUS(status, "Can't get string binding:", RESUME);

    rpc_string_binding_parse(       /* get components of string binding ❷*/
        string_binding,                     /* the string of binding data */
        NULL,                       /* an object UUID string is not obtained */
        &protseq,                   /* a protocol sequence string IS obtained */
        NULL,                   /* a network address string is not obtained */
        NULL,                       /* an endpoint string is not obtained */
        NULL,                   /* a network options string is not obtained */
        &status
    );
    CHECK_STATUS(status, "Can't parse string binding:", RESUME);

    strcpy(protocol_seq, (char *)protseq);
```

Example 3-6: Interpreting Binding Information (continued)

```
                /* free all strings allocated by other runtime routines ❸*/
        rpc_string_free(&string_binding,  &status);
        rpc_string_free(&protseq,         &status);
        return;
}
```

❶ The *rpc_binding_to_string_binding* routine converts binding information to its string representation. The binding handle is passed in and the
string holding the binding information is allocated.

❷ The *rpc_string_binding_parse* routine obtains the binding information
items as separate allocated strings. The components include an object
UUID, a protocol sequence, a network address, an endpoint, and network options. If any of the components are null on input, no data is
obtained for that parameter.

❸ The *rpc_string_free* routine frees strings allocated by other RPC runtime
routines.

Finding a Server from a Name Service Database

The usual way for a client to obtain binding information is from a name service database using the name service RPC runtime routines (routines beginning with *rpc_ns_*). This method assumes that the server you want has
exported binding information to the name service database.

The name service database contains entries of information, each identified
by a name used in programs, environment variables, and commands. A
name is used to begin a search for compatible binding information in the
database. Some entries contain binding information about specific servers;
some contain a group of database names that represent a set of servers; and
some entries contain a search list. Use RPC name service runtime routines
to search entries in the name service database for binding information. The
example in this section does a very simple search. See Chapter 6 for a more
detailed name service description.

Importing a binding handle

Since the same interface can be supported on many systems of the network, a client needs a way to select one system. The runtime import routines obtain information for one binding handle at a time from the name
service database, selecting from the available list of servers supporting the
interface.

Example 3-7 shows how an application obtains binding information from a name service database.

Example 3-7: Importing a Binding Handle

```
/* FILE NAME: do_import_binding.c */
/* Get binding from name service database. */
#include <stdio.h>
#include "inventory.h"
#include "check_status.h"
void do_import_binding(entry_name, binding_h)
char                    entry_name[];       /* entry name to begin search */
rpc_binding_handle_t    *binding_h;         /* a binding handle (rpcbase.h) */
{
    unsigned32      status;                     /* error status (nbase.h) */
    rpc_ns_handle_t import_context;     /* required to import (rpcbase.h) */
    char            protseq[20];                /* protocol sequence */

    rpc_ns_binding_import_begin(/* set context to import binding handles❶*/
        rpc_c_ns_syntax_default,                    /* use default syntax */
        (unsigned_char_t *)entry_name,      /* begin search with this name */
        inventory_v1_0_c_ifspec,  /* interface specification (inventory.h) */
        NULL,                       /* no optional object UUID required */
        &import_context,                    /* import context obtained */
        &status
    );
    CHECK_STATUS(status, "Can't begin import:", RESUME);

    while(1) {
        rpc_ns_binding_import_next(              /* import a binding handle❷*/
            import_context,     * context from rpc_ns_binding_import_begin */
            binding_h,                      /* a binding handle is obtained */
            &status
        );
        if(status != rpc_s_ok) {
            CHECK_STATUS(status, "Can't import a binding handle:", RESUME);
            break;
        }

     /* application-specific selection criteria (by protocol sequence)  ❸*/
        do_interpret_binding(*binding_h ,protseq);
        if(strcmp(protseq, "ncacn_ip_tcp") == 0)        /* select connection */
                                                        /* protocol */
            break;
        else {
            rpc_binding_free(       /* free binding information not selected❹*/
                binding_h,
                &status
            );
            CHECK_STATUS(status, "Can't free binding information:", RESUME);
        }
    } /*end while */
```

Example 3-7: Importing a Binding Handle (continued)

```
rpc_ns_binding_import_done(              /* done with import context ❺*/
    &import_context,      /* obtained from rpc_ns_binding_import_begin */
    &status
);
return;
}
```

❶ The *rpc_ns_binding_import_begin* routine establishes the beginning of a search for binding information in a name service database. An entry name syntax of *rpc_c_ns_syntax_default* uses the syntax in the RPC-specific environment variable RPC_DEFAULT_SYNTAX.

In this example, the entry to begin the search is /.:/inventory_group, which is passed as a parameter. If you use a null string for the entry name, the search begins with the name in the RPC environment variable RPC_DEFAULT_ENTRY. In this example, an object UUID is not required, so we use a null value. The interface handle inventory_v1_0_c_ifspec refers to the interface specification. It is generated by the IDL compiler and defined in file *inventory.h*.

Finally, the import context and error status are output. You use the import context in other import routines to select binding information from the name service database or to free the context memory when you have finished with it.

❷ The *rpc_ns_binding_import_next* routine obtains binding information that supports the interface, if any exists. The routine accesses the database and does not communicate with the server. The import handle, established with the *rpc_ns_binding_import_begin* call, controls the search for compatible binding handles.

❸ Once binding information is obtained, any criteria required by the application may be used to decide whether it is appropriate. In this example, the application-specific procedure, do_interpret_binding, shown in Example 3-6, is used to interpret binding information by returning the protocol sequence in a parameter. The do_import_binding procedure then selects the binding information if it contains the connection protocol.

❹ Each call to *rpc_ns_binding_import_next* requires a corresponding call to the *rpc_binding_free* routine that frees memory containing the binding information and sets the binding handle to null. Free the binding handle after you finish making remote procedure calls.

❺ The *rpc_ns_binding_import_done* routine signifies that a client has finished looking for a compatible server in the name service database. This routine frees the memory of the import context created by a call to *rpc_ns_binding_import_begin*. Each *rpc_ns_binding_import_begin* call must have a corresponding call to *rpc_ns_binding_import_done*.

Looking up a set of binding handles

Runtime routines whose names begin with *rpc_ns_binding_lookup_* obtain a set of binding handles from the name service database. You can then select individual binding handles from the set with the *rpc_ns_binding_select* routine or you may use your own selection criteria. Lookup routines give a client program a little more control than import routines because *rpc_ns_binding_import_next* returns a random binding handle from a list of compatible binding handles. Use the lookup routines when you want to select a server or servers by more specific binding information; for example, to select a server that is running on a system in your building or to use servers supporting a specific protocol sequence.

Finding a Server from Strings of Binding Data

If you bypass the name service database, you need to construct your own binding information and binding handles. Binding information may be represented with strings. You can compose a binding handle from appropriate strings of binding information or interpret information that a binding handle refers to.

The minimum information required in your application to obtain a binding handle is:

- A protocol sequence of communication protocols

- A server network address or host name

Remember that an endpoint is required for a remote procedure call to complete, but you can let the RPC runtime library obtain one for you. To set a binding handle, obtain and present the binding information to RPC runtime routines.

Example 3-8 shows a procedure to set a binding handle from strings of binding information. The `remote_file` application uses this procedure. A network address or host name is input for this procedure and the protocol sequence is obtained. This procedure creates a partially bound binding handle, so the RPC runtime library obtains the endpoint when a remote procedure uses the binding handle.

Example 3-8: Setting a Binding Handle from Strings

```
/* FILE NAME: do_string_binding.c */
/* Find a server binding handle from strings of binding information */
/* including protocol sequence, host address, and server process endpoint. */
```

Example 3-8: Setting a Binding Handle from Strings (continued)

```
#include <stdio.h>
#include <dce/rpc.h>
#include "check_status.h"              /* contains the CHECK_STATUS macro */

int do_string_binding(host, binding_h)/* return=0 if binding valid, else -1 */
char            host[];      /* server host name or network address input ❶*/
rpc_binding_handle_t *binding_h;    /* binding handle is output (rpcbase.h) */
{
    rpc_protseq_vector_t *protseq_vector;              /* protocol sequence */
                                                       /* list (rpcbase.h)*/
    unsigned_char_t     *string_binding; /*string of binding info. (lbase.h)*/
    unsigned32          status;               /* error status (nbase.h) */
    int                 i, result;

    rpc_network_inq_protseqs(   /* obtain list of valid protocol sequences ❷*/
        &protseq_vector,                /* list of protocol sequences obtained */
        &status
    );
    CHECK_STATUS(status, "Can't get protocol sequences:", ABORT);

    /* loop through protocol sequences until a binding handle is obtained */
    for(i=0; i < protseq_vector->count; i++) {
        rpc_string_binding_compose(  /* make string binding from components ❸*/
            NULL,                           /* no object UUIDs are required */
            protseq_vector->protseq[i],           /* protocol sequence */
            (unsigned_char_t *)host,       /* host name or network address */
            NULL,                          /* no endpoint is required */
            NULL,                          /* no network options are required */
            &string_binding,               /* the constructed string binding */
            &status
        );
        CHECK_STATUS(status, "Can't compose a string binding:", RESUME);

        rpc_binding_from_string_binding(            /* convert string to */
                                                    /* binding handle ❹*/
            string_binding,                  /* input string binding */
            binding_h,                      /* binding handle is obtained here */
            &status
        );
        if(status != rpc_s_ok) {
            result = -1;
            CHECK_STATUS(status, "Can't get binding handle from string :", RESUME);
        }
        else
            result = 0;

        rpc_string_free(                   /* free string binding created ❺*/
            &string_binding,
            &status
        );
        CHECK_STATUS(status, "Can't free string binding:", RESUME);
        if(result == 0)  break;                    /* got a valid binding */
    }
```

Example 3-8: Setting a Binding Handle from Strings (continued)

```
rpc_protseq_vector_free(       /* free the list of protocol sequences ❻*/
    &protseq_vector,
    &status
);
CHECK_STATUS(status, "Can't free protocol sequence vector:", RESUME);
return(result);
}
```

❶ The network address or host name on which a server is available is required binding information. For this example, the information is input as a parameter.

❷ The *rpc_network_inq_protseqs* routine creates a list of valid protocol sequences. This example uses each protocol sequence from the list until a binding handle is created.

❸ The *rpc_string_binding_compose* routine creates a string of binding information in the argument `string_binding` from all the necessary binding information components. The component strings include an object UUID, a protocol sequence, a network address, an endpoint, and network options.

❹ The *rpc_binding_from_string_binding* routine obtains a binding handle from the string of binding information. The string of binding information comes from the *rpc_string_binding_compose* routine or from the *rpc_binding_to_string_binding* routine.

When you are finished with the binding handle, use the *rpc_binding_free* routine to set the binding handle to null and to free memory referred to by the binding handle. In this example, another part of the application frees the binding handle.

❺ The *rpc_string_free* routine frees strings allocated by other RPC runtime routines. This example frees the string `string_binding` allocated by the *rpc_string_binding_compose* routine.

❻ The *rpc_protseq_vector_free* routine is called to free the list of protocol sequences. An earlier call to *rpc_network_inq_protseqs* requires a corresponding call to *rpc_protseq_vector_free*.

Customizing a Binding Handle

The basic binding handles we have seen so far are **primitive binding handles**. A **customized binding handle** adds some information that your application wants to pass between client and server. You can use a customized binding handle when application-specific data is appropriate to use for finding a server, and the data is also needed as a procedure parameter.

For example, in the `transfer_data` application, a structure contains a host name and a remote filename. The application creates the necessary binding information from the host name, and the filename is passed with the binding information so the server knows what data file to use. You can use a customized binding handle with the explicit or implicit binding methods, but the automatic method uses only primitive binding handles.

Figure 3-2 shows how a customized binding handle works during a remote procedure call.

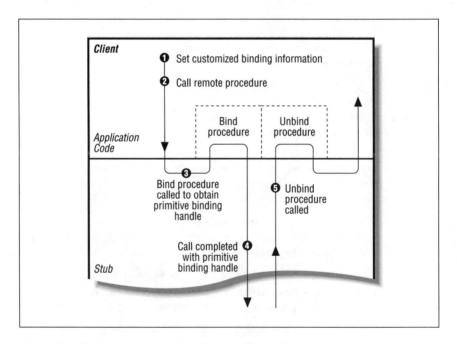

Figure 3-2: How a customized binding handle works

To define a customized binding handle, apply the `handle` attribute to a type definition in an interface definition.

You can use a customized binding handle in a client just like a primitive binding handle, but you must write special **bind** and **unbind** procedures. Your code does not call these procedures; the client stub calls them during each remote procedure call. For a primitive binding handle, the client stub already has the necessary code to prepare the binding information for the call. For application-specific binding information, you must supply the code. The tasks of the bind and unbind procedures are to obtain a primitive binding handle and do application cleanup when finished with the binding handle.

Manipulate the data structure in your application the same as any structure, including passing data in the remote procedure call. However, the client stub uses the special procedures to manage the binding. The customized binding handle must be the first parameter in a remote procedure (or the global handle for the implicit method) to act as the binding handle for the call. A customized handle acts as a standard parameter if it is not the first parameter.

Example 3-9 shows how to define a customized binding handle in the `transfer_data` interface definition (see Appendix I).

Example 3-9: Defining a Customized Binding Handle

```
/* FILE NAME: transfer_data.idl */
[
uuid(A6876974-F555-11CA-BAE1-08002B245A28),
version(1.0)
]
interface transfer_data     /* data transfer to and from a remote system */
{
    const long NAME_LENGTH = 200;

    typedef [handle] struct {               /* a customized handle type ❶*/
        char host[NAME_LENGTH+1];
        char filename[NAME_LENGTH+1];
    } file_spec;                                            /*❷*/
    .
    .
    .
```

Example 3-9: Defining a Customized Binding Handle (continued)

```
void send_floats(       /* send pipe of floats to a file on the server ❸*/
    [in] file_spec cust_binding_h,    /* customized binding for server */
    [in] pipe_type data               /* input pipe of float data      */
);
    .
    .
    .
```

❶ Use the `handle` attribute in the interface definition to associate a customized binding handle with a data type.

❷ The `file_spec` data type is a structure whose members are file specifications. This is application-specific information used by the bind procedure to obtain server binding information.

❸ The customized binding handle is the first parameter of a procedure declaration. This is an example of explicit binding.

You must implement bind and unbind procedures (see Example 3-10).

Example 3-10: Bind and Unbind Procedures

```
/* FILE NAME: binding.c */
#include "transfer_data.h"       /* header created by the IDL compiler */
#include "check_status.h"        /* contains the CHECK_STATUS macro    */

handle_t file_spec_bind(spec)   /* "bind" procedure for customized handle❶*/
file_spec spec;
{
    rpc_binding_handle_t binding_h;
    if(do_string_binding(spec.host, &binding_h) < 0) {
        fprintf(stderr, "Cannot get binding\n");
        exit(1);
    }
    return(binding_h);
}

void file_spec_unbind(spec, binding_h) /* "unbind" for customized handle❷*/
file_spec spec;
handle_t binding_h;
{
    unsigned32 status;   /* error status */

    rpc_binding_free(&binding_h, &status);
    CHECK_STATUS(status, "Can't free binding handle:", RESUME);
    return;
}
```

❶ The bind procedure takes an input parameter of the customized handle data type, and returns a primitive binding handle. You construct the procedure name from the data type name, *file_spec*, to which you append *_bind*. In this example *file_spec_bind* calls the application-specific `do_string_binding` procedure (defined in the `remote_file` application and shown in Example 3-8) to obtain a primitive binding handle.

❷ The unbind procedure takes input parameters of the customized handle data type and a primitive binding handle. You construct the procedure name from the data type name, *file_spec*, to which you append *_unbind*. In this example *file_spec_unbind* calls the RPC runtime routine, *rpc_binding_free*, to free the binding handle.

Example 3-11 shows how a `transfer_data` application client uses a customized binding handle.

Example 3-11: A Client with a Customized Binding Handle

```
/* FILE NAME: client_send.c */
    .
    .
    .
main(argc, argv)
int argc;
char *argv[];
{
    file_spec   cust_binding_h;          /* customized binding handle❶*/
    char        local_source[100];
    .
    .
    .
    void        send_floats();

    /* get user input */
    if(argc < 4) {
        printf("USAGE: %s  local_source  host  file\n", argv[0]);
        exit(0);
    }
    /* initialize customized binding handle structure */          /*❷*/
    strcpy(local_source, argv[1]);
    strcpy(cust_binding_h.host, argv[2]);
    strcpy(cust_binding_h.filename, argv[3]);
    .
    .
    .
    send_floats(cust_binding_h, data); /* remote procedure with input❸*/
}
```

❶ The application allocates the customized binding handle.

❷ Initialize the customized binding information in the client before calling the remote procedure. For this example, when we invoke the client, we input the server host name and remote data filename as arguments.

❸ The remote procedure is called with the customized binding handle as the first parameter.

Error Parameters or Exceptions

DCE RPC client applications require special error-handling techniques to deal with errors that may occur during a remote procedure call. The following discussion pertains to both client and server development.

Server and communication errors are raised to the client as exceptions during a remote procedure call. RPC exceptions are equivalent to the RPC error status codes. For example, the exception `rpc_x_comm_failure` is the same as the error code `rpc_s_comm_failure`.*

Types of exceptions include the following:

- Exceptions raised on the client system, such as when the client process is out of memory (`rpc_x_no_memory`).

- Exceptions raised to the client application by the client stub due to communication errors, such as crashes on the remote system (`rpc_x_comm_failure`).

- Exceptions raised by the client stub on behalf of the server. These errors can occur in the server stub (`rpc_x_fault_remote_no_memory`), in the remote procedures (`rpc_x_call_faulted`), in pipe support routines (`rpc_x_fault_pipe_order`), or in the server's RPC runtime library.

A distributed application can have errors from a number of sources, so you will need to decide whether you want to handle errors with exception

---

*The RPC runtime routines define error status codes as `unsigned32` so data type naming is consistent. The IDL compiler-generated header file contains procedure definitions whose error parameters are defined as `error_status_t` so data type naming in IDL is consistent. The data types `unsigned32` and `error_status_t` are equivalent. The applications in this book use the data type `unsigned32` for exceptions and error parameters.

handling code or error parameters. This may simply be a matter of personal preference or consistency.

Using Exception Handlers in Clients or Servers

You can handle exceptions by writing exception handler code in the application to recover from an error or gracefully exit the application. DCE threads supply macros as a framework to handle exceptions in your client or server code. (Example 5-6 uses exception handling macros.)

Using Remote Procedure Parameters To Handle Errors

In your ACF, you can add error parameters to remote procedures in order to conveniently handle communication and server errors. The RPC runtime library then stores errors values in these parameters rather than raising exceptions. You can also use a combination of exception handlers and error parameters.

The following procedure is declared in the interface definition for the inventory application. Notice that there is one input parameter:

```
boolean is_part_available(    /* Return true if part is in inventory */
    [in] part_num number      /* input part number */
);
```

To establish an error parameter for the procedure, include the following statement in an ACF:

```
is_part_available([comm_status, fault_status] status);
```

The ACF attributes, comm_status and fault_status, establish a parameter in which to report communication and server errors, if they occur during this remote procedure call. These ACF attributes can be associated with one parameter or separate parameters. In a client, the remote procedure call to this procedure now has an additional parameter written as follows:

```
unsigned32 status;
    .
    .
    .
available = is_part_available(part.number, &status);
CHECK_STATUS(status, "", ABORT);
```

Notice the added error parameter at the end of the parameter list. In this example, if a communication or server error occurs during the remote procedure call, the error code is assigned to status when the call returns. You can interpret the error code by calling the RPC runtime routine *dce_error_inq_text*. Example 3-12 shows this routine in the application-specific CHECK_STATUS macro.

Example 3-12: The CHECK_STATUS Macro

```
/* FILE NAME: check_status.h */
#include <stdio.h>
#include <dce/dce_error.h>/* required to call dce_error_inq_text routine */
#include <dce/pthread.h>          /* needed if application uses threads */
#include <dce/rpcexc.h> /* needed if application uses exception handlers */

#define RESUME 0
#define ABORT  1

#define CHECK_STATUS(input_status, comment, action) \
{ \
  if(input_status != rpc_s_ok) { \
    dce_error_inq_text(input_status, error_string, &error_stat); \
    fprintf(stderr, "%s %s\n", comment, error_string); \
    if(action == ABORT) \
    exit(1); \
  } \
}

static int            error_stat;
static unsigned char  error_string[dce_c_error_string_len];

void exit();
```

For most applications that use ACFs, you compile the interface separately for the client and server because their header files are different. Each shows the correct number, order, and type of parameters where the client has the error parameter, but the server does not. If an error occurs during a remote procedure call, the stubs deliver and assign the value to the additional error parameter in the client.

If an error parameter already exists for the procedure in the interface definition, the comm_status and fault_status ACF attributes can be applied to that parameter to override the exception mechanism. In this case, the error parameter must be a pointer to the error_status_t type and be an output parameter with the out directional attribute. For example, the following procedure declaration in an interface definition has an error parameter:

```
proc([out] error_status_t *status);
```

The ACF must have the following declaration to report communication errors through the parameter:

```
proc([comm_status] *status);
```

Compiling and Linking Clients

Figure 3-3 shows the files and libraries required to produce an executable client. If needed, the IDL compiler produces the client stub auxiliary file (*appl_*caux.o) when the interface is compiled. The following features cause the production of a client auxiliary file:

- Self-referential pointers in the interface definition

- The out_of_line attribute in an ACF

To compile the implicit client of the inventory application, type the following from the *implicit* directory:

1. Compile all the client modules with the C compiler.

    ```
    C> cc -c implicit_client.c do_import_binding.c \
    do_interpret_binding.c
    ```

2. Link the client application, client stub, and client auxiliary object files (if available) with the DCE libraries to produce the executable client. The IDL compiler does not produce auxiliary files for the inventory interface.

    ```
    C> cc -o implicit_client.exe \
    implicit_client.o do_import_binding.o do_interpret_binding.o \
    inventory_cstub.o -ldce -lcma
    ```

Local Testing

You can compile a local version of your client to test and debug remote procedures without using remote procedure calls. To do a local test, compile the client object files and remote procedure implementations without the stub or auxiliary files. The code that finds a server is also unnecessary for a local test. Applications in this book use the compiler directive, −DLO-CAL, to distinguish a test compilation used in a local environment from a compilation used in a distributed environment. Type the following from the *implicit* directory:

```
C> cc -I../ -I../../arithmetic -DLOCAL -o local_implicit_client.exe \
implicit_client.c ../i_procedures.c ../implement_inventory.c
```

Be sure to delete the object files created with the −DLOCAL compiler directive so they do not interfere with a build for the distributed version of the applications.

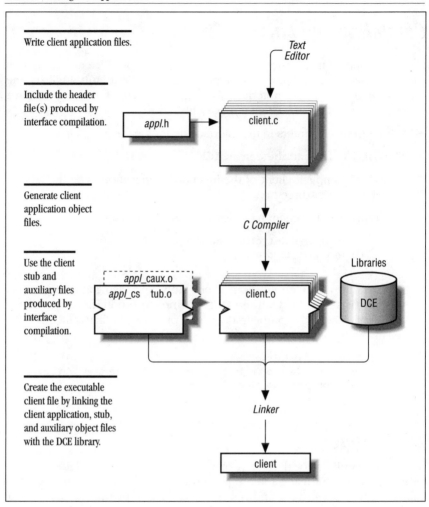

Write client application files.

Include the header file(s) produced by interface compilation.

Generate client application object files.

Use the client stub and auxiliary files produced by interface compilation.

Create the executable client file by linking the client application, stub, and auxiliary object files with the DCE library.

Figure 3-3: Producing a client

4

Pointers and Arrays

In C, pointers and arrays have a close correlation due to the way applications access the information they contain. Pointers and arrays work essentially the same in distributed and local applications. But there are a few restrictions in distributed applications because the client and server have different address spaces. In most of this chapter we discuss pointers and arrays for clients. See also Chapter 5 for a discussion of memory allocation for pointers and arrays in remote procedures.

To make your applications more efficient, IDL offers several kinds of pointers and arrays to reduce network traffic and stub overhead. This chapter uses the inventory application to demonstrate the use of pointers and arrays in distributed applications.

Kinds of Pointers

A pointer is a variable containing the address of another data structure or variable. As in C, you declare a pointer in an interface definition by using an asterisk (*) followed by a variable. For example, the inventory application has the following procedure declaration:

```
void whatis_part_price(              /* get part price from inventory */
    [in]  part_num   number,
    [out] part_price *price
);
```

In a distributed application, the client and server do not share the same address space. This means the data a pointer refers to in the client is not available in the remote procedure of the server. The opposite is also true. Therefore, pointer data is copied between the client and server address spaces during a remote procedure call. For the whatis_part_price procedure, data that the pointer argument refers to on the server is copied back to the client and placed in the memory referred to by the `price` pointer. This copying of pointer data does not occur during a local procedure call. IDL has two kinds of pointers: full pointers and reference pointers.

A **full pointer** has all the capabilities usually associated with pointers. Interface definitions require full pointers for the following:

- When a remote procedure call allocates new memory for the client. The client stub actually allocates the memory.

- When the value of the pointer is NULL, as with an optional parameter.

- When two pointers refer to the same address, as in a double-linked list.

The `ptr` attribute specifies a full pointer in an interface definition. Full pointer capability comes at a cost of significant stub overhead, so IDL provides a second kind of pointer, a reference pointer.

A **reference pointer** is used to refer to existing data. A reference pointer has a performance advantage over a full pointer because stub overhead is reduced. For example, the `whatis_part_price` procedure uses a reference pointer. This procedure passes by reference a pointer to an allocated `part_price` data structure. The remote procedure returns output data to the same memory location with the part price. Thus for reference pointers, the data can change, but not the address itself. The `ref` attribute specifies a reference pointer in an interface definition.

A pointer attribute must be applied where the pointer is defined with an asterisk. For instance, if you define a typedef that resolves to a pointer, you cannot apply the pointer attribute where you use the typedef.

The following sections discuss the use of pointers, and tell you when you need a reference or full pointer. Table 4-1 and Example 4-5 summarize what you need to know to declare and use pointers.

Pointers as Output Parameters

Due to the overhead of transmitting data, you have to declare IDL parameters to be input, output, or both. In IDL, as in C, input parameters are passed in by value, which means a copy of each input parameter is available in the procedure. Passing input parameters by value makes sense for remote procedure calls since data must be copied and transmitted from the client to the server anyway. However, passing by value also means that any change to the variable in the procedure cannot reflect back to the original parameter when the call completes.

To fill in data for an output parameter (or modify an input/output parameter), both C and IDL must pass by reference a memory address using a pointer or array parameter. During a remote procedure call, the parameter refers to existing memory, which is passed by reference to the client stub.

When the remote procedure completes execution, data is sent back by the server stub to the client stub, which unmarshalls it into the memory referred to by the pointer. Therefore, the data is available to the client application when the client stub returns to the application.

Example 4-1 shows an output parameter in the whatis_part_price procedure declaration from the inventory interface definition. Pointer parameters (*price) are reference pointers by default.

Example 4-1: Defining an Output Parameter

```
void whatis_part_price(            /* get part price from inventory */
    [in]  part_num   number,
    [out] part_price *price                    /* reference pointer */
);
```

The `part_price` structure must be allocated in the client prior to the remote procedure call, but values are assigned in the remote procedure and transmitted back. The `whatis_part_price` remote procedure call in the client looks like this:

```
part_record part;          /* structure for all data about a part */
    .
    .
    .
    case 'p': whatis_part_price(part.number, &(part.price));
              printf("price:%10.2f\n", part.price.per_unit);
              break;
```

In the server, whatis_part_price reads a part record from the database for the part number input. It then assigns the values from the part record to the price structure members. Finally, the procedure returns and the price information is marshalled and transmitted by the server stub. The whatis_part_price remote procedure looks like this:

```
void whatis_part_price(number, price)
part_num   number;
part_price *price;
{
    part_record *part;                 /* a pointer to a part record */

    read_part_record(number, &part);
    price->units = part->price.units;
    price->per_unit = part->price.per_unit;
    return;
}
```

You can see from the preceding explanation that an output parameter must refer to existing storage on the client, and therefore that it is always a reference pointer. In fact, the IDL compiler refuses to let you declare an output-only parameter with the ptr attribute.

Suppose we don't know how much memory should be allocated for output data, so we want a procedure to return data in a parameter as newly allocated memory. We cannot just allocate some memory and hope it's enough because if the data output is greater, data will overwrite into other memory. To solve this, we pass a pointer to a pointer. We describe how to do this later in the chapter.

A parameter used as both input and output is passed by reference. Programs commonly modify data by passing a pointer to a data structure into a procedure, which passes back the same pointer, but with modified data. Pointer features including optional parameters and pointer aliasing can apply to input/output parameters. These features apply to the input and are described in the following section.

Pointers as Input Parameters

Suppose our inventory interface has the following procedure declaration:

```
void store_parts(
    [in] part_record *part1,
    [in] part_record *part2
);
```

Assume this procedure adds new parts to the database. The procedure takes as parameters two pointers to structures of type part_record, (already defined in the interface) to store all data about a part.

The remote procedure call in a client can look like the following:

```
part_record *part1, *part2;
part1 = (part_record *)malloc(sizeof(part_record));
part2 = (part_record *)malloc(sizeof(part_record));
/* part structures are filled in */
part1->number = 123;
part2->number = 124;
    .
    .
    .
store_parts(part1, part2);
```

In this simple case, the client stub marshalls and transmits the data the pointers refer to. (This procedure is not implemented in any applications in this book, so no server code is shown.)

One reason that reference pointers reduce overhead is that the stubs make certain assumptions about the use of the pointer. Since pointer parameters are reference pointers by default, one of these assumptions is that a pointer parameter points to valid data of the type specified.

Suppose we want optional parameters in our procedure definition. In this case, the client passes a null pointer value for the parameter, so the remote procedure knows to ignore it. For the stubs to know the parameter is a null value, the parameter must be a full pointer so the stubs do not attempt to copy any data for the parameter.

Example 4-2 shows how to modify our store_parts procedure declaration so that both parameters are full pointers.

Example 4-2: Defining Optional Procedure Parameters

```
void store_parts_1(                      /* ❶ */
    [in,ptr] part_record *part1,
    [in,ptr] part_record *part2
);
    .
    .
    .
typedef [ptr] part_record *part_record_ptr;
void store_parts_2(                      /* ❷ */
    [in] part_record_ptr part1,
    [in] part_record_ptr part2
);
```

❶ To specify an optional parameter, use the ptr attribute on an input (or input/output) parameter.

❷ As an alternative to method 1 for specifying an optional parameter, define a full pointer data type and use the data type for the procedure parameter.

The client can now supply a NULL pointer:

```
store_parts_1(part1, NULL);
```

If an input/output parameter is a full pointer with a null value on input, it is also null on output because the client does not have an address to store a return value.

Full pointers allow two pointers to refer to the same data. This is known as **pointer aliasing**:

To minimize overhead, stubs cannot manage more than one reference pointer referring to the same data in a single remote procedure call. For example, suppose our store_parts procedure does something useful if we pass in the same pointer for both arguments. The following type of remote procedure call causes unpredictable behavior:

```
store_parts(part1, part1); /* WRONG - do not use ref pointer aliasing */
```

This call will *not* work as expected because the parameters (reference pointers) both point to the same address. Reference pointers do not allow two pointers to refer to the same data.

The following call will work correctly, however, because the pointers are specifically defined in the interface definition as full pointers with the `ptr` attribute:

```
store_parts_1(part1, part1);    /* full pointers allow aliasing */
```

Using Pointers to Pointers for New Output

A pointer refers to a specific amount of memory. For a procedure parameter to output newly allocated memory, we use a pointer to refer to another pointer that refers to data (or to another pointer and so on). This is also known as multiple levels of indirection.

If you use just one pointer for a procedure parameter, you would have to make two remote procedure calls to allocate new memory. The first remote procedure call obtains the size of the server's data structure. Then the client allocates memory for it. The second remote procedure call obtains data from the server and fills the previously allocated memory. In a distributed application, using two pointers allows the client and server stubs to allocate all the necessary memory in one remote procedure call. The client stub must generate a copy of the memory allocated on the server.

The `whatare_subparts` procedure in the inventory application contains a parameter with a pointer to a pointer:

```
[out] part_list **subparts
```

The procedure allocates memory for the left pointer, and the right pointer is a parameter passed by reference to return the address of the left pointer. To accomplish this, IDL must use both kinds of pointers:

The right pointer is a reference pointer and the left pointer is a full pointer. The reference pointer by itself cannot have new memory automatically allocated because it will point to the same address throughout the remote call. However, for the full pointer, the amount of memory allocated by the server is allocated automatically by the client stub when the call returns.

When a pointer attribute is applied in an interface definition where there are pointers to pointers, it applies only to the right pointer and does not propagate to any other pointers.

Example 4-3 demonstrates how to return data in a parameter by using two pointers. The procedure needs to output a data structure (in this case a structure with a conformant array). The final size of the data structure is unknown when you call the remote procedure.

Example 4-3: Defining Pointers to Pointers for Memory Allocation

```
[
    .
    .
    .
pointer_default(ptr)            /* the pointer default is a full pointer❶*/
] interface inventory
{
    .
    .
    .
    void whatare_subparts(      /* get list of subpart numbers for a part */
        [in]  part_num  number,
        [out] part_list **subparts          /* a pointer to a pointer❷*/
    );
```

❶ Parameters or type definitions with multiple pointers use a pointer default to specify the kind of pointer for all but the right one. To establish a pointer default, use the `pointer_default` attribute in the interface definition header. In this example, the `ptr` argument establishes a full pointer default.

❷ If memory is allocated during remote procedure execution, output parameters require multiple pointers. By default, the right pointer of a procedure parameter is a reference pointer. The left pointer must be a full pointer. This is accomplished through the `pointer_default` attribute.

The `part_list` structure is allocated during the remote procedure call. On the server, the remote procedure allocates memory and assigns data. The server stub marshalls and transmits the data back to the client, and then frees the memory allocated in the remote procedure. The client stub then allocates memory and unmarshalls the transmitted data into the new memory. The remote procedure call in a client for `whatare_subparts` looks like:

```
part_record part;            /* structure for all data about a part  */
part_list    *subparts;      /* pointer to parts list data structure */
    .
    .
    .
    case 's': whatare_subparts(part.number, &subparts);
             for(i = 0; i < subparts->size; i++)
                 printf("%ld  ", subparts->numbers[i]);
             printf("\ntotal number of subparts:%ld\n", subparts->size);
```

When you are finished with the data, free the memory allocated by full pointers:

```
        free(subparts);
        break;
```

See Example 5-8 for the server implementation of the remote procedure `whatare_subparts`.

Pointers as Procedure Return Values

As we have described previously, the client must allocate memory for reference pointer data before it is used in a remote procedure call. This simplifies the client stub by giving unmarshalling code a place to put data after the server sends it. Now consider the following remote procedure call in client application code:

```
idl_long_int *a;
a = proc();
```

The address of the procedure assignment, a, is available only when the procedure returns, and not during its execution. Therefore, we cannot use the method just described for a reference pointer: allocate memory in the client prior to the call, and expect the stub to complete the assignment for us. Procedures that return pointer results always return full pointers, so that the stub allocates any necessary memory and unmarshalls data into it for us. Example 4-4 shows an example of a procedure that returns a pointer.

Example 4-4: Defining a Procedure that Returns a Pointer

```
typedef [string, ptr] char *paragraph;          /* description of part ❶*/
    .
    .
    .
paragraph get_part_description(          /* return a pointer to a string ❷*/
    [in]  part_num  number
);
```

❶ A pointer attribute (`ptr`) on a pointer data type (`char *paragraph`) specifies the kind of pointer for that data type wherever it is used in the interface. (If a pointer data type does not have a pointer attribute, the pointer specified with the `pointer_default` attribute applies.) To specify a pointer to a string, apply the `string` attribute as well.

❷ Procedures that return a pointer result always return a full pointer. A procedure result cannot be a reference pointer because new storage is always allocated by the client stub, which copies data into it when the call returns.

The call to `get_part_description` looks like:

```
part_record part;              /* structure for all data about a part */
    .
    .
    .
    case 'd': part.description = get_part_description(part.number);
              printf("description:\n%s\n", part.description);
```

When you are finished with the data, free the memory allocated by full pointers:

```
if(part.description != NULL)
    free(part.description);          /* free memory allocated */
```

On the server, the remote procedure allocates memory that the server stub copies and transmits back to the client. The server stub then frees the memory allocated. Example 5-7 shows how to allocate memory in the `get_part_description` remote procedure.

Pointer Summary

Reference pointers require less overhead than full pointers, but they have some restrictions. Therefore, you must differentiate between a full and reference pointer in the interface definition. Table 4-1 summarizes and compares reference pointers and full pointers. Example 4-5 shows how to recognize which kind of pointer applies in an interface definition. A visible `ref` or `ptr` pointer attribute overrides a default.

Table 4-1: A Summary of Reference and Full Pointers

	Reference Pointer	Full Pointer
Attribute name	ref	ptr
Characteristics	Provides indirection where the value is always the address of valid data	Indirection and full pointer capabilities
Stub overhead	Minimum	Maximum
Value of NULL	Cannot be NULL	Can be NULL
Address value	Never changes when a call returns	May change when a call returns
Storage	Storage exists prior to the call	Storage is allocated automatically if needed
Input and output parameter	Data is written into existing storage when the call returns	The storage location of data on output may be different than the storage location on input. If the input value is NULL, the output value is also NULL.
Output parameter	Parameter is a reference pointer by default	Not allowed
Input parameter	Data is read from existing storage	Data is read from existing storage; if the value is NULL, no data is read.
Pointer aliasing	Not allowed	Allowed

Example 4-5: How to Determine Kinds of Pointers

```
[
    .
    .
    .
pointer_default(ptr);                  /*❶*/
] inventory interface
{
    .
    .
    .
typedef [string, ptr] char *paragraph;  /*❷*/
    .
    .
    .
```

Example 4-5: How to Determine Kinds of Pointers (continued)

```
paragraph get_part_description(          /*❸*/
    [in] part_num number,
);
        .
        .
        .

void whatis_part_price(
    [in]  part_num   number,
    [out] part_price *price               /*❹*/
);
        .
        .
        .

void whatare_subparts(
    [in]  part_num  number,
    [out] part_list **subparts            /*❺*/
);
        .
        .
        .

typedef struct {                          /*❻*/
    [ref] part_num      *number;
    [ref] part_quantity *quantity;
    [ref] account_num   *account;
} part_order;
        .
        .
        .

void store_parts_1(                       /*❼*/
    [in,ptr] part_record *part1,
    [in,ptr] part_record *part2
);
}
```

❶ The IDL compiler attempts to automatically assign the appropriate kind
of pointer to pointers without a `ptr` or `ref` attribute. The
`pointer_default` interface header attribute specifies which kind of
pointer applies when one cannot be automatically determined. The
`pointer_default` attribute has an argument of either `ref` or `ptr`. If
a pointer attribute is not specified for the data type, the interface
requires a pointer default to specify the kind of pointer for the following
cases:

— Pointers in typedefs (see callout 2)

— Multiple pointers other than the right pointer (see callout 5)

— Pointers that are members of structures or cases of
discriminated unions (see callout 6)

❷ A pointer type attribute specifies the kind of pointer used. In this example, all occurrences that use the `paragraph` data type are full pointers. If neither the `ref` nor `ptr` attribute is present in the typedef, the `pointer_default` attribute specifies the kind of pointer.

❸ A pointer return value of a procedure is always a full pointer because new memory is allocated. The `paragraph` data structure is a pointer to a string.

❹ A pointer parameter of a procedure is a reference pointer by default. Parameter reference pointers must always point to valid storage, never null (see also callout 7).

❺ With multiple pointers, the `pointer_default` attribute specifies all pointers except the right-most pointer. In this example, the right pointer is a reference pointer because it is a parameter pointer. The left pointer is determined by the pointer default. In this procedure, the left pointer must be a full pointer so the array of parts in the `subparts` structure is automatically allocated by the client stub when the call returns.

❻ When a structure member or discriminated union case is a pointer, you must assign it a `ptr` or `ref` attribute, either explicitly or through the `pointer_default` attribute. This interface definition specifies the structure members as reference pointers to override the full pointer default. Full pointers are unnecessary for these structure members; therefore, it is more efficient to use reference pointers to minimize the overhead associated with full pointers.

❼ An input or input/output pointer parameter can be made an optional procedure parameter by applying the `ptr` attribute. This is required if you pass a value of NULL, or alias pointers in a call.

Kinds of Arrays

You can use the following kinds of arrays in RPC applications:

- **Fixed arrays** contain a specific number of elements defined in the interface definition. They are defined just like standard C declarations.

- **Varying arrays** have a fixed size but clients and servers select a portion to transmit during a remote procedure call. The interface definition specifies subset bound variables used by the clients and servers to set the bounds.

- **Conformant arrays** have their size determined in the application code. The interface definition specifies an array size variable that the clients and servers use to control the amount of memory allocated and data transmitted.

Selecting a Portion of a Varying Array

For some clients or servers you need to use only a portion of an array in a remote procedure call. If this is the case, it is more efficient to transmit only the needed portion of the array. Procedures or structures that use varying arrays with data limit variables allow you to select the portion of an array that is processed by a remote procedure call.

A varying array has a fixed size when the application is compiled, but the portion of the array that contains the relevant, transmissible data is determined at runtime. For example, given the varying array `arr[100]`, you can specify any index values in the range $0 \le L \le U \le 99$, where L represents the lower data limit of the array and U represents the upper data limit.

An array is varying if you declare it in your interface definition with two extra attributes: `first_is` to indicate where transmission starts (L), and either `length_is` or `last_is` to indicated where transmission stops (U). Whether you use `length_is` or `last_is` depends on convenience.

Suppose that the following procedure appears in an interface definition:

```
const long SIZE = 100;

void proc(
    [in] long first,
    [in] long length,
    [in, first_is(first), length_is(length)] data_t arr[SIZE]
);
```

To select a portion of the array to transmit, assign values to the variables `first` and `length`. For input parameters, the client sets them prior to the remote procedure call. Be sure the upper data limit value does not exceed the size of the array; for example:

```
long first = 23;
long length = 54;
data_t arr[SIZE];

proc(first, length, arr);
```

The transmitted array portion is represented by the indices $\boxed{23}$ . . . $\boxed{76}$ (23 + 54 - 1). The entire array is available in the client and the server, but only the portion represented by the data limit variables is transmitted and meaningful for the given remote procedure call. If the data limit parameters are also output, the remote procedure can set them to control the portion of the array transmitted back to the client.

A structure is an alternate way to define a varying array in an interface definition; for example:

```
typedef struct varray_t {
   long first;
   long length;
   [first_is(first), length_is(length)] data_t arr[SIZE];
} varray_t;

proc([in] varray_t varray);
```

Managing the Size of a Conformant Array

Conformant arrays are defined in an interface definition with empty brackets or an asterisk (*) in place of the first dimension value.

```
. . . c1[*] . . .
. . . c2[][10] . . .
```

The conformant array `c1[*]` has index values $\boxed{0}$ . . . $\boxed{M}$ in which the dimension variable, *M*, represents the upper bound of the array. The dimension variable is specified in the interface definition and used in the application code at runtime to establish the array's actual size.

To specify an array size variable or a maximum upper bound variable, use one of the array size attributes, `size_is` or `max_is`, in an interface definition. These variables are used in the application to represent the size of the array. You can use either one; depending on which you find most convenient. Example 4-6 shows how a conformant array is defined in a structure.

Example 4-6: A Conformant Array in an Interface Definition

```
     .
     .
     .
typedef struct part_list{                    /* list of part numbers */
   long                    size;       /* number of parts in array ❶*/
   [size_is(size)] part_num numbers[*];  /* conformant array of parts❷*/
} part_list;

typedef struct part_record {                    /* data for each part */
   part_num       number;
   part_name      name;
   paragraph      description;
   part_price     price;
   part_quantity  quantity;
   part_list      subparts; /* Conformant array or struct must be last❸*/
} part_record;
     .
     .
     .
```

Example 4-6: A Conformant Array in an Interface Definition (continued)

```
void whatare_subparts(              /* get list of subparts numbers for a part */
    [in]  part_num  number,
    [out] part_list **subparts                                /*❹*/
);
    .
    .
    .
```

❶ When an array member of a structure (`numbers[*]`) has an array attribute, the dimension variable (`size`) must also be a structure member. This assures that the dimension information is always available with the array when it is transmitted. The dimension variable member must be, or must resolve to, an integer.

❷ The `size_is` attribute specifies a variable (size) that represents the number of elements the array dimension contains. In the application, the array indices are $\boxed{0}$ ... $\boxed{\text{size-1}}$. For example, if `size` is equal to 8 in the application code, then the array indices are $\boxed{0}\boxed{1}\boxed{2}\boxed{3}\boxed{4}\boxed{5}\boxed{6}\boxed{7}$.

❸ If a conformant array is a member of a structure, it must be last so that your application can allocate any amount of memory needed. A conformant structure (structure containing a conformant array member) must also be the last member of a structure containing it.

❹ Use a conformant structure and multiple levels of indirection for remote procedures that allocate a conformant array. Chapter 5 implements this procedure.

To specify a variable that represents the highest index value for the first dimension of the array rather than the array size, use the `max_is` attribute instead of the `size_is` attribute. For example, the conformant structure defined in Example 4-6 can also be defined as follows:

```
typedef struct part_list{
    long  max;
    [max_is(max)] part_num numbers[*];
} part_list;
```

The variable `max` defines the maximum index value of the first dimension of the array. In the application, the array indices are $\boxed{0}$ ... $\boxed{\text{max}}$. For example, if max is equal to 7 in the application code, then the array indices are $\boxed{0}\boxed{1}\boxed{2}\boxed{3}\boxed{4}\boxed{5}\boxed{6}\boxed{7}$.

To avoid making mistakes in application development, be consistent in the interface definitions you write. Use either the `size_is` attribute or the `max_is` attribute for all your conformant arrays.

Conformant arrays as procedure parameters

When you call a remote procedure that contains a conformant array, you must pass the number of elements contained by the array. When a client calls the whatare_subparts remote procedure of Example 4-3, the dimension information is available in the part_list structure. However, if an array is passed as a parameter, the dimension information must also be an in parameter of the procedure.

For example, instead of obtaining an array of all the subparts for a part (as the whatare_subparts procedure does) you may want only the first five subparts. This procedure is defined as follows:

```
void get_n_subparts(                /* get n subpart numbers for a part */
    [in]   part_num    number,
    [in]   long        n,
    [out,size_is(n)] part_num subparts[]
);
```

In the client, the input includes the part number, a five representing the number of subparts desired, and a previously allocated array large enough for the five subpart numbers. The output is the array with the first five subpart numbers. (The get_n_subparts procedure is not defined in the inventory interface definition.)

Dynamic memory allocation for conformant arrays

Suppose the following procedures appear in interface definitions:

```
proc1([in] long size, [in, size_is(size)] data_t arr[]);
proc2([in] long max,  [in, max_is(max)]   data_t arr[]);
```

You have to allocate memory for each array needed in the application. To allocate dynamic memory for conformant arrays, use a scheme such as the following:

```
idl_long_int s,m;            /* IDL data type generated in header */
data_t       *s_arr, *m_arr; /* pointers to some data structures  */

    /* some application specific constants */
s = SIZE;
m = MAX;

    /* allocation of the arrays */
s_arr = (data_t *)malloc( (s)   * sizeof(data_t) );
m_arr = (data_t *)malloc( (m+1) * sizeof(data_t) );

    /* the remote procedure calls */
proc1(s, s_arr);
proc2(m, m_arr);
```

In this example, SIZE is defined in the client to represent an array size and MAX is defined to represent the maximum index value of an array. Notice an array that has the `max_is` attribute in its interface definition must have an extra array element allocated because arrays begin with an index value of 0.

Memory allocation for conformant structures

Structures containing a conformant array require memory allocation in the client before they are input to a remote procedure call because a statically allocated conformant structure has storage for only one array element. For example, the following is the `part_list` structure of the inventory interface:

```
typedef struct part_list{
    long                    size;
    [size_is(size)] part_num numbers[*]
} part_list;
```

The structure in the header file generated by the IDL compiler has an array size of only one, as follows:

```
typedef struct part_list {
    idl_long_int size;
    part_num numbers[1];
} part_list;
```

The application is responsible for allocating memory for as much of the array as it needs. Use a scheme such as the following to allocate more memory for a conformant structure:

```
part_list *c;       /* a pointer to the conformant structure */
long s;
s = 33;             /* the application specific array size   */

c = (part_list *)malloc(sizeof(part_list) + (sizeof(part_num)*(s-1)));
```

Notice that since the declared structure's size contains an array of one element representing the conformant array, the new memory allocated needs one array element less than the requested array size.

5

How to Write a Server

DCE servers are more complicated than clients—at least at this introductory stage—because the servers have a more complicated role: they have to be continuously active and be prepared to handle multiple calls in any order. This chapter uses the inventory example as the basis for showing the various issues required by servers.

Before reading this chapter, it's a good idea to read Chapter 1, *Overview of an RPC Application,* for an overview of a distributed application, and Chapter 2 *Using a DCE RPC Interface,* for features of interface definitions. You should also read Chapter 3, *How to Write Clients,* to understand how clients use servers.

You write the following two distinct portions of code for all servers:

- Server **initialization** includes most of the RPC-specific details including RPC runtime routines. This code is executed when the server begins, before it processes any remote procedure calls.

- The **manager** portion, or remote procedure implementations, include special techniques for memory management.

Some Background on Call Processing

Chapter 1 describes how a typical distributed application works:

- Figure 1-9 shows the initialization steps to prepare a server before it processes remote procedure calls.

- Figure 1-10 shows how a client finds a server using the automatic binding method.

- Figure 1-11 shows the basic steps during a remote procedure call after the client finds the server.

To understand server initialization, it is useful at this point to explain how the RPC runtime library handles an incoming call. Figure 5-1 shows how the server system and RPC runtime library handle a client request.

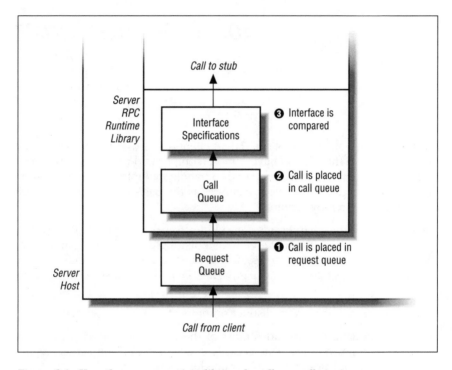

Figure 5-1: How the server runtime library handles a call

❶ A call request for the server comes in over the network. The request is placed in a request queue for the endpoint. (The server initialization can select more than one protocol sequence on which to listen for calls, and each protocol sequence can have more than one endpoint associated with it.) Request queues temporarily store all requests, thus allowing multiple requests on an endpoint. If a request queue fills, however, the next request is rejected.

❷ The RPC runtime library dequeues requests one at a time from all request queues and places them in a single call queue. The server can process remote procedures concurrently, using threads. If a thread is available, a call is immediately assigned to it. (Server initialization can select the number of threads for processing remote procedure calls.) In this figure, only one thread is executing. If all threads are in use, the call remains in the call queue until a thread is available. If the call queue is full, the next request is rejected.

❸ After a call is assigned to a thread, the **interface specification** of the client call is compared with the interface specifications of the server. An interface specification is an opaque data structure containing information (including the UUID and version number) that identifies the interface. **Opaque** simply means the details are hidden from you. If the server supports the client's interface, processing goes to the stub code. If the server does not support the client's interface, the call is rejected.

When the call finally gets to the stub, it unmarshalls the input data. Unmarshalling involves memory allocation (if needed), copying the data from the RPC runtime library, and converting data to the correct representation for the server system.

Initializing the Server

The server initialization code includes a sequence of runtime calls that prepare the server to receive remote procedure calls. The initialization code typically includes the following steps:

1. Register the interface with the RPC runtime library.

2. Create server binding information by selecting one or more protocol sequences for the RPC runtime library to use in your network environment.

3. Advertise the server location so the clients have a way to find it. A client uses binding information to establish a relationship with a server. Advertising the server usually includes storing binding information in a name service database. Occasionally an application stores server binding information in an application-specific database, or displays it, or prints it.

4. Manage endpoints in a local endpoint map.

5. Listen for remote procedure calls.

During server execution, no remote procedure calls are processed until the initialization code completes execution. RPC runtime routines are used for server initialization. (Table B-2 lists all the RPC runtime routines for servers.)

Example 5-1 shows the necessary header files and data structures for server initialization of the inventory application.

Example 5-1: Server Header Files and Data Structures

```
/* FILE NAME: i_server.c */
#include <stdio.h>
#include <ctype.h>
#include "inventory.h"          /* header created by the IDL compiler❶*/
#include "check_status.h"          /* contains the CHECK_STATUS macro */
#define STRINGLEN 50

main (argc, argv)
int argc;
char *argv[];
{
    unsigned32            status;                  /* error status (nbase.h) ❷*/
                                                   /* RPC vectors❸*/
    rpc_binding_vector_t *binding_vector;          /* binding handle list */
    rpc_protseq_vector_t *protseq_vector;          /*protocol sequence list */
                                                   /* list(rpcbase.h)*/

    char entry_name[STRINGLEN];                    /* name service entry name */
    char group_name[STRINGLEN];                    /* name service group name */
    char annotation[STRINGLEN];            /* annotation for endpoint map */
    char hostname[STRINGLEN];
    char *strcpy(), *strcat();

    .
    .
    .
/* For the rest of the server initialization, register interfaces,     */
/* create server binding information, advertise the server,            */
/* manage endpoints, and listen for remote procedure calls.           */
```

❶ Always include the C language header file (created by the IDL compiler) from all interfaces the server uses. This file contains the definitions of data types and structures that are needed by the RPC runtime routines.

❷ An `unsigned32` variable is needed to report errors that may occur when an RPC runtime routine is called.

❸ Some RPC runtime routines use a data structure called a vector. A **vector** in RPC applications contains a list (array) of other data structures and a count of elements in the list. Vectors are necessary because the number of elements on the list is often unknown until runtime. The `rpc_binding_vector_t` is a list of binding handles in which each handle refers to some binding information. The `rpc_protseq_vec-tor_t` is a list of protocol sequence information representing the communication protocols available to a server. RPC runtime routines create vectors, use vectors as input, and free the memory of vectors.

Many header files such as *idlbase.h* and *rpc.h* are included in the interface header *inventory.h*. The *rpc.h* file in turn has included within it header files such as *nbase.h*, *idlbase.h*, and *rpcbase.h*. Many of these header files are associated with RPC-specific interface definitions. These interface definitions contain data structure definitions you may need to refer to in order to access structure members and make runtime calls.

Object UUIDs, discussed in Chapter 7, are scattered throughout the RPC runtime routines. They support applications that need to keep track of more than one resource, such as a database, on the server.

Registering Interfaces

All servers must register their interfaces so that their information is available to the RPC runtime library. This information is used when a call from a client comes in, so that the client is sure the server supports the interface, and the call can be correctly dispatched to the stub.

Before a client makes a call, it checks its interface against the one advertised in the server's binding information. But that does not guarantee that the server supports the client's interface. For example, it is possible for a complex server to temporarily suspend support for a specific interface. Therefore, when a remote procedure call arrives, a comparison is made between the client's and server's interface specifications. If the server supports the client's interface, the RPC runtime library can dispatch the call to the stub.

Use an interface handle to refer to the interface specification in application code. An **interface handle** is a pointer defined in the C language header file and generated by *idl*. For example, the server interface handle for the inventory application is `inventory_v1_0_s_ifspec`. The interface handle name contains the following:

- The interface name given in the interface definition header (`inventory`).

- The version numbers in the `version` attribute (`v1_0`). If the interface definition has no version declared, version 0.0 is assumed.

- The letter `s` or `c` depending on whether the handle is for the server or client portion of the application.

- The word `ifspec`.

Example 5-2 is a portion of C code that registers one interface.

Example 5-2: Registering an Interface with the Runtime Library

```
/* The header files and data structures precede registering interfaces. */
     .
     .
     .
/*********************** REGISTER INTERFACE ***********************/
```

Example 5-2: Registering an Interface with the Runtime Library (continued)

```
rpc_server_register_if(                                    /*❶*/
    inventory_v1_0_s_ifspec, /* interface specification (inventory.h) */
    NULL,
    NULL,
    status
);
CHECK_STATUS(status, "Can't register interface:", ABORT);   /*❷*/
.
.
.
/* For the rest of the server initialization, create server binding  */
/* information, advertise the server, manage endpoints, and listen for */
/* remote procedure calls.                                            */
```

❶ The *rpc_server_register_if* routine is a required call to register each interface that the server supports. The interface handle, `inven-
tory_v1_0_s_ifspec`, refers to the interface specification.

❷ The CHECK_STATUS macro is defined in the *check_status.h* file. It is an
application-specific macro used in this book to process status values
returned from RPC runtime calls (see Example 3-12).

Multiple interfaces may be registered from a single server by calling the
rpc_server_register_if routine with a different interface handle.

The second and third arguments to the *rpc_server_register_if* call are used
in complex applications to register more than one implementation for the
set of remote procedures. When only one implementation exists, these
arguments are set to NULL. Also, in the event of a symbol name conflict
between the remote procedure names of an interface and other symbols in
your server (such as procedure names), you can use these arguments to
assign different names to the server code's remote procedures.

Creating Server Binding Information

Server binding information is created when you select protocol sequences
during server initialization. RPC uses protocol sequences (described in
Chapter 3) to identify the combinations of communications protocols that
RPC supports.

Most servers offer all available protocol sequences so that you do not limit
the opportunities for clients to communicate with the server. For testing
purposes, however, you may want to select a specific protocol sequence.
For example, to debug your server, use the connection protocol sequence
`ncacn_ip_tcp`, because the process will timeout when the debugger
stops it if you use the datagram protocol sequence, `ncadg_ip_udp`.

Recall that besides a protocol sequence, binding information includes a host network address. A server process runs on only one host at a time, so this binding information is obtained from the system and not controlled in your server code.

When a protocol sequence is selected, an endpoint is also obtained. You have several choices when obtaining endpoints.

Using dynamic endpoints

Chapter 3 describes the difference between dynamic and well-known endpoints. Most servers use dynamic endpoints for their flexibility and to avoid the problem of two servers using the same endpoints. Dynamic endpoints are selected for you by the RPC runtime library and vary from one invocation of the server to the next. When the server stops running, dynamic endpoints are released and may be reused by the server system.

Example 5-3 is a portion of the inventory server initialization showing the selection of one or all protocol sequences and dynamic endpoints. For this example, invoke the server with a protocol sequence argument to select a specific protocol sequence. If you invoke this server without an argument, the server uses all available protocols.

Example 5-3: Creating Server Binding Information

```
/* Registering interfaces precedes creating server binding information. */
    .
    .
    .
    /*************** CREATING SERVER BINDING INFORMATION ***************/
    if(argc > 1) {
        rpc_server_use_protseq(                    /* use a protocol sequence❶*/
            (unsigned_char_t *)argv[1],     /* the input protocol sequence */
            rpc_c_protseq_max_calls_default,          /* (rpcbase.h) */
            &status
        );
        CHECK_STATUS(status, "Can't use this protocol sequence:", ABORT);
    }
    else {
        puts("You can invoke the server with a protocol sequence argument.");
        rpc_server_use_all_protseqs(      /* use all protocol sequences ❷*/
            rpc_c_protseq_max_calls_default,          /* (rpcbase.h) */
            &status
        );
        CHECK_STATUS(status, "Can't register protocol sequences:", ABORT);
    }

    rpc_server_inq_bindings(    /* get all binding information for server❸*/
        &binding_vector,
        &status
    );
    CHECK_STATUS(status, "Can't get binding information:", ABORT);
```

Example 5-3: Creating Server Binding Information (continued)

```
        .
        .
        .

/* For the rest of the server initialization, advertise the server,   */
/* manage endpoints, and listen for remote procedure calls.           */
```

❶ The *rpc_server_use_protseq* routine is called with the chosen protocol sequence string. This call selects one protocol sequence on which the server listens for remote procedure calls. For this example, when the server is invoked, `argc` is the number of arguments on the command line, and `argv[1]` is the protocol sequence string argument. The constant `rpc_c_protseq_max_calls_default` sets the request queue size for the number of calls an endpoint can receive at any given moment. At this time, DCE RPC uses a system-dependent default so you cannot control request queue size (see Figure 5-1).

❷ The *rpc_server_use_all_protseqs* routine is called to select all available protocol sequences on which the RPC runtime library listens for remote procedure calls.

❸ The *rpc_server_inq_bindings* routine is a required call to obtain the set of binding handles referring to all of this server's binding information.

Dynamic endpoints must be registered with the server system's local endpoint map using the *rpc_ep_register* routine, so that clients can look them up when they try to find a server.

Using well-known endpoints

An endpoint is well-known if it is specifically selected and assigned to a single server every time it runs. Well-known endpoints are more restrictive than dynamic endpoints because, to prevent your servers from using the same endpoints as someone else, you need to register well-known endpoints with the authority responsible for a given transport protocol. For example, the ARPANET Network Information Center controls the use of well-known endpoint values for the Internet Protocols.

Well-known endpoints are often employed for widely-used applications such as core DCE servers. One server that needs well-known endpoints is the RPC daemon, *rpcd*. This daemon runs on each system hosting DCE RPC servers to maintain the database that maps servers to endpoints. When a client has a partially bound handle, and it needs to obtain an endpoint for its application's server, the client RPC runtime library contacts the server system's *rpcd* process. In short, *rpcd* is required for finding dynamic endpoints. For clients to contact it, *rpcd* itself must have a well-known end-point.

Although you do not need to register well-known endpoints in the server system's endpoint map, you are encouraged to so that clients are unrestricted in finding your servers. Use the *rpc_ep_register* routine to register endpoints in the endpoint map.

Table 5-1 shows the RPC runtime routines to create server binding information with well-known endpoints.

Table 5-1: Creating Binding Information with Well-known Endpoints

RPC Runtime Routine	Description
rpc_server_use_protseq_ep	Uses a specified protocol sequence and well-known endpoint, supplied in application code, to establish server binding information. Even though the endpoint is not dynamically generated, clients do not have an obvious way to get it, so the servers must register the endpoint in the server system's endpoint map.
rpc_server_use_protseq_if	Uses a specified protocol sequence, but well-known endpoints are specified in the interface definition with the **endpoint** attribute. Both clients and servers know the endpoints through the interface definition.
rpc_server_use_all_protseqs_if	Uses all supported protocol sequences, but well-known endpoints are specified in the interface definition with the **endpoint** attribute. Both clients and servers know the endpoints through the interface definition.

Advertising the Server

Advertising the server means that you make the binding information available for clients to find this server. You can advertise the server by one of the following methods:

- Export to a name service database.

- Store binding information in an application-specific database.

- Print or display binding information for clients.

The method you use depends on the application, but the most common way is through a name service database. Binding information and the interface specification are first exported to a server entry in the database. The information is associated with a recognizable name appropriate for the application. This information can now be retrieved by a client using this name. When the client imports binding information, the RPC runtime library compares the interface specifications of the client and the name service entries, to be sure the client and server are compatible.

The convention for naming RPC server entries includes the interface name and the host name. However, this requires that your client know the specific server entry name (including the host on which a server is running) in order to find a server. A name service group associates a general group name with a set of server entries, so your client does not need to know the server entry name. The convention for naming RPC group entries includes the interface name. The server entry name is added as a member of the group. When the client imports binding information using the group name, the group members are searched until a compatible server entry is found.

Using a group name to begin a name service search eliminates the need for clients to know the specific server entry name, but now clients must know the group name. Chapter 6 describes how to set up a slightly more sophisticated naming scheme in the name service.

Example 5-4 is a portion of the inventory initialization code that uses the name service database to advertise the server.

Example 5-4: Advertising the Server to Clients

```
/* Registering interfaces and creating server binding information    */
/* precede advertising the server.                                   */
  .
  .
  .
  /*********************** ADVERTISE SERVER ***********************/
  strcpy(entry_name, "/.:/inventory_");
  gethostname(hostname, STRINGLEN);
  strcat(entry_name, hostname);
  rpc_ns_binding_export(           /* export to a name service database❶*/
    rpc_c_ns_syntax_default,       /* syntax of entry name (rpcbase.h) */
    (unsigned_char_t *)entry_name, /* name of entry in name service */
    inventory_v1_0_s_ifspec,/* interface specification (inventory.h) */
    binding_vector,                        /* binding information */
    NULL,                          /* no object UUIDs exported */
    &status
  );
  CHECK_STATUS(status, "Can't export to name service database:", RESUME);
```

Example 5-4: Advertising the Server to Clients (continued)

```
strcpy(group_name, "/.:/inventory_group");
rpc_ns_group_mbr_add(        /* add as member of name service group❷*/
    rpc_c_ns_syntax_default,     /* syntax of group name (rpcbase.h) */
    (unsigned_char_t *)group_name,  /* name of group in name service */
    rpc_c_ns_syntax_default,     /* syntax of member name (rpcbase.h) */
    (unsigned_char_t *)entry_name, /* name of member in name service */
    &status
);
CHECK_STATUS(status, "Can't add member to name service group:", RESUME);

  .
  .
  .
/* For the rest of the server initialization, manage endpoints and    */
/* listen for remote procedure calls.                                 */
```

❶ The *rpc_ns_binding_export* routine exports the server binding information to a name service database. The constant `rpc_c_ns_syntax_default` establishes the syntax the RPC runtime library uses to interpret an entry name. (DCE currently has only one syntax.) The entry name is the recognizable name used in the database for this binding information.

The interface handle (`inventory_v1_0_s_ifspec`) is needed so interface information is associated with the binding information in the name service database. The binding vector is the list of binding handles that represents the binding information exported. (The NULL value represents an object UUID vector. For this application, no object UUIDs are used.)

❷ The *rpc_ns_group_mbr_add* routine adds the server entry exported with the *rpc_ns_binding_export* call as a member of a name service group, `/.:/inventory_group`. The binding information of an inventory server can be accessed in the name service database through the general group name, `/.:/inventory_group`, rather than a specific server entry name `/.:/inventory_serverhost`.

If all inventory servers use this combination of RPC runtime routines, clients will be able to find one of the servers.

There are three ways to manipulate the name service database:

- Use the *rpc_ns_binding_export* and other RPC runtime routines in the server initialization code (see Example 5-4).

- Use the RPC control program (*rpccp*) to export binding information (*rpccp* is discussed in Chapter 6).

- Use the *rpc_ns_mgmt_entry_create* and other RPC runtime routines in a separate management application. Management application development is an advanced subject not discussed in this book.

Exporting to the name service database requires both read and write access permission. If your access to the name service database is restricted, your name service administrator can use *rpccp* to export the binding information for you.

The *rpc_ns_binding_export* routine exports well-known endpoints to the name service database along with other binding information, but, because of their temporary nature, dynamic endpoints are not exported. Performance of the name service will degrade if it becomes filled with obsolete endpoints generated when servers restart. Also, clients will fail more often trying to bind to servers of nonexistent endpoints. Since dynamic endpoints are not in a name service database, clients need to find them from another source. The next section discusses how to manage endpoints.

Managing Server Endpoints

When the server uses dynamic endpoints, clients need a way to find them, because neither the name service database nor the interface specification store dynamic endpoints. The **endpoint map** is a database on each RPC server system that associates endpoints with other server binding information. As a general rule, have your server store all endpoints (dynamic and well-known) in the endpoint map. If all endpoints are placed in the endpoint map, system administrators have an easier time monitoring and managing all RPC servers on a host system.

The RPC daemon (*rpcd*) process maintains the endpoint map for the particular host system. Access the endpoint map through the RPC daemon with calls to RPC runtime routines or with the RPC control program (*rpccp*).

When a client uses a partially bound binding handle for a remote procedure call, the RPC runtime library obtains an endpoint from the server system's endpoint map. (However, if a well-known endpoint is available in the interface specification, the server's endpoint map is not used.) To find a valid endpoint, the client's interface specification and binding information (protocol sequence, host, and object UUID) are compared to the information in the endpoint map. When an endpoint of an appropriate server is finally obtained, the resulting fully bound binding handle is used to complete the connection at that endpoint. Example 5-5 shows how a server registers its endpoints in the endpoint map.

Example 5-5: Managing Endpoints in an Endpoint Map

```
/* Registering interfaces, creating server binding information, and    */
/* advertising the server precede managing endpoints.                  */
  .
  .
  .

    /*********************** MANAGE ENDPOINTS ***********************/
    strcpy(annotation, "Inventory interface");
    rpc_ep_register(                    /* add endpoints to local endpoint map❶*/
        inventory_v1_0_s_ifspec, /* interface specification (inventory.h) */
        binding_vector,                 /* vector of server binding handles */
        NULL,                           /* no object UUIDs to register */
        (unsigned_char_t *)annotation,          /* annotation supplied */
                                                /* (not required) */
        &status
    );
    CHECK_STATUS(status, "Can't add endpoints to endpoint map:", RESUME);

    rpc_binding_vector_free(            /* free server binding handles❷*/
        &binding_vector,
        &status
    );
    CHECK_STATUS(status, "Can't free server binding handles:", RESUME);

    open_inventory();                   /* application-specific procedure */

  .
  .
  .

/* For the rest of the server initialization, listen for remote       */
/* procedure calls.                                                    */
```

❶ The *rpc_ep_register* routine registers the server endpoints in the local endpoint map. Use the same interface handle, binding vector, and object UUID vector as you used in the *rpc_ns_binding_export* routine (see Example 5-4). An annotation argument is recommended so the information in the endpoint map can be read more easily when using *rpccp*.

❷ The *rpc_binding_vector_free* routine is a required call that frees the memory of the binding vector and all binding handles in it. Each call to *rpc_server_inq_bindings* (see Example 5-3) requires a corresponding call to *rpc_binding_vector_free*. Make this call prior to listening for remote procedure calls, so the memory is available when remote procedure calls are processed.

The *rpc_ep_register* call is required if dynamic endpoints are established with the *rpc_server_use_protseq* or *rpc_server_use_all_protseqs* runtime routines, because each time the server is started, new endpoints are created (see Example 5-3). If well-known endpoints are established with the *rpc_server_use_protseq_ep* runtime routine, you should use the *rpc_ep_register* routine because even though the endpoint may always be the same, a client needs to find the value. Well-known endpoints need not be registered if they are established with the *rpc_server_use_protseq_if* or *rpc_server_use_all_protseqs_if* call because the client has access to the endpoint values through the interface specification.

When a server stops running, endpoints registered in the endpoint map become outdated. The RPC daemon maintains the endpoint map by removing outdated endpoints. However, an unpredictable amount of time exists in which a client can obtain an outdated endpoint. If a remote procedure call uses an outdated endpoint, it will not find the server and the call will fail. To prevent clients from receiving outdated endpoints, use the *rpc_ep_unregister* routine before a server stops executing.

There are several ways to manage endpoints in the endpoint map:

- Use the *rpc_ep_register* and other RPC runtime routines in the server initialization code (see Example 5-5).

- Use the RPC control program (*rpccp*) to show or remove mapping information.

- Use the *rpc_mgmt_ep_elt_inq_begin* and other RPC runtime routines in a separate management application to manage a local or remote endpoint map. Managing an endpoint map with a management application is not discussed in this book.

Listening for Remote Procedure Calls

The final requirement for server initialization code is to listen for remote procedure calls.

Many of the RPC runtime routines used in this book have an error status variable, used to determine whether the routine executed successfully. However, when the server is ready to process remote procedure calls, the *rpc_server_listen* runtime routine is called. The *rpc_server_listen* runtime routine does not return unless the server is requested to stop listening by another process, or by one of its own remote procedures using the *rpc_mgmt_stop_server_listening* routine.

Any errors occurring during stub code or remote procedure execution are reported as exceptions, and, unless your code is written to handle exceptions, it will abruptly exit. You can use a set of macros from DCE threads to help process exceptions. The macros TRY, FINALLY, and ENDTRY delineate code sections in which exceptions are controlled. If an exception occurs in the TRY section, code in the FINALLY section is executed to handle any necessary error recovery or cleanup.

The FINALLY section contains clean-up code that does such things as remove outdated endpoints from the endpoint map. The TRYs+1 and FINALLY sections end with the ENDTRY macro.

Example 5-6 is a portion of C code that shows how the inventory server listens for remote procedure calls and handles exceptions.

Example 5-6: Listening for Remote Procedure Calls

```
/* Registering interfaces, creating server binding information,      */
/* managing endpoints, and advertising the server precede listening  */
/* for remote procedure calls.                                       */
.
.
.

/***************** LISTEN FOR REMOTE PROCEDURE CALLS *****************/
TRY                             /* thread exception handling macro❶*/
rpc_server_listen(                                          /*❷*/
    1,                /* process one remote procedure call at a time */
    &status
);
CHECK_STATUS(status, "rpc listen failed:", RESUME);

FINALLY                            /* error recovery and cleanup */
close_inventory();                 /* application specific procedure */
rpc_server_inq_bindings(              /* get binding information❸*/
    &binding_vector,
    &status
);
CHECK_STATUS(status, "Can't get binding information:", RESUME);

rpc_ep_unregister(     /* remove endpoints from local endpoint map❹*/
    inventory_v1_0_s_ifspec, /* interface specification (inventory.h) */
    binding_vector,            /* vector of server binding handles */
    NULL,                           /* no object UUIDs */
    &status
);
CHECK_STATUS(status,"Can't remove endpoints from endpoint map:",RESUME);

rpc_binding_vector_free(            /* free server binding handles❺*/
    &binding_vector,
    &status
);
CHECK_STATUS(status, "Can't free server binding handles:", RESUME);

puts("\nServer quit!");
ENDTRY
} /* END SERVER INITIALIZATION */
```

❶ The TRY macro begins a section of code in which you expect exceptions to occur. For this example, the TRY section contains only the *rpc_server_listen* routine. If an exception occurs during the remote procedure execution, the code section beginning with the FINALLY macro is executed to handle application-specific cleanup.

❷ The *rpc_server_listen* routine is a required call that causes the runtime to listen for remote procedure calls. The first argument sets the number of threads the RPC runtime library uses to process remote procedure calls. In this example, the RPC runtime library can process one remote procedure call at a time. If your remote procedures are not thread safe, set this value to 1.

❸ The *rpc_server_inq_bindings* routine obtains a set of binding handles referring to all of the server's binding information.

❹ The *rpc_ep_unregister* routine removes the server endpoints from the local endpoint map. If the server registered endpoints with a call to *rpc_ep_register*, this call is recommended before the process is removed (see Example 5-5).

❺ The *rpc_binding_vector_free* routine is called to free the memory of a binding vector and all the binding handles in it. Each call to *rpc_server_inq_bindings* requires a corresponding call to *rpc_binding_vector_free*.

The server initialization code for the inventory application is now complete. All of the server initialization code is shown in Example D-6, and Table B-2 lists all the runtime routines that servers can use.

Writing Remote Procedures

When writing your remote procedures, consider the issues of memory management, threads, and client binding handles.

Remote procedures require special memory management techniques. Suppose a procedure allocates memory for data that it returns to the calling procedure. In a local application, the calling procedure can free allocated memory because the procedure and calling procedure are in the same address space. However, the client (calling procedure) is not in the same address space as the server (remote procedure), so the client cannot free memory on the server. Repeated calls to a remote procedure that allocates memory, without some way to free the memory, will obviously waste the server's resources.

You must manage memory for remote procedures using special **stub support routines** in remote procedures. Stub support routines enable the server stub to free memory allocated in remote procedures, after the remote procedure completes execution.

Recall that the *rpc_server_listen* routine in server initialization determines the number of threads a server uses to process remote procedure calls. If the server listens on more than one thread, the remote procedures need to be thread safe. For example, the remote procedures should not use server global data unless locks are used to control thread access. In the inventory application, when reading from or writing to the inventory application database, a lock may be needed so data is not changed by one thread while another thread is reading it. The inventory application is single-threaded. Details of multithreaded application development are beyond the scope of this book.

So far, we have used server binding handles and server binding information to allow clients to find servers. When a server receives a call from a client, the client RPC runtime library supplies information about the client side of the binding to the server RPC runtime library. **Client binding information** is used in server code to inquire about the client. This client binding information includes:

- The RPC protocol sequence used by the client for the call.

- The network address of the client.

- The object UUID requested by the client. This can be simply a nil UUID; other options are discussed in Chapter 7.

- The client authentication and authorization information (optional).

To access client binding information in remote procedures use a **client binding handle**. If the client binding handle is available, it is the first parameter of the remote procedure. If you require client binding information, and the procedure declarations in the interface definition do not have a binding handle as the first parameter, you must generate the server stub and header file using an ACF with the `explicit_handle` attribute.

Managing Memory in Remote Procedures

In typical applications, you use the C library routines, *malloc* and *free*, or your own allocation scheme, to allocate and free memory that pointers must refer to. In RPC servers, when implementing a remote procedure that returns a pointer to newly allocated memory to the client, use stub support routines to manage memory in the remote procedures. Use the stub support routine *rpc_ss_allocate* instead of the C library routine *malloc* so bookkeeping is maintained for memory management. This also ensures that memory on the server is automatically freed by the server stub after the remote procedure has completed execution. Memory allocation will not accumulate on the server and get out of control.

For reference pointers, memory on the client side must already exist, so no memory management is required for remote procedures whose output parameters are reference pointers. After you make the remote procedure call, first the server stub automatically allocates necessary memory and copies the data for the reference pointer into the new memory. Then it calls the implementation of the remote procedure. Finally, the remote procedure completes, output data is transmitted back to the client stub and the server stub frees the memory it allocated.

On both the client and server, more complex memory management occurs for full pointers than for reference pointers. If a remote procedure allocates memory for an output parameter, the server stub copies and marshalls the data, then the stub frees the memory that was allocated in the remote procedure. When the client receives the data, the client stub allocates memory and copies the data into the new memory. It is the client application's responsibility to free the memory allocated by the client stub.

Example 5-7 shows how to use the *rpc_ss_allocate* routine to allocate memory for full pointers. The procedure `get_part_description` of the inventory application returns a string of characters representing the description of a part in the inventory. The call in the client is as follows:

```
part_record part; /* structure for all data about a part  */
   .
   .
   .
part.description = get_part_description(part.number);
```

Example 5-7: Memory Management in Remote Procedures

```
paragraph get_part_description(number)
part_num number;
{
    part_record *part;                    /* a pointer to a part record */
    paragraph description;
    int size;
    char *strcpy();

    if( read_part_record(number, &part) ) {
        /* Allocated data that is returned to the client must be allocated */
        /* with the rpc_ss_allocate stub support routine.               */
        size = strlen((char *)part->description) + 1;            /*❶*/
        description = (paragraph)rpc_ss_allocate((unsigned)size);    /*❷*/
        strcpy((char *)description, (char *)part->description);
    }
    else
        description = NULL;
    return(description);
}
```

❶ An additional character is allocated for the null terminator of a string.

❷ The remote procedure calls the *rpc_ss_allocate* stub support routine to allocate memory in the remote procedure.

When the procedure completes, the server stub automatically frees the memory allocated by *rpc_ss_allocate* calls. When the remote procedure call returns, the client stub automatically allocates memory for the returned string. When the client application code is finished with the data, it frees the memory allocated by the client stub as follows:

```
if(part.description != NULL)
    free(part.description);
```

For more complex memory management, there is a stub support counterpart to the C library routine *free* called *rpc_ss_free*.

The only time you don't use the *rpc_ss_allocate* and *rpc_ss_free* routines for memory management is when you use context handles. Memory allocated for context on the server must not use these routines because subsequent calls by the client must have access to the same context as previous calls. See Chapter 7 for more information on context handles.

Allocating Memory for Conformant Arrays

The whatare_subparts procedure of the inventory application allocates memory for a conformant array in a structure, and returns a copy of the conformant structure to the client. The whatare_subparts procedure is declared in the interface definition as follows:

```
typedef struct part_list{               /* list of part numbers    */
    long                    size;        /* number of parts in array */
    [size_is(size)] part_num numbers[*]; /* conformant array of parts */
} part_list;
    .
    .
    .
void whatare_subparts(      /* get list of subpart numbers for a part */
    [in]  part_num  number,
    [out] part_list **subparts  /* the structure containing the array */
);
```

Output pointer parameters are reference pointers, which must have memory allocated in the client prior to the call. Therefore, you need a full pointer in order for new memory to be automatically allocated by the client stub for the **subparts structure when the whatare_subparts procedure returns. A pointer to a pointer is required so that the reference pointer points to a full pointer, which in turn points to the structure.

Example 5-8 shows how to allocate memory in the remote procedure for a conformant structure. The call in the client is as follows:

```
part_record part;           /* structure for all data about a part  */
part_list   *subparts;      /* pointer to parts list data structure */
 .
 .
 .

   whatare_subparts(part.number, &subparts);
```

Example 5-8: Conformant Array Allocation in a Remote Procedure

```
void whatare_subparts(number, subpart_ptr)
part_num  number;
part_list **subpart_ptr;
{
    part_record *part;                          /* pointer to a part record */
    int i;
    int size;

    read_part_record(number, &part);

    /* Allocated data that is output to the client must be allocated with */
    /* the rpc_ss_allocate stub support routine.  Allocate for a part_list */
    /* struct plus the array of subpart numbers.  Remember the part_list   */
    /* struct already has an array with one element, hence the -1.         */
    size = sizeof(part_list)
            + (sizeof(part_num) * (part->subparts.size-1));        /*❶*/
    *subpart_ptr = (part_list *)rpc_ss_allocate((unsigned)size);   /*❷*/

    /* fill in the values */
    (*subpart_ptr)->size = part->subparts.size;
    for(i = 0; i < (*subpart_ptr)->size; i++)
        (*subpart_ptr)->numbers[i] = part->subparts.numbers[i];
    return;
}
```

❶ The allocated memory includes the size of the conformant structure plus enough memory for all the elements of the conformant array. The conformant structure generated by the IDL compiler already has an array of one element, so the new memory allocated for the array elements is one less than the number in the array.

❷ Use the RPC stub support routine *rpc_ss_allocate* to allocate memory so bookkeeping is maintained for memory management, and so the server stub automatically frees memory on the server after the remote procedure completes execution.

When the data for the conformant structure is returned to the client, the client stub allocates memory and copies the data into the new memory. The client application code uses the data and frees the memory allocated, as follows:

```
for(i = 0; i < subparts->size; i++)
    printf("%ld ", subparts->numbers[i]);
printf("\nTotal number of subparts:%ld\n", subparts->size);
free(subparts); /* free memory allocated for conformant structure */
```

Compiling and Linking Servers

Figure 5-2 shows the files and libraries required to produce an executable server. If needed, the IDL compiler produces the server stub auxiliary file (*appl_***saux.o**) when the interface is compiled. The following features cause the production of a server auxiliary file:

- Self-referential pointers in the interface definition

- The **pipe** data type in the interface definition

- The **out_of_line** attribute in an ACF

No stub auxiliary files are produced for the inventory application.

To compile and link the server for the inventory application, perform the following steps:

1. Compile all the server application modules with the C compiler including the server initialization code and the remote procedures. The *arithmetic* directory is included with the compiler directive **-I** because this is where the *check_status.h* header file resides.

   ```
   S> cc -I../arithmetic -c i_server.c i_procedures.c \
   implement_inventory.c
   ```

2. Link the server application and server stub object files with the DCE libraries to produce the executable server.

   ```
   S> cc -o i_server.exe i_server.o i_procedures.o \
   implement_inventory.o inventory_sstub.o -ldce -lcma
   ```

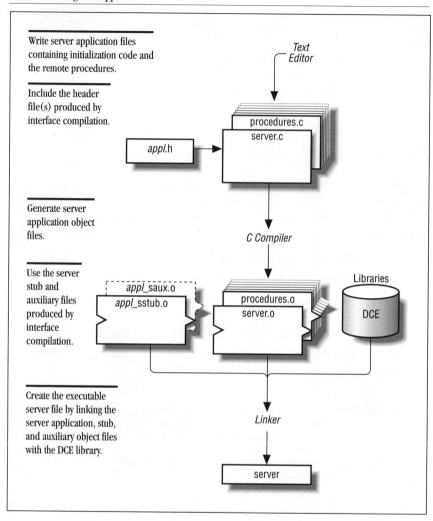

Figure 5-2: Producing a server

6

Using a Name Service

We have seen in earlier chapters that clients query a name service to find a host where a server is running. We have set up our environment in a simplistic, if not inconvenient, manner so we could avoid discussing details about the name service. For instance, in Chapter 1, we made the RPC_DEFAULT_ENTRY environment variable point to a specific server entry for the arithmetic application, before we ran the client.

We already discussed programming access to the name service in Chapter 3 (which shows how a client imports binding information from it), and Chapter 5 (which shows how servers export binding information to it). In this chapter we discuss administration rather than programming, and show how to make the search in the name service more flexible. After a brief introduction to the name service and its naming conventions, we discuss administration for individual servers, groups of servers, and profiles that tailor a search to your needs.

Naming

A name service accesses and maintains a distributed database of server location information (binding information). An entry name is associated with each entry in the database. You use the name in programs, commands, and environment variables to access and search the database.

DCE supplies the Cell Directory Service (CDS) as the name service used by RPC applications to locate servers. CDS tracks many kinds of resources in DCE, but its most important purpose is to provide clients with binding information so they can connect to servers.

The name service database can be quite complex and extensive. The portion that deals with your applications is only one small part of the entire distributed database.

If you are working under DCE, you already know that it divides a network into cells. CDS maintains information on the servers and other resources in a cell, where they are organized into a hierarchy in the same way that files are organized into directories. Cells have unique names themselves and are represented in a larger hierarchy, but we do not discuss this level of organization in this chapter.

The following is an example of an entry name in DCE syntax:

```
/.:/product_development/test_servers/arithmetic_YAK
```

The forward slash divides the different portions of an entry name and is part of the CDS name syntax. Represent your local cell name with /.: as a prefix to all name service entries. Each cell also has a global name that begins with the /... prefix. If the cell name for this example is /.../amoeba, the global name for the same entry looks like this:

```
/.../amoeba/product_development/test_servers/arithmetic_YAK
```

Entry names have a hierarchy that to a file system hierarchy. For the above entry, the directory pathname is product_development/test_servers. A leaf name identifies a specific entry for a directory pathname in the name service database. In our example, the leaf name is arithmetic_YAK, in which arithmetic represents the interface the server supports, and YAK represents the server host name.

The creation of name service entries is generally a management activity and may require special user permission. For example, assume that only our cell administrator has permission to create or delete directories immediately under /.:/. And perhaps the system administrators for product development have permission to create or delete directories under product_development, and set appropriate user permissions for its subdirectories. Finally, the test_servers directory may be available for some developers to read and write entries.

You manage leaf names with the RPC control program, *rpccp*, or with RPC runtime routines that begin with *rpc_ns_* in client, server, or management programs. Use the Cell Directory Service control program (*cdscp*) to control global cell naming and to create or remove directory pathnames. We do not describe the use of *cdscp* in this book.

If an entry does not exist when information is stored in the database, it is created automatically. When new information is added to the same entry, the information in the database is updated and no entries are created or removed. For example, servers that frequently stop executing and then restart (such as during testing) have their binding information updated for the same entry. The name service operates more efficiently if you update an entry rather than remove an old entry and create a new one each time a server starts.

Environment Variables

Recall that with the automatic binding method, the job of finding a server is done for you by the client stub. If your client uses this method of binding management, you must set the RPC-specific environment variable, RPC_DEFAULT_ENTRY, to a valid entry name, so the client stub can begin to search the name service database.

DCE uses CDS as its name service. If, however, your system uses a name service other than CDS, you must set the RPC-specific environment variable, RPC_DEFAULT_ENTRY_SYNTAX, to the value designated for that name service.

Server Entries

A name service **server entry** stores binding information for an RPC server. Figure 6-1 depicts server entries in the name service database.

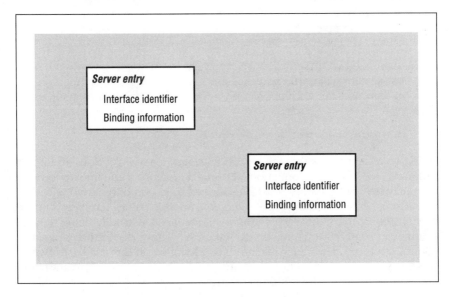

Figure 6-1: Server entries in the name service database

A server entry contains the following information:

- An **interface identifier** consists of an interface UUID and a version number. During the search for binding information, RPC name service routines use this identifier to determine if a compatible interface is found.

- **Binding information** is needed by a client so it can find a server. This information includes one or more sets of protocol sequence and host address combinations. Well-known endpoints can also be part of the binding information, but dynamic endpoints cannot.

- Some applications use optional **object UUIDs** to identify application-specific objects or resources. These are discussed in Chapter 7.

A reasonable naming scheme for server entries combines the host system name and a meaningful definition of what the server offers. For example, the arithmetic interface on a host system named **YAK** can have the following name service entry:

```
/.:/arithmetic_YAK
```

In this way, using a simple convention that all servers can follow, you are assured that each server at your site has a unique name—as long as you have only one server per host.

Most host systems need only one server for an interface; however, if your system has multiple servers offering the same interface, you need to distinguish each server with separate name service entries and unique entry names. For example, one server might be `/.:/arithmetic1_YAK`, and another `/.:/arithmetic2_YAK`.

If you organized your name service directory pathname to point to a particular host system, using the name of the system in the leaf name is redundant. In this case, the arithmetic application might have the following entry name:

```
/.:/product_development/test_servers/host_YAK/arithmetic
```

When your client uses the name service to find a server, it does an **import** or **lookup** for binding information, starting at an entry name known to be in the database. Entry names must be supplied to you in one of two ways: by the name service administrator who knows the name service database organization, or by the server administrator. You use RPC name service routines to search the name service database. These routines compare the client's interface identifier with interface identifiers in the database. When there is a match and the entry contains compatible binding information, the compatible binding information is returned.

Figure 6-2 shows how the arithmetic application uses a server entry in the name service database. The arithmetic server uses the *rpc_ns_binding_export* runtime routine to export binding information to the `/.:/arithmetic_YAK` server entry. The arithmetic server's use of *rpc_ns_binding_export* is shown in Example 1-4.

The arithmetic client uses the automatic binding method, so the client stub finds the server. The RPC-specific environment variable, RPC_DEFAULT_ENTRY, is set to `/.:/arithmetic_YAK` on the client system

DUB, so the client stub has a name with which to start a name service search. In this example, the name service simply begins and ends the search with the server entry name `/.:/arithmetic_YAK`. The server entry's binding information is returned and the remote procedure call is completed.

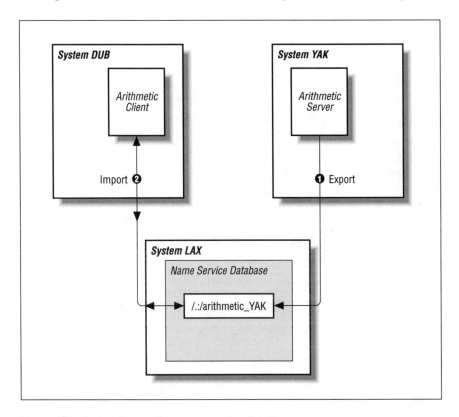

Figure 6-2: A simple use of a name service database

Creating a Server Entry and Exporting Binding Information

Suppose the server code for the arithmetic application does not export binding information to the name service. To create a server entry, export binding information, and display the information exported, type the following sequence of *rpccp* commands:

1. Use *rpccp* to export binding information to the name service database for an entry named `/.:/arithmetic_YAK`. If the entry does not exist, the control program creates it automatically.

```
> rpccp export /.:/arithmetic_YAK \
 -i C985A380-255B-11C9-A50B-08002B0ECEF1,0.0 \
 -b ncacn_ip_tcp:YAK -b ncadg_ip_udp:YAK

>>> binding information exported
```

/.:/arithmetic_YAK   The name of the server entry.

-i C985A380-255B-11C9-A50B-08002B0ECEF1,0.0
> The interface identifier contains the UUID and version number
> for the arithmetic interface. The **uuid** and **version** attributes
> in the interface definition contain the values.

-b ncacn_ip_tcp:YAK **-b** ncadg_ip_udp:YAK
> The binding information including a protocol sequence and
> server host name (or network address) is added to the entry.

2. Display the binding information for the server entry created. The name
   service stores the host address rather than the host name. (Objects can
   also be exported to a server entry. If no objects are stored, a message is
   displayed.)

```
> rpccp show server /.:/arithmetic_YAK

>>> no matching objects found

binding information:

 <interface id>   C985A380-255B-11C9-A50B-08002B0ECEF1,0.0
 <string binding> ncadg_ip_udp:16.20.16.83[]
 <string binding> ncacn_ip_tcp:16.20.16.83[]
```

If you expect the server to be removed from service for a long period of
time or even permanently, you should remove the server binding information from the name service using the *rpc_ns_binding_unexport* runtime
routine or the *rpccp unexport* command.

To simplify the typing of *rpccp* commands that require an interface identifier, you can set an application-specific environment variable to represent
the identifier, and then use the environment variable in the *rpccp* commands. To set an environment variable that represents the arithmetic interface identifier, type the following:

```
> setenv ARITHMETIC_ID C985A380-255B-11C9-A50B-08002B0ECEF1,0.0
```

Group Entries

A **group entry** is a name service entry that corresponds to a set of servers, usually those offering the same interface. The members of a group can include server entries and other groups. The name service runtime routines search the members of a group to find a server. A group offers the advantage of storing server entries from many systems under a single name. Figure 6-3 depicts a group and its members in the name service database.

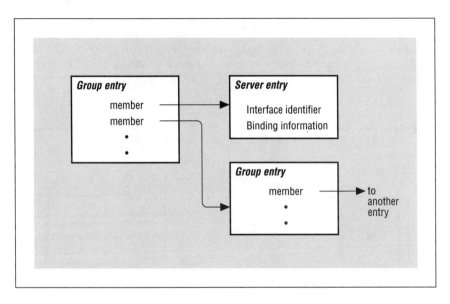

Figure 6-3: Group entries in a name service database

A group contains one or more **group members**, which are simply names referring to other entries (server entries or groups) in the name service database. Use a group name appropriate for all the members of a group. For example, the inventory application uses the group name /.:/inventory_group to refer to all servers that offer the inventory interface.

Figure 6-4 shows how the inventory application uses a group and a server entry in the name service database. The inventory server uses the runtime routine *rpc_ns_binding_export* to export binding information to the /.:/inventory_YAK server entry. The inventory server then uses the runtime routine *rpc_ns_group_mbr_add* to add the server entry name as a group member to the /.:/inventory_group. The inventory server's use of these routines is shown in Example 5-4.

To find the inventory server, clients begin a search with the group entry named /.:/inventory_group. The client that uses the automatic binding method needs the RPC-specific environment variable, RPC_DEFAULT_ENTRY, set to /.:/inventory_group, so the client stub can find a server. The clients that use the implicit and explicit binding methods use the RPC name service import routines (RPC runtime routines that begin with *rpc_ns_binding_import*) to find a server. Example 3-7 shows how to use these routines.

The search goes from the group entry to the group members and returns the binding information found in a valid server entry. The search is recursive, so if a group member is itself another group, its members are searched in the same way. The RPC name service import routines automatically select one valid server entry at a time during a search. For this example, /.:/inventory_YAK is the only member for the search to find.

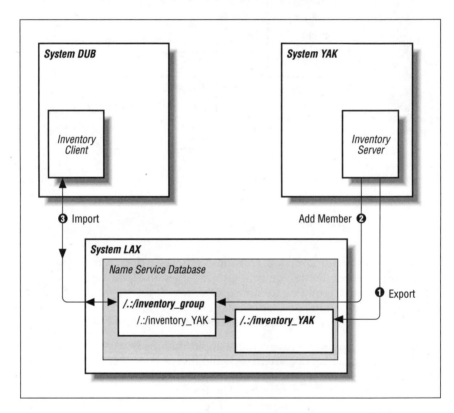

Figure 6-4: A simple search in a name service database

Creating a Group Entry and Adding a Member

Suppose the server code for the inventory application does not add the server entry name to the group entry in the name service. To create a group entry, add a member to it, and display the information in the entry, then type the following *rpccp* commands:

1. Assume `/.:/inventory_YAK` is a server entry in the name service database. Use *rpccp* to add the `/.:/inventory_YAK` server entry as a member to the group `/.:/inventory_group`.

   ```
   > rpccp add member /.:/inventory_group -m /.:/inventory_YAK

   >>> group member added
   ```

`/.:/inventory_group`	The name of the group entry.
`-m /.:/inventory_YAK`	The name of the new member is the server entry name.

2. Display the members of the group. The name `/ . . . /amoeba` represents the cell's global name.*

   ```
   > rpccp show group /.:/inventory_group

   group members:

       /.../amoeba/inventory_YAK
   ```

3. Display all information for an entry, which in this example is a group entry. (Every entry has the capability to be a server, group, or profile. Since a group entry has no objects or binding information, only messages for these data are displayed.)

   ```
   > rpccp show entry /.:/inventory_group

   >>> no matching objects found

   >>> no matching binding information found

   group members:

       /.../amoeba/inventory_YAK
   ```

---

*When CDS encounters an entry with the /.: prefix, it expands it to a global name that includes the full name of the local cell.

Profile Entries

A client must always start its name service search with a known entry, but you can make that entry very specific or very inclusive, depending on the variety of servers you use. The client that uses an arithmetic server in Figure 6-2 starts its search with a specific server entry. The client that uses an inventory server in Figure 6-4 conducts a broader and probably more realistic search: it starts with a group entry representing a set of servers. Thus, it can choose a server at random (in the case of automatic binding) or select the exact server that it wants from the group (in the case of implicit and explicit binding).

Profiles represent yet another layer of flexibility in searching. A **profile entry** is a name service entry that defines a search list for finding servers in the name service database. You use profiles to gather all your services together. Profiles let you tailor the database search so that all your clients begin a search from a single, general entry name. With profiles, clients do not need to know specific entry names. You usually set the RPC-specific environment variable, RPC_DEFAULT_ENTRY, to a profile entry name.

Like the group members discussed in the previous section, profiles contain **elements**, each possessing an interface identifier and information about another entry in the database. The elements of a profile can refer to server entries, groups, and other profiles. Figure 6-5 depicts a profile and its elements in the name service database.

Each profile element corresponds to a specific interface and contains the following information:

- The **interface identifier** consists of an interface's UUID and version number.

- A **member name** refers to another entry (server entry, group, or other profile) in the database. The RPC name service routines use this name during a search, to go to that entry for server information.

- A **priority value** (from a high of 0 to a low of 7) controls the search order of profile elements. If a profile contains more than one element for the same interface, the search uses the higher priority elements first. A priority is very useful in giving you more specific control during a database search. For example, you may prefer to specify a higher priority for servers running on nearby systems, and a lower relative priority for servers running on a system much further away. In this way, the nearby servers are tried first.

- An **annotation** is optional documentation to help users and administrators understand the entry. It has no effect on the name service search.

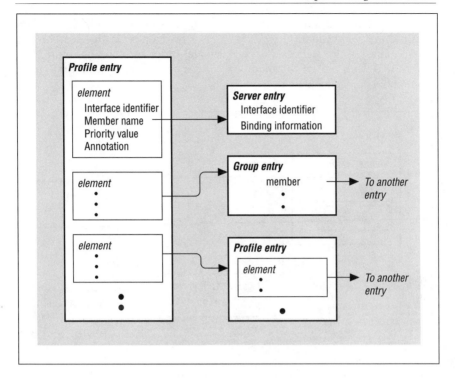

Figure 6-5: Profile entries in a name service database

Names can be descriptive. For example, /.:/johns_profile is the name of a profile the author created to organize searches for applications that were coded and tested for the book.

Figure 6-6 shows a name service database with a new profile entry and associations we can create so that the clients for both the arithmetic and inventory applications need only one general name service entry, /.:/johns_profile, to find any server. When a search begins at a profile, it looks for a matching interface identifier. If only one is found, it uses that to go to the next entry for information. If more than one element has the desired interface identifier, the search uses the one with the highest priority. In the case of equal priority, one is randomly chosen.

When an arithmetic application client begins a search in this database with the profile /.:/johns_profile, the search goes to a profile element whose interface identifier matches the arithmetic application's interface identifier. The search uses the element's member name as the next entry. In the case of the arithmetic application, the search goes to the server entry /.:/arithmetic_YAK. This server entry is the end of the search and the binding information is returned.

For the inventory application, an extra search is required. In this case, the group entry /.:/inventory_group is the next entry in the search. The group members are searched in no particular order and binding information is returned from one of the members. If a member is itself another group, its members are also searched.

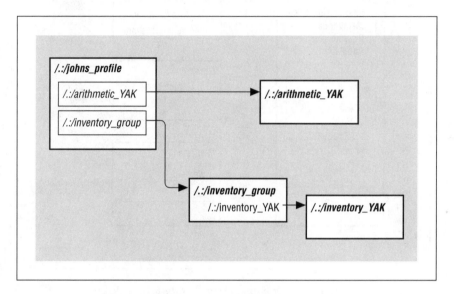

Figure 6-6: Organizing entries in a name service database

Creating a Profile and Adding Elements

Profiles tend to be created manually, through *rpccp* commands, by users customizing their environments. Programs can also create or manage profiles, using RPC routines that begin with *rpc_ns_profile_*. The following sequence of commands show how to create and add elements to the profile shown in Figure 6-6.

1. Use *rpccp* to add an element to the profile /.:/johns_profile. The member name for the element is the arithmetic server entry /.:/arithmetic_YAK. If the profile does not exist, the control program creates it automatically.

   ```
   > rpccp add element /.:/johns_profile \
     -i C985A380-255B-11C9-A50B-08002B0ECEF1,0.0 \
     -m /.:/arithmetic_YAK \
     -a "Arithmetic IF"

   >>> profile element added
   ```

/.:/johns_profile   The name of the profile to which the element is added.

-i C985A380-255B-11C9-A50B-08002B0ECEF1, 0.0

The interface identifier contains the UUID and version number for the server interface.

-m /.:/arithmetic_YAK   The member name of the element added to the profile is /.:/arithmetic_YAK.

-a "Arithmetic IF"   An annotation in the profile is Arithmetic IF.

2. Add another element to the profile /.:/johns_profile. The member name for this element is the entry /.:/inventory_group.

```
> rpccp add element /.:/johns_profile \
    -i 008B3C84-93A5-11C9-85B0-08002B147A61,1.0 \
    -m /.:/inventory_group \
    -a "Inventory IF"

>>> profile element added
```

/.:/johns_profile   The name of the profile to which the element is added.

-i 008B3C84-93A5-11C9-85B0-08002B147A61,1.0

The interface identifier contains the UUID and version number for the server interface.

-m /.:/inventory_group   The member name of the element added to the profile is /.:/inventory_group.

-a "Inventory IF"   An annotation in the profile is Inventory IF.

3. Display the elements of the profile.

```
> rpccp show profile /.:/johns_profile

profile elements:

    <interface id>   C985A380-255B-11C9-A50B-08002B0ECEF1,0.0
    <member_name>    /.../amoeba/arithmetic_YAK
    <priority>       0
    <annotation>     Arithmetic IF

    <interface id>   008B3C84-93A5-11C9-85B0-08002B147A61,1.0
    <member_name>    /.../amoeba/inventory_group
    <priority>       0
    <annotation>     Inventory IF
```

Since some clients use the automatic binding method, set the RPC-specific environment variable RPC_DEFAULT_ENTRY, to /.:/johns_profile prior to testing:

```
C> setenv RPC_DEFAULT_ENTRY /.:/johns_profile
```

Clients that use name service import and lookup routines can begin their search at the value specified in the RPC_DEFAULT_ENTRY environment variable, by using NULL for the entry name argument. You can also change clients to use /.:/johns_profile as an entry name.

Accessing the Database Hierarchy with Default Elements

So far we have described how to use a profile to organize a hierarchy of servers from entries you know. In a typical distributed environment, however, you want access not only to your servers, but to servers for many kinds of resources, across many levels of your organization.

For example, suppose your program makes a remote procedure call to an interface that manages a database of people in your organization. You should not have to obtain entry names and include them in your profile every time you want another interface already in use by your organization. Profiles not only allow you to create a top-down hierarchy of your servers, they also give you bottom-up access to the name service database hierarchy in a way that frees you from knowing about the details of the hierarchy.

Figure 6-7 shows how your profile can access more of the database hierarchy. Every profile can contain one **default element**, which is used as the last resort during a search of that profile. If none of a profile's elements match the interface identifier being sought, the search uses the default element to continue. The default element refers to another profile that is usually the next level up in your name service database hierarchy. The search starts over again with the new profile. If the new profile does not contain an appropriate element, that profile's default element is used, and the search continues until a server is found or the search is exausted. Thus your personal profile can inherit upper levels of the name service database hierarchy by using a default profile.

The default element has a NULL interface identifier, and since there can be only one default element per profile, the priority of a profile element is not relevant.

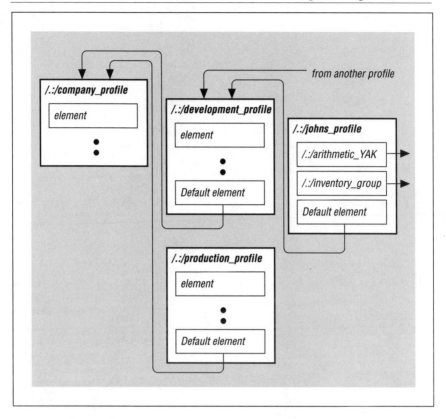

Figure 6-7: Default elements in a name service database

7

Using Object UUIDs

Up to this point, all of our servers and clients have exported or imported binding information solely on the basis of the interface. That is, the choice of a server has been determined by the name assigned in the interface statement in the header of the IDL file. For instance, in the inventory application the server exports to server entries whose names are based on the application's interface and host name (`inventory_YAK`). The inventory client imports from a group based on the application's interface name (`inventory_group`).

DCE allows you to specify another piece of information—an object UUID—in addition to the interface, whenever you create or refer to a binding. The purpose of object UUIDs and the methods for using them are the subjects of this chapter.

Servers and Resources

In this chapter we shift the focus from the interfaces offered by servers to the objects that servers manage.

Focusing on the interface implemented by a server makes good sense for some applications—ones where other elements of the server system don't matter. The arithmetic application provides an example of this. Presumably the arithmetic servers have been installed only on those hosts that have array processing hardware. In this case, arithmetic clients do not care which arithmetic server they bind to, since any server that implements the arithmetic interface can perform array processing.

However, for many applications it is not sufficient for a client to locate a server based solely on an interface. The interface identifies just the set of remote procedures executed by the server. In addition to offering an interface, many servers manage resources on behalf of clients. Take as an example a printing service. When you want a document printed, you, as a client, need to bind to a print application. But you do not want just any print server, you want the one that will print your document on the post-script printer nearest your office. In this case, you are interested in a partic-ular **resource** as well as the interface.

The inventory application is another example where the focus could shift from the interface alone to both an interface and a resource. For instance, the current inventory application provides access to a single database. However, it is easy to imagine a single inventory server providing access to multiple databases. Figure 7-1 shows such a server. In this case the inven-tory server manages one database for the parts that make an electric clothes dryer and another for the parts that make a gas version of the dryer.

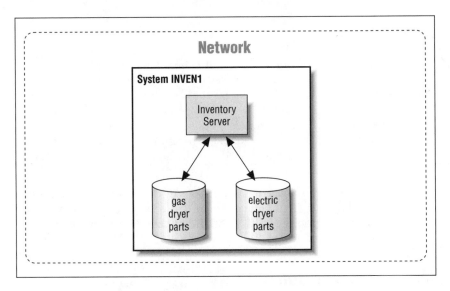

Figure 7-1: Inventory server with multiple databases

Different copies of the inventory server could provide access to completely different databases. For example, in addition to one server maintaining the clothes dryer databases, a server on a different host provides access to the parts databases for stoves, as shown in Figure 7-2. In this case, not only must a client locate an inventory server, the client must locate the particular server that provides access to the database of interest.

There are several ways for advertising and locating servers based on resource rather than by interface:

- Using resource-based server entry names

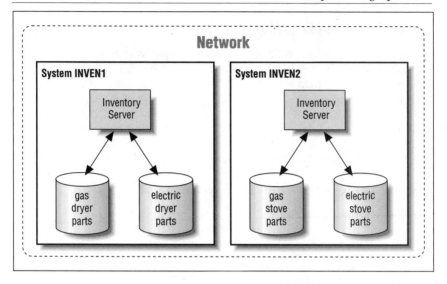

Figure 7-2: Multiple inventory servers

- Exporting object UUIDs to server entries and groups

- Importing by resource using object UUIDs

The chapter includes strategies for using the namespace to accomplish these functions.

Ways to Advertise and Locate Servers by Resource

Previous chapters have already shown how a server exports an interface to the name service and to the endpoint map, and how a client specifies the interface to import a binding. We refer to this focus as **exporting by interface** and **importing by interface**.

For server applications offering access to some resource, the focus from the client's point of view shifts. For example, in the inventory application the client is less interested in finding a server that offers the inventory interface than in finding a server that provides access to a particular database.

When dealing with applications that offer access to some resource, we can think of servers **exporting by resource**.

When importing by interface, the client application specifies an entry name based on the interface of interest, obtains a binding handle for a compatible server, and makes RPC calls. When importing by resource, we would like to maintain that same order of events and level of simplicity: import based on a meaningful name, obtain a binding handle, make your RPC calls.

Advertising and Locating Resources by Name Only

As a sort of strawman, we'll show a very simple way to change the focus from interface to resource. Just base the server entries in the name service on resource rather than interface. When exporting by resource in this way, the arguments passed to *rpc_ns_binding_export* are essentially the same as when exporting by interface. Since this simple approach does not use object UUIDs, only the entry name argument would be different. Example 7-1 shows how the inventory application server on host INVEN1 from Figure 7-1 would advertise itself when exporting by resource.

Example 7-1: Exporting by Resource: Dryer Parts Databases

```
unsigned char *entry_name[2] = {  "/.:/gas_dryer_parts",
                                   "/.:/electric_dryer_parts" };

for (i = 0; i < 2; ++i)
{
   rpc_ns_binding_export (
   rpc_c_ns_syntax_default,
   entry_name[i],
   inventory_v1_0_s_ifspec,
   binding_vector,
   NULL,
   &status
   );
}
```

Since the INVEN1 inventory server manages two resources, the gas dryer parts database and the electric dryer parts database, the server exports twice; once for each resource. The entry name provided to *rpc_ns_binding_export* reflects the name of the offered resource. The server application decides how to name that entry.

Similarly, the inventory server on host INVEN2 would export by resource to the namespace entries /.:/gas_stove_parts and /.:/electric_ stove_parts.

Figure 7-3 shows how the namespace would look after the two inventory servers from Figure 7-2 advertise themselves when exporting by resource. This usage results in storing multiple copies of each server's interface identifier and binding information in the namespace.

We refer to these entries as **resource entries**, since the information contained within the entry provides an importing client with access to the server that manages the specified resource.

Unlike Example 5-4, there is no need for either server to add its entry to a group. Because inventory clients are interested in accessing a particular database, they import by resource directly from the resource entry of interest. To do this, the client uses one of the entry names shown in Figure 7-2 as the *entry_name* argument to the *rpc_ns_binding_import_begin* routine.

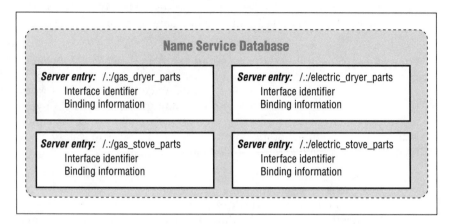

Figure 7-3: Resource-based server entries in the name service database

If, however, the inventory interface contained an operation allowing a client to create a new parts database, each inventory server would advertise itself based on interface, in addition to exporting by resource. In this situation, a group entry would be used as in Example 5-4. Since any of the inventory servers can create a new database on behalf of the client, a client that needs to create a new database would import from the inventory group entry to bind to any inventory server.

For this situation, the inventory server on host INVEN1 could export by interface to server entry `/.:/inventory_INVEN1`, and the inventory server on host INVEN2 could export by interface to server entry `/.:/inventory_INVEN2`. Each server then adds its server entry as a member of the group `/.:/inventory_group`. The resulting entries in the namespace, and their use, are essentially the same as shown in Figure 6-4.

Shortcoming

Creating resource entries in this fashion provides clients with a simple mechanism to import by resource. However, this method has the following drawbacks:

• Although the client knows the name of the resource, the server does not. When the server receives an RPC request, it does not know which resource the RPC is for. This means that the resource must become an additional argument to one or more operations in the interface definition, so that the client can tell the server the resource on which to operate. For the inventory interface, the parts database name must be passed as an argument in one or more operations.

We will see later that object UUIDs remove this burden from the argument of the remote call. The resources represented by object UUIDs can be automatically communicated from the client to server as part of the binding handle.

- For every resource offered by the server, the namespace contains multiple copies of interface and binding information. In the inventory application of Figure 7-2 and Figure 7-3, the interface and binding information for each server appears twice in the namespace, since each inventory server manages and exports two resources. For servers managing many resources, the binding information would be duplicated many times. This is an inefficient use of the namespace.

- If your application becomes more sophisticated so that multiple servers provide access to a single resource, the naming model provided by this inventory example fails. In this case, multiple servers would be trying to store their interface and binding information to a single resource entry. In order to avoid coordination problems when maintaining the binding information in the entry, multiple servers should not share a single name service entry. As an example of what could go wrong, suppose one server were to call the runtime routine *rpc_ns_binding_unexport* to remove its binding information from an entry. It would also remove the binding information of other servers that exported to the entry.

As we will see in the next section, we can eliminate these disadvantages by using object UUIDs as a key element of exporting by resource.

Advertising and Locating Resources by Object UUID

Up until now our applications have used UUIDs to distinguish among interfaces on the network. UUIDs can also be used to distinguish among resources on the network. DCE provides **object UUIDs** for this purpose. DCE RPC allows you to store object UUIDs in the namespace and in the endpoint map, and it allows you to communicate an object UUID between client and server in a binding handle.

There are three uses for object UUIDs:

- During the binding process, DCE RPC uses an object UUID to select server binding information.

- During an RPC call, a server manager routine uses an object UUID to identify which resource to operate on.

- During an RPC call, DCE RPC uses an object UUID to select which implementation of a manager routine to execute. This involves grouping object UUIDs by type and is an advanced topic beyond the scope of this book.

DCE RPC provides a number of API routines for manipulating object UUIDs. When a client wants access to a particular resource, DCE uses object UUIDs in the selection criteria for locating servers of that resource. For a client of a resource to successfully locate an appropriate server, your server application must store the object UUIDs for its resources in the namespace, in the local endpoint map, and in a database maintained by the server.

To support the use of object UUIDs, all of the appropriate DCE routines (for example, *rpc_ns_binding_export*, the *rpc_ns_binding_import_** routines, and *rpc_ep_register*) contain an argument for specifying object UUIDs.

Object UUIDs in the name service

Just as your applications can use the name service to advertise the interfaces they offer, they can use it to advertise resources. As we'll see later, your server applications assign an object UUID to each resource the server manages. Unlike interface UUIDs which can be stored only in server entries, RPC allows you to store object UUIDs in all of the RPC entries: server entries, group entries, and profile entries. However, there is rarely any reason to store object UUIDs in profile entries. You can even store several object UUIDs in an entry.

An object UUID in a server entry is treated as part of the server's binding information when a client imports from the entry. As we'll see later, when storing an object UUID in a group entry, an application can apply that UUID to all of the group's members.

DCE stores object UUIDs independently of the other RPC data in an entry. This minimizes having to store the same UUID multiple times. For example, if a server listens for remote procedure calls over both the `ncacn_ip_tcp` and `ncadg_ip_udp` protocol sequences, its server entry contains separate binding information for each. If the server also manages a resource, call requests to operate on that resource can be received over both protocol sequences. Rather than storing the object UUID of that resource twice, once with the binding information for each protocol sequence, DCE stores the UUID separately and applies it to all the binding information.

Figure 7-4 shows a server entry and group entry that contain object UUIDs.

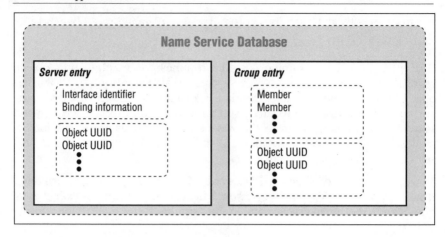

Figure 7-4: Object UUIDs in name service database entries

Object UUIDs in the endpoint map

If you use an object UUID to mark a resource, the server must store it in the local endpoint map along with the other binding information we have seen before.

Recall from Chapter 5 that when a client uses a partially bound binding handle for a remote procedure call, the RPC runtime library obtains a server endpoint from the remote host's endpoint map. If the client used an object UUID to import by resource, in addition to matching the interface identifier and binding information, the selected endpoint must be for a server that registered an object UUID matching the client-specified object UUID.

Local object UUID/resource map

Each time the server executes, it must know about its resources. To do this, the server maintains its own database, probably in a file, that maps each resource to its object UUID. Since each copy of your server application may offer different resources, each server maintains its own private mapping.

The information stored in this map is application-specific. For instance, in a banking application, the actual resource, a savings account, might be stored as a file. In the inventory application, the resource might be a database. In some other application, the resource might be in-memory data.

When your server starts execution, it reads its object UUID/resource map to determine which object UUIDs to export to the name service and register in the local endpoint map.

Object UUIDs and the Binding Process

The rest of this chapter shows an actual program for managing bank accounts. Each bank account here is considered a resource. This means that a server has to create a UUID for each bank account, and register that UUID in the endpoint map and name service. There are several ways to organize the namespace, and its important to choose a robust one so you can get the most out of the application. So this chapter will explore solutions and explain why one of them is the best.

The next two figures, Figure 7-5 and Figure 7-6, show the binding process for a server application that exports by resource and the corresponding client that imports by resource. Figure 7-5 shows how the banking server uses object UUIDs to export by resource.

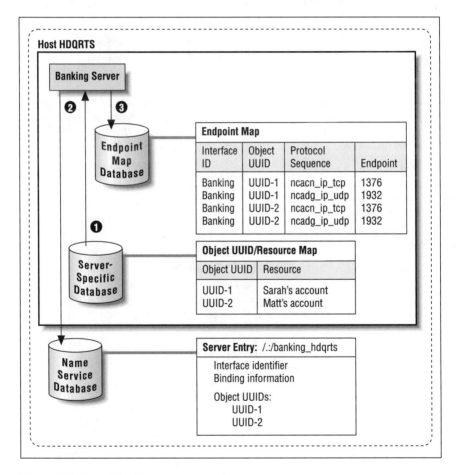

Figure 7-5: Exporting by resource

The bullets in Figure 7-5 show the sequence of events in exporting and importing.

❶ When your server begins execution, it reads its object UUID/resource map to determine which object UUIDs to export to the namespace and register in the local endpoint map. If your server creates a new resource while running, the server generates a new object UUID, adds an entry to the object UUID/resource map, exports the new object UUID to the namespace, and registers it in the local endpoint map.

❷ Using *rpc_ns_binding_export*, the banking application server creates its server entry /.:/banking_hdqrts. In addition to the interface specification and vector of binding handles, the server calls *rpc_ns_binding_export* with a list of object UUIDs. In this way, the server advertises that it offers both the banking interface and the resources assigned UUID-1 and UUID-2 as object UUIDs.

❸ Using *rpc_ep_register*, your server application adds its interface identifier, binding information, managed object UUIDs, and endpoints to the local endpoint map.

Figure 7-6 shows how the corresponding banking client uses an object UUID to import by resource. In the figure, steps 1 through 3 are taken directly by the client, while steps 4 through 6 are performed by the RPC runtime library on behalf of the client. The sequence of events is as follows:

❶ A banking client that needs to access a particular bank account uses the routines beginning with *rpc_ns_binding_import_* to obtain a binding handle for an appropriate server. The client specifies the object UUID (in this example the UUID can be thought of as the account number) of interest to the *rpc_ns_binding_import_begin* routine.

When you provide an object UUID to *rpc_ns_binding_import_begin*, in addition to finding a suitable server based on the interface identifier and protocol sequence, the import operation also checks that the server exported the object UUID the client specified.

❷ If a suitable server was located, the *rpc_ns_binding_import_next* routine returns a binding handle for that banking server. The returned binding handle automatically contains the object UUID the client specified in the *rpc_ns_binding_import_begin* routine. In this example, the binding handle is partially bound (it doesn't contain an endpoint), since the banking server uses dynamic endpoints.

For example, if the client specified /.:/banking_hdqrts as the entry name argument and UUID-1 as the object UUID argument to the *rpc_ns_binding_import_begin* routine, the returned binding handle would be to the banking server on host HDQRTS and would contain UUID-1 as the object UUID.

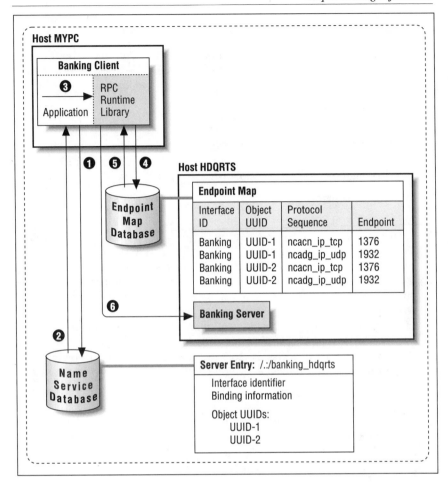

Figure 7-6: Importing by resource

❸ The client makes a remote procedure call using the returned binding handle.

❹ Detecting a partially bound binding handle, the RPC runtime library contacts the *rpcd* on host HDQRTS to obtain the endpoint for a server whose interface identifier, binding information, and object UUID matches that found in the binding handle.

❺ The *rpcd* returns the endpoint for a server that offers the banking interface and manages the object UUID found in the partially bound binding handle. This example chooses either endpoint 1376 or 1932, depending on the protocol sequences supported on the client's host.

❻ Using the now fully bound binding handle, the RPC runtime library forwards the RPC request to the banking server on host HDQRTS.

Representing UUIDs

DCE provides two methods for representing UUIDs. Although the focus of this chapter is on object UUIDs, these methods can be applied to interface UUIDs, as well as any other use of UUIDs in your application.

- Binary representation

  This is the internal format that programs use to store and retrieve UUIDs. DCE provides the uuid_t data type for storing a UUID in binary representation. To create a new UUID in binary representation, your applications call the runtime routine *uuid_create*.

- String representation

  As you saw in Chapter 1 when you created an interface definition, UUIDs can also be stored as a string of hexadecimal digits and hyphens. This is necessary for writing interface definitions and other text files that refer to UUIDs. To create a new UUID in string representation, you run the *uuidgen* utility. Your applications can create a binary UUID from a string representation of a UUID by calling the runtime routine *uuid_from_string*. Your applications can create a string representation of a binary UUID by calling the runtime routine *uuid_to_string*.

In addition to the UUIDs created to represent interfaces and objects, RPC recognizes a special UUID value: the nil UUID. The string representation of the nil UUID is:

```
00000000-0000-0000-0000-000000000000
```

Those runtime routines that have an object UUID argument usually tell you to provide the NULL value when there is no UUID. In those cases, NULL is equivalent to providing the nil UUID.

Your application can create the nil UUID by calling the runtime routine *uuid_create_nil*, and can determine if a UUID is the nil UUID by calling the runtime routine *uuid_is_nil*.

An OK Usage Model for Exporting by Resource

Although DCE RPC provides API routines for creating, storing, and using object UUIDs, and for manipulating namespace server entries and group entries, it does not prescribe exactly how applications should use object UUIDs. In this and the following section, through two variations of a banking application, we will make those recommendations and show how to implement them.

For the banking example, suppose the bank has two offices, the headquarters and a branch, and that customers can open savings accounts at either office. Each office has one computer (host **hdqrts** and host **branch**) that maintains the accounts for that office.

The application described in this chapter lets you open an account, close an account, and perform some transactions like a withdrawal. We concentrate on opening and closing, since they involve manipulation of the namespace. Appendices E and F contain the complete programs.

In this application each bank account is considered a resource. Thus, there is an object UUID for each bank account, and the object UUID is stored in the name service.

This section provides a simple model for using object UUIDs to identify and locate a server. It shows how your server application assigns an object UUID to a resource, and how that object UUID can be stored in a server entry. It is a good start, but not the way you will probably use UUIDs in production.

To make the client's importing task as easy as possible, each banking server adds itself as a member of a group entry. With all servers added to a group, a banking client that knows an object UUID (in the banking application, the client has a bank account number) can import from that group and bind to the server that manages the account.

Figure 7-7 shows the name service entries for the banking example in which the headquarters office manages three accounts and the branch office manages two accounts. Except for the addition of object UUIDs in the server entries, this usage is similar to that shown in Figure 6-4 for the inventory application. The name service entries in this usage model, corresponding to the callouts in Figure 7-6, are as follows:

❶ Server entries

Each server exports both its binding information and a list of object UUIDs to a server entry whose name is based on the server's interface name and host name. This is the same as the server entry naming described in Chapter 6.

❷ Server group

Each server adds itself as a member of the group that contains all the servers of an interface. Clients start their import search at this entry regardless of whether they are importing by resource or interface.

The remainder of this section details how to create and use those namespace entries in your application. Although this model familiarizes us

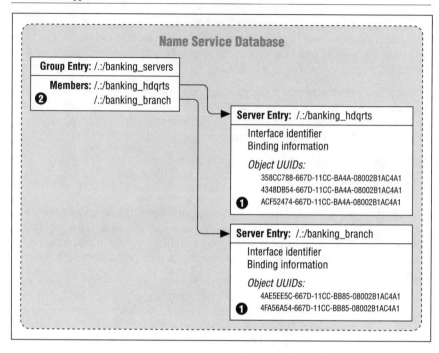

Figure 7-7: Simple banking example name service database usage

with using object UUIDs, its use of object UUIDs is relatively simple, and has a number of shortcomings as a model for developing rigorous applications. At the close of the section we will discuss those shortcomings in preparation for our second and more complete model for using object UUIDs.

Initializing the Server

In addition to the usual server initialization code discussed in Chapter 5, a server managing resources has to:

- Obtain the list of its managed resources and their associated object UUIDs.

- Export the resources' object UUIDs to the server's namespace server entry.

- Register the object UUIDs in the local endpoint map.

Example 7-2 shows the necessary header files and data structures for the banking server initialization.

Example 7-2: Banking Server Header Files and Data Structures

```
#include <stdio.h>
#include <dce/dce_cf.h>      /* DCE configuration file, DCE provided */❶
#include "banking.h"         /* Application specific, IDL generated  */❷
#include "check_status.h"    /* Contains macros to check status      */❸
#include "svr_support.h"     /* Defines obj UUID/res map data type   */❹
#define bank_c_max_map_size 50   /* Obj UUID/res map size           */

res_map_list_t     *res_map_list;    /* Object UUID/resource map  */ ❺
rpc_binding_vector_t *binding_vector; /* Binding handle list       */ ❻
unsigned_char_t  server_entry_name[STRINGLEN];
unsigned_char_t  server_group_name[STRINGLEN];

main ()
{
     uuid_vector_t    *uuid_list;     /* Object UUID list */      ❼
     uuid_vector_t    resource_uuid;  /* Object UUID list */      ❽
     unsigned_char_t  annotation[STRINGLEN];
     unsigned_char_t  *host_name;
     unsigned32       status;
     int              i;
     boolean32        mgmt_auth_fn();  /* Management operations
                                        * authorization function   */
```

❶ DCE provides a number of API routines, beginning with *dce_cf_*, that are used to access a host-specific configuration file. The configuration file is created when DCE is installed on the host. This **include** statement includes the DCE-provided header file required when using those routines. Later, in Example 7-5, we will use a *dce_cf_* routine to get the name by which this host is known in the DCE cell.

❷ Include the C language header file, created by the IDL compiler, for the banking interface. This is just like Chapter 5.

❸ Each operation in the banking interface returns two status codes: a bank status code specific to the application and an RPC status code. This header file contains the macros CHECK_DCE_STATUS and CHECK_BANK_STATUS to check each code.

The application-specific status codes are defined in *banking.idl* (see Appendix E). Each procedure of the interface contains *bank_status* as an explicit parameter. The RPC status code for each procedure in the interface is declared in *banking.acf* (also in Appendix E) using the ACF attributes comm_status and fault_status. These attributes cause the IDL compiler to automatically add an additional parameter to each procedure in the interface. These ACF attributes are described in Chapter 3.

❹ This header file defines the application-specific data structures used by the banking server to store its object UUID/resource map.

❺ Many functions that make up the banking server process the object UUID/resource map. This declaration makes the map available to those functions.

❻ This is the same as in Chapter 5.

❼ Some of the RPC runtime routines accept a vector (or list) of object UUIDs. The uuid_vector_t data type is a list of pointers to the binary representation of object UUIDs and a count of the UUIDs in the list. The definition of uuid_vector_t can be found in the DCE-provided header file *uuid.h*. However, your applications do not need to include *uuid.h* since it is already included by *banking.h*.

Frequently, your application does not know the number of elements in the list until run time. In this case, your application must dynamically create and initialize UUID vectors for use by the RPC runtime routines.

In this application, *uuid_list* is a pointer to a vector of object UUIDs that the server dynamically allocates.

❽ The uuid_vector_t data type itself is a list containing one element. When your application needs to call one of the RPC runtime routines for processing a single object UUID, your application still uses a UUID vector. However, in this case your application doesn't need to dynamically allocate the vector, it can statically allocate a uuid_vector_t to hold the one UUID. *resource_uuid* is used in this way.

Registering the interface

The banking application server follows the same steps as the other programs in this book for registering the application's interface with the RPC runtime library. Example 7-3 shows the portion of the banking server initialization code for registering the banking interface.

Example 7-3: Registering an Interface with the RPC Runtime Library

```
/*
 * Register the interface with the RPC runtime library.
 * The two NULL arguments are the default manager type and manager EPV.
 */
rpc_server_register_if (banking_v1_0_s_ifspec, NULL, NULL, &status); ❶

CHECK_DCE_STATUS (status, "rpc_server_register_if failed:", ABORT);
```

❶ Registering the banking interface uses code similar to that described in Chapter 5.

Creating server binding information

The banking application server follows the typical steps for creating server binding handles with dynamic endpoints and obtaining the list of binding handles from the RPC runtime library. Example 7-4 shows the portion of the banking server initialization code for creating the server binding handles.

Example 7-4: Creating Server Binding Handles

```
/*
 * Use all available protocol sequences.
 */
rpc_server_use_all_protseqs (rpc_c_protseq_max_calls_default,
    &status);                                                        ❶

CHECK_DCE_STATUS (status, "rpc_server_use_all_protseqs failed:", ABORT);

/*
 * Get the server's binding information.
 */
rpc_server_inq_bindings (&binding_vector, &status);                  ❷

CHECK_DCE_STATUS (status, "rpc_server_inq_bindings failed:", ABORT);
```

❶ This is the same as in Chapter 5.

❷ This is the same as in Chapter 5.

Advertising the server's interface

Example 7-5 shows the portion of the banking server initialization code for exporting its interface and binding information to the namespace, and registering the same information plus endpoints in the local endpoint map.

In this usage model, advertising a server's interface is a three step process including:

- Exporting interface and binding information to a server entry.

- Adding the server entry to a group.

- Registering interface, binding information, and endpoints in the local endpoint map.

The individual steps are identical to those discussed in Chapter 5.

Example 7-5: Advertising by Interface

```
/*
 * Create the server entry name for export.
 * Make it: <interface-name>_<host-name>.
 */

dce_cf_get_host_name (&host_name, (unsigned long *) &status);        ❶

CHECK_DCE_STATUS (status, "dce_cf_get_host_name failed:", ABORT);

/*
 * Since the returned hostname is relative to the cell root
 * (for ex: hosts/hdqrts), we need to extract the leaf name
 * (the host's name) from the returned pathname and use it
 * to create the server entry name.
 */
sprintf ((char *) server_entry_name, "/.:/banking_%s",
         strrchr (host_name, '/')+1);

/*
 * Deallocate the returned host name.
 */
free (host_name);                                                    ❷

/*
 * Create interface group name.
 * Using: <interface-name>_servers.
 */
strcpy ((char *) server_group_name, "/.:/banking_servers");

/*
 * Export binding information to namespace server entry.
 */
rpc_ns_binding_export (                                              ❸
    rpc_c_ns_syntax_default,    /* Syntax of server entry name.  */
    server_entry_name,          /* Namespace server entry name.  */
    banking_v1_0_s_ifspec,      /* Exporting interface info.     */
    binding_vector,             /* Exporting binding info.       */
    NULL,                       /* Not exporting object UUIDs.   */
    &status
    );

CHECK_DCE_STATUS (status,
    "Can't export interface.\nrpc_ns_binding_export failed:", ABORT);

/*
 * Add the server entry to the interface's server group.
 */
rpc_ns_group_mbr_add (
    rpc_c_ns_syntax_default,    /* Syntax of group entry name.   */
    server_group_name,          /* Namespace group entry name.   */
    rpc_c_ns_syntax_default,    /* Syntax of server entry name.  */
    server_entry_name,          /* Namespace server entry name.  */
    &status
    );
```

Example 7-5: Advertising by Interface (continued)

```
CHECK_DCE_STATUS (status,
    "Can't add server to interface group.\nrpc_ns_group_mbr_add failed:",
    ABORT);

/*
 * Register the binding information and dynamic endpoints in the
 * endpoint map. No objects are registered here.
 */
rpc_ep_register (banking_v1_0_s_ifspec, binding_vector, NULL,          ❹
    (unsigned_char_t *) "banking server", &status);

CHECK_DCE_STATUS (status, "rpc_ep_register failed: ", ABORT);
```

❶ The DCE routine *dce_cf_get_host_name* returns this host's name relative to the cell root. The host name is assigned when DCE is installed and the system joins a DCE cell. Please note that a system's DCE host name can differ from the Internet host name returned by calling the *gethostname* routine.

❷ Since *dce_cf_get_host_name* allocates memory using *malloc* to store the host name, the server must call *free* to deallocate the memory.

❸ The NULL argument specifies that we are not exporting any object UUIDs to the namespace. *rpc_ns_binding_export* allows you to export by interface and by resource in a single call. But in this application, for clarity, we have chosen to export by interface and export by resource as separate application tasks. Example 7-7 contains the code for exporting resources.

❹ The NULL argument specifies that we are not registering any object UUID in the endpoint map. Like *rpc_ns_binding_export*, *rpc_ep_register* allows you to specify an interface and its resources in a single call. But we have not taken advantage of that flexibility here. Example 7-9 contains the code for registering resources.

Advertising the server's resources

In addition to advertising its interface and binding information, a server that manages resources must also handle object UUIDs. This means exporting its object UUIDs (representing the managed resources) to the server entry in the name service, and registering those object UUIDs in the local endpoint map.

To advertise its resources, a server must know what they are. Therefore, each copy of the server typically maintains a local database of its managed resources and the object UUID of each one. In the banking application, the server maintains the object UUID/resource map in a file. Each time the server begins execution it reads the file.

The format of the mapping file is simply a UUID in string format followed by the name of the resource. Here are a few sample entries:

```
CF4FD9A0-9BE3-11CC-8B76-08002B245A45 debra.dat
B56ACEC0-9C59-11CC-8FBE-08002B245A45 dianne.dat
59A6D8A0-9C5D-11CC-8627-08002B245A45 marty.dat
```

Step 1: Read the Object UUID/Resource Map

Each copy of the banking server maintains its own database that maps object UUIDs to managed resources. For the banking server, each resource is a savings account maintained as a file. The mapping pairs an object UUID to a filename. As we'll see later, each time the server creates or deletes a resource, the server updates the map and writes it to a file.

Example 7-6 shows the portion of the banking server initialization code for reading its object UUID/resource map database.

Example 7-6: Initializing the Object UUID/Resource Map

```
/*
 * Allocate an object UUID/resource map for bank_c_max_map_size
 * entries.
 */
res_map_list = (res_map_list_t *) malloc (sizeof(res_map_list_t) + ❶
    (bank_c_max_map_size - 1) * sizeof(res_map_element_t));

/*
 * Get the list of server-managed resources, if any.
 */
read_resources_map ("banking.dat", res_map_list); ❷
```

❶ Here the server allocates memory for a fixed sized object UUID/resource map database. Consequently, each banking server is limited to managing up to *bank_c_max_map_size* resources. A more rigorous implementation would allow the object UUID/resource map database to vary in size. The `res_map_list_t` and `res_map_ele-ment_t` data types are defined in *svr_support.h* (see Appendix E) as follows:

```
typedef struct  {
    uuid_t   resource_id;           /* Resource ID    */
    char     resource_file[128];    /* Associated file */
    } res_map_element_t;

typedef struct   {
    int       count;
    res_map_element_t   map_element[1];
} res_map_list_t;
```

The object UUID/resource map list data type, `res_map_list_t`, contains a count member, *count*, followed by an array of elements, *res_map_element_t*. Each *res_map_element_t* represents an object UUID/filename pair. The value of *count* specifies the number of *res_map_element_t* elements in the array. The *malloc* statement allocates enough space for one *count* field plus the desired number of *res_map_element_t* fields.

❷ In this example, the banking server maintains its local object UUID/resource map in the file *banking.dat*. This server application function (*read_resources_map*) reads the map from the file into an in-memory structure. In this way each banking server remembers the resources it manages from server execution to server execution. For example, if the server's host crashes, the server reads the map from the file when it restarts. The code for this routine is in *svr_support.c* (see Appendix E). The following code fragment shows the portion of *read_resources_map* that reads a record from the file and converts the string UUID to a binary UUID:

```
/* Get the resource ID stored as a string UUID and the associated
 * resource filename.
 */
fscanf (res_map, "%s%s", buffer,
    res_map_list->map_element[i].resource_file);

/*
 * Convert the UUID from string representation to binary
 * representation.
 */
uuid_from_string (buffer, &res_map_list->map_element[i].resource_id,
    &status);

CHECK_DCE_STATUS (status, "uuid_from_string failed\n", ABORT);
```

The *read_resources_map* routine first reads a record from the map file. The string representation of the object UUID is read into the character string *buffer*, while the filename is read directly into the server's in-memory UUID/resource map data structure. Next, the routine calls the RPC runtime routine *uuid_from_string* to convert the string representation of the resource's object UUID to its binary representation. The binary form is stored in the server's in-memory UUID/resource map data structure.

Step 2: Export UUIDs to the Name Service

Once the server knows the object UUIDs of its managed resources, it can advertise those resources in the name service and endpoint map. A client that knows the object UUID of a particular resource can use that object UUID to find the individual copy of a server that manages that resource.

When exporting object UUIDs to a namespace entry, the server application is responsible for allocating and initializing a UUID vector. Each time the server starts running, it creates a UUID vector large enough to hold the object UUIDs for all of its managed resources. In the banking application, this means allocating a vector with one element for each account managed by the banking server.

Example 7-7 shows the portion of the banking server initialization code for exporting object UUIDs to the name service.

Example 7-7: Exporting Resources to the Namespace

```
/*
 * Only if there are active accounts, should we export resources.
 */
if (res_map_list->count > 0)
{
    /*
     * From the resource map list, gather up the resource IDs and
     * create a UUID vector.
     */
    create_uuid_list (res_map_list, &uuid_list);                    ❶
    /*
     * Export the UUIDs to the namespace server entry.          */
    rpc_ns_binding_export (                                         ❷
        rpc_c_ns_syntax_default,    /* Syntax of server entry name.   */
        server_entry_name,          /* Namespace server entry name.   */
        NULL,                       /* Not exporting interface info.  */
        NULL,                       /* Not exporting binding info.    */
        uuid_list,                  /* Exporting only object UUIDs.   */
        &status
        );

    CHECK_DCE_STATUS (status,
        "Can't export resource.\nrpc_ns_binding_export failed:", ABORT);

    /*
     * Free the UUID vector allocated in create_uuid_list.
     */
    free (uuid_list);                                              ❸
}
```

❶ Earlier, we said you would have to create space for the UUIDs dynamically and initialize it with the UUIDs. This is what *create_uuid_list* does. It allocates and initializes a UUID vector to contain the object UUIDs of all of the server managed resources. The full implementation of this function is shown in Example 7-8.

❷ When your server application creates a resource and assigns it an object UUID, the server uses the RPC runtime routine *rpc_ns_binding_export* to store the object UUID in a namespace entry. In one call to the *rpc_ns_binding_export* routine, you can store both binding information and a list of object UUIDs. But since the banking server has already exported its binding information, here it exports only object UUIDs. When calling *rpc_ns_binding_export* to store only object UUIDs, you specify a NULL value for the interface specification and binding vector arguments.

At this point, the namespace contains the entries as shown in Figure 7-7.

❸ The application is responsible for freeing the memory it allocated for a UUIDvector.

The purpose of *create_uuid_list* is to reformat UUID information into a uuid_vector_t structure that *rpc_ns_binding_export* can read. The uuid_vector_t data type is a structure with two members: an integer *count* and an array of pointers to UUIDs called *uuid*. Suppose that a banking server managed two accounts. When the server begins running and wants to export the object UUIDs for those accounts, it must allocate and initialize a UUID vector with two elements. In the banking example, the server initializes each element in the *uuid* array to point to an object UUID in the server's object UUID/resource map. This is shown in Figure 7-8. Although the figure shows string UUIDs, they are stored as binary UUIDs in the object UUID/resource map.

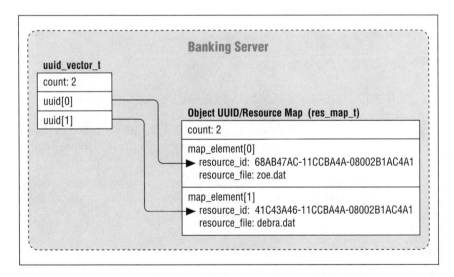

Figure 7-8: Example UUID vector

Example 7-8 shows the code used by the banking server to create and initialize its UUID vector.

Example 7-8: Creating a UUID List

```
void create_uuid_list (res_map_list, uuid_list)
res_map_list_t    *res_map_list;
uuid_vector_t     **uuid_list;
{
    unsigned32      status;
    int             i;

    /*
     * Allocate enough memory to hold all of the resource IDs.
     */
    *uuid_list = (uuid_vector_t *) malloc (sizeof(uuid_vector_t) +        ❶
        (res_map_list->count - 1) * sizeof(uuid_t *) );

    /*
     * Save the number of UUIDs in the list.
     */
    (*uuid_list)->count = res_map_list->count;                           ❷

    /*
     * For each element in the map...
     */
    for (i = 0; i < res_map_list->count; ++i)
    {
        /*
         * Place a pointer to the resource ID in the UUID list.
         */
        (*uuid_list)->uuid[i] = &res_map_list->map_element[i].resource_id; ❸
    }
}
```

❶ DCE defines the *uuid* member of the uuid_vector_t structure as a
   one element array of pointers to *uuid_t* (that is: uuid_t *uuid[0]).
   This means that when allocating memory for a uuid vector to hold multiple UUIDs, your application subtracts one from the needed *uuid* array
   size.

   This also means that if your application is processing only a single
   object UUID, there is no need to dynamically allocate a uuid_vec-
   tor_t. Your application can statically allocate a variable of type
   uuid_vector_t.

❷ Always assign a value to the *count* member of a UUID vector.

❸ Assign each element in the *uuid* array the address of a binary representation of a UUID (that is, the address of a uuid_t variable).

Step 3: Register in the Endpoint Map

When registering their binding information and endpoints in the local endpoint map, servers that manage resources include the object UUIDs of
those resources. When a client wishes to access a particular resource, it
includes the resource's object UUID in the binding handle. If the binding
handle is a partially bound handle when the client makes a remote procedure call, the RPC runtime library obtains an endpoint from the server system's endpoint map. In addition to comparing the client's interface specification and binding information to the data in the endpoint map, the runtime
library also looks for the endpoint of a server that registered with a matching object UUID. If a match is found, the runtime library adds that endpoint
to the binding handle and completes the connection to that endpoint.

Example 7-9 shows the portion of the banking server initialization code for
registering object UUIDs in the local endpoint map.

Example 7-9: Registering Resources in the Endpoint Map

```
/*
 * For each resource in the object UUID/resource map...
 */
for (i = 0; i < res_map_list->count; ++i)
{
    /*
     * Create an annotation string (that is, a documentation string)
     * using the interface name and the resource name.
     */
    sprintf ((char *) annotation, "banking object: %s",          ❶
        res_map_list->map_element[i].resource_file);

    /*
     * Place the object UUID for the current resource into a UUID
     * list which is one element long.
     */
    resource_uuid.count = 1;
    resource_uuid.uuid[0] = &res_map_list->map_element[i].resource_id; ❷

    /*
     * For this managed resource, add binding information
     * and endpoints to the local endpoint map.
     */
    rpc_ep_register (banking_v1_0_s_ifspec, binding_vector,       ❸
        &resource_uuid, annotation, &status);

    CHECK_DCE_STATUS (status, "rpc_ep_register failed:", ABORT);
}
```

❶ For each managed resource, the server generates a unique annotation
string to use in the endpoint registration. In this way each entry in the
endpoint map is labeled with easily understood documentation. When
you use the *rpccp* command *show mapping*, the resulting display contains this annotation string.

❷ When registering object UUIDs in the endpoint map, your application must provide the RPC routine *rpc_ep_register* with a UUID vector. In the banking example, the server calls *rpc_ep_register* once for each object UUID so that a different annotation string can be applied to each registration. Since the `uuid_vector_t` structure allows you to list one UUID, there is no need for the server to dynamically allocate a larger vector.

❸ The *rpc_ep_register* routine registers the server's endpoints, interface specification, binding information, and object UUID in the local endpoint map. If the server uses multiple protocol sequences, this registration results in multiple entries in the endpoint map; one for each protocol sequence.

If this example were using the same annotation string for every resource, the server could have passed a UUID vector with multiple object UUIDs to register all the resources in one call to *rpc_ep_register*.

Registering a management authorization function

The RPC runtime library allows a server application to specify a function that the runtime library automatically calls each time the server receives a remote call for one of the RPC-provided management routines (those routines beginning with *rpc_mgmt_*). In this way, the server application can write a routine to check if the calling client is authorized to perform the requested management operation. Chapter 9 discusses how servers can authorize clients.

Example 7-10 shows how the server registers its authorization function.

Example 7-10: Registering a Management Authorization Function

```
/*
 * Register a management authorization function to control client
 * access to RPC-provided management routines.
 */
rpc_mgmt_set_authorization_fn (&mgmt_auth_fn, &status); ❶

CHECK_DCE_STATUS(status, "rpc_mgmt_set_authorization_fn failed:", ABORT);
```

❶ The server calls the *rpc_mgmt_set_authorization_fn* routine to register the server-provided function *mgmt_auth_fn* with the RPC runtime library. In the banking application, whenever a client calls *rpc_mgmt_stop_server_listening* to shut down the server, the runtime library automatically calls *mgmt_auth_fn* prior to executing the management routine. Details of *mgmt_auth_fn* are discussed in Example 7-15.

Listening for remote procedure calls

Finally, the server is ready to accept client requests to execute remote procedure calls. Example 7-11 shows the portion of the banking server initialization code for this. The process is the same as in Chapter 5.

Example 7-11: Listening for Remote Procedure Calls

```
/*
 * Begin listening for one remote procedure call at a time.
 */
rpc_server_listen (1, &status);

CHECK_DCE_STATUS (status, "rpc_server_listen failed:", ABORT);
```

Server Manager Code

When your server application uses object UUIDs and manages resources, the manager routines use RPC runtime routines to:

- Obtain the object UUID for the resource to operate on.

- If necessary, create a new resource, assign it an object UUID, export the resource's UUID to the namespace, and register it with the local endpoint map.

- If necessary, delete a resource, remove the resource's UUID from the namespace, and remove it from the local endpoint map.

For instance, the banking server creates new bank accounts at the client's request. This entails creating a new object UUID and repeating the steps required to register it. When the banking server closes an account at the client's request, it must repeat the steps to unregister the object UUID.

Identifying a resource

An object UUID can be referenced by a binding handle. The UUID automatically gets passed to the server, which can retrieve it from the binding handle using the RPC routine *rpc_binding_inq_object*. The object UUID referred to by the binding handle represents the resource on which the server operates. In this way, RPC provides a mechanism to automatically communicate the object UUID of a resource between client and server. Example 7-12 shows how this is done in the banking application manager code.

The code for this and the other manager routines is in *ok_mgr.c* (see Appendix E).

Example 7-12: Getting an Object UUID and Resource

```
void transaction (
     rpc_binding_handle_t   binding_handle,                              ❶
     trans_type             trans_code,
     unsigned32             amount,
     unsigned32             *balance,
     unsigned32             *bank_status,
     unsigned32             *dce_status
     )
{
     uuid_t            resource_id;

     /*
      * Get the object UUID from the binding handle.
      */
     rpc_binding_inq_object (binding_handle, &resource_id, dce_status);  ❷

     CHECK_DCE_STATUS (*dce_status, "rpc_binding_inq_object failed: ",
              ABORT);

     /*
      * Read the savings account info.
      */
     read_account (&resource_id, filename, &name, balance, bank_status); ❸
```

❶ Your server application manger code needs to know the resource on which to operate. Since the binding handle contains the object UUID of the resource, the manager code needs the binding handle.

To obtain a binding handle as an argument, procedures must take a handle_t data type as the first argument. Alternatively, you can specify the explicit_handle attribute in the ACF file so that all operations have, as their first argument, a binding handle.

❷ The manager code uses the *rpc_binding_inq_object* routine to obtain the object UUID of the requested resource from the binding handle. The routine returns the binary representation of the object UUID in a variable of data type uuid_t.

❸ Using the object UUID from the binding handle, the *read_account* function determines the associated savings account file by looking in the server's object UUID/resource map. The manager routine can then read the file.

Creating a new resource

Each time your server application creates a new resource, it must generate an object UUID, add an entry to its object UUID/resource map, and advertise the resource. In the banking application, this activity takes place each time a client calls the remote procedure *create_account* to open a new savings account. Example 7-13 shows portions of the code for this routine.

Example 7-13: Creating and Advertising a New Resource

```
uuid_t create_account (                                              ❶
    rpc_binding_handle_t  binding_handle,
    account_name          name,
    unsigned32            opening_balance,
    unsigned32            *bank_status,
    unsigned32            *dce_status
    )
{
    uuid_vector_t    uuid_list;
    uuid_t           resource_id;
         .
         .
         .
    unsigned_char_t  annotation[STRINGLEN];

    /*
     * Create a resource ID for the account.
     */
    uuid_create (&resource_id, dce_status);                          ❷

    CHECK_DCE_STATUS (*dce_status, "uuid_create failed:", ABORT);
         .
         .
         .
    /*
     * Create a UUID vector containing the new resource ID.
     */
    uuid_list.count = 1;
    uuid_list.uuid[0] = &resource_id;                                ❸

    /*
     * Export only the UUID to the namespace server entry.
     */
    rpc_ns_binding_export (                                          ❹
        rpc_c_ns_syntax_default,  /* Syntax of server entry name. */
        server_entry_name,        /* Namespace server entry name. */
        NULL,                     /* Not exporting interface info.*/
        NULL,                     /* Not exporting binding info.  */
        &uuid_list,               /* Exporting only object UUIDs. */
        &status
        );

    CHECK_DCE_STATUS (status,
        "Can't export resource.\nrpc_ns_binding_export failed:", ABORT);
```

Example 7-13: Creating and Advertising a New Resource (continued)

```
/*
 * Register the resource with the endpoint map.
 */
sprintf ((char *) annotation, "banking object: %s", filename);

rpc_ep_register (banking_v1_0_s_ifspec, binding_vector, &uuid_list, ❺
    annotation, dce_status);

CHECK_DCE_STATUS (*dce_status, "rpc_ep_register failed: ", ABORT);

*bank_status = bank_s_ok;

return (resource_id);                                          ❻
```

❶ Since a client calling this remote procedure wants to create a new account, the binding handle passed to the *create_account* manager routine does not contain an object UUID. This routine creates a new object UUID (savings account number), which is sent to the client as the manager routine's return value.

❷ The RPC runtime routine *uuid_create* generates a new UUID and returns it in binary form.

❸ Although this routine creates and advertises only one new account at a time, the RPC runtime routines for advertising object UUIDs require the UUID to be passed as a UUID vector argument. Consequently, the server creates a UUID vector with one element pointing to the newly generated object UUID.

❹ The new object UUID is exported to the name service in the same way as during server initialization (Example 7-7) except the UUID vector here always contains one UUID.

❺ The new object UUID is registered in the local endpoint map in the same way as during server initialization (Example 7-9). We don't show the portions of the *create_account* routine that create a new file for the new account and add an entry to the object UUID/resource map. See *ok_mgr.c* in Appendix E for the full implementation.

❻ The routine returns the newly created object UUID to the calling client.

Deleting an existing resource

Each time your server application deletes a resource, it must remove the entry from its object UUID/resource map, and stop advertising the resource. In the banking application, this activity takes place each time a client calls the remote procedure *delete_account* to close a savings account.

Example 7-14 shows portions of the code for this routine.

Example 7-14: Deleting and Removing a Resource

```
void delete_account (
        rpc_binding_handle_t   binding_handle,
        unsigned32             *bank_status,
        unsigned32             *dce_status
        )
{
        uuid_t                 resource_id;
        uuid_vector_t          uuid_list;
        char                   filename[STRINGLEN];
        unsigned32             status;

        /*
         * Get the object UUID from the binding handle.
         */
        rpc_binding_inq_object (binding_handle, &resource_id, dce_status);  ❶

        CHECK_DCE_STATUS (*dce_status, "rpc_binding_inq_object failed: ",
            ABORT);

        /*
         * See if we can find this resource.
         */
        resource_to_filename (res_map_list, &resource_id, &filename,      ❷
            bank_status);

        /*
         * If we found the account...
         */
        if (*bank_status == bank_s_ok)
        {
                .
                .
                .
                /*
                 * Create a UUID vector containing the resource ID to unexport.
                 */
                uuid_list.count = 1;
                uuid_list.uuid[0] = &resource_id;                        ❸

                /*
                 * Unexport only the uuid_list to namespace entry entry_name.
                 */
                rpc_ns_binding_unexport (                                ❹
                    rpc_c_ns_syntax_default, /* Syntax of server entry name. */
                    server_entry_name,       /* Namespace server entry name. */
                    NULL,                    /* Not unexporting bindings.    */
                    &uuid_list,              /* Unexporting only an object UUID. */
                    &status
                    );
```

Example 7-14: Deleting and Removing a Resource (continued)

```
                CHECK_DCE_STATUS (status,
                    "Can't unexport resource.\nrpc_ns_binding_unexport failed:",
                    ABORT);
                                .
                                .
                                .
                /*
                 * Unregister the resource from the endpoint map.
                 */
                rpc_ep_unregister (banking_v1_0_s_ifspec, binding_vector,  ❺
                        &uuid_list, dce_status);

                CHECK_DCE_STATUS (*dce_status, "rpc_ep_unregister failed: ",
                                ABORT);
                                .
                                .
                                .
                *bank_status = bank_s_ok;
        }
        return;
}
```

❶ This is the same as in Example 7-12.

❷ This routine checks the object UUID/resource map and returns the filename for the account corresponding to the object UUID. The routine is in *svr_support.c*.

❸ This is the same as in Example 7-13.

❹ The RPC runtime routine *rpc_ns_binding_unexport* removes a server's binding information and/or object UUIDs from a namespace entry. In this situation, the server removes only the object UUID referred to by the UUID vector. The NULL argument specifies not to remove any binding information from the namespace entry.

❺ Unregistering the object UUID removes its information from the local endpoint map. This information includes the interface specification, binding information, and endpoints for the object UUID(s) provided in the UUID vector argument. The entries for other object UUIDs remain in the map.

We haven't shown the portions of the *delete_account* routine that delete the file for the account and remove its entry from the object UUID/resource map. See *ok_mgr.c* in Appendix E for the full implementation.

Server Termination

If a server is to become unavailable for an extended period of time, it makes sense to remove its binding information from the namespace and its endpoints from the local endpoint map. Otherwise, clients that import from the namespace may waste time attempting to bind to a server that is no longer running.

In our application, the server will shut down only at the request of a client. This determines where we put our server shutdown code, and gives us a chance to illustrate another feature of DCE: the management authorization function.

A management authorization function is necessary because you usually want to limit the ability of a client to do management, such as shutting down the server. You may want the server to check that the client is who it says it is, and whether that client has the right to shut down the server—in other words, you want to do some authentication and authorization. In Chapters 8 and 9, we see how authentication and authorization is done. In this chapter, we just leave an empty spot where you can plug them in.

A management authorization function is one that the RPC runtime library calls automatically when the client requests some aspect of server management. We will call our function *mgmt_auth_fn*. It is installed in the server's main function, as shown in Example 7-10, by calling *rpc_mgmt_set_authorization_fn*. Example 7-15 shows portions of the code for the *mgmt_auth_fn* routine.

Example 7-15: Shutting Down a Server

```
boolean32 mgmt_auth_fn (client_binding, requested_mgmt_operation, status) ❶
rpc_binding_handle_t    client_binding;
unsigned32              requested_mgmt_operation;
unsigned32              *status;
{
    uuid_vector_t    *uuid_list = NULL;
    unsigned_char_t  *string_binding;
    void             print_uuids();

    /*
     * In a more rigorous application, at this point we would
     * perform an authentication check to see if the calling client
     * is who he says he is.
     *
     * For this example, we trust all clients.
     */

    switch (requested_mgmt_operation)
    {
        case rpc_c_mgmt_stop_server_listen:

            /*
```

Example 7-15: Shutting Down a Server (continued)

```
 * In a more rigorous application, at this point we would
 * perform an authorization check to see if the calling client
 * should be allowed to perform this operation.
 *
 * For this example, all clients are allowed to shutdown the
 * server.
 */

/*
 * Only if there are active accounts, do we need an object UUID
 * vector for exporting resources.
 */
if (res_map_list->count > 0)
{
    /*
     * Create a list of resource object UUIDs from the
     * object UUID/resource map
     */
    create_uuid_list (res_map_list, &uuid_list);              }

/*
 * Unexport both the interface and any object UUIDs from the
 * namespace server entry.
 */
rpc_ns_binding_unexport (                                     ❷
    rpc_c_ns_syntax_default, /* Syntax of server entry name. */
    server_entry_name,        /* Namespace server entry name. */
    banking_v1_0_s_ifspec, /* Unexport bindings for this i/f */
    uuid_list,                /* Unexporting object UUIDs */
    status
    );

CHECK_DCE_STATUS (*status,
    "Can't unexport.\nrpc_ns_binding_unexport failed:", ABORT);

/*
 * Remove the server entry from the interface's server group.
 */
rpc_ns_group_mbr_remove (                                     ❸
    rpc_c_ns_syntax_default, /* Syntax of group entry name.  */
    server_group_name,        /* Namespace group entry name.  */
    rpc_c_ns_syntax_default, /* Syntax of server entry name. */
    server_entry_name,        /* Namespace server entry name. */
    status
    );

CHECK_DCE_STATUS (*status,
    "Can't remove server from interface group. \
    \nrpc_ns_group_mbr_remove failed:", ABORT);

if (uuid_list != NULL)
{
```

Example 7-15: Shutting Down a Server (continued)

```
                    /*
                     * Remove endpoints from local endpoint map for each object.
                     */
                    rpc_ep_unregister (banking_v1_0_s_ifspec, binding_vector,❹
                        uuid_list, status);

                    CHECK_DCE_STATUS (*status, "rpc_ep_unregister failed:",
                      ABORT);

                    /*
                     * Free the UUID list returned from create_uuid_list.
                     */
                    free (uuid_list);                                    ❺
                }

                /*
                 * Remove endpoints from local endpoint map for the interface
                 * itself.
                 */
                rpc_ep_unregister (banking_v1_0_s_ifspec, binding_vector,    ❻
                    NULL, status);

                CHECK_DCE_STATUS (*status, "rpc_ep_unregister failed:", ABORT);

                /*
                 * Free server binding handles
                 */
                rpc_binding_vector_free (&binding_vector, status);          ❼

                CHECK_DCE_STATUS (*status, "rpc_binding_vector_free failed:",
                    RESUME);

                return (true);                                              ❽
            }
        }
```

❶ The RPC API specifies the server-provided management authorization function. The first argument is a binding handle representing the client that called the *rpc_mgmt_* routine.

The second argument is a constant specifying which *rpc_mgmt_* routine is being called by the client. For example, when a client calls *rpc_mgmt_stop_server_listening*, the value of the *requested_mgmt_ operation* argument is rpc_c_mgmt_stop_server_listen.

boolean32, an RPC-defined data type, signifies that the authorization function returns a boolean value. When the authorization function returns true, the RPC runtime library allows the requested *rpc_mgmt_* routine to execute. Otherwise, the runtime library does not execute the *rpc_mgmt_* routine and an error is returned to the calling client.

❷ To remove binding information from a server entry, call the RPC routine *rpc_ns_binding_unexport* with the IDL-generated interface specification. *rpc_ns_binding_unexport* removes all binding information for that interface from the server entry. In the same call, you can remove object UUIDs from a server entry by providing an object UUID vector. In this version of the banking application, unexporting object UUIDs is not required to unadvertise a server.

Removing a server's binding information from the namespace is sufficient to unadvertise a server. However, the notion of unexporting both resources and interfaces becomes important in the Better version of the application later in this chapter, so we have done that here as well.

❸ The RPC runtime routine *rpc_ns_group_mbr_remove* removes a member from a namespace group entry. After this, clients that begin their import at the */.:/banking_servers* group entry will not know about this server.

❹ This is the same as in Example 7-14, except in this routine the UUID vector may point to more than one object UUID.

❺ The application is responsible for deallocating UUID vectors it allocated.

❻ During server initialization, the banking server registered its interface and endpoints without any object UUIDs (see Example 7-4). Consequently, the server must now unregister those endpoints.

In this example there is one endpoint per protocol sequence without an object UUID. The use of *rpc_ep_unregister* is discussed in Chapter 5.

❼ Up to this point, the banking server needed its list of binding handles for registering new object UUIDs in the endpoint map. Now the binding vector can be freed. This is discussed in Chapter 5.

❽ A return value of `true` signals the RPC runtime library that it can execute *rpc_mgmt_stop_server_listening* and thereby stop accepting new remote procedure calls. After this call executes and the server program completes execution of all active remote procedure calls, the server program returns from the call to *rpc_server_listen*. This is discussed in Chapter 5.

Client Initialization

Banking clients are interested in locating a banking server in one of two ways:

• By interface—to open a new account, in which case any compatible banking server will do.

• By resource—to access the server that manages a particular account.

Chapter 3 discussed the ways in which a client obtains a fully bound binding handle for communications with a compatible server. Although that discussion implicitly referred to importing by interface, those same methods, with some modifications, can be used for importing by resource as well.

Finding a Server Based on Interface

Recall from Chapter 3 that a server's binding information always contains a place for an object UUID. None of this book's previous examples used object UUIDs, and so the client didn't need to bother with them. When object UUIDs aren't used by an application, the RPC runtime library automatically places the nil UUID in binding handles.

However, when an application uses object UUIDs, as in the banking example, the client is responsible for managing the object UUID in binding handles. This is necessary whether your client is interested in locating an interface or a particular resource.

If a nil UUID is in a binding handle, an object (a resource) is not being referenced. This has been the case until this chapter; none of the examples in previous chapters used object UUIDs. Since this banking example does use object UUIDs, the client is responsible for managing the object UUID in the binding handle.

Example 7-16 shows how the banking client finds a banking server and manages the object UUID in the returned binding handle.

Example 7-16: Locating a Server Based on Interface

```
extern unsigned_char_t        server_group_name[STRINGLEN];

void import_interface (if_name, if_spec, binding_h, status)
unsigned_char_t      *if_name;
rpc_if_handle_t      if_spec;
rpc_binding_handle_t *binding_h;
unsigned32           *status;
{
    rpc_ns_handle_t   import_context;
    unsigned32        temp_status;

    /*
     * Import binding information from the namespace server group.
     */
    rpc_ns_binding_import_begin (                                    ❶
        rpc_c_ns_syntax_default,    /* Syntax for server group name.  */
        server_group_name,          /* Namespace server group name.   */
        if_spec,                    /* Interface to import            */
        NULL,                       /* Not importing an object UUID.  */
        &import_context,            /* Import context.                */
        status
        );
```

Example 7-16: Locating a Server Based on Interface (continued)

```
CHECK_DCE_STATUS (*status,
    "Can't import by interface\nrpc_ns_binding_import_begin failed",
    ABORT);

do
{
    /*
     * Get a server binding handle.
     */
    rpc_ns_binding_import_next (import_context, binding_h, status); ❷

                        .
                        .
                        .

    /*
     * Get an endpoint for the binding.
     */
    rpc_ep_resolve_binding (*binding_h, if_spec, status);              ❸

    CHECK_DCE_STATUS (*status, "rpc_ep_resolve_binding failed:",
        ABORT);

    /*
     * Verify the server is available.
     */
    if (rpc_mgmt_is_server_listening (*binding_h, &temp_status))       ❹
    {
        break;
    }
    else
    {
        CHECK_DCE_STATUS (temp_status,
            "Server not listening \
            \nrpc_mgmt_is_server_listening failed:", RESUME);
                        .
                        .
                        .

    }
} while (*status == rpc_s_ok);

/*
 * If we have a binding...
 */
if (*status == rpc_s_ok)
{
    /*
     * Make sure the returned binding doesn't reference an
     * existing account.
     */
```

Example 7-16: Locating a Server Based on Interface (continued)

```
    rpc_binding_set_object (*binding_h, NULL, status);          ❺

    CHECK_DCE_STATUS (*status, "rpc_binding_set_object failed:", ABORT);
  }

  return;
}
```

❶ This sets up the import context to search for banking servers. It begins the search at a group entry that contains server entries as members. Since the client is interested in any banking server—not a server for a particular account—the client provides a NULL value for the object UUID. This routine is discussed in Chapters 3 and 6.

❷ *rpc_ns_binding_import_next* returns a single binding handle for a server. Because an object UUID is part of a server's binding information, *rpc_ns_binding_import_next* (and *rpc_ns_binding_lookup_next*) always include an object UUID in the returned binding handle. Suppose you specified either a NULL value for the object UUID argument or the nil object UUID in *rpc_ns_binding_import_begin*. If the *rpc_ns_binding_import_next* routine found a compatible binding in a server entry and it contained object UUIDs, then the returned binding handle would contain, at random, one of those object UUIDs.

In this banking example, once a server has created the first savings account, the server entries do contain object UUIDs and so the returned binding handles contain a non-nil object UUID.

❸ This ensures that the returned binding handle is fully bound with an endpoint. If you call a remote procedure from an interface that is offered by multiple servers, and pass a partially bound handle without an endpoint, the RPC runtime library either returns an error or may return the endpoint for a different server than expected. Calling the *rpc_ep_resolve_binding* routine supplies the missing endpoint and avoids this problem.

When you try to resolve a partially bound binding, some aspect of the server recorded by the endpoint map must be unique—either the interface UUID, or one of the object UUIDs.

At this point in the program, we want to call an *rpc_mgmt_* routine. If we did so right now, the RPC runtime library wouldn't know which server to query, since all servers are automatically registered for the management interface. So the *rpc_mgmt_* call would fail with an error.

To resolve this ambiguity, we first call the *rpc_ep_resolve_binding* routine with the client's interface specification handle. Using the interface UUID from the handle, *rpc_ep_resolve_binding* can select the correct server from the endpoint map. When importing by interface, this works so long as only a single server on each host exports that client's interface. When multiple hosts export the interface, you need to provide *rpc_ep_resolve_binding* with an object UUID to further select among servers.

❹ To be certain that the selected server is available to receive remote procedure requests, the client calls the RPC runtime routine *rpc_mgmt_is_server_listening*.

❺ When importing by interface, it is a good practice to set the object UUID of binding handles returned from the *rpc_ns_binding_import_next* routine to be the nil object UUID. You can specify a NULL value to signify the nil UUID. Otherwise, you may see unexpected behavior.

For example, the server manager routine for creating a new account could have been implemented to verify that the binding handle contains a nil UUID, since a non-nil UUID means the client is trying to operate on an existing account. If the create account manager routine encountered a non-nil UUID, the operation would fail.

Additionally, if the server is using type UUIDs to form groups of object UUIDs, your remote procedure call request might not execute as you expected, since such a server may contain multiple manager routines for that procedure. Type UUIDs are an advanced topic beyond the scope of this book.

Finding a server based on resource

When importing by resource, the client must provide the object UUID for the resource of interest. In the banking application, the account number is the object UUID. The client specifies an object UUID argument in the *rpc_ns_binding_import_begin* routine. As the *rpc_ns_binding_import_next* routine examines the server entries in the import search path, the routine looks for a server entry with a matching object UUID, in addition to a compatible protocol sequence, interface, and so on. Example 7-17 shows how the banking client application obtains a binding handle for the banking server that manages a particular account.

Example 7-17: Locating a Server Based on Resource

```
void get_id_and_binding (binding_h)
rpc_binding_handle_t   *binding_h;
{
    uuid_t            account_id;
    unsigned_char_t   string_account_id[UUID_STRING_LEN];
    unsigned32        status;
```

Example 7-17: Locating a Server Based on Resource (continued)

```
          .
          .
          .
     printf ("\nEnter account ID: ");
     scanf ("%s", string_account_id);

     /*
      * Convert the string UUID to a binary UUID.
      */
     uuid_from_string (string_account_id, &account_id, &status);          ❶

     CHECK_DCE_STATUS (status, "uuid_from_string failed:", RESUME);
     ...
     import_resource ("banking", banking_v1_0_c_ifspec,
         &account_id, binding_h, &status);
          .
          .
          .
}

void import_resource (if_name, if_spec, account_id, binding_h, status)
unsigned_char_t      *if_name;
rpc_if_handle_t      if_spec;
uuid_t               *account_id;
rpc_binding_handle_t *binding_h;
unsigned32           *status;
{
     rpc_ns_handle_t    import_context;
     unsigned32         temp_status;

     /*
      * Import binding information from the namespace group entry_name.
      */
     rpc_ns_binding_import_begin (                                        ❷
         rpc_c_ns_syntax_default,    /* Syntax for server group name.  */
         server_group_name,          /* Namespace server group name.   */
         if_spec,                    /* Interface to import            */
         account_id,                 /* Importing for an object UUID.  */
         &import_context,            /* Import context.                */
         status
         );

     CHECK_DCE_STATUS (*status,
         "Can't import by resource\nrpc_ns_binding_import_begin failed:",
         ABORT);

     do
     {
         /*
          * Get a server binding handle.
          */
```

Example 7-17: Locating a Server Based on Resource (continued)

```
        rpc_ns_binding_import_next (import_context, binding_h, status); ❸

    if (*status == rpc_s_ok)
    {
        /*
         * Verify the server is available.
         */
        if (rpc_mgmt_is_server_listening (*binding_h, &temp_status)) ❹
        {
            break;
        }
        else
        {
            CHECK_DCE_STATUS (temp_status,
                "Server not listening \
                \nrpc_mgmt_is_server_listening failed:", RESUME);
                .
                .
                .
        }
    }
        .
        .
        .

} while (*status == rpc_s_ok);

return;
}
```

❶ After prompting the user for an account ID, the client calls the RPC routine *uuid_from_string* to convert the string representation of a UUID to
   its binary representation.

❷ This sets up the import context to search for servers. It begins the
   search at a namespace group entry that contains server entries as members. Since you provide an object UUID (*account_id*), the search
   returns binding handles only for those servers that exported the same
   UUID.

❸ This returns a single binding handle for a server. The binding handle
   contains the object UUID specified in *rpc_ns_binding_import_next*.

❹ This call ensures the selected server is available to receive remote procedure requests. Unlike importing by interface, as in Example 7-16,
   there is no need for the client to call *rpc_ep_resolve_binding*. In this
   case, if a partially bound binding handle was returned to the client, the
   runtime library finds the endpoint of a server based on the object UUID
   in the handle.

As we've seen, this version of the banking application requires clients to have an object UUID to locate an appropriate server. One way to make this version more friendly for users of the client application would be to implement the client so that it, too, maintained an object UUID/resource map database similar to the one maintained by each server. The client's database could map a customer name to their account object UUID. In this way, users of the client would enter their name instead of an object UUID.

However, this approach limits each client to accessing only accounts that were created using that particular client. That is to say, a customer that opened an account at one bank branch would be unable to transact business on that account at any other bank branch. Using the account ID, as we did in this version, allows all clients to access any account. The Better banking example, shown later in this chapter, provides a namespace usage model that allows clients to enter names rather than UUIDs, without the restriction of doing business only at one branch office.

Finding a server from strings of binding data

Alternately, your client can bypass the namespace and construct a binding handle using the string representation of binding information. If your client needs to access a particular resource, the string representation must contain an object UUID, in addition to a protocol sequence and server network address or host name.

One way to obtain a binding handle from the string representation of binding information is to construct a string of binding information by calling *rpc_string_binding_compose*.

This includes providing a string representation of an object UUID as a routine argument. You can then call the *rpc_binding_from_string_binding* routine to convert the string representation to a binding handle. Example 3-8 can be easily modified to do this. The necessary changes are shown below in Example 7-18.

Example 7-18: Binding Handle with an Object UUID from String

```
int do_string_binding (host, object, binding_h)
char     host[];
char     *object;  /* String representation of an object UUID */  ❶
rpc_binding_handle_t *binding_h;
{    .
        .
        .
  rpc_string_binding_compose (
    (unsigned_char_t *) object,     /* Object UUID for binding handle. */  ❷
    protseq_vector->protseq[i],
    (unsigned_char_t *) host,
    NULL,
    NULL,
```

Example 7-18: Binding Handle with an Object UUID from String (continued)

```
    &string_binding,
    &status
 )
      .
      .
      .
}
```

❶ The string representation of an object UUID is passed to the routine.

❷ The string representation of the object UUID is passed to the *rpc_string_binding_compose* routine.

When you associate an object UUID with a binding handle, the string representation of the binding information also contains the object UUID. For example, the string representation of a fully bound binding handle with a non-nil object UUID returned from calling the *rpc_binding_to_string_binding* routine is:

```
    A4672167-F555-11CA-BAE1-08002B245A28@ncacn_ip_tcp:128.10.2.30[1025]
```

The @ character separates the string UUID from the protocol sequence.

On the other hand, when your application converts a binding handle to its string representation, the returned string contains a UUID only if it is non-nil. If an object UUID is not associated with a binding handle, the binary UUID returned by calling the *rpc_binding_inq_object* routine is the nil UUID.

Shortcomings

Although a logical extension to the namespace usage described in Chapter 6, this model of exporting multiple object UUIDs to each server's server entry has the following drawbacks:

- Resources are identified only by object UUID. Consequently, the user of a client application must know in advance the object UUID of the resource. For the banking application, it may seem reasonable for you to know your account number, but for many applications that would be a burden.

- The binding handle returned from *rpc_ns_binding_import_next* may contain the object UUID for some resource, even though a client may want to import by interface only.

- Exporting object UUIDs of resources to each server entry prevents you from uniquely identifying individual servers on a single host. For some applications, multiple copies of the server will run on a single host.

When this happens, you may need to uniquely distinguish each of the servers for management purposes. This distinction can be made only if each server copy manages a unique set of resources, or each server copy stores, in its server entry, a single object UUID to identify that server copy. This means the object UUIDs of the server-managed resources must be stored elsewhere. Although the details of distinguishing between copies of a server on a single host is an advanced topic not covered in this book, the namespace usage described in the next section enables you to add that capability when necessary.

The next section provides a more complete namespace usage model that overcomes these shortcomings.

A Better Usage Model for Exporting by Resource

The previous section introduced object UUIDs with a relatively simple application. This section provides a more sophisticated solution for using object UUIDs to identify and locate a server that manages a resource. The namespace usage described in this section addresses the shortcomings identified when exporting and importing by resource name only, as well as those identified in the previous model of exporting resources' object UUIDs to server entries.

This section's model of namespace usage has the following advantages:

- It allows clients to import by resource name.

- It automatically communicates the resource's object UUID from client to server.

- It requires only one copy of each server's binding information to be stored in the namespace.

- It supports a single resource managed by multiple servers without server binding information collisions in the namespace.

- When importing by interface, the returned binding handle does not contain the object UUID of some resource.

- Through a single group entry, the application can browse a list of all resources.

- In the future, you can store an object UUID in each server entry to uniquely identify each copy of the server.

For this model, each server continues to export its address information to a server entry, and continues to add itself as a member of an interface-based group for those clients interested in importing by interface (for example, to create a new resource). However, instead of storing the object UUIDs of resources in the server entry, this model uses an RPC group entry as a resource entry and assigns an object UUID to that resource. The use of a group entry as a resource entry allows users of client applications to specify resource names rather than object UUIDs for locating servers of a resource. Figure 7-9 contains the resulting namespace entries.

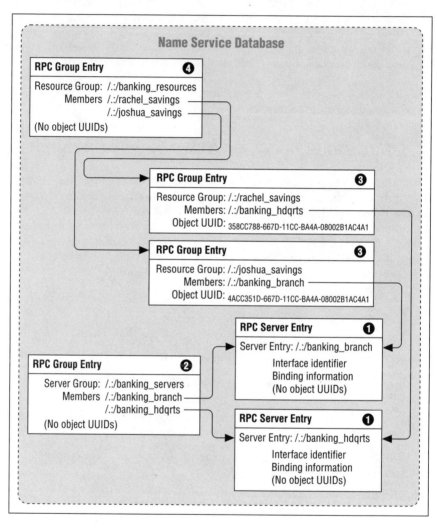

Figure 7-9: Banking example using group entries as resource entries

Each callout describes a different type of entry.

❶ Server entries

Each server exports its binding information to a server entry whose name is based on the server's interface name and host name, as described in Chapter 6. Object UUIDs of managed resources are not exported to server entries.

❷ Server group

Each server adds itself as a member of the group that contains all the servers of an interface. Clients that need to import by interface start their import search at this entry, as described in Chapter 6.

❸ Resource entry

For each resource managed by a server, the server creates a group entry whose name is resource-based. The server adds itself as a member of that group and exports the resource's object UUID to the entry. Clients that need to import by resource start their import search at the appropriate resource entry.

❹ Resource group

Servers add each resource entry to a group that contains all resources. Clients or servers can thus browse the list of all resources managed by all servers of a given interface.

End users of this application can now provide their name to the banking client command which constructs the resource entry name for their savings account and then imports from that group.

Initializing the Server

The initialization of the banking server is almost the same as in the OK Usage Model. The differences are that for each managed resource, the server:

- Creates a resource entry.
- Exports the resource's object UUID to that entry.
- Adds itself as a group member to the resource entry.
- Adds the resource entry as a member of the resource group.

This replaces the technique of storing all object UUIDs in the server entry.

In this section only the code that differs from the OK Usage Model is shown in the examples. This code also appears in Appendix F.

Advertising the server's resources

The server creates a name service entry for each managed savings account. This is a group entry, so it can contain pointers to multiple servers if necessary. The server names the resource entry based on the account owner's name. The server stores the resource's object UUID in the entry and finally adds itself as a member of the group.

Example 7-19 shows the portion of the banking server initialization code that differs from the OK example for exporting existing accounts to resource entries.

Example 7-19: Exporting Resources to the Namespace

```
unsigned_char_t   resource_group_name[STRINGLEN];
        .
        .
        .
uuid_vector_t     resource_uuid;        /* Object UUID list  */
unsigned_char_t   resource_entry_name[STRINGLEN];
unsigned_char_t   annotation[STRINGLEN];
char              resource_name[STRINGLEN];
unsigned32        status;
int               i;
        .
        .
        .
/*
 * Create resource group name.
 * Using:   <interface-name>_resources
 */
strcpy ((char *) resource_group_name, "/.:/banking_resources");
        .
        .
        .
/*
 * For each resource in the object UUID/resource map...
 */
for (i = 0; i < res_map_list->count; ++i)
{
    /*
     * Place the object UUID for the current resource into a
     * UUID list that is one element long.
     */
    resource_uuid.count = 1;
    resource_uuid.uuid[0] = &res_map_list->map_element[i].resource_id; ❶

    /*
     * Remove ".dat" from the resource filename.
     */
    strcpy (resource_name, res_map_list->map_element[i].resource_file);
    *(strchr(resource_name, '.')) = '\0';

    /*
     * Create resource entry name.
     * Using:   <account-name>_savings
     */
```

Example 7-19: Exporting Resources to the Namespace (continued)

```
        sprintf ((char *) resource_entry_name, "/.:/%s_savings",         ❷
            resource_name);

        /*
         * Export the resource's object UUID to namespace resource entry.
         */
        rpc_ns_binding_export (                                            ❸
            rpc_c_ns_syntax_default,   /* Syntax of resource entry name  */
            resource_entry_name,       /* Namespace resource entry name. */
            NULL,                      /* Not exporting interface info.  */
            NULL,                      /* Not exporting binding info.    */
            &resource_uuid,            /* Exporting only an object UUID. */
            &status
            );

        CHECK_DCE_STATUS (status,
            "Can't export resource.\nrpc_ns_binding_export failed:", ABORT);

        /*
         * Add the server entry as a member of the resource entry
         * (which is a group).
         */
        rpc_ns_group_mbr_add (                                             ❹
            rpc_c_ns_syntax_default, /* Syntax of resource entry name  */
            resource_entry_name,     /* Namespace resource entry name  */
            rpc_c_ns_syntax_default, /* Syntax of server entry name     */
            server_entry_name,       /* Namespace server entry name     */
            &status
            );

        CHECK_DCE_STATUS (status,
            "Can't add server to resource entry. \
            \nrpc_ns_group_mbr_add failed:", ABORT);

        /*
         * Add the resource entry as a member of the resource group.
         */
        rpc_ns_group_mbr_add (                                             ❺
            rpc_c_ns_syntax_default,   /* Syntax of resource group name */
            resource_group_name,       /* Namespace resource group name */
            rpc_c_ns_syntax_default,   /* Syntax of resource entry name */
            resource_entry_name,       /* Namespace resource entry name */
            &status
            );

        CHECK_DCE_STATUS (status,
            "Can't add resource entry to resource group. \
            \nrpc_ns_group_mbr_add failed:", ABORT);
}
```

❶ Only a single object UUID is stored in each namespace resource entry.
    Consequently, the server does not need to dynamically allocate a UUID
    vector for exporting object UUIDs.

❷ Each banking server names the resource entry for each savings account based on the owner's name. For example, `/.:/zoe_savings` and `/.:/rachel_savings` are the resource entries for Zoe's and Rachel's savings accounts. A more rigorous application would need to use a more sophisticated naming convention to ensure unique resource entry names for all customers.

❸ This creates the resource entry and stores the object UUID for the account in the entry. Since the server does not store binding information in the resource entry, a NULL value is specified for both the interface specification and the binding vector.

❹ This adds the server's server entry as a group member to the resource entry. If only a single server manages the resource, the resource entry has only a single group member. However, in an industrial-strength banking application it is likely that multiple servers manage each account. In that case, the resource entry contains multiple group members, one for each server managing the account. Regardless of the number of servers that manage an account, each resource entry still has one object UUID shared by the servers.

❺ This adds the resource entry to the resource group `/.:/banking_resources`. The resource group has as its members all the resource entries for all of the accounts managed by all copies of the banking server. Clients use this group to browse the list of resources available through this application.

Server Manager Code

Creating a new resource

The code to create a new resource is identical to that in the OK example except for the way in which the server advertises the resource in the namespace.

The *create_account* manager routine for this example exports the newly created resource to a namespace resource entry and resource group exactly as was done in the server initialization for existing accounts (see Example 7-19).

Deleting an existing resource

Again, deleting is just like the OK example except for the way in which the server removes the resource from the namespace.

Example 7-20 shows the portion of the *delete_account* manager routine for unexporting a resource that differs from the OK example.

Example 7-20: Deleting and Removing a Resource

```
/*
 * See if we can find this resource.
 */
resource_to_filename (res_map_list, &resource_id, &filename, ❶
    bank_status);

/*
 * If we found the account...
 */
if (*bank_status == bank_s_ok)
{

                      .
                      .
                      .

    /*
     * Remove ".dat" from the resource filename.
     */
    strcpy (resource_name, filename);
    *(strchr(resource_name, '.')) = '\0';

    /*
     * Create resource entry name.
     * Using:  <account-name>_savings
     */
    sprintf ((char *) resource_entry_name, "/.:/%s_savings",
        resource_name);

    /*
     * Remove the resource entry from the namespace.
     */
    rpc_ns_mgmt_entry_delete (                               ❷
        rpc_c_ns_syntax_default, /* Default entry name syntax.  */
        resource_entry_name,     /* Namespace entry name.       */
        dce_status
        );

    CHECK_DCE_STATUS (*dce_status,
        "rpc_ns_mgmt_entry_delete failed: ", ABORT);

    /*
     * Remove the resource entry from the resource group.
     */
    rpc_ns_group_mbr_remove (                                ❸
        rpc_c_ns_syntax_default, /* Syntax for resource group name. */
        resource_group_name,     /* Namespace resource group name.  */
        rpc_c_ns_syntax_default, /* Synatx for resource entry name. */
        resource_entry_name,     /* Namespace resource entry name.  */
        dce_status
        );
```

Example 7-20: Deleting and Removing a Resource (continued)

```
CHECK_DCE_STATUS (*dce_status,
    "Can't remove resource entry from resource group. \
    \nrpc_ns_group_mbr_remove failed:", ABORT);
              .
              .
              .
```

❶ After the server obtained an object UUID from the binding handle, this routine returns the filename associated with that object UUID from the object UUID/resource map.

❷ The RPC runtime routine *rpc_ns_mgmt_entry_delete* deletes an entry and its contents from the name service. Using this routine here assumes that only one banking server manages each saving account, and so this server's server entry is the only member in the resource entry.

If the application supported multiply accessed resources—that is multiple servers that provide access to each account—then, at this point, instead of deleting the resource entry, the server would do the following:

- Call *rpc_ns_group_mbr_remove* to remove the server entry from the resource entry.

- Call the routines beginning with *rpc_ns_group_mbr_inq_* to see if the resource entry contains any other servers as members.

If the resource entry has no more members, it means the resource is no longer offered by any server. In this case, the server cleans up the namespace by calling *rpc_ns_mgmt_entry_delete* to remove the resource entry from the namespace. Otherwise, if the resource entry has at least one more member, it means the resource is still offered by another server. In this case, the server does not delete the resource entry.

❸ This removes the resource entry as a member of the resource group. Since the resource is no longer available, clients that browse the resource group should not see this resource entry.

If the application supported resources accessible from multiple servers, the server would remove the resource entry from the resource group only if the resource is no longer offered by any servers, and it had deleted the resource entry from the namespace.

Server Termination

The banking server *mgmt_auth_fn* function is identical to that in the OK example except for the way in which the server removes its resources from the namespace.

The *mgmt_auth_fn* function for this example removes resource entries from the namespace exactly as was done in the *delete_account* manager routine (see Example 7-20).

Client Initialization

As in the OK model, clients in this usage model are able to import by interface or by resource.

The banking client code differs from the client in the OK Usage Model in the following ways:

- To access an existing account, users enter their account name rather than the account ID.

- The client imports beginning at a resource entry rather than at the server group.

In this section, the examples show only the code that differs from the OK Usage Model.

Finding a server based on interface

When importing by interface, the client specifies the server group as the starting entry name. This corresponds to callout 2 in Figure 7-9. The client, not interested in any particular resource, provides a NULL value for the object UUID argument in the *rpc_ns_binding_import_begin* routine. This is the same as in the OK model.

In this usage model, neither the server group nor the individual server entries contain object UUIDs. Therefore, the binding handles returned from the *rpc_ns_binding_import_next* routine contain the nil object UUID. This means that unlike the *import_interface* routine in the OK model (see Example 7-16), when your client imports by interface, it does not need to set the object UUID to the nil object UUID.

Finding a server based on resource

When importing by resource, you provide the client with the name of the resource of interest; you no longer need to know the resource's object UUID. In this banking example, that means you provide your name rather than an account ID, as in the OK model. Example 7-21 shows the client code for importing based on account name.

Example 7-21: Locating a Server Based on Resource

```
void import_resource (if_spec, account_name, binding_h, status)
rpc_if_handle_t      if_spec;
unsigned_char_t      *account_name;
rpc_binding_handle_t *binding_h;
unsigned32           *status;
{
    rpc_ns_handle_t   import_context;
    rpc_ns_handle_t   obj_inq_context;
    unsigned_char_t   resource_entry_name[STRINGLEN];
    uuid_t            account_id;
    unsigned32        temp_status;

    /*
     * Create resource entry name for import.
     * Using:  <account-name>_savings
     */
    sprintf ((char *) resource_entry_name, "/.:/%s_savings",        ❶
        account_name);

    /*
     * Import binding information from the namespace resource entry.
     */
    rpc_ns_binding_import_begin (                                   ❷
        rpc_c_ns_syntax_default,    /* Syntax for resource entry name.  */
        resource_entry_name,        /* Namespace resource entry name.   */
        if_spec,                    /* Interface to import              */
        NULL,                       /* Importing without object UUID.   */
        &import_context,            /* Import context.                  */
        status
        );

    CHECK_DCE_STATUS (*status,
        "Can't import by resource\nrpc_ns_binding_import_begin failed:",
        ABORT);

    do
    {
        /*
         * Get a server binding handle.
         */
        rpc_ns_binding_import_next (import_context, binding_h, status); ❸

        if (*status == rpc_s_ok)
        {
          /*
           * Get the current resource's object UUID from the resource
           * entry (a group) and place it into the current
           * binding handle.
           */
          rpc_ns_entry_object_inq_begin (                          ❹
              rpc_c_ns_syntax_default, /* Syntax for resource entry name */
              resource_entry_name,     /* Namespace resource entry name. */
              &obj_inq_context,        /* Inquiry context handle.        */
```

Example 7-21: Locating a Server Based on Resource (continued)

```
        status
        );

    CHECK_DCE_STATUS (*status,
        "rpc_ns_entry_object_inq_begin failed:", ABORT);

    /*
     * Get the object UUID.
     */
    rpc_ns_entry_object_inq_next (obj_inq_context, &account_id, ❺
        status);

    CHECK_DCE_STATUS (*status,
        "rpc_ns_entry_object_inq_next failed:", ABORT);

    /*
     * End the search.
     */
    rpc_ns_entry_object_inq_done (&obj_inq_context, status);      ❻

    CHECK_DCE_STATUS (*status,
        "rpc_ns_entry_object_inq_done failed:", ABORT);

    /*
     * Place the UUID into the binding handle.
     */
    rpc_binding_set_object (*binding_h, &account_id, status);     ❼

    CHECK_DCE_STATUS (*status,
        "rpc_binding_set_object failed:", ABORT);

    /*
     * Verify the server is available.
     */
    if (rpc_mgmt_is_server_listening (*binding_h, &temp_status)) ❽
    {
        break;
    }
    else
    {
        CHECK_DCE_STATUS (temp_status,
            "Server not listening \
            \nrpc_mgmt_is_server_listening failed:", RESUME);
    }
}
else
{
  if (*status != rpc_s_no_more_bindings)
  {
      CHECK_DCE_STATUS (*status,
          "Can't import by resource \
          \nrpc_ns_binding_import_next failed:", RESUME);
  }
}
```

Example 7-21: Locating a Server Based on Resource (continued)

```
} while (*status == rpc_s_ok);

return;
}
```

❶ Using the account name entered by the user, the client constructs a resource entry name using the same naming convention as used by the banking server.

❷ When importing by resource, you provide the client with the name of the resource of interest; you no longer need to know the resource's object UUID. The client application code calls *rpc_ns_binding_import_begin* with the resource entry as the starting point, and with a NULL value for the object UUID. This sets up the import context to search for servers beginning with a group entry for the resources. The group entry contains server entries as members.

In Figure 7-9, the entries labeled 3 would be the possible starting entries for importing by resource.

❸ This returns a single binding handle for a server. The *rpc_ns_binding_import_next* routine examines object UUIDs only in server entries. Since the resource entry is a group entry, the import operation ignores the object UUID stored there. Furthermore, because the server entry members of the resource group themselves do not contain object UUIDs, the *rpc_ns_binding_import_next* routine always returns binding handles containing the nil object UUID.

Since the resource entry is a group whose members are server entries, the *rpc_ns_binding_import_next* routine searches the server entry for compatible binding information. In this banking application, each resource entry contains a single server entry name. However, if multiple servers provided access to a resource, each server would have added itself as a member of the resource entry. In this case, an importing client would obtain a binding handle for any of those servers.

❹ To obtain the object UUID for the selected account, the client calls the RPC runtime routines that begin with *rpc_ns_entry_object_inq_*. These routines return the object UUIDs stored in an RPC entry.

In particular, the *rpc_ns_entry_object_inq_begin* routine establishes a context for returning the object UUIDs from a resource entry.

❺ The *rpc_ns_entry_object_inq_next* routine returns a single object UUID, in binary form, from the resource entry. The client supplies a uuid_t variable to receive the UUID.

In the banking example, each resource entry contains a single object UUID, so the client calls this routine only once per import.

❻ The client calls the *rpc_ns_entry_object_inq_done* routine to free the context set up by *rpc_ns_entry_object_inq_begin*.

❼ Before using the binding handle returned from import for making remote procedure calls, the client sets the object UUID for this account into the handle using the RPC runtime routine *rpc_binding_set_object*.

In this way, the RPC runtime library automatically sends the object UUID for the resource to the server manager routine as part of the binding handle.

❽ This call ensures that the selected server is available to receive remote procedure requests. This is the same as in Example 7-17 of the OK example.

In this usage model, all servers add each resource entry to a resource group. Using the runtime routines that begin with *rpc_ns_group_mbr_inq_*, clients or servers can query for the members of a resource group to obtain the list of resources managed by servers of an interface. For example, callout 4 in Figure 7-9 contains the list of all savings accounts managed by all banking servers. Instead of prompting for an account name, the client application might have displayed the resource list as a menu of available resources.

Summary

Most applications can benefit from object UUIDs. You will find occasions to import a binding handle based either on the interface alone or on the interface plus a resource. The bank application shows how it's useful to have two indices into the namespace for your application: one giving access to all servers, and the other giving access to all resources.

The essential strategy we recommend is to:

1. Make each resource name a group entry.

2. Place server entries in that group entry, so they can be found through the resource name.

3. Create a group entry for servers, and another group entry for resources.

These steps, while they create a fairly complicated namespace, give you a great deal of flexibility to browse and organize your resources.

8

Using Authenticated RPC

A key issue omitted from the applications in the previous chapters is security.

In our experience, customers do not deploy RPC applications without adequate security. Production RPC applications need to ensure that the client and server identities are **authenticated** and that the right access controls exist to protect the data. These capabilities are provided in DCE by **authenticated RPC** and DCE Security Services.

This chapter will describe the use of authenticated RPC from a client application. We will motivate the discussion with a sample application, describe how this problem is modeled in DCE, and then illustrate the client code. The steps for writing a simple server that uses security will be described in Chapter 9.

RPC applications, because they operate in a more distributed and open environment, do not have the same inherent level of security as local applications. In the local case, applications can assume a relatively high level of security by default. The operating system knows the identities of all the user processes because users have to log in. The local file system controls access based upon file permission bits and the user/group IDs. File permissions also ensure the integrity of standard system commands like *ls*. When a user types *ls* to view the contents of a directory, for example, he or she does not usually need to worry about malicious intrusion. But to have a secure distributed application, you must consciously designed in security.

The Grade Server Application

Assume that we want to build a distributed online database of student grades using DCE RPC. Such an application would probably consist of multiple remote interfaces for updating, querying, and managing the database. In this book, we show just an interface for querying a student's grade point average (GPA). The interface definition is shown in Example 8-1.

Example 8-1: IDL File for Grade Server Application

```
/*
**    gpa.idl
*/
[uuid(f657c75c-277f-11cc-88c5-08002b1d3118),
    version(1.0)]
interface gpa
{
        typedef float           gpa_t;

        /*                                        .
         * Return the current GPA of the student whose name
         * is student_name.  If student_name is NULL, then
         * return the caller's GPA.
         */
        [idempotent]
        void get_GPA(
              [in]  handle_t            handle,
              [in, string] char  *student_name,
              [out] gpa_t         *gpa
           );
}
```

The implementation of this interface immediately raises a number of security issues. Consider the following scenarios:

* Joe Hacker, a Computer Science student, decides to make sure that he will graduate with top honors. He implements a new server, "Joe's Grade Server," which exports the same interface as the real Grade Server. Joe's Grade Server has a very desirable characteristic: it always returns 4.0 when asked for Joe Hacker's GPA.

* Slime Data, Inc., an information broker, makes available to all credit reporting agencies the grade point averages of any current or former student.

* Wiretap, Inc., a maker of value-added hardware equipment, sells a network analyzer that can read all the RPC packets on the network and decode their contents. Their next model will also be able to modify packets in real time.

If we were to implement an update interface, the following scenario would be possible:

- College Prep, Inc., guarantees that your GPA will be 4.0 within a month of enrolling in their program. They have never had a dissatisfied customer. When pressed for details, their salesperson refers to their customized interface to the Grade Server database.

As the examples show, real-world RPC applications need to address security issues. Clients need to verify the identity of the server so that they can trust the results; servers need to restrict the types of operations that are allowed, based upon the clients' identities; and there may be privacy and integrity issues associated with transmitting data over shared network media. Authenticated RPC and DCE Security provide a set of services that allows distributed applications to operate with the same level of security that users have come to expect from local applications.

The DCE Security Model

Figure 8-1 shows how to describe the Grade Server application in DCE terms and how DCE solves the problems described.

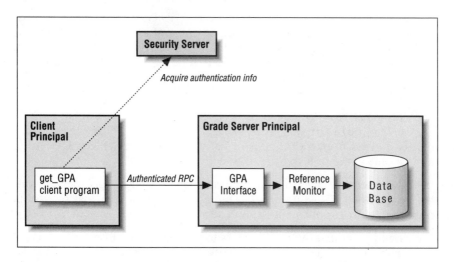

Figure 8-1: DCE security model for the grade server application

The application consists of the Grade Server that exports the gpa interface, and a client program, *get_GPA*, that calls a function named *get_GPA*. The Grade Server process and the user that runs the *get_GPA* client are **principals**. All principals trust the **Security Server** of the cell. The *get_GPA* client program and the Grade Server communicate using authenticated RPC. When such a remote procedure call is made, the Security Server is contacted to certify the identity of the client. The client identity is passed to the Grade Server, which can then make **authorization** decisions using the client identity.

An authorization decision simply determines whether a certain client has the right to request an operation. This authorization decision is made by a piece of code in the server manager called a **reference monitor**. If the reference monitor allows the access, then the operation proceeds. Otherwise, the operation is not carried out.

We will now describe this model in greater detail.

Principals

A DCE principal is an entity that is capable of bearing an identity and verifying another principal's identity. Authentication is the act of proving that an entity is what it claims to be. Principals, therefore, are the entities that you authenticate.

Users are principals. Less obviously, servers are also principals; servers need to know the identities of their clients to make the right access control decisions, and servers need to be principals so that clients can authenticate server identities. The Grade Server process is, therefore, a principal.

Client programs are usually not principals. This is because the client program is typically just an agent and not the entity of interest. For example, it does not help the Grade Server to know that it is being queried by the *get_GPA* client, unless it knows who is running *get_GPA*. In short, the Grade Server principal needs to know the identity of the principal (the user) rather than the agent (the client program).

Each principal has a **principal name** in the standard DCE format, such as `/ . . . /my_cell/grade_server`. Each principal also has a **secret key** that is derived from the principal's password. The secret key is a string known only to the principal and the Security Server.

Just like users on a local system, principals must **login** to the network before accessing DCE resources. During the login, a principal proves its own identity by supplying the proper secret key

We should point that the DCE login is logically separate from the local system login. DCE login gives you access to network-wide resources, while the local system login gives you access to only local resources. In practice, we expect that most vendors will integrate DCE login into the local system login. This allows a user, with a single login, to set up the security state needed to access both local as well as DCE-wide resources.

Secret Key Authentication

Authentication allows clients and servers to securely determine each other's identities. DCE Security uses a secret-key-based protocol to perform authentication. The authentication protocol used in DCE is based upon the Kerberos Version 5 authentication system developed by Project Athena at the Massachusetts Institute of Technology.

The security of secret-key-based authentication protocols relies upon encryption. Encryption is the process of transforming a plaintext message into another message that is unintelligible. Decryption is the process of taking an encrypted message and recovering the original plaintext message. The encryption and decryption algorithms use keys to compute their output

In DCE, each principal has a secret key that is known only by itself and the Security Server. The Security Server uses its knowledge of the secret key in two ways. First, the Security Server uses the secret key to directly authenticate a principal in the cell during login. The Security Server does this by encrypting some data using the principal's secret key and verifying that the principal was able to decrypt it, hence demonstrating that the principal knows the secret key.

The Security Server also uses the secret key to produce messages that the recipient can trust came from the Security Server. The Security Server does this by encrypting a message with the intended recipient's secret key. Since only the recipient and the Security Server know the recipient's secret key, successful decryption proves that the message originated from the Security Server.

It is not necessary for an application developer to understand the internals of the authentication protocol in order to use authenticated RPC. However, we will briefly describe how it works so that the reader can understand why it is secure. Readers who are not interested in this information can skip to the next section.

Kerberos authentication protocol

The Kerberos authentication protocol involves three parties—the client, the server, and the **key distribution center** (KDC). In DCE, the KDC is a component of the Security Server. The Kerberos authentication protocol defines a series of messages that allows a client to acquire a **ticket**. The ticket identifies the client and is destined for a specific server principal. Tickets are generated by the KDC and have expiration times, so they need to be reissued periodically

Obtaining a ticket

Figure 8-2 shows the flow of messages that are required to establish an authenticated conversation between a client and a server.

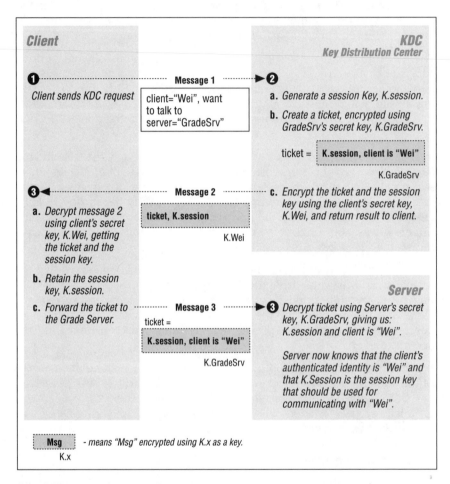

Figure 8-2: Kerberos authentication exchange

❶ A client begins by sending a message to the KDC to request a new ticket. This is message 1 in Figure 8-2. The request specifies the identity of the client, as well as that of the server that the client wishes to contact.

The KDC creates a ticket by generating a random **session key**, adding the identity of the client as well as some other information, and encrypting all of it using the server's secret key. The session key is a secret key whose only purpose is to authenticate this conversation. It is not used beyond that conversation. In DCE, a conversation corresponds to an

RPC connection between a client and a server. Since the ticket is encrypted using the server's secret key, only the target server will be able to decode the ticket and make use of the session key within the ticket.

❷ The KDC then encrypts the ticket and another copy of the session key using the client's secret key, and sends the result to the client. This corresponds to message 2 in Figure 8-2. The KDC includes another copy of the session key because the client cannot access the copy in the ticket; only the server (or someone who is in possession of the server's secret key) can decrypt and make sense of the information within the ticket.

❸ When the client receives the KDC's reply, it decrypts the message using the client's secret key. This yields the ticket (which contains the session key encrypted with the server's secret key), as well a copy of the session key that the client can use. Since the KDC's reply is encrypted with the client's secret key, only the client can recover the session key and the ticket from the message. Note that at this point, even the client cannot take apart the ticket itself. This is because the ticket is encrypted using the server's secret key.

The client retains the session key for later use and forwards the ticket (which is still encrypted with the server's secret key) to the server as is. The ticket is message 3 in Figure 8-2.

When the server gets the ticket, it decrypts it using its own secret key. Because the ticket was originally encrypted with the server's key, the server can decode the contents. The server, therefore, gets the identity of the client and the session key. This identity is certified by the KDC. The server knows that the ticket is authentic because only the KDC (besides the server itself) knows the server's secret key. This is how the server authenticates the client.

If the client requested mutual authentication (that is, the client wants to know the authenticated identity of the server also), the server would send back a message encrypted with the session key. Since the session key that was sent to the server was in the ticket that was encrypted using the server's secret key, the fact that the server possesses the right session key is proof that the server is the intended principal.

The authentication exchange described above forms the basis of the authentication protocol used by Kerberos and DCE Security. The actual protocol uses a **ticket granting ticket** (TGT), instead of the client's secret key. The client would obtain a TGT from the Ticket-Granting Server prior to acquiring tickets for any application servers. The Ticket-Granting Server is also a component of the DCE Security Server. The TGT is used instead of the secret key so that the secret keys themselves are not exposed unnecessarily. The initial acquisition of the TGT still involves the use of the client's secret key. But once this is done, subsequent tickets are obtained using the TGT.

Note that after the authentication exchange has been concluded, the client and the server share a common secret key (the session key). This session key is used for several purposes. First, it can be used to individually authenticate the RPC packets that are sent between the client and the server. This is done by computing a checksum, using this session key for each packet. Since only the client, server, and the KDC knows this key, the checksum is proof that the packets are authentic. The session key can also be used to provide higher levels of protection like user data encryption. All these services can be selected by the client using the *rpc_binding_set_auth_info* call that we will describe later.

The DCE Security Server uses Kerberos tickets to implement **credentials**. A credential is a set of attributes of the principal (for instance, its identity) that has been certified by some trusted authority (the Security Server in this case). DCE has defined a specific type of credential called the **Privilege Attribute Certificate** (PAC). A PAC captures identity information as well as group membership information (e.g., is the user an administrator? an operator? etc.) PACs are embedded in the tickets issued by the Security Server are designed so that the client can securely forward it to the server for use in authorization.

Authorization

Authentication allows one to determine a principal's real identity. Authentication lets a server know, for example, that the client is Joe Hacker. But authentication by itself is inadequate as a security mechanism. The missing piece is authorization.

Authorization is the use of the authenticated identity to make access-control decisions—determining, for example, whether Joe Hacker is allowed to update a student's grade. A secure authorization mechanism depends upon a secure authentication mechanism, since access controls cannot be properly applied unless you know the true identity of the principal that is attempting to access the data.

The code that implements an authorization policy is usually separated out into its own module called a **reference monitor**. The reference monitor checks each reference to see if it is allowed by the authorization policy. The authorization code is isolated in its own module so that programmers can easily examine its correctness.

A reference monitor should be implemented at the resource that is being accessed. For the RPC applications that we have been describing, the reference monitor should be implemented by the server manager routine—since that's where the resources are actually being accessed. Clients typically do not implement reference monitors. Clients are responsible only for supplying a PAC or other authorization information so that the reference monitor at the server can make the right authorization decisions.

Authenticated RPC

An application that wishes to use authentication and authorization can directly call the appropriate security services to obtain the necessary credentials. For example, this is how applications use other authentication services like raw Kerberos, which does not have the DCE enhancements. DCE simplifies this by providing an **authenticated RPC** facility. If authentication is requested, DCE RPC will automatically contact the Security Server to obtain a PAC or authenticated identity for the client. Whether an RPC will be authenticated is determined by the client. Whether the call actually gets processed is up to the server. In other words, the server decides what level of security to demand, and the client attempts to match this level. DCE RPC also allows a client to select an authorization service and determine how the messages are to be protected over the wire.

Authenticated RPC forwards the client's credentials to the server. Hence the server can trust the client's identity. It turns out that the protocol also authenticates the server to the client. This is because the Security Server seals the client's credentials with the server's secret key before giving it to the client. Thus, only the real server will be able to decode it. Therefore, if the server generates a response to the client, it must be the correct server principal.

Writing the get_GPA Client

To make an authenticated RPC, the only operation that a client needs to do is request authentication prior to calling the remote procedure. Since the authentication information is done on a client-server pair basis, DCE stores the authentication state as part of the RPC binding. Recall that a binding is a relationship between a client and a server. A client would, therefore, request authentication by annotating a specific binding. Doing so will cause authentication to be performed when an RPC is made over the indicated binding.

The following code fragment shows how the binding handle is annotated for authenticated RPC in the get_GPA client application.

Example 8-2: Structure of Client Code

```
rpc_binding_handle_t    binding_handle;
unsigned32              status;
rpc_ns_handle_t         import_context;
unsigned_char_t         *student_name;
gpa_t                   gpa;
```

Example 8-2: Structure of Client Code (continued)

```
...

/* Get server bindings from the Cell Directory Service. */
rpc_ns_import_begin (binding_h, ....                                    ❶
rpc_ns_import_next (binding_h,....
rpc_ns_import_done (binding_h,...

/* Annotate the binding handle for authentication. */
rpc_binding_set_auth_info (                                             ❷
      binding_h,
      "/.:/grade_server",       /* server princ. name */
      rpc_c_protect_level_default,   /* protection level */
      rpc_c_authn_dce_default, /* authentication service */
      NULL,                      /* default login context */
      rpc_c_authz_dce,           /* authorization service */
      &status);

/* Make the remote procedure call. */
get_GPA (binding_h, student_name, &gpa);                                ❸

rpc_binding_free (binding_h...                                          ❹
```

❶ The client would obtain a server binding as usual. This can be done either by importing it from the name service (as done here), or by using a string binding.

❷ The client then annotates the binding handle for authenticated RPC. The call to *rpc_binding_set_auth_info* specifies:

- A binding handle

  Since an explicit binding handle must be supplied to this call, authentication can only be used in conjunction with explicit or implicit binding methods.

- The server principal name

  In this case, we directly specify the name of the Grade Server. Later we'll discuss what to do if the client does not know the server's principal name.

- The desired protection level

  DCE RPC can protect the data that is sent over the network to prevent unauthorized modification or reading. Various protection levels are available, ranging from none to total encryption of all user data. For this call, we are requesting the default protection level; this causes a checksum to be computed for each packet so that RPC can detect any unauthorized modifications.

- The **authentication service**

  DCE RPC is designed to support multiple authentication services. Thus, this argument is provided to allow the application program to select one. At present, the only supported authentication services are **none** and **DCE private key** authentication; DCE private key is the default.

- The **login context** for this principal

  The security credentials associated with the current process are stored in the login context. We use NULL to specify the default login context. This causes RPC to use the login context of the process that is running the client application. Recall that this is the desired behavior since the real principal is the process that is running the client program as opposed to the client program itself

  An explicit login context is needed only when a client is its own principal or needs to act as multiple identities. Commonly, a client would use an explicit login context in which you have a client that is also a server.

- The **authorization service**

  Here we specify the default, DCE PAC-based authorization. This causes RPC to request a PAC from the Security Server when the remote procedure call is initiated, and then pass the PAC in the call. The other option is name-based authorization in which just the client's authenticated principal name is passed. The server must then make its access control decisions based upon the name only. This is highly restrictive and does not take advantage of the full capabilities of DCE. Therefore, to give the server maximum flexibility in implementing its reference monitor, PAC-based authorization should be used.

❸ Call the remote procedure. The call will be authenticated, a PAC will be passed for authorization, and the integrity of the messages that go over the network will be protected.

  Should the client need to make an unauthenticated call later, it can annotate the binding handle again via the *rpc_binding_set_auth_info* call, or by using another binding handle.

❹ Free the binding handle

The above steps are the only ones that a client needs to take to use authenticated RPC when it knows the identity of the server.

Selecting a Protection Level

In the example just presented, the client selected the default protection level in the call to *rpc_binding_set_auth_info*. This is a good choice for most applications. To flexibly tailor the amount of protection to match the needs of the application, DCE allows an application to select the exact protection level to use in the call.

There are six distinct protection levels:

- **none**

  Communication is unauthenticated.

- **connect**

  Client and server will mutually authenticate when the RPC connection is established. Subsequent calls over the same connection will not be individually authenticated.

- **call**

  Client and server will mutually authenticate on every call. In addition, RPC will compute a checksum on the protocol header of the first packet of each call to ensure that the header has not been modified by a third party. When running over a connection-oriented transport like TCP, this level is automatically upgraded to the next level, **packet**.

- **packet**

  Client and server will mutually authenticate on every call. In addition, a checksum is computed on each packet header to ensure that the headers have not been modified in transit. The user data is not protected.

- **integrity**

  Client and server will mutually authenticate on every call. In addition, a checksum is computed over each RPC packet; this includes the user data. This level will detect any tampering of either the RPC header or the user data. This is the level that is currently specified when an application selects the default protection level.

- **privacy**

  This is similar to integrity level, except that the user data is encrypted using DES to guard against wiretapping.

The selection of the appropriate protection level is a cost-benefit tradeoff. Both the level of security and the amount of application overhead increase with higher protection levels. Thus, an application should select the lowest protection level that suffices.

In practice, the protection levels really reduce to three: **connect**, **integrity**, and **privacy**. Level **none** is almost never used; an unauthenticated RPC should not be calling *rpc_binding_set_auth_info* in the first place. Level **connect** is used when the client and server want to mutually authenticate and where message modification attacks are not an issue. Levels **call** and **packet** do not offer much additional security. Level **integrity** should be used where malicious modification of the data being passed is an issue but privacy is not. Level **privacy** should be selected where the data is sensitive. Because the United States prohibits export of DES encryption, level **privacy** may not be available in all DCE implementations.

In the case of the Grade Server, we selected the default level, which is equivalent to selecting packet level **integrity**. This will allow us to detect fake client or server principals and guarantee that the grade point averages returned by the server are not tampered with. It does not, however, protect the data against active wire-tapping. We chose not to do so because we wanted to ensure that the application will run on all DCE implementations. A production server will likely require privacy protection, so no one will know the data except the client.

Determining the Server Principal Name

The example presented assumes that the client knows the principal name of the server. This is easy to do when, for example, there is only a single instance of a server. Sometimes, the client is interested in talking to one of a number of servers and does not care about the specific identity of the particular server. In that case, the client can ask the server for its principal name before calling *rpc_binding_set_auth_info*.

This needs to be done with care. A server could authenticate successfully and yet be untrustworthy. Authenticated RPC would tell you that the server is indeed Joe Hacker's Grade Server; authenticated RPC does not, however, tell you whether the server could be trusted to carry out the requested operation.

The client needs to determine whether the given principal has a certain attribute, for example, whether it is a trusted file server. This is done in DCE via the use of **groups**. Note that this is different from the group entries described in Chapter 6. Group entries are stored in the name service and are used to locate servers. The groups that we are describing here represent a collection of principals that share a common attribute. Groups are created for ease of management. Since group identity and membership are maintained by the Security Server, they can be trusted. We will discuss the use of groups in greater detail when we describe how to implement servers in Chapter 9.

A common technique for changing the server's authenticity is to inquire the server's principal name and then contact the Security Server to see if the principal is a member of a specified group.

Example 8-3 shows the code fragment to do this. The complete source code for the *get_GPA* client is in Appendix G. This example assumes that the DCE cell administrator has created a group named `grade_server` and made every Grade Server a member of this group. Thus, before a client calls a Grade Server, it will first verify that the server principal is indeed a member of this group. The administrative steps required to set up the example application are described at the end of this chapter.

Example 8-3: Inquiring the Server for Its Principal Name

```
rpc_binding_handle_t      binding_handle;
unsigned32                status;
sec_rgy_handle_t          rgy_handle;
sec_rgy_name_t            princ_name;
unsigned_char_t           *server_princ_name;
boolean32                 is_member;

rpc_ep_resolve_binding (binding_handle,                ❶
        gpa_v1_0_c_ifspec,      /* interface of server we want */
        &status);
CHECK_STATUS (status, "resolve_binding failed", ABORT);

rpc_mgmt_inq_server_princ_name (binding_handle,        ❷
        rpc_c_authn_dce_secret,  /* authn protocol */
        &server_princ_name,      /* server principal name */
        &status);
CHECK_STATUS (status, "inq princ_name failed", ABORT);

sec_rgy_site_open_query(NULL, &rgy_handle, &status);   ❸
CHECK_STATUS (status, "rgy_site_open failed", ABORT);

/* Translate the global principal name into a simple
   principal name. */
sec_id_parse_name (rgy_handle, server_princ_name,      ❹
        NULL, NULL, princ_name, NULL, &status);
CHECK_STATUS (status, "sec_id parse_name failed", ABORT);

is_member = sec_rgy_pgo_is_member (rgy_handle,         ❺
        sec_rgy_domain_group, "grade_server",
        princ_name, &status);
CHECK_STATUS (status, "is_member failed", ABORT);

sec_rgy_site_close(rgy_handle, &status);               ❻
CHECK_STATUS (status, "rgy_site_close failed", ABORT);

if (! is_member )
{
    fprintf (stderr, "got an imposter\n");
    exit(1);
}
```

Example 8-3: Inquiring the Server for Its Principal Name (continued)

```
rpc_binding_set_auth_info(binding_handle,              ❼
    server_princ_name, rpc_c_protect_level_default,
    rpc_c_authn_dce_secret, NULL /*default login context*/,
    rpc_c_authz_dce, &status);
}
```

❶ The binding handle returned from the namespace is normally a partially bound handle, that is, it does not contain the endpoint. To determine exactly which server the client will be calling, we need to fully resolve it. *rpc_ep_resolve_binding* contacts the endpoint map at the server's machine to fully resolve the binding to the gpa interface. For an Internet address, this would fill in the dynamic endpoint portion of the binding, thereby giving us an address of the form "ncacn_ip_tcp:136.12.125[2067]".

❷ Get the principal name of the server that is listening at the specified endpoint. This results into a call to the RPC management interface that is built into every DCE server. *rpc_mgmt_inq_server_princ_name* then returns the full principal name, for instance, "/ . . . /my_cell/grade_server_1".

❸ We now need to contact the Security registry to check on this server principal. Communications with the Security Server, like everything else in DCE, goes via DCE RPC. As with normal RPCs, initially we need to establish a binding to the Security Server. The Security code could have established this binding internally on every call, but that would be rather inefficient. Instead, the application is given full control of the binding process.

This brings up the issue of Security replication. The DCE Security Server is replicated; that is, there are a number of servers supporting the same interface. Updates are made at a master site, which then propagates the changes to a number of secondary sites. Therefore, if you want to update the Security registry, you need to bind to the master replica. Otherwise, you can bind to a secondary site. Since we are interested only in read access, we use *sec_rgy_site_open_query*. For updates, *sec_rgy_site_open_update* should be used.

The first argument is the registry site name. This argument is provided so that an application that cares can select a particular registry site. We pass in NULL because we are willing to bind to any available Security Server; this causes the default server to be used. The output of this call is a binding handle to the Security Server.

❹ Next, we need to check whether the Grade Server principal is a member of the `grade_server` group. The routine that checks for group membership takes a cell-relative name. The server principal name returned in callout 2 is a fully qualified name; it contains the cell name as well as the relative name within the cell. Therefore, we need to parse the name. For the Grade Server application, *sec_id_parse_name* will return "grade_server_1".

❺ We now contact the Security registry to see if the server is a member of the grade_server group. If so, we can proceed with the call; otherwise, we've got the wrong server.

❻ Close the registry site since we are done with the query. This causes the underlying binding handle to the Security Server to be freed.

❼ Annotate the binding handle for authentication as before, except we now pass in the server principal name that we've obtained dynamically.

The full source code for the client is in Appendix G.

Running the get_GPA Client

The get_GPA client program is built as a normal DCE application. The full makefile is in Appendix G.

Security Setup

Prior to running the client, we need to create the principals, groups, and accounts. In particular, we need to create the Grade Server and the student principals. We also need to create the Grade Server group and make the Grade Server a member of this group. The following shows a sequence of *rgy_edit* commands that we used to exercise the Grade Server application.

Example 8-4: Administrative Operations To Set Up the Grade Server

```
% dce_login cell_admin -dce-                                          ❶
% rgy_edit                                                            ❷
Current site is: registry server at /.../my_cell/subsys/dce/sec/master
rgy_edit=> domain group                                              ❸
Domain changed to: group
rgy_edit=> add grade_server
rgy_edit=> domain principal                                          ❹
Domain changed to: principal
rgy_edit=> add grade_server_1
rgy_edit=> add student_1
rgy_edit=> domain account                                            ❺
Domain changed to: account
rgy_edit=> add grade_server_1 -g grade_server -o none -pw -dce- -mp -dce-
rgy_edit=> add student_1 -g none -o none -pw -dce- -mp -dce-
```

Example 8-4: Administrative Operations To Set Up the Grade Server (continued)

```
rgy_edit=> ktadd -p grade_server_1 -pw -dce- -f /tmp/grade_server_tab    ❻
rgy_edit=> quit
bye.
%
% chown grade_server_1 /usr/users/grade_server/grade_server_tab
% chmod 0600 /usr/users/grade_server/grade_server_tab                    ❼
```

❶ Log in as the cell administrator so that we can update the Security registry. On a system such as DEC OSF/1 that has an integrated login, your normal system login program includes `dce_login`.

❷ Run the `rgy_edit` (registry edit) utility to create the necessary entries in the Security registry.

❸ First create the `grade_server` group.

❹ Create some principals. For now, we'll just create the Grade Server and a single student principal.

❺ Create accounts for the principals. When we create the account for the Grade Server principal (`grade_server_1`), we also make it a member of the `grade_server` group.

❻ Create a keytab file for the `grade_server_1` principal. We will explain how keytab files are used when we describe how servers are written in Chapter 9.

❼ We change the owner and permissions on the keytab file so that only the server can access it. This will be explained in Chapter 9.

These are all the Security setup steps required.

Running the Grade Server Application

At this point, we are ready to run the application. We begin by starting the server and then running the client program using a number of different input arguments.

Example 8-5: Running the Grade Server Application

Starting up the server

```
login: grade_server                                          ❶
passwd:
csh> server &                                                ❷
[1] 4502
csh> refresh login context thread started up
key mgmt thread started up
```

Example 8-5: Running the Grade Server Application (continued)

        Server ready.

Starting up the client:

        $ get_GPA
        rgy_site_open failed
         No currently established network identity for which context exists   ❸
         (dce / sec)
        $ dce_login student_1 -dce-   ❹
        csh> get_GPA   ❺
        GPA is: 3.200000
        csh> get_GPA student_1   ❻
        GPA is: 3.200000
        csh> get_GPA Peter   ❼
        GPA is: -1.000000
        csh> exit
        csh> $

❶ Log in to the local system as the grade_server so that we can access the server's keytab file.

❷ Start the server in the background. Since the server establishes its own identity, we do not need to log into DCE.

❸ Run *get_GPA* without having logged into DCE. As expected, the program fails for lack of network credentials.

❹ Log into DCE as the principal student_1; his password is -dce-. We now have the network identity of student_1.

❺ Run the *get_GPA* client program again. Passing no arguments specifies that we want our own, i.e., student_1's, grade. The response is 3.2.

❻ Run *get_GPA* again. This time, we explicitly specify student_1 as the name. We again get back 3.2.

❼ Now try to get the grade of another student. As expected, the attempt fails and -1.0 is returned.

9

Writing a Server that Uses Authenticated RPC

In this chapter, we discuss how to write a server that uses authenticated RPC and DCE Security. Chapter 8 gave an overview of the DCE security services and described the client side of security; Chapter 8 should be read before this chapter.

In Chapter 5, we described how to implement a server as two distinct pieces of code: server initialization code that is executed before the server processes any remote procedure calls, and the code that implements the remote procedures. In this chapter, we will describe the additional initialization steps that are required to implement a server that uses authenticated RPC and the code that is called by the remote procedures to perform authorization. We will illustrate the concepts by implementing the Grade Server described in Chapter 8. Note that the security policy is hard-coded into the server; the application does not support DCE access control lists (ACLs). ACLs are a major area of programming beyond the scope of this book.

Figure 9-1 shows the major steps that a server must perform in order to use authenticated RPC. The steps that are in bold are specifically added to use authenticated RPC; the rest are the same as those described in Chapter 5. As Figure 9-1 shows, the initialization code has to log in to DCE as a principal, maintain its login context, manage its own secret key, and register some authentication information with the RPC runtime library. The server must also implement a reference monitor that controls access to protected data. The server executes the reference monitor code when the actual remote procedure is called.

```
       log in

       maintain login context

       manage server secret key

       register authentication information

         register interfaces

         create server binding information

         advertising the server

         managing server endpoints

         listening for remote calls

         Implement remote procedures

       Implement reference monitor
```

Figure 9-1: Major steps in implementing a server

Server Login

RPC client programs do not need to log in since they are not principals; the process that is executing the client is the principal. Servers usually run in the background from a startup file. They cannot simply inherit rights from the root superuser; each server must establish itself as a separate principal.

A user generally thinks of logging in as a way to obtain a terminal, a home directory, and so forth. These things do not make much sense to a program such as a distributed application server. It is more fruitful to think of logging in as gaining a set of resources that you can use uniquely—a login context. An important element of these resources is a set of access rights; this aspect is the purpose for a server logging in.

A login context is the location in which the security credentials acquired by the current process are stored. A process can acquire a login context by either of two means: use the login context of a parent process, or establish its own login context via calls to DCE Security. Figure 9-2 illustrates the two alternatives.

Inheriting a Login Context

The default login context is part of the process context that is preserved when a subprocess starts (e.g., via *fork/exec*). Thus, a process can use its parent process' login context. Note that the login context is shared; the child process does not get a new copy.

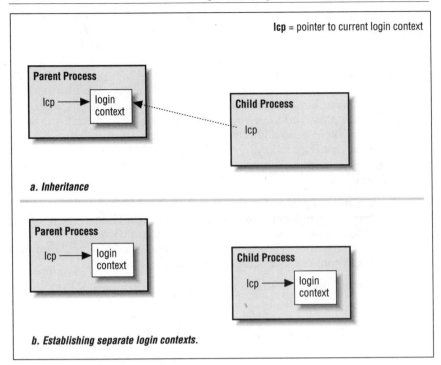

a. Inheritance

b. Establishing separate login contexts.

Figure 9-2: Establishing the login context

A server could, therefore, rely on its parent process to establish a login context. This could be useful in a development and debugging environment. The parent process would first log in to DCE under the identity of the server to establish the login context. Then the parent process would run the server program. Under UNIX, this would normally cause a child process to be forked, which would then *exec* the *grade_server* program. Example 9-1 below shows how to start the Grade Server in a shell script.

Example 9-1: Starting the Server from a Shell Script

```
dce_login grade_server_1 -dce-                          ❶
grade_server &                                          ❷
```

❶ Log in to DCE using the identity of the Grade Server principal, `grade_server_1`, and the password. This step causes a login context to be established for this process. Remember that the administrative steps at the end of the last chapter defined `grade_server_1` as the principal name of this Grade Server. If the Grade Server is replicated, then the other instances would have their own principal names.

❷ Run the `grade_server` program; this is the server code. The shell would create the Grade Server process. The Grade Server process can then inherit the login context that was established in item 1.

The advantage of this approach is simplicity. The server program does not need to worry about making the DCE Security calls to establish its own identity or manage keys. There are, however, drawbacks to this approach: First, the server password must be included in the script. If the file is properly protected, there is no additional security exposure from storing it in a file. Passwords and secret keys, however, should be changed periodically. Changing server passwords would be difficult if they are scattered across a large number of text files.

The second problem is lack of robustness. Under this approach, the server depends upon its parent process to establish the right login context. If not done correctly, the server could wind up with either no login context or, far worse, the wrong one. Therefore, we recommend that servers establish their own login contexts and manage their own keys.

The next section describes the steps required for a server to set up a login context.

Authenticating the Server

Secret-key based encryption is a commonly used technique for authenticating users to local systems. The local operating system might, for example, maintain a registry of users associated with their encrypted passwords. When a user logs in, the password is encrypted and compared with the entry stored in the registry. If they match, the user is assumed to be genuine and is, therefore, authenticated. Note that the algorithm that we have just described is simplified; in practice, the algorithm is more complicated to prevent various password guessing attacks.

A similar sequence of events occurs when a principal logs into DCE. Figure 9-3 shows the overall flow of a DCE login. The basic algorithm is altered so that the principal's password is not transmitted over the network. This is important because transmitting passwords over the network potentially exposes them to anyone that is monitoring the network traffic. Instead of sending the principal's name and the password, therefore, the login program just sends the user's principal name to the DCE Security Server. The DCE Security Server then constructs a message, encrypts it with the principal's secret key (which is known to the Security Server), and sends the resulting message back to the requesting system. In the case of DCE, the message contains the principal's network credentials.

After receiving the encrypted message, the DCE login program prompts the user for a password/secret key. This key is then used to decrypt the message. If the message is decrypted successfully, the principal must have supplied the right password and is therefore authenticated. Note that password validation is a local operation; the password (in either plaintext or encrypted form) is not sent over the network.

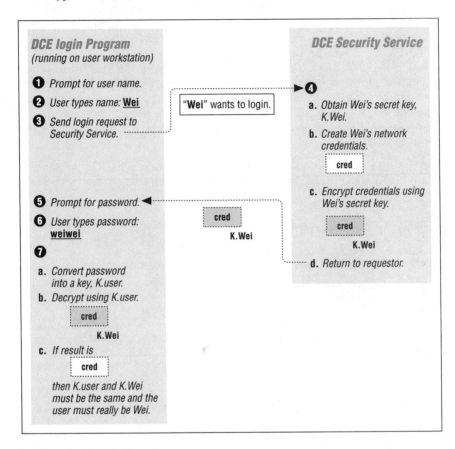

Figure 9-3: DCE login

Since the encrypted message contains the principal's network credentials, an important result of authenticating the user is that the user now has a set of valid network credentials that can be used to access network resources.

This brings up the issue of key management. A user remembers his or her password. (We use the words password and secret key interchangeably since you can derive the secret key from the password.) Unlike a real user that remembers his/her own secret key, a server principal keeps its secret key in a **key table**, or **keytab**, file. The keytab file can store multiple secret keys; each of these keys has a key version number. DCE Security retains old versions of the key so that a principal can decrypt messages that may have been encrypted with an older, unexpired key.

A process can either use its own keytab file or share the system-wide key-tab file in */krb5/v5srvtab*. Since the system-wide keytab file is readable and writeable only by root, each server that uses the global keytab file must be run under the root account. This is not a good practice; it grants the server program the same local privileges as the root process. A better approach is to have each server process run under a different local process ID and to create a separate keytab file for each server process. If this approach is taken, the permissions on the private keytab file should be set so that only the server process has read and write access because any process that can access the server's secret key will be able to impersonate the server. The administrative steps in setting up the keys were described in Chapter 8 and are also shown at the end of this chapter.

Example 9-2 is a portion of the C code that retrieves the Grade Server's sealed network credentials and then validates them using a key stored in a private keytab file.

Example 9-2: Get Grade_Server's Network Credentials

```
#define SERVER_PRINCIPAL_NAME "grade_server_1"
#define KEYTAB "/usr/users/grade_server/grade_server_tab"

sec_login_handle_t    login_context;
sec_login_auth_src_t  auth_src;
void                  *server_key;
error_status_t        status;
boolean32             identity_valid;
boolean32             reset_passwd;
    .
    .
    .
sec_login_setup_identity(SERVER_PRINCIPAL_NAME,           ❶
                         sec_login_no_flags,
                         &login_context, &status);
CHECK_STATUS (status,
             "Cannot retrieve network credentials",
             ABORT);

sec_key_mgmt_get_key(rpc_c_authn_dce_secret,             ❷
                     KEYTAB,       /* keytab file name */
                     SERVER_PRINCIPAL_NAME,
                     0,  /* key version number */
                     &server_key, &status);

CHECK_STATUS (status, "Cannot get my key", ABORT);

identity_valid =
    sec_login_validate_identity(login_context,          ❸
    server_key, &reset_passwd, &auth_src, &status);
CHECK_STATUS (status, "Validate failure", ABORT);
```

Example 9-2: Get Grade_Server's Network Credentials (continued)

```
sec_key_mgmt_free_key(&server_key, &status);          ❹
CHECK_STATUS (status, "Cannot free key", ABORT);

if (identity_valid &&                                 ❺
    (auth_src == sec_login_auth_src_network))
{
    /* We now have a valid login context */

}
else
{
    /* Fail and cleanup */
}
```

❶ We fetch the sealed network credentials for the Grade Server. Setting the second argument, *flags*, to `sec_login_no_flags` indicates that the credentials may be inherited by any children of the current process. The call returns a handle to the login context that will hold the DCE Security state of the current process.

❷ We now retrieve the Grade Server's secret key by calling *sec_key_mgmt_get_key*. For extensibility, this routine allows the caller to specify an authentication protocol. At present, the only supported authentication protocol is the secret key protocol. We also specify the keytab file as well as a key version number. We specify 0 to indicate that the most recent key should be used. The output of this call is the server's secret key.

❸ We have the network credentials now, but sealed by the secret key. The next step is to unseal them; this step simultaneously verifies the server's password. We pass in a handle to the current login context that contains the sealed network credentials from item 1 and the server's key/password that we obtained from item 2. If the key is valid, the credentials in the login context will be updated. As discussed earlier, this is a local operation; the secret key is not transmitted over the network, thus eliminating another potential security threat.

In addition to whether the key is valid, *sec_login_validate_identity* will set the third argument, *reset_passwd*, to let the caller know if the key has expired and should be changed. Notification of an expired key is informational only; the Security Server does not force you to change the key immediately. Thus, a server set up a key management thread to change it later; this is discussed in a later section of this chapter.

The login context will be validated by the network unless the Security Server was unavailable or the local system has explicitly disabled this capability. The fourth argument, *auth_src*, lets the caller know whether the login context was validated by the network (i.e., the Security Server) or by the local operating system.

❹ Secret keys, like passwords, should not be preserved on the system because that increases the chances of their being compromised. Hence, the key should be freed as soon as it has been used for validating the login context.

❺ We now check to make sure that the identity is valid and that the login context was validated by the Security Server before continuing.

Certifying the login context

Under some circumstances, the server should take special care in establishing its identity. If the server sets the local process identity based upon the information returned by the Security Server, then the server must make sure that it is communicating with a legitimate Security Server.

The DCE Security registry stores each principal's local process identity as well as its network credentials. In the case of UNIX systems, the local identity consists of the local user and group IDs. These values can be retrieved by using the *sec_login_get_pwent* and *sec_login_get_groups* calls. Some applications, such as a system login program that is integrated with DCE login, may set the local user and group IDs to be those registered in DCE Security. If the local user and group IDs returned by DCE Security are used, the server's login code must certify the authenticity of the Security Server that supplied the login context. If this were not done, it would be possible for an illegitimate Security Server to improperly assign a user the local system identity of root, for example, and open the local file system to attack.

The Grade Server application does not set the local user and group IDs based upon the data in DCE Security. Hence, this is not an issue. Should the server application need to do so, however, an alternate call, *sec_login_valid_and_cert_ident*, should be used instead. This call performs the same functions as *sec_login_validate_identity* but goes one step further and engages in another authentication exchange to verify that the Security Server is legitimate. Since this involves more overhead, this call should not be used unless required.

We do not need to certify the identity of the Security Server if we use only the network credentials. This is because an illegitimate Security Server would not know the principals' secret keys. Thus, the network credentials that are generated would not be usable and the principal would detect this case when it tries to make an authenticated RPC.

Setting the Default Login Context

It is a good practice, after a login context has been validated, to make it the default login context. This allows it to be selected by default when, for example, the server calls *rpc_binding_set_auth_info* to annotate binding handles for making authenticated RPCs. The following call does that:

```
sec_login_set_context(login_context, &status);
CHECK_STATUS (status,"unable to set default context",ABORT);
```

Maintain Server Login Context

The credentials within a login context have expiration times. When a login context expires (or more precisely, when the credentials within a login context expire), the login context is no longer valid. This means, for example, that authenticated remote procedure calls using this login context will fail.

When a user's login context expires, he or she can simply log in again (or run *kinit*) to refresh the login context. To maintain uninterrupted service, a user could refresh the login context before it expires. (The expiration time of login context's is set by *rgy_edit*.) A process that is maintaining its own login context should likewise periodically refresh its login context. DCE provides a routine, *sec_login_refresh_identity*, that refreshes login contexts.

sec_login_refresh_identity should be run from a dedicated thread, which is needed because the routine repeatedly sleeps until it is time to refresh the login context. Example 9-3 shows how to create the thread and the code that the thread executes.

Example 9-3: Starting Up a Thread To Maintain the Login Context

```
sec_login_handle_t login_context;
pthread_t          refresh_login_context_thread;
void               refresh_login_context_rtn ();

/* login code */

/*
 * Start up a thread to refresh the login context when it
 * expires.
 */
    if (( pthread_create (&refresh_login_context_thread,      ❶

            pthread_attr_default,
            (pthread_startroutine_t) refresh_login_context_rtn,
        (pthread_addr_t)login_context) ) == -1)              ❷
        exit (1);

/* rest of code in server initialization */
```

Example 9-3: Starting Up a Thread To Maintain the Login Context (continued)

```
#include <sys/time.h>
/*
 * A thread to periodically refresh the credentials contained in a
 * login context.
 */
void refresh_login_context_rtn (login_context)                      ❸
sec_login_handle_t login_context;
{
    struct timeval      current_time;
    struct timespec         delay;
    signed32            expiration;
    signed32            delay_time;
    unsigned32          used_kvno;
    boolean32           reset_passwd;
    boolean32           identity_valid;
    void                *server_key;
    sec_login_auth_src_t auth_src;
    error_status_t      status;

#define MINUTE 60

    while (1)
    {
      /*
       * Wait until the login context is about to expire.
       */
      sec_login_get_expiration (login_context,
            &expiration, &status);                                  ❹
      if ((status != rpc_s_ok) && (status != sec_login_s_not_certified))
      {
          fprintf (stderr,
            "Cannot get login context expiration time\n");
          exit (1);
      }

      gettimeofday (&current_time);
      delay_time = expiration - current_time.tv_sec - (10*MINUTE);

      if (delay_time > 0)
      {
          delay.tv_sec = delay_time;
          delay.tv_nsec = 0;
          pthread_delay_np (&delay);                                ❺
      }

      sec_login_refresh_identity (login_context, &status);    ❻
      CHECK_STATUS (status, "cannot refresh identity",ABORT);

      sec_key_mgmt_get_key (rpc_c_authn_dce_secret, KEYTAB,
            SERVER_PRINCIPAL_NAME,
            0,     /* return most recent version */
```

Example 9-3: Starting Up a Thread To Maintain the Login Context (continued)

```
                    &server_key, &status);                         ❼
        CHECK_STATUS (status,"unable to retrieve key",ABORT);

        identity_valid = sec_login_validate_identity (login_context,
                server_key, &reset_passwd, &auth_src, &status);    ❽

        sec_key_mgmt_free_key (&server_key, &status);              ❾
        CHECK_STATUS (status,"unable to free key",ABORT);

        if (! identity_valid)
        {
            /* Fail and cleanup */
        }

    }       /* end while */
```

1. We create a separate thread (item 1) to keep the login context refreshed. It will start execution at *refresh_login_context_rtn* (item 3). *refresh_login_context_rtn* takes a single argument, the login context, which is passed in item 2.

2. The thread starts execution at *refresh_login_context_rtn* (item 3). The thread repeatedly calls *sec_login_get_expiration* (item 4) to see when the login context would expire, and calls *pthread_delay_np* (item 5) to suspend itself until shortly before the login context would expire.

3. When the proper amount of time has elapsed, the thread wakes up and calls *sec_login_refresh_identity* (item 6) to refresh the login context. Since the wake time was computed to be earlier than the expiration time, the current login context should still be valid.

4. The login context returned by *sec_login_refresh_identity*, like that returned by *sec_login_setup_identity*, needs to be validated. We therefore acquire the key from the keytab (item 7) and call *sec_login_validate_identity* (item 8).

As before, we destroy the server's secret key as soon as we are done with it (item 9).

Manage Server Key

Since anyone who knows a principal's secret key can become that principal and access any resource that the principal can access, the keys must be kept secret. Servers should, therefore, periodically change their keys to reduce the chance of compromising the server key. Like maintaining the login context, this is done by creating a separate thread that periodically changes a server's key. *sec_key_mgmt_manage_key* automatically changes a principal's key to a random value before it expires and updates both the

Security Server's registry and the keytab file. Example 9-4 shows how to create the key management thread from the initialization thread, and how to change the key automatically:

Example 9-4: Starting Up the Key Management Thread

```
#include <pthread.h>
#include <dce/sec_login.h>
pthread_t            key_mgmt_thread;
void                 key_mgmt_rtn ();


/* Login code */
/* Start up a thread to refresh the login context */

/* Start up a thread to manage our secret key */
  if (( pthread_create (&key_mgmt_thread,                    ❶
         pthread_attr_default,
         (pthread_startroutine_t) key_mgmt_rtn,             ❷
         (pthread_addr_t)NULL) ) == -1)
      exit (1);

/* rest of code in server initialization */


/*
 * A thread to periodically change the server's secret key.
 */

  void key_mgmt_rtn ()                                       ❸
{
     error_status_t   status;

   while (1)
     {
         sec_key_mgmt_manage_key (rpc_c_authn_dce_secret,
             KEYTAB, SERVER_PRINCIPAL_NAME, &status);
         CHECK_STATUS (status,"key mgmt failure",ABORT);
     }

}
```

❶ We create a separate thread to perform the key management operation.

❷ This thread executes *key_mgmt_rtn*, shown at item 3.

❸ The only operation that this thread needs to do is repeatedly call *sec_key_mgmt_manage_key*. This routine causes the thread to sleep until shortly before the key expires, change the key randomly, update this server's key, and then sleep again.

Register Principal Name with RPC

The final initialization step is to register the server's authentication information with the runtime library. The runtime library needs to know the principal name(s) under which the server will operate, and how to retrieve the server's secret key. When the client makes a call to the server, the runtime library uses the server credentials to decode the call.

Example 9-5 illustrates the call that the Grade Server would use.

Example 9-5: Register Authentication Information with RPC

```
/* Register authentication info with RPC runtime library. */
rpc_server_register_auth_info(SERVER_PRINCIPAL_NAME,
        rpc_c_authn_dce_secret, /* authn protocol */
    NULL  /*default key retrieval function*/,
    KEYTAB,      /* server keytab file */
    &status);
CHECK_STATUS (status,
        "server_register_auth_info failed",ABORT);
```

The server specifies the principal name and the authentication protocol to use. The only supported authentication protocol at present is secret-key based. In addition, *rpc_server_register_auth_info* allows the server to specify how the server's secret key is to be obtained. This is done through both a key retrieval function that RPC can call and an optional argument to pass to that function. Structuring the arguments this way allows the integration of other mechanisms (e.g., hardware-based schemes) for obtaining the server's secret key. The default key retrieval function supplied with DCE assumes that the key is in a keytab file and the name of the file is specified by the optional argument.

If a server operates under multiple identities, this routine must be called once per identity.

This completes the initialization steps for security. The server has logged into DCE, started up a thread to periodically change its secret key, and informed the RPC runtime library of its principal name and how to get at its secret key. After making the rest of the initialization calls (described in Chapter 5), the server will be able to accept incoming authenticated remote procedure calls. Example 9-6 shows the rest of the initialization code.

Example 9-6: Remaining Server Initialization Code

```
#include "gpa.h"
#include "check_status.h"

rpc_binding_vector_t     *bind_vector_p;
unsigned32               status;
```

Example 9-6: Remaining Server Initialization Code (continued)

```
    ...

    /* Register interface/type_uuid/epv associations with RPC. */
    rpc_server_register_if(gpa_v1_0_s_ifspec, NULL,
        NULL, &status);
    CHECK_STATUS (status,"unable to register i/f",ABORT);

    /* Tell RPC that we want to use all supported protocol sequences. */
    rpc_server_use_all_protseqs(rpc_c_protseq_max_reqs_default, &status);
    CHECK_STATUS (status,"use_all_protseqs failed",ABORT);

    rpc_server_inq_bindings(&bind_vector_p, &status);
    CHECK_STATUS (status,"server_inq_bindings failed",ABORT);

    /* Code to set up login context & start key mgmt thread */

    /* Register authentication information with RPC */

    /* Register binding info with endpoint map. */
    rpc_ep_register(gpa_v1_0_s_ifspec, bind_vector_p,
        NULL,
        (unsigned_char_t *)"GPA server, version 1.0", &status);
    CHECK_STATUS (status,"ep_register failed",ABORT);

    /* Export binding info to the namespace. */
    rpc_ns_binding_export(rpc_c_ns_syntax_dce, "/.:/grade",
        gpa_v1_0_s_ifspec, bind_vector_p,
        NULL, &status);
    CHECK_STATUS (status,"export failed",ABORT);

    /* Listen for service requests (semi-infinite loop). */
    fprintf(stderr, "Server ready.\n");
    rpc_server_listen(rpc_c_listen_max_calls_default, &status);
    CHECK_STATUS (status,"server_listen failed",ABORT);

    /* Returned from listen loop. We haven't arranged for this. */
    fprintf(stderr, "FAULT: %s:%d\n", __FILE__, __LINE__);
    exit(1);
```

The Reference Monitor

The initialization code described previously is called during startup, before the main server thread calls *rpc_server_listen*; it is called only once. The reference monitor, in contrast, must run at the start of every remote procedure call. The reference monitor is the piece of code that performs the authorization checks. For the Grade Server, the server code that implements the *get_GPA* remote procedure must call the reference monitor prior to executing the remote procedure. Figure 9-4 shows the flow of control.

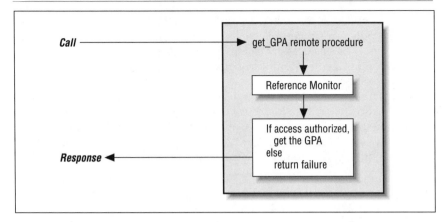

Figure 9-4: Reference monitor

The reference monitor can use the client's identity and group membership, along with the type of operation requested, to make its authorization decision. The general mechanism defined in DCE for authorization is the **access control list** (ACL). An ACL is a list of entries, each of which specifies the types of access (such as read, write, or modify) that a principal or group may have to a given object. To implement ACLs in DCE, a server must implement a standard RPC interface called an **ACL manager**, which is not described in this book. An ACL manager takes a client's PAC and determines the type of access that is permitted.

An ACL manager is a complex piece of software to write. It involves the implementation of a number of remote and local procedures to check permissions, etc. ACL managers are essential when one is implementing fine-grained protection of data. An example of this is the DCE Cell Directory Service, which uses ACLs to protect individual entries in the name space. For other applications like the Grade Server, it is much simpler to implement the reference monitor directly in the server code. In this section, we will show how to write a reference monitor that uses the client identity and group membership to make its authorization decisions.

Security Policy

Before we can implement a reference monitor, we need to specify the policy that the reference monitor should enforce. For the Grade Server, we will use the following:

> *A user can access his or her own GPA.*
> *If the user is a teacher, then he or she can access anyone's GPA.*
> *Otherwise, access is denied.*

A security policy is distinct from the underlying mechanism that implements the policy; a single policy can potentially be implemented in a number of ways. The easiest way to implement this policy is to use groups. In DCE, a group is a collection of principals that can be treated the same way for authorization purposes. Operators are an example of a group since principals that are operators share a common set of permissions (e.g., right to do backups, etc.) In addition to traditional groupings, applications can also define their own groups, such as teachers, who are principals that have access to anyone's grade. (Please do not confuse the DCE meaning use of the word "principal" with the principal of a school.)

The use of groups is fundamental to the Grade Server's security policy. Consider how one would implement the Grade Server without groups: each application that accesses the database would have to maintain a list of all the active teachers and explicitly check to see if the client principal is in the list. Since teachers can be hired or retired, we probably don't want to embed this list in the application. Thus, we would be driven to maintain this list in some central location (perhaps a file), thus increasing the administrative overhead of this application.

Groups eliminate the need for individual applications to take ad-hoc measures. Using groups, we can simply create a group named `teacher` and make every teacher a member of this group. The reference monitor would then need to check only the list of groups to which a client belongs to see if `teacher` is among them. We can also achieve a finer granularity of control by, for instance, assigning students to groups based upon their classes and granting access rights only to the teacher of that class.

Grade Server Reference Monitor

A reference monitor checks to see whether the authentication parameters specified by the client are acceptable, and then performs the actual access check.

Checking authentication parameters

Authenticated RPC guarantees that if the server's remote procedure is invoked, the client has been authenticated. It is up to the server application, however, to determine if the other aspects of the authenticated call are acceptable. In particular, the client sets a number of authentication parameters when it calls *rpc_binding_set_auth_info* (see Chapter 8). These parameters include the protection level, the authentication protocol, and the authorization protocol. The server needs to determine if the values that the client has selected are acceptable. Example 9-7 shows the code that performs this check for the Grade Server.

Example 9-7: Checking Authentication Parameters

```
#include <dce/id_base.h>

#include "gpa.h"
#include "check_status.h"

void get_GPA(
        rpc_binding_handle_t      handle,
        char                      *student_name,
        gpa_t                     *gpa)
{
    sec_id_pac_t          *pac;
    unsigned_char_t       *server_principal_name;
    sec_rgy_name_t        client_principal_name;
    unsigned32            protection_level;
    unsigned32            authn_svc;
    unsigned32            authz_svc;
    error_status_t        status;

    ...

    rpc_binding_inq_auth_client (binding_handle,           ❶
            (rpc_authz_handle_t *) &pac,
            &server_principal_name, &protection_level,
            &authn_svc, &authz_svc, &status);
    CHECK_STATUS (status, "inq_auth_client failed",
            ABORT);

    if (!((protection_level == rpc_c_protect_level_pkt_integ)  ❷
            &&
        (authn_svc == rpc_c_authn_dce_secret)
            &&
        (authz_svc == rpc_c_authz_dce) ))
    {
        *gpa = -1.0;        /* signal failure */
        return;
    }
```

❶ The server first retrieves the parameters that the client used to set up the authenticated RPC. *rpc_binding_inq_auth_client* gets the values that the client specified in its call to *rpc_binding_set_auth*.

The most important output argument is the Privilege Atttribute Certificate (PAC). This is the credential that specifies the client identity and any groups to which it may belong. We will use this later in our access check. For now, we are interested in the other arguments. This call returns, in addition to the client PAC, the server principal name that the client specified, the protection level, the authentication service, and the authorization service.

The server principal name argument is useful when the server process has registered several principal names. The protection level, authentication, and authorization service parameters specify those actually used for the current call.

❷ The server must now check that the authentication, authorization, and protection levels specified by the client are acceptable. DCE RPC relies upon the server application to check these values so the server can take application-specific actions (such as audit the failure).

In the case of the Grade Server, the reference monitor requires that the transmitted data be integrity-protected, the authentication service be DCE private key, and the authorization protocol be DCE (i.e., PAC-based). If the checks fail, the call fails.

Performing the access check

Once we are satisfied with the authentication parameters specified by the client, we can perform the actual access check to see if the security policy permits this particular remote procedure call. We use the PAC obtained from *rpc_binding_inq_auth_client* to do so. The PAC contains the identity of the principal and the list of groups to which the principal belongs. After obtaining the client PAC, the server needs to perform a check for group membership.

In principle, the check for group membership can be performed based upon only the information in the PAC. This is because the PAC includes a list of all the groups to which the client belongs. However, the PAC encodes groups as UUIDs. Thus, we need to contact the Security registry to translate between the UUID and the name. If we need to contact the Security registry anyway, we might as well ask it to perform the membership test directly. The code fragment in Example 9-8 does this by making a call to *sec_rgy_pgo_is_member*.

Example 9-8 shows the code fragment that performs the access check and then invokes the actual routine, *lookup_gpa*, to return the data if the client is authorized. Note that the remote procedure assumes that when the client passes in a null string for the student_name, that means "look up my own name." The administrative steps needed to set up this program, including the creation of a group named `teacher`, appear at the end of this chapter.

Example 9-8: A Reference Monitor

```
#include <dce/binding.h> /* binding to registry */
#include <dce/pgo.h>    /* registry i/f */
#include <dce/secidmap.h>     /* translate global name -> princ name */

#include <dce/id_base.h>

#include "gpa.h"
#include "check_status.h"
```

Example 9-8: A Reference Monitor (continued)

```
void lookup_gpa ();
          /* forward declaration */

void get_GPA(

    rpc_binding_handle_t      handle,
    char                      *student_name,
    gpa_t                     *gpa)
{

    sec_rgy_handle_t      rgy_handle;
    sec_id_pac_t          *pac;
    sec_rgy_name_t        client_principal_name;
    boolean32             is_teacher;
    error_status_t        status;
      ...

    sec_rgy_site_open_query(NULL,     /* registry site name */
            &rgy_handle,              /* output: binding to the registry */
              &status);                                                ❶
    CHECK_STATUS (status, "rgy_site_open failed", ABORT);

    sec_rgy_pgo_id_to_name (rgy_handle,                                ❷
            sec_rgy_domain_person,    /* this is a principal */
            &(pac->principal.uuid),   /* principal's UUID */
          client_principal_name,      /* output: name */
            &status);
    CHECK_STATUS (status, "pgo_id_to_name failed", ABORT);

    is_teacher = sec_rgy_pgo_is_member (rgy_handle,                    ❸
            sec_rgy_domain_group,     /* this is a group */
            "teacher",                /* group=teacher */
            client_principal_name,    /* principal in question */
            &status);
    CHECK_STATUS (status, "is_member failed", ABORT);

    sec_rgy_site_close(rgy_handle,&status);                            ❹
    CHECK_STATUS (status, "rgy_site_close failed", ABORT);
    /*
     * If you are a teacher, then you can lookup anyone's
     * GPA.
     * Else, if you are looking up your own GPA, it's ok.
     * else, access is denied; just return -1.0.
     */
    if (is_teacher)                                                   ❺
        lookup_gpa (student_name, gpa);                               ❻
    else if ((! strcmp (student_name, client_principal_name)) ||
            (student_name[0] == '\0'))
      lookup_gpa (client_principal_name, gpa);
    else
        *gpa = -1.0;

}
```

❶ We establish an RPC binding to the Security Server in preparation for our group membership test. We call *sec_rgy_site_open_query* since we are interested only in queries. The output is the binding that we will use when we need to query the Security registry. Like the client code in Chapter 8, we pass in NULL for the registry site name since we don't care which Security server services our requests.

❷ The PAC stores the principal identity in the form of UUIDs. For our group membership query, we need the client's principal name. Thus, we need to convert the uuid into a name. We do this by querying the Security registry using the handle that we obtained in (1). The output of this call is a principal name (e.g., `/ . . . /my_cell/student_1`).

❸ We now query the Security registry again to see if the principal is a member of the `teacher` group.

❹ We close the registry site since we are done with the queries. This call releases the binding handle (and also any underlying network resources) that we have established to the Security registry.

❺ Now we know the identity of the client as well as whether it belongs to the `teacher` group. The `if` block here implements the rest of the reference monitor. As noted earlier, the code assumes that if a null string is passed in for the student name, then the client is asking for his/her own GPA.

❻ *lookup_gpa* is the actual application code that implements the guts of the remote procedure—retrieving the GPA. Note that it is only invoked after the reference monitor code has been executed.

This completes the code that the Grade Server application needs to run as an authenticated principal. We have shown how to implement the server initialization code to set up its own identity, manage its own keys, and register its authentication information with RPC. We then gave an example of a reference monitor that performs checks on every remote procedure call.

Although we are done with the code, we still need to perform a number of administrative operations to deploy the Grade Server application. Specifically, we need to set up the Security registry information and the name space entry for the server.

Administrative Operations

The implementation of the Grade Server assumes that the server can export to the name service and that the principal identities and groups have been created. It also assumes that the keytab file exists and can be accessed by the Grade Server process. These operations are done outside of the program by an administrator, using the management utilities supplied with

DCE. We start with Security setup since that step creates the principal identities that are needed for the name space operation.

Security Setup

We assume that the Grade Server will execute with the local identity of `grade_server` and that it owns the directory */usr/users/grade_server.* */etc/passwd* should be updated if necessary to make this the case. The Grade Server needs the local identity so that it can access its keytab file.

We need to create the principals for the Grade Server, students, and teachers. Note that the grade_server group is not used by the server; it is used by clients to authenticate the server (see Chapter 8 for how this is used). We also need to create groups for both Grade Servers and teachers. Finally, we also need to create the keytab file for the server. Example 9-9 shows a sequence of *rgy_edit* commands that we used to exercise the Grade Server application.

Example 9-9: Administrative Operations Setup

```
% dce_login cell_admin -dce-                                              ❶
% rgy_edit
Current site is: registry server at /.../my_cell/subsys/dce/sec/master
rgy_edit=> domain group                                                  ❷
Domain changed to: group
rgy_edit=> add grade_server
rgy_edit=> add teacher
rgy_edit=> domain principal                                              ❸
Domain changed to: principal
rgy_edit=> add grade_server_1
rgy_edit=> add student_1
rgy_edit=> add teacher_1
rgy_edit=> domain account                                                ❹
Domain changed to: account
rgy_edit=> add grade_server_1 -g grade_server -o none -pw -dce- -mp -dce-
rgy_edit=> add student_1 -g none -o none -pw -dce- -mp -dce-
rgy_edit=> add teacher_1 -g teacher -o none -pw -dce- -mp -dce-
rgy_edit=> ktadd -p grade_server_1 -pw -dce- \
           -f /usr/users/grade_server/grade_server_tab                   ❺
rgy_edit=> quit
bye.
%
% chown grade_server_1 /usr/users/grade_server/grade_server_tab
% chmod 0600 /usr/users/grade_server/grade_server_tab                    ❻
%
```

❶ Log in as `cell_admin`.

❷ Create the groups that we will use. In this case, we create the `teacher` and `grade_server` groups.

❸ Create some principals.

❹ Create accounts for the principals. We make `grade_server_1` a member of the `grade_server` group and `teacher_1` a member of the `teacher` group.

❺ Create a keytab file for the `grade_server_1` principal.

❻ Change the file permissions on the keytab file so that it is accessible only by the grade_server process.

CDS set up

The Grade Server exports its bindings into the CDS entry named `/.:/grade` via a call to *rpc_ns_binding_export*. This call will automatically create the entry if it does not exist during the export operation. In the presence of security, however, this will not work if the Grade Server principal does not have the right permissions on that CDS entry.

Therefore, we explicitly create the CDS entry in which the Grade Server will export its bindings using the *cdscp* utility, and then use *acl_edit* to modify the entry's ACL to allow the `grade_server_1` principal to read from and write to the name space entry (see Example 9-10).

Example 9-10: Setting the Right Permissions in the Namespace

```
csh> cdscp create obj /.:/grade                          ❶
csh> acl_edit -e /.:/grad                                ❷
sec_acl_edit> list                                       ❸

# SEC_ACL for /.:/grade:
# Default cell = /.../mycell
unauthenticated:r--t-
user:cell_admin:rwdtc
group:subsys/dce/cds-admin:rwdtc
group:subsys/dce/cds-server:rwdtc
any_other:r--t-
sec_acl_edit> modify user:grade_server_1:rw              ❹
sec_acl_edit> list

# SEC_ACL for /.:/grade:
# Default cell = /.../mycell
unauthenticated:r--t-
user:cell_admin:rwdtc
user:grade_server_1:rw---                                ❺
group:subsys/dce/cds-admin:rwdtc
group:subsys/dce/cds-server:rwdtc
any_other:r--t-
sec_acl_edit> exit
csh>
```

❶ Create the object in CDS. This is the entry to which the Grade Server exports its bindings.

❷ Run *acl_edit* to examine and change the ACL associated with this name space entry. We use the −e option to indicate that we want to modify the RPC entry /.:/grade rather than the CDS object whose name is /.:/grade.

❸ List the current ACL on this entry. Note that only the cell administrator, the CDS administrator, and the CDS server are allowed to write to the entry.

❹ Modify the ACL to allow the grade_server_1 principal read and write access.

❺ List the current ACL again and verify that grade_server_1 is now included.

Running the Grade Server Application

At this point, we are ready to run the application. We begin by starting up the server. Since it will establish its own i DCE identity, the process that starts the Grade Server does not need to log into DCE. We do need to log into its local account so that it can access its keytab file (see Example 9-11).

Example 9-11: Running the Application

Starting up the server:

```
login: grade_server
password:
csh> server &
[1] 4502
csh> refresh login context thread started up
key mgmt thread started up
Server ready.
csh> exit
```

Running the client:

```
$ dce_login student_1 -dce-                        ❶
csh> get_GPA student_1                             ❷
GPA is: 3.200000
csh> get_GPA Peter                                 ❸
GPA is: -1.000000
csh> exit                                          ❹
csh> flute.lkg.dec.com> dce_login teacher_1 -dce-
csh> get_GPA student_1                             ❺
```

Example 9-11: Running the Application (continued)

```
GPA is: 3.200000
csh> get_GPA Peter
GPA is: 4.000000
csh> exit
csh> $
```

❶ Log in under the student_1 principal.

❷ Ask for our own GPA; we get back 3.2.

❸ Ask for another student's GPA. Since we are not running under Peter's identity and we are not a teacher, this query is not permitted and the server returns −1.0 to signal failure.

❹ Exit our shell (to eliminate any credentials that we may have established), and log into DCE again. This time, we log in as a teacher.

❺ Ask for student_1 and Peter's GPAs. Since we are running under the identity of a teacher, both calls succeed.

10

Context Handles

Some applications require that a server maintain information between remote procedure calls. This is called **maintaining context** (or maintaining state). Global data is one way a local application can maintain information between procedure calls. In a distributed application, however, the client and server are in different address spaces so the only data common to each are passed as parameters. Even if a set of remote procedures use server global data, there is nothing to prevent more than one client from making calls that modify the data. A **context handle** is the mechanism that maintains information on a particular server for a particular client. An **active context handle** refers to valid (non-null) context, and includes binding information because a specific server maintains information for a particular client.

The Remote_file Application

The `remote_file` application is a simple file transfer example that copies text from the client to the server.* A client uses a context handle to refer to server context. The server context is the file handle used by remote procedures to open, write, and close the file. In this application, the filename on the server may be the same or different from the filename on the client, but the server does not overwrite an existing file on the server system.

If you do not select any filenames, this application uses standard input (*stdin*) of the client and standard output (*stdout*) of the server to transfer a message from the client to the server. The complete `remote_file` application is shown in Appendix H.

---

*We use remote file access here as a simple demonstration of how to use a context handle. See Chapter 11, *Using Pipes for Large Quantities of Data*, for a more efficient way to transfer files.

Declaring Context in an Interface Definition

A file handle in a local application is analogous to a context handle in a distributed application. The information a file handle refers to is maintained by the C library and the operating system, not your application. You call some library routines to open or close the file, and other routines to read from or write to the file.

A context handle is maintained by the stubs and RPC runtime library, not by your application code. What you have to write is a remote procedure that returns an active context handle, and one that frees the context when you are finished with it. Other remote procedures can access or manipulate the active context.

Example 10-1 shows how to define context handles in the remote_file interface definition.

Example 10-1: Defining Context Handles

```
/* FILE NAME: remote_file.idl */
[
uuid(016B2B80-F9B4-11C9-B31A-08002B111685),
version(1.0)
]
interface remote_file          /* file manipulation on a remote system  */
{
    typedef [context_handle] void *filehandle;  /*❶*/
    typedef                  byte buffer[];

filehandle remote_open(        /* open for write ❷*/
    [in] handle_t binding_h,   /* explicit primitive binding handle     */
    [in, string] char name[],  /* if name is null, use stdout in server */
    [in, string] char mode[]   /* values can be "r", "w", or "a"        */
);

long remote_send(
    [in] filehandle fh,                        /*❸*/
    [in, max_is(max)] buffer buf,
    [in] long max
);

void remote_close(
    [in,out] filehandle *fh                    /*❹*/
);
}
```

❶ To define a context handle data type, apply the **context_handle** attribute to a `void *` type (or a type that resolves to `void *`) in a type definition. If the client-server communication breaks down or the client fails, a context handle data type allows the server to automatically clean up the user-defined context with a call to a **context rundown**

procedure. If a context handle is applied in a type definition, then the server application developer must write a context rundown procedure.

❷ At least one remote procedure initializes the context handle and returns it to the client for later use. A procedure returning a context handle result always returns a new active context handle. Also, if a parameter is an out-only context handle, the procedure creates a new active context handle.

❸ A procedure with a context handle parameter that is input only must use an active context handle.

❹ When the client application is finished with the server context, the context must be freed.

If the context handle is null upon return from a procedure, the remote procedure on the server has freed the context and the client stub has freed the context handle. A remote procedure that frees a context handle requires the parameter to have the in directional attribute so the server can free the context, and the out directional attribute so the client stub can also free the client's copy of the context handle.

Using a Context Handle in a Client

The client uses a context handle to refer to the server context through the remote procedure calls. In the client, the context handle refers to an **opaque structure**, meaning that the data is hidden and cannot be manipulated by the client application code. The context handle can be tested for null, but not assigned any values by the client application. The server code accomplishes all context modification, but the status of the context is communicated to the client through the context handle. The client stub manipulates the context handle in the client on behalf of the server. Example 10-2 shows a typical sequence of remote procedure calls when using context handles.

Example 10-2: Using a Context Handle in a Client

```
/* FILE NAME: r_client.c */
#include <stdio.h>
#include <string.h>
#include "remote_file.h"
#define MAX 200         /* maximum line length for a file */

main(argc, argv)
int argc;
char *argv[];
{
    FILE        *local_fh;      /* file handle for client file input */
    char        host[100];    /* name or network address of remote host */
```

Example 10-2: Using a Context Handle in a Client (continued)

```
    idl_char     remote_name[100];              /* name of remote file */
    rpc_binding_handle_t binding_h;                /* binding handle */
    filehandle   remote_fh;                        /* context handle */
    buffer       *buf_ptr;              /* buffer pointer for data sent */
    int          size;                     /* size of data buffer */
    void exit();
    char *malloc();

    get_args(argc, argv, &local_fh, host, (char *)remote_name);
#ifndef LOCAL
    if(do_string_binding(host, &binding_h) < 0) {              /*❶*/
        fprintf(stderr, "Cannot get binding\n");
        exit(1);
    }
#endif
    remote_fh = remote_open(binding_h, remote_name, (idl_char *)"w"); /*❷*/
    if(remote_fh == NULL) {
        fprintf(stderr, "Cannot open remote file\n");
        exit(1);
    }
    /* The buffer data type is a conformant array of bytes; */
    /* memory must be allocated for a conformant array.     */
    buf_ptr = (buffer *)malloc((MAX+1) * sizeof(buffer));

    while( fgets((char *)buf_ptr, MAX, local_fh) != NULL) {
        size = (int)strlen((char *)buf_ptr); /* data sent won't include */
        if( remote_send(remote_fh, (*buf_ptr), size) < 1) {        /*❸*/
            fprintf(stderr, "Cannot write to remote file\n");
            exit(1);
        }
    }
    remote_close(&remote_fh);                                   /*❹*/
}
```

❶ Before a context handle becomes valid, a client must establish a binding with the server that will maintain the context. For the explicit or implicit binding methods, your application has to perform this step. For the automatic binding method, binding occurs in the client stub during the first remote procedure call. Then, to find the server after the context handle is established, subsequent calls use it instead of a binding handle. The do_string_binding procedure is an application-specific procedure that creates a binding handle from a host input and a generated protocol sequence. It is shown in Chapter 3.

The symbol LOCAL is used in applications in this book, to distinguish compiling this client to test in a local environment, from compiling to run in a distributed environment.

❷ To establish an active context handle, a procedure must either return the context handle as the procedure result or have only the out directional attribute on a context handle parameter. The context handle cannot be used by any other procedure until it is active. For the `remote_open` procedure, an explicit binding handle is the first parameter.

❸ Procedures using only an active context handle can be employed in any way the application requires. Note that for a procedure to use the context handle, a context handle parameter must have at least the `in` attribute. The `remote_send` procedure sends a buffer of text data to the server, where the remote procedure writes the data to the file referred to by the context handle.

❹ When you have finished with the context, free the context handle to release resources.

Binding Handles and Context Handles

A procedure can use a binding handle and one or more context handles. However, make sure all handles in the parameter list refer to the same server because a remote procedure call cannot directly refer to more than one server at a time.

Table 10-1 shows how to determine whether a binding handle or a context handle directs the remote procedure call to the server.

Table 10-1: Binding Handles and Context Handles in a Call

Procedure Format	Other Parameters	Handle that Directs Call
`proc( . . . )`	No binding or context handles	The interface-wide automatic or implicit binding handle directs the call.
`proc( [in] bh . . . )`	May include context handles	The explicit binding handle, bh, directs the call.
`proc( . . . [in] ch . . . )`	May include other context handles but no binding handles	The first context handle that is an input only parameter directs the call. If it is null, the call will fail.

Table 10-1: Binding Handles and Context Handles in a Call (continued)

Procedure Format	Other Parameters	Handle that Directs Call
proc(. . . [in,out]ch. . .)	May include other input/output or output-only context handles but no binding handles or input only context handles	The first non-null context handle that is an input/output parameter directs the call. If all are null, the call will fail.

Managing Context in a Server

When more than one remote procedure call from a particular client needs context on a server, the server stub and server application maintain the context. This section describes how to implement the procedures that manipulate context in a server.

A **server context handle** refers to context in the server code. It communicates the status of the context back to the client. From the perspective of the server developer, a server context handle is an untyped pointer that can be tested for null, assigned null, or assigned any value.

Once the server context handle is active (non-null), the server maintains the context for the particular client until one of the following occurs:

• The client performs a remote procedure call that frees the context.

• The client terminates while context is being maintained.

• Communication breaks between the client and server.

If the client terminates or the client-server communication breaks while the server maintains context, the server's RPC runtime library may invoke a context rundown procedure to clean up user data.

Writing Procedures That Use a Context Handle

Example 10-3 shows how to implement a procedure that obtains an active context handle, one that uses the active context handle, and one that frees the context handle.

Example 10-3: Procedures that Use Context Handles

```
/* FILE NAME: r_procedures.c */
#include <stdio.h>
#include <string.h>
#include <unistd.h>
#include "remote_file.h"

filehandle remote_open(binding_h, name, mode)   /*❶*/
rpc_binding_handle_t binding_h;
idl_char           name[];
idl_char           mode[];
{
    FILE *FILEh;

    if(strlen((char *)name) == 0)                    /* no filename given */
        if(strcmp((char *)mode, "r") == 0)
            FILEh = NULL;                   /* cannot read nonexistent file */
        else FILEh = stdout;                      /* use server stdout */

    else if(access((char *)name, F_OK) == 0)          /* file exists */
        if(strcmp((char *)mode, "w") == 0)
            FILEh = NULL;              /* do not overwrite existing file */
        else FILEh = fopen((char *)name, (char *)mode); /*open read/append */

    else                                       /* file does not exist */
        if(strcmp((char *)mode, "r") == 0)
            FILEh = NULL;                   /* cannot read nonexistent file */
        else FILEh = fopen((char *)name, (char *)mode);/*open write/append */

    return( (filehandle)FILEh );    /* cast FILE handle to context handle */
}

idl_long_int remote_send(fh, buf, max)           /*❷*/
filehandle fh;
buffer buf;
idl_long_int max;
{
    /* write data to the file (context), which is cast as a FILE pointer */
    return( fwrite(buf, sizeof(buffer), max, (FILE *)fh) );
}

void remote_close(fh)                           /*❸*/
filehandle *fh;  /* the client stub needs the changed value upon return */
{
    if( (FILE *)(*fh) != stdout )
        fclose( (FILE *)(*fh) );
    (*fh) = NULL;          /* assign NULL to the context handle to free it */
    return;
}
```

❶ Initialize data as required by later calls, and assign the application context to the server context handle. In this example, a file handle is obtained and assigned to the context handle when the procedure returns. Outside of the server process this file handle is meaningless, but when the client makes subsequent calls, the server uses this file handle to write data or close the file.

❷ Use the server context handle parameter defined with the `in` directional attribute. This procedure must have an active context handle as input. For this example, the buffer (`buf`) of `max` number of items is written to the file. Cast the server context handle to the context's data type (`FILE *`).

❸ Free the context by using a procedure whose context handle parameter is defined with the `in` and `out` directional attributes. This procedure must have an active context handle as input. To free the context, assign null to the server context handle and use the C library procedure *free* or a corresponding method to clean up your application. In this example, before freeing the file handle, the context is tested to be sure it does not refer to *stdout*. The server context handle is cast to the context's data type.

When this procedure returns to the client, the client stub automatically frees the context handle on the client side if the server context handle is set to NULL.

If memory must be allocated for the context, use the C library procedure *malloc* or another method. Do *not* use the stub support procedure *rpc_ss_allocate* because you do not want the allocated memory to be automatically freed by the server stub after the procedure completes.

Writing a Context Rundown Procedure

A context rundown procedure allows orderly cleanup of the server context. The server RPC runtime library automatically calls it when a context is maintained for a client, and either of the following occurs:

• The client terminates without requesting that the server free the context.

• Communication breaks between the client and server.

In our example, the interface definition defines the following type as a context handle:

```
typedef [context_handle] void *filehandle;
```

Example 10-4 shows the context rundown procedure to implement in the server code. The procedure name is created by appending `_rundown` to the type name (`filehandle`). The procedure does not return a value and the only parameter is the context handle. In this example, when the context rundown procedure executes, it closes the file that represents the context.

Example 10-4: A Context Rundown Procedure

```
/* FILE NAME: context_rundown.c */
#include <stdio.h>
#include "remote_file.h"

void filehandle_rundown(remote_fh)
filehandle remote_fh;                   /* the context handle is passed in  */
{
    fprintf(stderr, "Server executing context rundown\n");
    if( (FILE *)remote_fh != stdout )
       fclose( (FILE *)remote_fh );  /* file is closed if client is gone */
    remote_fh = NULL;                    /* must set context handle to NULL  */
    return;
}
```

The context handle must be defined as a type in the interface definition for the server runtime to automatically call the context rundown procedure. And if you define the context handle as a type, then you must implement a context rundown procedure in the server.

11

Using Pipes for Large Quantities of Data

A **pipe** in a DCE application is an efficient way to pass very large or incrementally produced quantities of data in a remote procedure call. The following kinds of data are candidates for pipes:

- Large quantities of data

- Data of unknown size that cannot be in memory all at once

- Data incrementally produced or consumed and not in memory all at once

The purpose of a pipe is to put the RPC mechanism in charge of data transfer because it can use the underlying transport protocol more efficiently than the high-level application can. A pipe is defined in the IDL interface definition, and encompasses a collection of data structures, procedures, and stub routines. In the remote procedure declaration, a pipe can appear as a parameter with the same in and out attributes as other parameters.

As an input parameter, the pipe transfers data from client to server, while as an output parameter it transfers data from server to client. Unlike the familiar pipes of UNIX shell commands, you can use an RPC pipe to transfer data in both directions.

Transfer through a pipe starts after the client issues a remote procedure call and while the server executes the remote procedure. The server and client now enter loops in which the stubs transfer chunks of data. The server calls special stub routines that load or unload a buffer of pipe data, and the client calls application programmer's procedures that allocate buffers and load or unload them. Because the server controls the loops, we use the term **pull** for an input pipe (transferring data from client to server), and **push** for an output pipe (transferring data from server to client).

The Transfer_data Application

The `transfer_data` application (see Appendix I) shows how pipes are used to transfer binary data to and from the server. As defined in Chapter 3, a customized binding handle controls binding.

Defining Pipes in an Interface Definition

Example 11-1 shows how pipes are defined in an interface definition.

Example 11-1: Defining Pipes

```
/* FILE NAME: transfer_data.idl */
[
uuid(A6876974-F555-11CA-BAE1-08002B245A28),
version(1.0)
]
interface transfer_data    /* data transfer to and from a remote system */
{
  const long NAME_LENGTH = 200;

    typedef [handle] struct {              /* a customized handle type */
        char host[NAME_LENGTH+1];
        char filename[NAME_LENGTH+1];
    } file_spec;

    typedef pipe float pipe_type;              /* a pipe data type❶*/

void send_floats(        /* send pipe of floats to a file on the server */
    [in] file_spec  cust_binding_h,    /* customized binding for server */
    [in] pipe_type data                 /* input pipe of float data❷*/
);

void receive_floats(   /* get pipe of floats from a file on the server */
    [in] file_spec  cust_binding_h,    /* customized binding for server */
    [out] pipe_type *data                /* output pipe of float data❸*/
);
}
```

❶ You define a pipe in a type definition using the keyword `pipe`. The base type for a pipe defines the size of one element in the transfer buffer. In this example, the base type is a `float`.

❷ In this procedure, we use an input pipe to transfer data of type `float` from the client to a file on the server system.

❸ In this procedure, we use an output pipe to transfer data of type `float` to the client from a file on the server system.

When you pass the interface definition of Example 11-1 through the IDL compiler, it creates a C structure in the output header file for the pipe data type. The structure outline is shown in Example 11-2 and contains pointers to procedures and a pipe state. We describe the parameters required for each procedure later in this chapter.

Example 11-2: A Pipe Structure Generated by the IDL Compiler

```
       .
       .
       .
typedef struct pipe_type {
  void (* pull)(
       .
       .
       .
  );
  void (* push)(
       .
       .
       .
  );
  void (* alloc)(
       .
       .
       .
  );
  rpc_ss_pipe_state_t state;
} pipe_type;
```

Figure 11-1 shows where an application defines and uses the procedures, stub routines, and pipe state. Your client has to manage the data. For an input pipe, write a *pull* procedure that provides a chunk of data (for instance, by reading it from a file). For an output pipe, write a *push* procedure that processes a chunk of data (for instance, by writing it to a file). In both cases, write an *alloc* procedure that allocates or points to a buffer of memory for each chunk. Finally, to coordinate these procedures over multiple calls, define an application-specific state structure. Your client application never calls the procedures directly; instead, the client stub calls them during each pass in its internal loop.

During data transfer, the following information is required:

• The size of the chunk transferred each time

• Where the data transfer starts (for instance, the beginning of a file or the first element of an array)

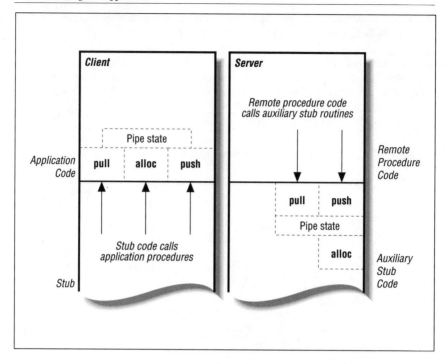

Figure 11-1: Structure of pipe application code

- Where the data transfer ends (for instance, check for the end of the file, or count the number of elements being transferred and stop at the end of the array). A chunk of zero length indicates the end of pipe data.

For the server, the IDL compiler generates the pipe state and *alloc*, *pull*, and *push* stub routines, and places them in a server auxiliary stub file. Your server calls the *pull* stub routine for an input pipe and the *push* stub routine for an output pipe in loops from the remote procedure. On the server side, the *alloc* stub routine and the pipe state are used exclusively by the stub.

This chapter describes the rules that you must follow to make pipes work. The examples show an input pipe first, and then an output pipe that performs the reverse operation.

The Pipe State

A pipe state is application-specific and local to each side. That is, the client and the server each have a separate state that is used just to communicate between application code and stub code. For most applications, the state is a structure.

The client developer defines and manipulates the pipe state for the client. The main task of the state for all applications is to keep track of where to find or place the data. For example, if you are transferring chunks of data from a large array in memory, you set a structure member of the state to start at zero for the first element. During each *pull* or *push* loop cycle, you update the member so that it points to the starting element for the next transfer. The example in this chapter transfers data from one file to another, so all that is needed for the state is the file handle. It keeps track internally of the current data location in the file.

Many clients have additional uses for the state structure and can define extra members to meet these needs. For example, suppose you are using a pipe for both input and output in a remote procedure call. Your application may need to perform specific activities after input data is transferred to the server, but before output data is transferred back to the client. For the *pull* and *push* procedures to coordinate and perform these activities, the state can include whatever data is necessary. For example, let's assume pipe data from a file on a client is transferred to a server for processing, and then the pipe data is transferred back to the same file on the client. If the file is opened and the data in it is transferred to the server with an input pipe, the file must be reset to write data back to the file with an output pipe. If the last time the *pull* procedure is called it closes the file, the *push* procedure needs the filename in the state structure to reopen the file.

In the server, the IDL compiler generates the pipe state structure. It is used only in the server stub. The server developer does not manipulate the pipe state.

Example 11-3 shows the pipe state structure used by the client of the transfer_data application.

Example 11-3: A Pipe State Structure

```
/* FILE NAME: pipe_state.h */
/* Definition of application-specific state structure of client pipe data.*/
typedef struct pipe_state {
    int  filehandle;          /* handle of client data file❶*/
    char *filename;           /* name of client data file  ❷*/
} pipe_state;
```

❶ This application requires the handle of the opened data file so our *pull* procedure can find the data and so our *push* procedure knows where to put the data.

❷ The name of the client data file is part of this pipe state structure, so the file can be opened in the *pull* and *push* procedures. The application requires this information for a pipe that is both input and output, so the file can be reset from read to write.

Using an Input Pipe

In this section, we first describe how to write a client for an input pipe parameter. Then we describe how to write a remote procedure to manage an input pipe for a server.

Using an Input Pipe in a Client

For an input pipe, you write the following:

- An *alloc* procedure, that the client stub calls to allocate a buffer of client memory for pipe data

- A *pull* procedure, that the client stub calls to load the allocated buffer

- A `pipe state` structure that coordinates *alloc* and *pull*

Figure 11-2 shows how the client processes pipe data that is transferred to the server.

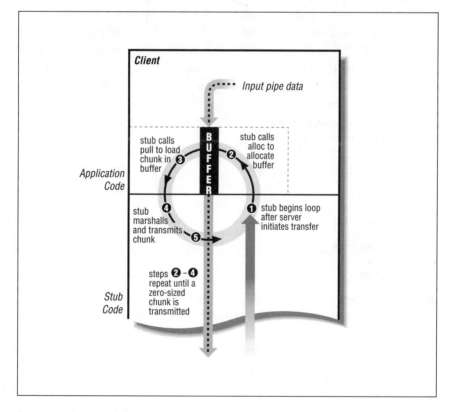

Figure 11-2: Pipe data transfer from a client

When the server initiates data transfer, the client stub begins to process data in a loop. On each pass, the stub calls the *alloc* procedure to create a buffer, then it calls the *pull* procedure to fill the buffer, and finally it marshalls and transmits data from the buffer to the server. The loop repeats until the stub transmits a zero-sized chunk of data. Example 11-4 shows an example of a remote procedure call with an input pipe parameter.

Example 11-4: Using an Input Pipe in a Client

```
/* FILE NAME: client_send.c */
/* Client for customized handle and input pipe test */
#include <stdio.h>
#include "transfer_data.h"
#include "pipe_state.h"  /* definition of state structure for pipe data❶*/

main(argc, argv)
int argc;
char *argv[];
{
    file_spec  cust_binding_h;             /* customized binding handle */
    pipe_state state;
    pipe_type  data;                  /* a pipe structure is allocated❷*/
    char       local_source[100];
               /* procedures in other modules */
    void       client_alloc(), in_pull();
    void       send_floats();
               /* get user input */
    if(argc < 4) {
      printf("USAGE: %s  local_source  host  file\n", argv[0]);
      exit(0);
    }
    /* initialize customized binding handle structure */
    strcpy(local_source, argv[1]);
    strcpy(cust_binding_h.host, argv[2]);
    strcpy(cust_binding_h.filename, argv[3]);

    /* initialize pipe structure */
    state.filehandle = -1;
    state.filename = local_source;
    data.state = (rpc_ss_pipe_state_t)&state;    /* initialize pipe state❸*/
    data.alloc = client_alloc;    /* initialize alloc procedure for a pipe❹*/
    data.pull = in_pull;       /* Initialize pull procedure for input pipe❺*/

    send_floats(cust_binding_h, data);/* remote procedure with input pipe❻*/
}
```

❶ Example 11-2 shows the `pipe_state` structure. This structure allows your *pull* and *alloc* procedures to coordinate activities during the data transfer loop.

❷ Allocate a pipe structure.

❸ To initialize the pipe state, assign your application-specific state structure to the `state` member of the pipe structure. Since you define the
state to be anything appropriate for your application, cast your application state structure when it is assigned to the `state` member.

❹ To initialize the *alloc* procedure, assign your application procedure,
`client_alloc`, to the *alloc* member of the pipe structure. Then,
when the client stub needs a buffer for pipe data, it calls `cli-
ent_alloc`. This procedure is shown in Example 11-5.

❺ To initialize the *pull* procedure, assign your application procedure,
`in_pull`, to the *pull* member of the pipe structure. Then, when the client stub needs input pipe data, it calls `in_pull`. This procedure is
shown in Example 11-6.

❻ Call the remote procedure that has the input pipe parameter. The
`send_floats` procedure takes an input pipe of floating-point file data
and copies it to the target file on the server.

Example 11-5 shows the *alloc* procedure for the input pipe of Example
11-4. This example simply returns a pointer to the same array each time the
client stub calls this procedure. Sophisticated applications may need to
allocate a different amount of memory each time the stub calls this procedure.

Example 11-5: A Client Alloc Procedure for a Pipe

```
/* FILE NAME: client_alloc.c */
#include <stdio.h>
#include "transfer_data.h"
#include "pipe_state.h"

#define BUFFER_SIZE 2000
idl_short_float client_buffer[BUFFER_SIZE];

void client_alloc(state, bsize, buf, bcount)    /* allocation for a pipe❶*/
pipe_state          *state;         /* coordinates pipe procedure calls❷*/
idl_ulong_int       bsize;          /* desired size of buffer in bytes❸*/
idl_short_float     **buf;                        /* allocated buffer❹*/
idl_ulong_int       *bcount;        /* allocated buffer size in bytes  ❺*/
{
    *buf = client_buffer;
    *bcount = BUFFER_SIZE;
    return;
}
```

❶ The header file generated by the IDL compiler specifies arguments that
you must include in your *alloc* procedure.

❷ The pipe state is available to coordinate calls that the stub makes to the
pipe procedures. In this example, the state is not used.

❸ The stub passes in the number of bytes it would prefer to use for the transfer buffer. This value is set by the IDL compiler and is read-only in your *alloc* procedure. In this example, this value is not used.

❹ The procedure obtains a pointer to the allocated buffer.

❺ The procedure obtains the actual size of the buffer in bytes.

After the client stub calls your *alloc* procedure, the stub calls your *pull* procedure to load a chunk of data into the buffer. This procedure must perform the following tasks:

* Find the chunk of data, usually by referring to the state structure.

* Read the chunk of data into the buffer, usually from a data structure, file, or device.

* Set the number of bytes to be transferred. To indicate the end of data, set this argument to zero.

* Do application-specific cleanup when all data is transferred. Cleanup can include tasks in preparation for the transfer of output data back through the pipe.

Example 11-6 shows the *pull* procedure and the arguments you must include for the input pipe of Example 11-4. In this example, the procedure opens the source file on the client and reads a chunk of data.

Example 11-6: A Client Pull Procedure for an Input Pipe

```
/* FILE NAME: in_pull.c */
#include <stdio.h>
#include <sys/file.h>
#include "transfer_data.h"
#include "pipe_state.h" /* definition of a state structure for pipe data */

void in_pull(state, buf, esize, ecount)/* input pipe uses pull procedure❶*/
pipe_state      *state;             /* coordinates pipe procedure calls❷*/
idl_short_float *buf;               /* buffer of data pulled          ❸*/
idl_ulong_int   esize;              /* maximum element count in buffer ❹*/
idl_ulong_int   *ecount;            /* actual element count in buffer  ❺*/
{
    /* for this application, open local source file if not open already */
    if(state->filehandle == -1) {
        state->filehandle = open(state->filename, O_RDONLY);
        if(state->filehandle == -1) {
            fprintf(stderr, "Cannot open file %s for read\n", state->filename);
            exit(0);
        }
    }
    /* process buffer for your application */
    *ecount = read(state->filehandle, buf, (sizeof(float)*esize)) /
                sizeof(float);
```

Example 11-6: A Client Pull Procedure for an Input Pipe (continued)

```
/* To signal the end of data, pull procedure must set count to 0.   ❻*/
if(*ecount == 0) {      /* end of data reached, do application cleanup❼*/
   close(state->filehandle);
}
return;
}
```

❶ The required parameters are declared in the pipe structure of the header file generated by IDL.

❷ You refer to the pipe state to find the start of a chunk of data, and any other state information you need. In this example, the state contains a filename and handle for the open file.

❸ The stub passes in a pointer to the buffer allocated by the previous call to the *alloc* procedure.

❹ The stub passes in the size of the buffer in terms of data elements. You should try to read this amount of data into the buffer. In this example, a pipe data element is a float.

❺ The procedure returns the actual number of pipe data elements in the buffer. The stub needs this value to marshall and transmit the correct amount of data.

❻ Send one empty data buffer by setting the element count to 0. This is the signal to the stub that it has reached the end of data. In this example, the last read from a file returns 0 elements in ecount, so the pull procedure simply passes it back to the client stub.

❼ Do application-specific cleanup. If an input parameter is also an output parameter, some preparation may be necessary before the stub calls the *push* procedure. In this example, the data file is closed.

Some applications use a pipe when data already has the proper form in memory, such as an array of pipe type elements. You can use your *alloc* procedure to assign the data to the buffer and make your *pull* procedure a null procedure.

Managing an Input Pipe in the Server

Figure 11-3 shows how the remote procedure processes input pipe data. You initiate data transfer by calling the server stub's *pull* routine in a loop. This routine tells the client stub to begin transmitting chunks of pipe data. It also unmarshalls the data into the server's buffer for use by the remote procedure. The loop repeats until the remote procedure receives a zero-sized chunk of data.

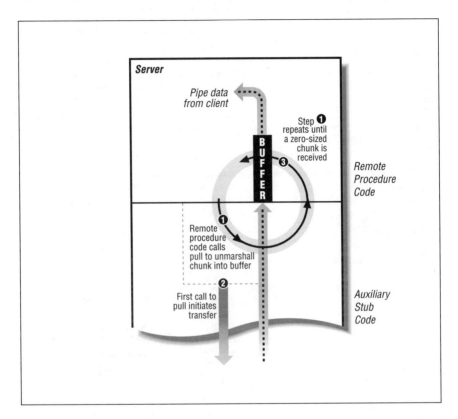

Figure 11-3: Input pipe data transfer to a server

Example 11-7 shows the steps to process an input pipe in a remote procedure implementation. Your remote procedure must call the *pull* stub routine in a loop until all data elements are received. Parameters passed to the stub routine include the pipe state (controlled by the stub) and the maximum number of data elements requested. Parameters returned include the buffer for the data and the actual count of elements pulled.

The stub puts into the buffer no more elements than the maximum requested. It could put in less. For instance, in this application, when the last chunk of data from the client's input file is sent, it could be shorter than the rest.

When a zero-sized chunk is received, the process loop can quit. Exiting the loop before this leads to an exception condition. Once the pipe is empty, the *pull* stub routine must not be called for this parameter again.

Example 11-7: Processing an Input Pipe in a Remote Procedure

```
/* FILE NAME: send_floats.c */
#include <stdio.h>
#include <sys/file.h>
#include "transfer_data.h"
#define MAX_ELEMENTS  1000

void send_floats(c_b_h, in_data)     /* copy input data to a server file */
file_spec  c_b_h;                    /* customized binding handle        */
pipe_type in_data;
{
    int             file_h;
    idl_short_float buf[MAX_ELEMENTS];                /* pipe data buffer */
    idl_ulong_int   element_count;          /* number of elements pulled */

    /* open local file on server for write */
    file_h = open(c_b_h.filename, O_CREAT | O_TRUNC | O_WRONLY, 0777);
    if(file_h < 0)  /* If can't open file, need to discard the pipe data */
        file_h = open("/dev/null", O_WRONLY);

    while(true) {                          /* entire pipe must be processed❶*/
        (in_data.pull)(           /* pull routine is used for an input pipe❷*/
            in_data.state,                 /* state is controlled by the stub */
            buf,                                  /* the buffer to be filled */
            MAX_ELEMENTS,        /* maximum number of data elements in buffer */
            &element_count       /* actual number of elements in the buffer */
        );
        if(element_count == 0) break;   /* 0 count signals pipe is empty❸*/
        /****          application specific process of buffer       **** ❹*/
        write(file_h, buf, (sizeof(idl_short_float) * element_count));
    }

    close(file_h);
    return;
}
```

❶ Keep looping until all data is received.

❷ Call the *pull* stub routine to obtain pipe data from the client.

❸ A chunk of data with 0 elements indicates that the pipe is empty.

❹ Process the data buffer appropriately for your implementation. In this example, the chunk of data is written to a file on the server.

Using an Output Pipe

Using an output pipe is similar to using an input pipe. However, an output pipe requires a *push* procedure instead of a *pull* procedure. In this section we first describe how to write a client for an output pipe parameter. Then we describe how to write a remote procedure to manage an output pipe for a server.

Using an Output Pipe in a Client

For an output pipe, you write the following:

- An *alloc* procedure, which the client stub calls to allocate a buffer of client memory for the pipe data.

- A *push* procedure, which the client stub calls to unload the allocated buffer.

- A **pipe state** structure that coordinates *alloc* and *push*.

Figure 11-4 shows how the client processes pipe data that is transferred from the server.

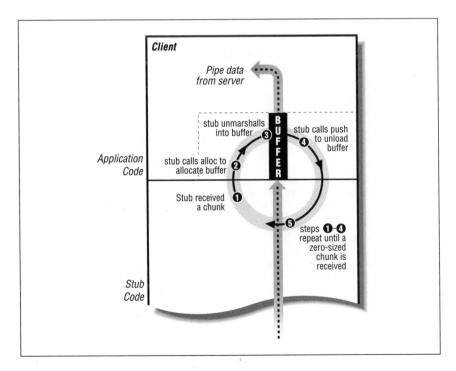

Figure 11-4: Pipe data transfer to a client

The client stub enters a loop in which it receives a chunk of data, calls the *alloc* procedure to create a buffer, unmarshalls data into the buffer, and calls the *push* procedure to use the data. The size of the chunk sent by the server can be different from the size allocated by your *alloc* procedure. If the chunk sent is larger than your allocated buffer, the stub repeats this sequence for the remainder of the chunk sent. The loop repeats until the stub receives a zero-sized chunk of data. Example 11-8 shows a remote procedure call with an output pipe parameter. In this example, the `state` structure and the *alloc* procedure are the same as those used for the input pipe in Example 11-4.

Example 11-8: Using an Output Pipe in a Client

```
/* FILE NAME: client_receive.c */
/* Client for customized handle and output pipe test */
#include <stdio.h>
#include "transfer_data.h"
#include "pipe_state.h"  /* definition of state structure for pipe data❶*/

main(argc, argv)
int argc;
char *argv[];
{
    file_spec  cust_binding_h;              /* customized binding handle */
    pipe_state state;
    pipe_type  data;                        /* a pipe structure is allocated❷*/
    char       local_target[100];
               /* procedures in other modules */
    void       client_alloc(),out_push();
    void       receive_floats();

    /* get user input */
    if(argc < 4) {
       printf("USAGE: %s  local_target  host  file\n", argv[0]);
       exit(0);
    }
    /* initialize customized binding handle structure */
    strcpy(local_target, argv[1]);
    strcpy(cust_binding_h.host, argv[2]);
    strcpy(cust_binding_h.filename, argv[3]);

    /* initialize pipe structure */
    state.filehandle = -1;
    state.filename = local_target;
    data.state = (rpc_ss_pipe_state_t)&state;   /* initialize pipe state❸*/
    data.alloc = client_alloc; /* initialize alloc procedure for a pipe ❹*/
    data.push = out_push;    /* initialize push procedure for output pipe❺*/

    receive_floats(cust_binding_h, &data); /* procedure with output pipe❻*/
}
```

❶ Example 11-3 defined the `pipe_state` structure. This structure allows your *push* and *alloc* procedures to coordinate activities during the data transfer loop. In this example, the state is a structure of client data file information including the filename and the handle of the open file.

❷ Allocate a pipe structure.

❸ To initialize the pipe state, assign the client-specific state structure to the `state` member of the pipe structure.

❹ To initialize the *alloc* procedure, assign your application procedure, `client_alloc`, to the *alloc* member of the pipe structure. Then, when the client stub needs a buffer for pipe data, it calls `client_alloc`. The procedure is the same one used for the input pipe (see Example 11-5).

❺ To initialize the *push* procedure, assign your application procedure, `out_push`, to the *push* member of the pipe structure. Then, when the client stub has output pipe data, it calls `out_push`. This procedure is shown in Example 11-9.

❻ Call the remote procedure that has the output pipe parameter. The `receive_floats` procedure copies a server file of floating-point data to the target file on the client.

After the client stub calls your *alloc* procedure to allocate the buffer for a chunk of output pipe data, the stub unmarshalls data into the buffer. The stub then calls your *push* procedure to unload the chunk of data from the buffer to your application. This procedure must perform the following tasks:

- Check the number of data elements transferred. If the number is zero, data transfer is finished.

- Take the chunk of data from the buffer, and process it or store it as required by the application.

Example 11-9 shows the *push* procedure and the arguments you must include for the output pipe of Example 11-8. For each chunk of data the server sends, the client stub calls this procedure to retrieve the data in a manner appropriate to your application.

Example 11-9: A Client Push Procedure for an Output Pipe

```
/* FILE NAME: out_push.c */
#include <stdio.h>
#include <sys/file.h>
#include "transfer_data.h"
#include "pipe_state.h" /* definition of a state structure for pipe data */
```

Example 11-9: A Client Push Procedure for an Output Pipe (continued)

```
void out_push(state, buf, ecount)   /* output pipe needs push procedure ❶*/
pipe_state       *state;            /* coordinates pipe procedure calls ❷*/
idl_short_float *buf;               /* buffer of data pushed            ❸*/
idl_ulong_int   ecount;             /* number of elements for buffer    ❹*/
{
    /* for this application, open local target file if not open already   */
    if(state->filehandle == -1) {
        if(ecount <= 0)       /* if first buffer is empty, don't do anything */
            return;
        state->filehandle = open(state->filename,
                                O_CREAT | O_TRUNC | O_WRONLY, 0777);
        if(state->filehandle == -1) {
            fprintf(stderr, "Cannot open file %s for write\n", state->filename);
            exit(0);
        }
    }
    /* To detect end of data, push routine must test the count for 0.   ❺*/
    if(ecount == 0)                     /* do application specific cleanup */
        close(state->filehandle);
    else                                /* process buffer for application */
        write(state->filehandle, buf, (sizeof(float) * ecount));
    return;
}
```

❶ The required parameters are declared in the pipe structure of the header file, generated by IDL.

❷ The pipe state coordinates calls that the stub makes to your pipe procedures. In this example, the state is used to determine whether the input file is open and to hold the file handle.

❸ The client stub passes in a pointer to the buffer containing a chunk of data.

❹ The client stub passes in the number of data elements in the buffer.

❺ The procedure must test the element count for 0, indicating that the end of data has been reached. In this example, if the element count is 0, the procedure closes the file; otherwise the data in the buffer is written to the file.

Managing an Output Pipe in the Server

Figure 11-5 shows how the remote procedure processes output pipe data. You initiate data transfer by calling the server stub's *push* routine in a loop. This stub routine marshalls and transmits chunks of pipe data. The loop repeats until a zero-sized chunk of data is sent. Example 11-10 shows the steps needed to process an output pipe in a remote procedure. Your remote procedure must call the *push* stub routine in a loop until all data items are sent. Parameters passed to the stub routine include the pipe state (controlled by the stub), the buffer of data, and the number of data elements to send.

Example 11-10: Processing an Output Pipe in a Remote Procedure

```
/* FILE NAME: receive_floats.c */
#include <stdio.h>
#include <sys/file.h>
#include "transfer_data.h"
#define MAX_ELEMENTS  1000

void receive_floats(c_b_h, out_data) /* copy server file data to a client */
file_spec c_b_h;           /* customized binding handle */
pipe_type *out_data;
{
    int             file_h;
    idl_short_float buf[MAX_ELEMENTS];      /* pipe data buffer      */
    idl_ulong_int   element_count;          /* number of elements pushed */
    int             nbytes;

    /* open local file on server for read */
    file_h = open(c_b_h.filename, O_RDONLY);
    nbytes = sizeof(idl_short_float) * MAX_ELEMENTS;

    if(file_h > 0) {
        while(true)  {
            /*****         application specific process of buffer      *****❶*/
            element_count = read(file_h, buf, nbytes) / sizeof(idl_short_float);
            if(element_count == 0) break;

            out_data->push(     /* push routine is used for an output pipe ❷*/
                out_data->state,     /* the state is controlled by the stub */
                buf,                 /* the buffer of data to send      */
                element_count        /* the number of data elements to send */
            );
        }
        close(file_h);
    }

    out_data->push(out_data->state, buf, 0);   /* 0 indicates end of pipe❸*/
    return;
}
```

❶ Process the data buffer for the given implementation. In this example, we read a chunk of data from a file.

❷ Call the *push* stub routine to transfer data to the client. The pipe state is an input parameter, and is controlled by the stub. Other input parameters include the buffer of data to send and the number of elements to push.

❸ The last call to the *push* stub routine for this pipe must have an element count of 0 to indicate the end of the data.

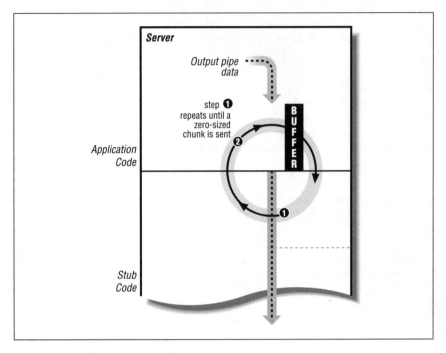

Figure 11-5: Output pipe data transfer from a server

Managing Multiple Pipes

IDL assumes that the client and server have a stream-like connection between them when they use pipes. This means data for a remote procedure transmits in a specific order, without "handshaking" in between transmission of parameters. This allows the underlying network protocol to transmit data in the most efficient way it can. For example, data for all non-pipe parameters are transmitted first, followed by data for each input pipe parameter. This means that when a remote procedure has more than one pipe, each must be completely processed and in a specific order. Suppose the following procedure is declared in an interface definition:

```
void proc([in,out] pipe_type *a, [out] pipe_type *b, [in] pipe_type c);
```

For this example, assume **pipe_type** is any valid pipe previously defined in the interface definition. Example 11-11 demonstrates the order in which the pipes must be processed in the remote procedure implementation. Example 11-7 and Example 11-10 show the details of processing the individual input and output portion of a pipe.

Example 11-11: Processing Multiple Pipes in a Remote Procedure

```
void proc(a, b, c)
pipe_type *a;     /* in, out pipe */
pipe_type *b;     /* out pipe     */
pipe_type c;      /* in pipe      */
{
    .
    .
    .
    while(true) {/* process first input pipe with its pull stub routine ❶*/
      (a->pull) ( . . . )
      .
      .
      .
    while(true) {/* process next input pipe with its pull stub routine  ❷*/
      (c.pull) ( . . . )
      .
      .
      .
    while(true) {/* process first output pipe with its push stub routine❸*/
      .
      .
      .
      (a->push) ( . . . )
      .
      .
      .
    while(true) {/* process next output pipe with its push stub routine ❹*/
      .
      .
      .
      (b->push) ( . . . )
      .
      .
      .
    return;      /* return only when all pipes are completely processed  ❺*/
}
```

❶ Obtain all data from the first input pipe of the parameter list. The output portion is not processed until all input pipes are processed.

❷ Obtain all data from the rest of the input pipes of the parameter list, one parameter at a time.

❸ Send data for the first output pipe only after all input pipes are complete. All output pipes are processed in the order shown in the parameter list.

❹ Send all data from the rest of the output pipes of the parameter list, one parameter at a time.

❺ The procedure returns only when all pipes have been completely processed.

A

IDL and ACF Attributes Quick Reference

All IDL attributes are shown in Tables A-1 through A-8, and all ACF attributes are shown in Table A-9, but not all are demonstrated in this book.

Table A-1: IDL Interface Header Attributes

Attribute	Description
uuid(*uuid_string*)	A universal unique identifier is generated by the *uuidgen* utility and assigned to the interface to distinguish it from other interfaces. This attribute is required unless the local attribute is used.
version(*major.minor*)	A particular version of a remote interface is identified when more than one version exists.
pointer_default(*kind*)	The default treatment for pointers is specified. Kinds of pointers include reference (ref) and full (ptr).
endpoint(*string*)	An endpoint is a number representing the transport-layer address of a server process. This attribute specifies a well-known endpoint on which servers will listen for remote procedure calls. Well-known endpoints are usually established by the authority responsible for a particular transport protocol.
local	The IDL compiler can be used as a C language header file generator. When this attribute is used, all other interface header attributes are ignored and no stub files are generated by the IDL compiler.

Table A-2: IDL Array Attributes

Attribute	Description
string	An array is specified to have the properties of a string.
Conformant Array Attributes	
size_is (*size*)	A variable is defined in the interface definition and used at runtime to establish the array size.
max_is (*max*)	A variable is defined in the interface definition and used at runtime to establish the maximum index value.
Varying Array Attributes	
first_is (*Ærst*)	A variable is defined in the interface definition and used at runtime to establish the lowest index value of transmitted data. The value is not necessarily the lowest bound of the array.
last_is (*last*)	A variable is defined in the interface definition and used at runtime to establish the highest index value of transmitted data. The value is not necessarily the highest bound of the array.
length_is (*length*)	A variable is defined in the interface definition and used at runtime to establish the number of elements transmitted for a portion of the array.

Table A-3: IDL Pointer Type Attributes

Attribute	Description
ptr	A pointer is specified as a full pointer with the ptr attribute, which gives all the capabilities usually associated with pointers.
ref	A pointer is specified as a reference pointer with the ref attribute. This attribute gives basic indirection without the implementation overhead associated with full pointers.
string	A pointer is specified as pointing to a string.

Table A-4: IDL Data Type Attributes

Attribute	Description
pointer type attributes	A data type with a visible pointer operator may be specified with a pointer type attribute (see Table A-3).
context_handle	A state is maintained on a particular server between remote procedure calls from a specific client by maintaining a context handle as a data type. The context handle identifies the state.
handle	A defined data type is specified as a customized handle so that the client-server binding information is associated with it.
transmit_as (*type*)	A data type that is manipulated by clients and servers may be specified so that it is converted to a different data type for transmission over the network.

Table A-5: IDL Structure Member Attributes

Attribute	Description
array attributes	A structure member can have array attributes if it has array dimensions or a visible pointer operator. A structure member that has a visible pointer operator and the size_is or max_is attribute defines a pointer to a conformant array, not an array structure member (see Table A-2).
pointer type attributes	A structure member can have a pointer type attribute if it has a visible pointer operator (see Table A-3).
ignore	Do not transfer the data in this structure member (a pointer) during a remote procedure call. This can save the overhead of copying and transmitting data to which the pointer refers.

Table A-6: IDL Union Case Attributes

Attribute	Description
pointer type attributes	A union case can have a pointer type attribute if it has a visible pointer operator (see Table A-3).

Table A-7: IDL Procedure Parameter Attributes

Attribute	Description
in	The parameter is input when the remote procedure is called.
out	The parameter is output when the remote procedure returns.
array attributes	A parameter with array dimensions can have array attributes. A conformant array is a procedure parameter with a visible pointer operator and the size_is or max_is attribute (see Table A-2).
pointer type attributes	A parameter with a visible pointer operator can have a pointer type attribute (see Table A-3).
context_handle	A parameter that is a void * type can have the context handle attribute.

Table A-8: IDL Procedure Attributes

Attribute	Description
Procedure Result Attributes	
string	A procedure result is specified to have the properties of a string with the string attribute.
ptr	A procedure that returns a pointer result always returns a full pointer. It may be specified with the ptr attribute but this is not necessary. Full pointers give all the capabilities normally associated with pointers.
context_handle	A procedure returns a context handle result in order to indicate a state on a particular server, which is then referred to in successive remote procedure calls from a specific client.
Procedure Execution Attributes	
idempotent	An idempotent procedure, when invoked multiple times, does not cause any state to change in the called procedure.
broadcast	A procedure can be broadcast to all hosts on the network. The client receives output from the first reply to return successfully.
maybe	A procedure is specified with the maybe attribute if it does not need to execute every time it is invoked, or if it does not require a response.

Most of the ACF attributes affect only the client side of an application, but `in_line`, `out_of_line`, and `represent_as` also affect the server side. The `heap` and `enable_allocate` attributes affect only the server side.

Table A-9: ACF Attributes

Attribute	Description
Binding Methods	
auto_handle	The automatic binding method is selected.
implicit_handle (*type name*)	The implicit binding method is selected.
explicit_handle	The explicit binding method is selected.
Exceptions as Parameters	
comm_status	Names a parameter or the procedure result to which a status code is written if a communication error is reported by the client runtime to the client stub. If an error is reported and this attribute is not used, the client stub raises an exception.
fault_status	Names a parameter or the procedure result to which a status code is written if an error is reported by the server runtime to the server stub, an exception occurs in the server stub, or an exception occurs in the remote procedure. If an error is reported and this attribute is not used, the client stub raises an exception.
Excluding Unused Procedures	
code	All or selected procedures from the interface have the associated client stub code generated by the IDL compiler.
nocode	All or selected procedures from the interface do not have the associated client stub code generated by the IDL compiler.
Controlling Marshalling	
in_line	The code for marshalling and unmarshalling data is stored in the flow of stub code rather than in generated routines.
out_of_line	The code for marshalling and unmarshalling data is in routines in auxiliary files generated by the IDL compiler.

Table A-9: ACF Attributes (continued)

Attribute	Description
Other ACF Attributes	
represent_as (*type*)	Data types in an interface definition are represented as local data types from your application code.
enable_allocate	The memory allocation stub support routine *rpc_ss_allocate* is enabled for use in a server. This routine is automatically enabled for remote procedures that use full pointers.
heap	Parameters are specified for allocation in server heap memory. If this attribute is not specified, the parameter may be allocated on the server stub's stack.

B

DCE RPC Runtime Routines Quick Reference

The following tables organize the RPC runtime routines so you can determine which ones you need. Table B-1 shows all the routines client applications can use, and Table B-2 shows all the routines server applications can use. All DCE RPC runtime routines are shown in these tables but not all are used in examples in this book.

The following abbreviations are used in RPC runtime routine names:

auth	authentication, authorization
com	communication
dce	distributed computing environment
dflt	default
elt	element
ep	endpoint
exp	expiration
fn	function
id	identifier
if	interface
inq	inquire
mbr	member
mgmt	management
ns	name service
protect	protection
protseq	protocol sequence
princ	principal
rpc	remote procedure call
stats	statistics

Table B-1 Client RPC Runtime Routines

Manage Binding Handles	Manage Name Service Expirations
rpc_binding_copy	rpc_ns_mgmt_inq_exp_age
rpc_binding_free	rpc_ns_mgmt_set_exp_age
rpc_binding_reset	rpc_ns_mgmt_handle_set_exp_age
rpc_ep_resolve_binding	**Manage Name Service Entries**
rpc_binding_inq_object	rpc_ns_mgmt_entry_create
rpc_binding_set_object	rpc_ns_entry_object_inq_begin
rpc_binding_inq_auth_info	rpc_ns_entry_object_inq_next
rpc_binding_set_auth_info	rpc_ns_entry_object_inq_done
rpc_binding_vector_free	rpc_ns_entry_expand_name
rpc_string_binding_compose	rpc_ns_mgmt_entry_inq_if_ids
rpc_binding_from_string_binding	rpc_ns_mgmt_binding_unexport
rpc_binding_to_string_binding	rpc_ns_mgmt_entry_delete
rpc_string_binding_parse	**Manage Name Service Groups**
Inquire of Protocol Sequences	rpc_ns_group_mbr_add
rpc_network_is_protseq_valid	rpc_ns_group_mbr_inq_begin
rpc_network_inq_protseqs	rpc_ns_group_mbr_inq_next
rpc_protseq_vector_free	rpc_ns_group_mbr_inq_done
Manage Interface Information	rpc_ns_group_mbr_remove
rpc_if_inq_id	rpc_ns_group_delete
rpc_if_id_vector_free	**Manage Name Service Profiles**
General Utility	rpc_ns_profile_elt_add
dce_error_inq_text	rpc_ns_profile_elt_inq_begin
rpc_string_free	rpc_ns_profile_elt_inq_next
Manage UUIDs	rpc_ns_profile_elt_inq_done
uuid_create_nil	rpc_ns_profile_elt_remove
uuid_create	rpc_ns_profile_delete
uuid_from_string	**Manage the Client**
uuid_to_string	rpc_mgmt_inq_com_timeout
uuid_is_nil	rpc_mgmt_set_com_timeout
uuid_equal	rpc_mgmt_inq_dflt_protect_level
uuid_compare	rpc_mgmt_set_cancel_timeout
uuid_hash	**Manage Local or Remote Applications**
Find Servers from a Name Service	rpc_mgmt_is_server_listening
rpc_ns_binding_import_begin	rpc_mgmt_stop_server_listening
rpc_ns_binding_import_next	rpc_mgmt_inq_if_ids
rpc_ns_binding_import_done	rpc_mgmt_inq_server_princ_name
rpc_ns_binding_inq_entry_name	rpc_mgmt_inq_stats
rpc_ns_binding_lookup_begin	rpc_mgmt_stats_vector_free
rpc_ns_binding_lookup_next	**Manage an Endpoint Map**
rpc_ns_binding_select	rpc_mgmt_ep_elt_inq_begin
rpc_ns_binding_lookup_done	rpc_mgmt_ep_elt_inq_next
	rpc_mgmt_ep_unregister
	rpc_mgmt_ep_elt_inq_done

Table B2: Server RPC Runtime Routines

Manage Binding Handles	Manage Name Service Expirations
rpc_binding_copy	rpc_ns_mgmt_inq_exp_age
rpc_binding_free	rpc_ns_mgmt_set_exp_age
rpc_binding_reset	rpc_ns_mgmt_handle_set_exp_age
rpc_ep_resolve_binding	**Manage Name Service Entries**
rpc_binding_inq_object	rpc_ns_mgmt_entry_create
rpc_binding_set_object	rpc_ns_entry_object_inq_begin
rpc_binding_inq_auth_info	rpc_ns_entry_object_inq_next
rpc_binding_set_auth_info	rpc_ns_entry_object_inq_done
rpc_binding_vector_free	rpc_ns_entry_expand_name
rpc_string_binding_compose	rpc_ns_mgmt_entry_inq_if_ids
rpc_binding_from_string_binding	rpc_ns_mgmt_binding_unexport
rpc_binding_to_string_binding	rpc_ns_mgmt_entry_delete
rpc_string_binding_parse	**Manage Name Service Groups**
Inquire of Protocol Sequences	rpc_ns_group_mbr_add
rpc_network_is_protseq_valid	rpc_ns_group_mbr_inq_begin
rpc_network_inq_protseqs	rpc_ns_group_mbr_inq_next
rpc_protseq_vector_free	rpc_ns_group_mbr_inq_done
Manage Interface Information	rpc_ns_group_mbr_remove
rpc_if_inq_id	rpc_ns_group_delete
rpc_if_id_vector_free	**Manage Name Service Profiles**
General Utility	rpc_ns_profile_elt_add
dce_error_inq_text	rpc_ns_profile_elt_inq_begin
rpc_string_free	rpc_ns_profile_elt_inq_next
Manage UUIDs	rpc_ns_profile_elt_inq_done
uuid_create_nil	rpc_ns_profile_elt_remove
uuid_create	rpc_ns_profile_delete
uuid_from_string	**Manage the Client**
uuid_to_string	rpc_mgmt_inq_com_timeout
uuid_is_nil	rpc_mgmt_set_com_timeout
uuid_equal	rpc_mgmt_inq_dflt_protect_level
uuid_compare	rpc_mgmt_set_cancel_timeout
uuid_hash	**Manage Local or Remote Applications**
Find Servers from a Name Service	rpc_mgmt_is_server_listening
rpc_ns_binding_import_begin	rpc_mgmt_stop_server_listening
rpc_ns_binding_import_next	rpc_mgmt_inq_if_ids
rpc_ns_binding_import_done	rpc_mgmt_inq_server_princ_name
rpc_ns_binding_inq_entry_name	rpc_mgmt_inq_stats
rpc_ns_binding_lookup_begin	rpc_mgmt_stats_vector_free
rpc_ns_binding_lookup_next	**Manage an Endpoint Map**
rpc_ns_binding_select	rpc_mgmt_ep_elt_inq_begin
rpc_ns_binding_lookup_done	rpc_mgmt_ep_elt_inq_next
	rpc_mgmt_ep_unregister
	rpc_mgmt_ep_elt_inq_done

C

The Arithmetic Application

The arithmetic application makes a remote procedure call to a procedure named *sum_arrays*, which adds together the values for the same array index in two long integer arrays, and returns the sums in another long integer array.

The application demonstrates the basics of a distributed application with a remote procedure call and includes these features:

- Defining a simple array in an interface definition
- Using the automatic binding method
- Exporting a server to the name service
- Checking the error status of RPC runtime calls

How To Run the Application

To run the nondistributed local test of the application, type the following:

```
C> make local
C> local_client
```

To run the server of the distributed application, set the application-specific environment variable ARITHMETIC_SERVER_ENTRY to the server entry name /.:/arithmetic_*serverhost*, where *serverhost* is the name of your server system. Type the following:

```
S> make server
S> setenv ARITHMETIC_SERVER_ENTRY /.:/arithmetic_serverhost
S> server
```

To run the client of the distributed application, set the RPC environment variable RPC_DEFAULT_ENTRY to the server entry name /.:/arithme-tic_*serverhost*. The *serverhost* is the server host name, not the client host name. Type the following:

```
C> make client
C> setenv RPC_DEFAULT_ENTRY /.:/arithmetic_serverhost
C> client
```

Application Files

Makefile contains descriptions of how the application is compiled. Use the compilation make all to create all the executable files for the application (see Example C-1).

client.sh is a shell script to set the environment and execute the client (see Example C-2).

server.sh is a shell script to set the environment and execute the server (see Example C-3).

arithmetic.idl contains the description of the constants, data types, and procedures for the interface (see Example C-4).

client.c initializes two arrays, calls the remote procedure *sum_arrays*, and displays the results of the returned array (see Example C-5).

procedure.c is the remote procedure implementation (see Example C-6).

server.c initializes the server with a series of RPC runtime calls (see Example C-7).

check_status.h defines the CHECK_STATUS macro, which interprets error status codes that may return from RPC runtime calls (see Example C-8).

Example C-1: The Makefile for the Arithmetic Application

```
# FILE NAME: Makefile
# Makefile for the arithmetic application
#
# definitions for this make file
#
APPL=arithmetic
IDLCMD=idl -v
LIBS = -ldce -lpthreads -lc_r -lmach -lm        # DEC Alpha OSF/1
CFLAGS= -D_SHARED_LIBRARIES -Dalpha -D_REENTRANT -w    # DEC Alpha OSF/1
CC=cc
```

Example C-1: The Makefile for the Arithmetic Application   (continued)

```
#
# COMPLETE BUILD of the application
#
all:   local interface client server


#
# LOCAL BUILD of the client application to test locally
#
local:interface client.c procedure.c
        $(CC)   -DLOCAL -o local_client client.c procedure.c
# remove object files so they do not interfere with a real build
        rm client.o procedure.o


#
# INTERFACE BUILD
#
interface:   $(APPL).h $(APPL)_cstub.o $(APPL)_sstub.o
$(APPL).h $(APPL)_cstub.o $(APPL)_sstub.o: $(APPL).idl
        $(IDLCMD) $(APPL).idl


#
# CLIENT BUILD
#
client:      $(APPL).h client.o $(APPL)_cstub.o
        $(CC) $(CFLAGS) -o client client.o $(APPL)_cstub.o $(LIBS)


#
# SERVER BUILD
#
server:      $(APPL).h server.o procedure.o $(APPL)_sstub.o
        $(CC) $(CFLAGS) -o server server.o procedure.o $(APPL)_sstub.o $(LIBS)
```


Example C-2: The Client Shell Script for the Arithmetic Application

```
# FILE NAME: client.sh
setenv RPC_DEFAULT_ENTRY /.:/arithmetic_serverhost
client
```

Example C-3: The Server Shell Script for the Arithmetic Application

```
# FILE NAME: server.sh
setenv ARITHMETIC_SERVER_ENTRY /.:/arithmetic_serverhost
server
```

Example C-4: The IDL File of the Arithmetic Application

```
/* FILE NAME: arithmetic.idl */
/* This Interface Definition Language file represents a basic arithmetic   */
/* procedure that a remote procedure call application can use.             */
[
uuid(C985A380-255B-11C9-A50B-08002B0ECEF1)          /* Universal Unique ID  */
]
interface arithmetic                           /* interface name is arithmetic */
{
   const unsigned short ARRAY_SIZE = 10;/* an unsigned integer constant     */
   typedef long long_array[ARRAY_SIZE]; /* an array type of long integers   */

   void sum_arrays ( /* The sum_arrays procedure does not return a value    */
      [in] long_array a,                      /* 1st parameter is passed in  */
      [in] long_array b,                      /* 2nd parameter is passed in  */
      [out] long_array c                      /* 3rd parameter is passed out */
   );
}
```

Example C-5: The Client File of the Arithmetic Application

```
/* FILE NAME: client.c */
/* This is the client module of the arithmetic example. */
#include <stdio.h>
#include "arithmetic.h"    /* header file created by IDL compiler    */

long_array a ={100,200,345,23,67,65,0,0,0,0};
long_array b ={4,0,2,3,1,7,5,9,6,8};

main ()
{
   long_array    result;
   int i;

   sum_arrays(a, b, result);              /* A Remote Procedure Call    */
   puts("sums:");
   for(i = 0; i < ARRAY_SIZE; i++)
      printf("%ld\n", result[i]);
}
```

Example C-6: Remote Procedure of the Arithmetic Application

```
/* FILE NAME: procedure.c */
/* An implementation of the procedure defined in the arithmetic interface. */
#include <stdio.h>
#include "arithmetic.h"              /* header file produced by IDL compiler   */

void sum_arrays(a, b, c)     /* implementation of the sum_arrays procedure   */
    long_array a;
    long_array b;
    long_array c;
    {
        int i;

        for(i = 0; i < ARRAY_SIZE; i++)
            c[i] = a[i] + b[i];     /* array elements are each added together   */
    }
```

Example C-7: Server Initialization of the Arithmetic Application

```
/* FILE NAME: server.c */
#include <stdio.h>
#include "arithmetic.h"                 /* header created by the idl compiler */
#include "check_status.h"               /* header with the CHECK_STATUS macro */

main ()
{
    unsigned32          status;                     /* error status (nbase.h) */
    rpc_binding_vector_t *binding_vector; /*set of binding handles(rpcbase.h)*/
    unsigned_char_t     *entry_name; /*entry name for name service (lbase.h)*/
    char *getenv();

    rpc_server_register_if(     /* register interface with the RPC runtime   */
        arithmetic_v0_0_s_ifspec,   /* interface specification (arithmetic.h) */
        NULL,
        NULL,
        &status                                         /* error status */
    );
    CHECK_STATUS(status, "Can't register interface\n", ABORT);

    rpc_server_use_all_protseqs(                /* create binding information   */
        rpc_c_protseq_max_reqs_default,   /* queue size for calls (rpcbase.h) */
        &status
    );
    CHECK_STATUS(status, "Can't create binding information\n", ABORT);

    rpc_server_inq_bindings(   /* obtain this server's binding information   */
        &binding_vector,
        &status
    );
    CHECK_STATUS(status, "Can't get binding information\n", ABORT);

    entry_name = (unsigned_char_t *)getenv("ARITHMETIC_SERVER_ENTRY");
    rpc_ns_binding_export(       /* export entry to name service database   */
```

Example C-7: Server Initialization of the Arithmetic Application (continued)

```
            rpc_c_ns_syntax_default,     /* syntax of the entry name   (rpcbase.h) */
            entry_name,                  /* entry name for name service            */
            arithmetic_v0_0_s_ifspec,    /* interface specification (arithmetic.h) */
            binding_vector,              /* the set of server binding handles      */
            NULL,
            &status
        );
        CHECK_STATUS(status, "Can't export to name service database\n", ABORT);

        rpc_ep_register(             /* register endpoints in local endpoint map   */
            arithmetic_v0_0_s_ifspec,    /* interface specification (arithmetic.h) */
            binding_vector,              /* the set of server binding handles      */
            NULL,
            NULL,
            &status
        );
        CHECK_STATUS(status, "Can't add address to the endpoint map\n", ABORT);

        rpc_binding_vector_free(         /* free set of server binding handles     */
            &binding_vector,
            &status
        );
        CHECK_STATUS(status, "Can't free binding handles and vector\n", ABORT);

        puts("Listening for remote procedure calls...");
        rpc_server_listen(                              /* listen for remote calls    */
            rpc_c_listen_max_calls_default, /*concurrent calls to server (rpcbase.h)*/
            &status
        );
        CHECK_STATUS(status, "rpc listen failed\n", ABORT);
}
```

Example C-8: The Check Error Status Macro

```
/* FILE NAME: check_status.h */
#include <stdio.h>
#include <dce/dce_error.h> /* required to call dce_error_inq_text routine   */
#include <dce/pthread.h>   /* needed if application uses threads            */
#include <dce/rpcexc.h>    /* needed if application uses exception handlers */

#define RESUME 0
#define ABORT  1
```

Example C-8: The Check Error Status Macro (continued)

```
#define CHECK_STATUS(input_status, comment, action) \
{ \
   if(input_status != rpc_s_ok) { \
      dce_error_inq_text(input_status, error_string, &error_stat); \
      fprintf(stderr, "%s %s\n", comment, error_string); \
      if(action == ABORT) \
         exit(1); \
   } \
}

static int            error_stat;
static unsigned char  error_string[dce_c_error_string_len];

void exit();
```

D

The Inventory Application

The inventory application allows a user to inquire about and order from a simple inventory. Data structures are defined for the following items:

- Part number (to identify a part)
- Part name
- Part description
- Part price
- Quantity of part
- Part list
- Account number (to identify a user)

Procedures are also defined in the interface definition to do the following:

- Confirm if a part is available
- Obtain a part name
- Obtain a part description
- Obtain a part price
- Obtain the quantity of parts available
- Obtain a list of subpart numbers
- Order a part

The application demonstrates many features of DCE application development including:

- Using strings, pointers, structures, a union, and a conformant array.

- Allocating new memory in a remote procedure for data returned to the client using stub support routines. The *get_part_description* and *whatare_subparts* remote procedures demonstrate server allocation of a string and a conformant structure.

- Managing protocol sequences, interpreting binding information, selecting binding information, and using exception handler macros.

- Variations on a client using ACFs and the automatic, implicit, and explicit binding methods.

- Finding a server by importing from a name service database.

How To Run the Application

To run the local test of the client, type the following:

```
C> make local
C> local_i_client.exe
```

To run the server of the distributed application, type the following:

```
S> make server
S> i_server.exe
```

Before you run the client that uses the automatic binding method for the first time, set the RPC environment variable, RPC_DEFAULT_ENTRY, to the name service group name for the inventory application. Type the following:

```
C> make client
C> setenv RPC_DEFAULT_ENTRY /.:/inventory_group
C> i_client.exe
```

To run a nondistributed local test of the implicit client, type the following in the *implicit* subdirectory:

```
C> make local
C> local_implicit_client.exe
```

To run the implicit client of the distributed application, type the following in the *implicit* subdirectory:

```
C> make client
C> implicit_client.exe
```

To run the explicit client of the distributed application, type the following in the *explicit* subdirectory:

```
C> make client
C> explicit_client.exe
```

Application Files

Makefile contains descriptions of how the application is compiled. Some files depend on the header file *check_status.h* from the arithmetic application for the CHECK_STATUS macro (see Example D-1).

i_client.sh is a shell script to set the environment and execute the client that uses automatic binding management (see Example D-2).

inventory.idl contains the description of the constants, data types, and procedures for the interface (see Example D-3).

i_procedures.c is the implementation of all the remote procedures defined in this interface (see Example D-4).

implement_inventory.c is the implementation of the inventory database. For simplicity, only three inventory items are included. The part numbers for these are printed when the inventory is opened (see Example D-5).

i_server.c initializes the server with a series of runtime calls prior to servicing remote procedure calls. In addition to the required calls, this server also selects a specific protocol sequence, uses exception handling macros, and does some basic cleanup when the server quits (see Example D-6).

i_client.c displays the instructions for the user and processes user input in a loop until exit is selected. Each remote procedure is exercised depending on the input from the user (see Example D-7).

implicit/implicit_client.c imports a binding handle from the name service database (see Example D-8).

explicit/explicit_client.c imports a binding handle from the name service database. All procedures have a binding handle as the first parameter (see Example D-9).

implicit/Makefile contains descriptions of how the implicit client is compiled. Some files depend on the header file *check_status.h* from the arithmetic application for the CHECK_STATUS macro.

The server for the implicit client is the same as the one for the automatic client (see Example D-10 for the Makefile).

implicit/inventory.acf customizes how you use an interface. In this application it is used to select the implicit binding method (see Example D-11).

implicit/do_import_binding.c contains the *do_import_binding* procedure, which shows how to import a binding handle from the name service database (see Example D-12).

implicit/do_interpret_binding.c contains the *do_interpret_binding* procedure, which shows how to obtain the binding information to which a binding handle refers (see Example D-13.

explicit/Makefile contains descriptions of how the explicit client is compiled. Some files depend on the header file *check_status.h* from the arithmetic application for the CHECK_STATUS macro. The compilation depends on some files from the implicit client development.

The server for the explicit client is the same as the one for the automatic and implicit clients (see Example D-14 for the Makefile).

explicit/inventory.acf customizes how you use an interface. In this application it is used to select the explicit binding method for all remote procedures in the interface (see Example D-15).

Example D-1: The Makefile for the Inventory Application

```
# FILE NAME: Makefile
# Makefile for the inventory application
#
# definitions for this make file
#
APPL=inventory
IDLCMD=idl -v
CHECK=../arithmetic      # directory containing check_status.h
LIBS = -ldce -lpthreads -lc_r -lmach -lm         # DEC Alpha OSF/1
CFLAGS= -D_SHARED_LIBRARIES -Dalpha -D_REENTRANT -w    # DEC Alpha OSF/1
CC= cc


#
# COMPLETE BUILD of the application.
#
all:   local interface client server


#
# LOCAL BUILD of the application to test locally.
#
local: interface i_client.c i_procedures.c implement_inventory.c
        $(CC) $(CFLAGS) -DLOCAL -o local_i_client.exe i_client.c \
            i_procedures.c implement_inventory.c
#remove the object files so they do not interfere with a real build
        rm i_client.o i_procedures.o implement_inventory.o


#
# INTERFACE BUILD
#
interface:   $(APPL).h $(APPL)_cstub.o $(APPL)_sstub.o
```

Example D-1: The Makefile for the Inventory Application (continued)

```
$(APPL).h $(APPL)_cstub.o $(APPL)_sstub.o: $(APPL).idl
        $(IDLCMD) $(APPL).idl


#
# CLIENT BUILD
#
client:     i_client
i_client:   i_client.o $(APPL)_cstub.o
        $(CC) $(CFLAGS) -o i_client.exe i_client.o $(APPL)_cstub.o $(LIBS)


#
# SERVER BUILD
#
server:     i_server
i_server:   $(APPL).h i_server.o i_procedures.o implement_inventory.o \
   $(APPL)_sstub.o
        $(CC) $(CFLAGS) -I$(CHECK) -o i_server.exe i_server.o i_procedures.o \
            implement_inventory.o \
            $(APPL)_sstub.o $(LIBS)
i_server.o: i_server.c
        $(CC) $(CFLAGS) -I$(CHECK) -c i_server.c
```

Example D-2: The Client Shell Script for the Inventory Application

```
# FILE NAME: i_client.sh
setenv RPC_DEFAULT_ENTRY /.:/inventory_group
i_client.exe
```

Example D-3: The IDL File of the Inventory Application

```
/* FILE NAME: inventory.idl */
[                                       /* brackets enclose attributes */
uuid(008B3C84-93A5-11C9-85B0-08002B147A61), /* universal unique identifier */
version(1.0),                           /* version of this interface */
pointer_default(ptr)                    /* pointer default */
] interface  inventory                  /* interface name */
{
   const long MAX_STRING = 30;              /* constant for string size */

   typedef long      part_num;             /* inventory part number */

   typedef [string] char part_name[MAX_STRING+1];     /* name of part */

   typedef [string, ptr] char *paragraph;    /* description of part */

   typedef enum {
      ITEM, GRAM, KILOGRAM
   } part_units;                           /* units of measurement */
```

Example D-3: The IDL File of the Inventory Application (continued)

```
typedef struct part_price {                          /* price of part    */
    part_units units;
    double     per_unit;
} part_price;

typedef union switch(part_units units) total {     /* quantity of part   */
    case ITEM:    long int number;
    case GRAM:
    case KILOGRAM: double   weight;
} part_quantity;

typedef struct part_list{                          /* list of part numbers  */
    long                      size;       /* number of parts in array  */
    [size_is(size)] part_num numbers[*];     /* conformant array of parts */
} part_list;

typedef struct part_record {                       /* data for each part */
    part_num       number;
    part_name      name;
    paragraph      description;
    part_price     price;
    part_quantity quantity;
    part_list      subparts;
} part_record;

typedef long account_num;                          /* user account number */

/*********************** Procedure Declarations ***********************/
boolean is_part_available(        /* return true if in inventory      */
    [in] part_num number               /* input part number */
);

void whatis_part_name(            /* get part name from inventory      */
    [in]  part_num  number,            /* input part number */
    [out] part_name name               /* output part name   */
);

paragraph get_part_description(   /* return a pointer to a string      */
    [in] part_num  number
);

void whatis_part_price(           /* get part price from inventory     */
    [in]  part_num   number,
    [out] part_price *price
);
```

Example D-3: The IDL File of the Inventory Application (continued)

```
    void whatis_part_quantity(           /* get part quantity from inventory */
       [in]  part_num     number,
       [out] part_quantity *quantity
    );

    void whatare_subparts(               /* get list of subpart numbers      */
       [in]  part_num  number,
       [out] part_list **subparts        /* structure containing the array   */
    );

    /* Order part from inventory with part number, quantity desired, and   */
    /* account number.  If inventory does not have enough, output lesser   */
    /* quantity ordered.  Return values: 1=ordered OK,                     */
    /* -1=invalid part, -2=invalid quantity, -3=invalid account.           */

    long order_part(    /* order part from inventory, return OK or error code */
       [in]      part_num      number,
       [in,out]  part_quantity *quantity,                /* quantity ordered  */
       [in]      account_num   account
    );
} /* end of interface definition */
```

Example D-4: Remote Procedures of the Inventory Application

```
/* FILE NAME: i_procedures.c */
/** Implementation of the remote procedures for the inventory application. **/
#include <stdio.h>
#include "inventory.h"
#ifdef LOCAL
    /* stub support procedures are redefined for a local test of application */
#define rpc_ss_allocate malloc
    /* In a distributed RPC application, rpc_ss_free is called automatically */
    /* by the server stub. In a local test, data is not automatically freed. */
#define rpc_ss_free free
#endif

idl_boolean is_part_available(number)
part_num number;
{
    part_record *part;                   /* a pointer to a part record */
    int found;

    found = read_part_record(number, &part);
    if(found)
       return(idl_true);
    else
       return(idl_false);
}


void whatis_part_name(number, name)
part_num  number;
```

Example D-4: Remote Procedures of the Inventory Application (continued)

```
part_name name;
{
    part_record *part;                        /* a pointer to a part record */
    char * strncpy();

    read_part_record(number, &part);
    strncpy((char *)name, (char *)part->name, MAX_STRING);
    return;
}

paragraph get_part_description(number)
part_num  number;
{
    part_record *part;                        /* a pointer to a part record */
    paragraph description;
    int size;
    char *strcpy();

    if( read_part_record(number, &part) ) {
        /* Allocated data that is returned to the client must be allocated */
        /* with the rpc_ss_allocate stub support routine.                  */
        size = strlen((char *)part->description) + 1;
        description = (paragraph)rpc_ss_allocate((unsigned)size);
        strcpy((char *)description, (char *)part->description);
    }
    else
        description = NULL;
    return(description);
}

void whatis_part_price(number, price)
part_num    number;
part_price  *price;
{
    part_record *part;                        /* a pointer to a part record */

    read_part_record(number, &part);
    price->units = part->price.units;
    price->per_unit = part->price.per_unit;
    return;
}
```

Example D-4: Remote Procedures of the Inventory Application (continued)

```
void whatis_part_quantity(number, quantity)
part_num        number;
part_quantity *quantity;
{
    part_record *part;                    /* a pointer to a part record */

    read_part_record(number, &part);
    quantity->units = part->quantity.units;
    switch(quantity->units) {
        case ITEM: quantity->total.number = part->quantity.total.number;
                break;
        case KILOGRAM:
        case GRAM: quantity->total.weight = part->quantity.total.weight;
                break;
    }
    return;
}


void whatare_subparts(number, subpart_ptr)
part_num number;
part_list **subpart_ptr;
{
    part_record *part;                          /* pointer to a part record */
    int i;
    int size;

    read_part_record(number, &part);

    /* Allocated data that is output to the client must be allocated with   */
    /* the rpc_ss_allocate stub support routine.  Allocate for a part_list  */
    /* struct plus the array of subpart numbers.  Remember the part_list    */
    /* struct already has an array with one element, hence the -1.          */
    size = sizeof(part_list) + (sizeof(part_num) * (part->subparts.size-1));
    *subpart_ptr = (part_list *)rpc_ss_allocate((unsigned)size);

    /* fill in the values */
    (*subpart_ptr)->size = part->subparts.size;
    for(i = 0; i < (*subpart_ptr)->size; i++)
        (*subpart_ptr)->numbers[i] = part->subparts.numbers[i];
    return;
}


idl_long_int order_part(number, quantity, account)
part_num        number;
part_quantity *quantity;
account_num    account;
{
    part_record *part;          /* pointer to a part record */

    long error = 1;  /* assume no error to start */
    /* Test for valid input */
    if( !read_part_record(number, &part) ) /* invalid part number input */
```

```
        error = -1;
    else if(quantity->units == ITEM)         /* invalid quantity input     */
        error = (quantity->total.number <= 0) ? -2 : error;
    else if(quantity->units == GRAM || quantity->units == KILOGRAM)
        error = (quantity->total.weight <= 0.0) ? -2 : error;
    /* else if()    invalid account, not implemented */
    /*     error = -3;                                    */
    if(error < 0)
        return(error);

    /* convert input quantity & units if units are not correct for part */
    if(quantity->units != part->quantity.units) {
        if(part->quantity.units == ITEM)      /* convert weight to items    */
            quantity->total.number = (idl_long_int)quantity->total.weight;
        else if(quantity->units == ITEM)      /* convert items to weight    */
            quantity->total.weight = (idl_long_float)quantity->total.number;
        else if(quantity->units == GRAM && part->quantity.units == KILOGRAM)
            quantity->total.weight /= 1000.0; /* convert grams to kilograms */
        else if(quantity->units == KILOGRAM && part->quantity.units == GRAM)
            quantity->total.weight *= 1000.0; /* convert kilograms to grams */
        quantity->units = part->quantity.units;
    }

    /* check if enough in inventory for this order */
    switch(part->quantity.units) {
    case ITEM:
        if(part->quantity.total.number > quantity->total.number)
            /* reduce quantity in inventory by amount ordered */
            part->quantity.total.number -= quantity->total.number;
        else {
            /* order all available and reduce quantity in inventory to 0 */
            quantity->total.number = part->quantity.total.number;
            part->quantity.total.number = 0;
        }
        break;
    case KILOGRAM:
    case GRAM:
        if(part->quantity.total.weight > quantity->total.weight)
            /* reduce quantity in inventory by amount ordered */
            part->quantity.total.weight -= quantity->total.weight;
        else {
            /* order all available and reduce quantity in inventory to 0.0 */
            quantity->total.weight = part->quantity.total.weight;
            part->quantity.total.weight = 0.0;
        }
        break;
    }

    write_part_record(part);    /* update inventory */

    return(1); /* order ok */
}
```

Example D-5: The Inventory Implementation

```
/* FILE NAME: implement_inventory.c */
/* A sample implementation of an inventory.                              */
/* For simplicity, a few inventory items are maintained in the inventory.  */
/* The valid numbers are printed when the open_inventory() procedure is   */
/* called so the user knows what numbers to test.                        */
#include <stdio.h>
#include "inventory.h"
#define MAX_PARTS    10       /* maximum number of parts in this inventory */
#define MAX_SUBPARTS 5        /* maximum number of subparts for a part     */

static part_record *rec[MAX_PARTS]; /* array of pointers for this inventory */
static inventory_is_open = 0;       /* flag is reset to non-zero when open  */

/* Data for empty record or unknown part number */
static part_record no_part = {0,"UNKNOWN"};
static part_num    no_subparts[MAX_SUBPARTS];

void open_inventory()  /***** setup inventory ******************************/
{
   int i,j;
   unsigned size;
   char *malloc(), *strcpy(), *strncpy();

   /* Allocate memory for the inventory array. Each part gets the size of  */
   /* a part_record plus enough memory for a subpart list. Since the       */
   /* subpart list is already defined in the part_record as an array of 1, */
   /* the new array memory only needs to be MAX_SUBPARTS-1 in size.        */
   for(i = 0; i < MAX_PARTS; i++) {
      size = sizeof(part_record) + (sizeof(part_num) * (MAX_SUBPARTS-1));
      rec[i] = (part_record *)malloc(size);
   }
   /* assign some data to the inventory array (part of an exercise machine) */
   rec[0]->number            = 102;
   strncpy((char *)rec[0]->name, "electronics display module", MAX_STRING);
   rec[0]->description = (paragraph)malloc(1000);
   strcpy((char *)rec[0]->description,
      "The electronics display module is a liquid crystal display containing\n\
a timer, counter, metronome, and calorie counter.");
   rec[0]->price.units       = ITEM;
   rec[0]->price.per_unit     = 7.00;
   rec[0]->quantity.units     = rec[0]->price.units;
   rec[0]->quantity.total.number = 432;
   rec[0]->subparts.size      = 4;  /* cannot be greater than MAX_SUBPARTS */
   for(i = 0; i < rec[0]->subparts.size; i++) /* values used are not relevant */
      rec[0]->subparts.numbers[i] = rec[0]->number + 1 + i;

   rec[1]->number            = 203;
   strncpy((char *)rec[1]->name, "base assembly", MAX_STRING);
   rec[1]->description = (paragraph)malloc(1000);
   strcpy((char *)rec[1]->description,
      "The base assembly rests on the floor to stabilize the machine.\n\
The arm and bench assemblies are attached to it.");
   rec[1]->price.units       = ITEM;
```

Example D-5: The Inventory Implementation (continued)

```
    rec[1]->price.per_unit        = 85.00;
    rec[1]->quantity.units        = rec[1]->price.units;
    rec[1]->quantity.total.number = 1078;
    rec[1]->subparts.size         = 5;  /* cannot be greater than MAX_SUBPARTS */
    for(i = 0; i < rec[1]->subparts.size; i++) /* values used are not relevant */
        rec[1]->subparts.numbers[i] = rec[1]->number + 17 + i;

    rec[2]->number                = 444;
    strncpy((char *)rec[2]->name, "ballast", MAX_STRING);
    rec[2]->description = (paragraph)malloc(1000);
    strcpy((char *)rec[2]->description,
        "The ballast is used to counter balance the force exerted by the user.");
    rec[2]->price.units           = KILOGRAM;
    rec[2]->price.per_unit        = 1.59;
    rec[2]->quantity.units        = rec[2]->price.units;
    rec[2]->quantity.total.weight = 13456.2;
    rec[2]->subparts.size         = 0;  /* cannot be greater than MAX_SUBPARTS */
    for(i = 0; i < MAX_SUBPARTS; i++)  /* zero out subpart array */
        rec[2]->subparts.numbers[i] = no_subparts[i];

    /* fill in rest of inventory as "empty" data */
    for(i = 3; i < MAX_PARTS; i++) {
        rec[i] = &no_part;
        for(j = 0; j < MAX_SUBPARTS; j++)
            rec[i]->subparts.numbers[j] = no_subparts[j];
    }
    puts("Part numbers in inventory:");
    for(i = 0; i < MAX_PARTS; i++)
        if(rec[i]->number > 0)
            printf("%ld\n", rec[i]->number);
    inventory_is_open = 1;
    return;
}


void close_inventory()   /**** close inventory ******************************/
{
    /* Undo whatever is done in open_inventory.  Free memory and so forth.   */
    /* (not implemented) */
    return;
}


int read_part_record(number, part_ptr) /** get record for this part number **/
part_num number;
part_record **part_ptr;
{
    int i;

    if(inventory_is_open == 0)
        open_inventory();
    *part_ptr = &no_part;                    /* initialize assuming no part */
    for(i = 0; i < MAX_PARTS; i++)           /* search the inventory        */
        if(rec[i]->number == number) {       /* found the part              */
```

Example D-5: The Inventory Implementation (continued)

```
            *part_ptr = rec[i];
            break;
        }
    if( (*part_ptr)->number > 0)
        return(1);
    else                                      /* not a valid part          */
        return(0);
}


int write_part_record(part)   /*** update inventory for this part number *****/
part_record *part;
{
    int i;

    if(inventory_is_open == 0)
        open_inventory();
    for(i = 0; i < MAX_PARTS; i++)
        if(rec[i]->number == part->number) {
            rec[i] = part;   /* overwrite inventory with new data */
            return(1);
        }
    return(0);
}
/*<COMMENT> dump the part data to the screen.
static dump_part_record(index)
int index;
{
    printf("number input:%ld  part number:%ld\n", number, rec[index]->number);
    printf("part name:%s\n", rec[index]->name);
    printf("description:%s\n", rec[index]->description);
    printf("price:%f per %s\n", rec[index]->price.per_unit,\
        (rec[index]->price.units == ITEM) ? "item" : "gram");
    printf("quantity:");
    switch(rec[index]->quantity.units) {
    case ITEM: printf("%ld items\n", rec[index]->quantity.total.number); break;
    case GRAM: printf("%f grams\n", rec[index]->quantity.total.weight); break;
    case KILOGRAM: printf("%f kilos\n", rec[index]->quantity.total.weight); break;
    }
    printf("subparts: ");
    for(i = 0; i < rec[index]->subparts.size; i++)
        printf("%ld  ", rec[index]->subparts.numbers[i]);
    printf("\n");
}<ENDCOMMENT>*/
```

Example D-6: Server Initialization of the Inventory Application

```
/* FILE NAME: i_server.c */
#include <stdio.h>
#include <ctype.h>
```

Example D-6: Server Initialization of the Inventory Application (continued)

```
#include "inventory.h"           /* header created by the IDL compiler    */
#include "check_status.h"        /* contains the CHECK_STATUS macro        */
#define STRINGLEN 50

main (argc, argv)
int argc;
char *argv[];
{
    unsigned32          status;          /* error status (nbase.h)          */
                                         /* RPC vectors                     */
    rpc_binding_vector_t *binding_vector; /* binding handle list (rpcbase.h) */
    rpc_protseq_vector_t *protseq_vector; /*protocol sequence list(rpcbase.h)*/

    char entry_name[STRINGLEN];          /* name service entry name         */
    char group_name[STRINGLEN];          /* name service group name         */
    char annotation[STRINGLEN];          /* annotation for endpoint map     */
    char hostname[STRINGLEN];
    char *strcpy(), *strcat();
/*********************** REGISTER INTERFACE **************************/
    rpc_server_register_if(                                          /*  */
        inventory_v1_0_s_ifspec,      /* interface specification (inventory.h) */
        NULL,
        NULL,
        &status
    );
    CHECK_STATUS(status, "Can't register interface:", ABORT);        /*  */

/***************** CREATING SERVER BINDING INFORMATION *****************/
    if(argc > 1) {
        rpc_server_use_protseq(             /* use a protocol sequence        */
            (unsigned_char_t *)argv[1],     /* the input protocol sequence    */
            rpc_c_protseq_max_calls_default, /* (rpcbase.h)                    */
            &status
        );
        CHECK_STATUS(status, "Can't use this protocol sequence:", ABORT);
    }
    else {
        puts("You can invoke the server with a protocol sequence argument.");
        rpc_server_use_all_protseqs(         /* use all protocol sequences     */
            rpc_c_protseq_max_calls_default,  /* (rpcbase.h)                    */
            &status
        );
        CHECK_STATUS(status, "Can't register protocol sequences:", ABORT);
    }

    rpc_server_inq_bindings(     /* get all binding information for server    */
        &binding_vector,
        &status
    );
    CHECK_STATUS(status, "Can't get binding information:", ABORT);

/*************************** ADVERTISE SERVER ****************************/
```

Example D-6: Server Initialization of the Inventory Application (continued)

```
strcpy(entry_name, "/.:/inventory_");
gethostname(hostname, STRINGLEN);
strcat(entry_name, hostname);
rpc_ns_binding_export(          /* export to a name service database    */
    rpc_c_ns_syntax_default,    /* syntax of entry name (rpcbase.h)     */
    (unsigned_char_t *)entry_name, /* name of entry in name service     */
    inventory_v1_0_s_ifspec,    /* interface specification (inventory.h) */
    binding_vector,             /* binding information                  */
    NULL,                       /* no object UUIDs exported             */
    &status
);
CHECK_STATUS(status, "Can't export to name service database:", RESUME);

strcpy(group_name, "/.:/inventory_group");
rpc_ns_group_mbr_add(           /* add as member of name service group  */
    rpc_c_ns_syntax_default,    /* syntax of group name (rpcbase.h)     */
    (unsigned_char_t *)group_name, /* name of group in name service     */
    rpc_c_ns_syntax_default,    /* syntax of member name (rpcbase.h)    */
    (unsigned_char_t *)entry_name, /* name of member in name service    */
    &status
);
CHECK_STATUS(status, "Can't add member to name service group:", RESUME);

/************************** MANAGE ENDPOINTS **************************/
strcpy(annotation, "Inventory interface");
rpc_ep_register(                /* add endpoints to local endpoint map  */
    inventory_v1_0_s_ifspec,    /* interface specification (inventory.h) */
    binding_vector,             /* vector of server binding handles     */
    NULL,                       /* no object UUIDs to register          */
    (unsigned_char_t *)annotation, /* annotation supplied (not required) */
    &status
);
CHECK_STATUS(status, "Can't add endpoints to local endpoint map:", RESUME);

rpc_binding_vector_free(                 /* free server binding handles  */
    &binding_vector,
    &status
);
CHECK_STATUS(status, "Can't free server binding handles:", RESUME);

open_inventory();               /* application specific procedure */

/****************** LISTEN FOR REMOTE PROCEDURE CALLS ******************/
TRY                             /* thread exception handling macro      */
    rpc_server_listen(                                       /*     */
        1,                      /* process one remote procedure call at a time */
        &status
    );
    CHECK_STATUS(status, "rpc listen failed:", RESUME);

FINALLY                                     /* error recovery and cleanup */
    close_inventory();                  /* application specific procedure */
    rpc_server_inq_bindings(            /* get binding information    */
        &binding_vector,
```

Example D-6: Server Initialization of the Inventory Application (continued)

```
            &status
        );
        CHECK_STATUS(status, "Can't get binding information:", RESUME);

        rpc_ep_unregister(      /* remove endpoints from local endpoint map   */
            inventory_v1_0_s_ifspec,  /* interface specification (inventory.h) */
            binding_vector,                 /* vector of server binding handles */
            NULL,                                      /* no object UUIDs */
            &status
        );
        CHECK_STATUS(status, "Can't remove endpoints from endpoint map:", RESUME);

        rpc_binding_vector_free(                /* free server binding handles   */
            &binding_vector,
            &status
        );
        CHECK_STATUS(status, "Can't free server binding handles:", RESUME);

        puts("\nServer quit!");
    ENDTRY
}   /* END SERVER INITIALIZATION */
```

Example D-7: The Automatic Client File of the Inventory Application

```
/* FILE NAME: i_client.c */
/******************** Client of the inventory application ********************/
#include <stdio.h>
#include <stdlib.h>
#include "inventory.h"          /* header file created by the IDL compiler */

char instructions[] = "Type character followed by appropriate argument(s).\n\
    Is part available?               a  [part_number]\n\
    What is part name?               n  [part_number]\n\
    Get part description.            d  [part_number]\n\
    What is part price?              p  [part_number]\n\
    What is part quantity?           q  [part_number]\n\
    What are subparts of this part?  s  [part_number]\n\
    Order part.                      o  part_number  quantity\n\
    REDISPLAY                        r\n\
    EXIT                             e\n";

main()
{
    part_record part;               /* structure for all data about a part   */
    part_list   *subparts;          /* pointer to parts list data structure  */
    account_num account = 1234;     /* a user account number                 */

    int i, num_args, done = 0;
    long result;
    char input[100], selection[20], quantity[20];
    char *strcpy();

    puts(instructions);
```

Example D-7: The Automatic Client File of the Inventory Application (continued)

```
part.number = 0;
strcpy(quantity, "");
while(!done) {                    /* user makes selections and each is processed */
    printf("Selection: "); fflush(stdout); gets(input);
    num_args = sscanf(input, "%s%ld%s", selection, &(part.number), quantity);

    switch (tolower(selection[0])) {
    case 'a': if (is_part_available(part.number))
                  puts("available: Yes");
              else
                  puts("available: No");
              break;
    case 'n': whatis_part_name(part.number, part.name);
              printf("name:%s\n", part.name);
              break;
    case 'd': part.description = get_part_description(part.number);
              printf("description:\n%s\n", part.description);
              if(part.description != NULL)
                  free(part.description);     /* free memory allocated */
              break;
    case 'p': whatis_part_price(part.number, &(part.price));
              printf("price:%10.2f\n", part.price.per_unit);
              break;
    case 'q': whatis_part_quantity(part.number, &(part.quantity));
              if(part.quantity.units == ITEM)
                  printf("total items:%ld\n", part.quantity.total.number);
              else if(part.quantity.units == GRAM)
                  printf("total grams:%10.2f\n", part.quantity.total.weight);
              else if(part.quantity.units == KILOGRAM)
                  printf("total kilos:%10.2f\n", part.quantity.total.weight);
              break;
    case 's': whatare_subparts(part.number, &subparts);
              for(i = 0; i < subparts->size; i++)
                  printf("%ld ", subparts->numbers[i]);
              printf("\ntotal number of subparts:%ld\n", subparts->size);
              free(subparts);        /* free memory for conformant struct */
              break;
    case 'o': if(num_args < 3) {
                  puts("Not enough arguments");
                  break;
              }
              /* Assume KILOGRAM units and assign quantity input */
              part.quantity.units = KILOGRAM;
              part.quantity.total.weight = atof(quantity);
              result = order_part(part.number, &(part.quantity), account);
              if(result > 0) {
                if(part.quantity.units == ITEM)
                  printf("order:%ld items\n", part.quantity.total.number);
                else if(part.quantity.units == GRAM)
                  printf("order:%10.2f grams\n", part.quantity.total.weight);
                else if(part.quantity.units == KILOGRAM)
                  printf("order:%10.2f kilos\n", part.quantity.total.weight);
```

Example D-7: The Automatic Client File of the Inventory Application (continued)

```
            }
            else { /* error cases */
                if(result == -1) puts("Invalid part number");
                else if(result == -2) puts("Invalid quantity");
                else if(result == -3) puts("Invalid account number");
            }
            break;
    case 'r':   /* redisplay selection or bad input displays instructions */
    default: puts(instructions);  break;
    case 'e': done = 1;  break;
    } /*end case */
  } /* end while */
} /* end main() */
```

Example D-8: The Implicit Client of the Inventory Application

```
/* FILE NAME: implicit_client.c */
/******* Client of the inventory application with implicit method **********/
#include <stdio.h>
#include <stdlib.h>
#include "inventory.h"          /* header file created by the IDL compiler */

char instructions[] = "Type character followed by appropriate argument(s).\n\
    Is part available?               a  [part_number]\n\
    What is part name?               n  [part_number]\n\
    Get part description.            d  [part_number]\n\
    What is part price?              p  [part_number]\n\
    What is part quantity?           q  [part_number]\n\
    What are subparts of this part?  s  [part_number]\n\
    Order part.                      o  part_number  quantity\n\
    REDISPLAY                        r\n\
    EXIT                             e\n";

main()
{
    part_record part;           /* structure for all data about a part  */
    part_list   *subparts;      /* pointer to parts list data structure */
    account_num account = 1234; /* a user account number                */

    int i, num_args, done = 0;
    long result;
    char input[100], selection[20], quantity[20];
    char *strcpy();

    puts(instructions);
    part.number = 0;
    strcpy(quantity, "");

#ifndef LOCAL                   /* find server in name service database */
    do_import_binding("/.:/inventory_group", &global_binding_h);
#endif
```

Example D-8: The Implicit Client of the Inventory Application (continued)

```
while(!done) {             /* user makes selections and each is processed */
    printf("Selection: ");  fflush(stdout);  gets(input);
    num_args = sscanf(input, "%s%ld%s", selection, &(part.number), quantity);

    switch (tolower(selection[0])) {
    case 'a': if (is_part_available(part.number))
                  puts("available: Yes");
              else
                  puts("available: No");
              break;
    case 'n': whatis_part_name(part.number, part.name);
              printf("name:%s\n", part.name);
              break;
    case 'd': part.description = get_part_description(part.number);
              printf("description:\n%s\n", part.description);
              if(part.description != NULL)
                  free(part.description);       /* free memory allocated */
              break;
    case 'p': whatis_part_price(part.number, &(part.price));
              printf("price:%10.2f\n", part.price.per_unit);
              break;
    case 'q': whatis_part_quantity(part.number, &(part.quantity));
              if(part.quantity.units == ITEM)
                  printf("total items:%ld\n", part.quantity.total.number);
              else if(part.quantity.units == GRAM)
                  printf("total grams:%10.2f\n", part.quantity.total.weight);
              else if(part.quantity.units == KILOGRAM)
                  printf("total kilos:%10.2f\n", part.quantity.total.weight);
              break;
    case 's': whatare_subparts(part.number, &subparts);
              for(i = 0; i < subparts->size; i++)
                  printf("%ld ", subparts->numbers[i]);
              printf("\ntotal number of subparts:%ld\n", subparts->size);
              free(subparts);         /* free memory for conformant struct */
              break;
    case 'o': if(num_args < 3) {
                  puts("Not enough arguments");
                  break;
              }
              /* Assume KILOGRAM units and assign quantity input */
              part.quantity.units = KILOGRAM;
              part.quantity.total.weight = atof(quantity);
              result = order_part(part.number, &(part.quantity), account);
              if(result > 0) {
                  if(part.quantity.units == ITEM)
                    printf("order:%ld items\n", part.quantity.total.number);
                  else if(part.quantity.units == GRAM)
                    printf("order:%10.2f grams\n", part.quantity.total.weight);
                  else if(part.quantity.units == KILOGRAM)
                    printf("order:%10.2f kilos\n", part.quantity.total.weight);
              }
```

Example D-8: The Implicit Client of the Inventory Application (continued)

```
                else { /* error cases */
                   if(result == -1) puts("Invalid part number");
                   else if(result == -2) puts("Invalid quantity");
                   else if(result == -3) puts("Invalid account number");
                }
                break;
      case 'r':   /* redisplay selection or bad input displays instructions */
      default:  puts(instructions);  break;
      case 'e': done = 1;  break;
      } /*end case */
   } /* end while */
} /* end main() */
```

Example D-9: The Explicit Client of the Inventory Application

```
/* FILE NAME: explicit_client.c */
/******* Client of the inventory application with explicit method ***********/
#include <stdio.h>
#include <stdlib.h>
#include "inventory.h"            /* header file created by the IDL compiler */

char instructions[] = "Type character followed by appropriate argument(s).\n\
   Is part available?                a  [part_number]\n\
   What is part name?                n  [part_number]\n\
   Get part description.             d  [part_number]\n\
   What is part price?               p  [part_number]\n\
   What is part quantity?            q  [part_number]\n\
   What are subparts of this part?   s  [part_number]\n\
   Order part.                       o  part_number  quantity\n\
   REDISPLAY                         r\n\
   EXIT                              e\n";

main()
{
    part_record part;            /* structure for all data about a part   */
    part_list    *subparts;      /* pointer to parts list data structure */
    account_num account = 1234;  /* a user account number                */

    handle_t     binding_h;      /* declare a binding handle */

    int i, num_args, done = 0;
    long result;
    char input[100], selection[20], quantity[20];
    char *strcpy();

    puts(instructions);
    part.number = 0;
    strcpy(quantity, "");
```

Example D-9: The Explicit Client of the Inventory Application (continued)

```
#ifndef LOCAL                           /* find server in name service database */
   do_import_binding("/.:/inventory_group", &binding_h);
#endif

   while(!done) {             /* user makes selections and each is processed */
     printf("Selection: ");  fflush(stdout);  gets(input);
     num_args = sscanf(input, "%s%ld%s", selection, &(part.number), quantity);

     switch (tolower(selection[0])) {
     case 'a': if (is_part_available(binding_h, part.number))
                    puts("available: Yes");
               else
                    puts("available: No");
               break;
     case 'n': whatis_part_name(binding_h, part.number, part.name);
               printf("name:%s\n", part.name);
               break;
     case 'd': part.description =
                    get_part_description(binding_h, part.number);
               printf("description:\n%s\n", part.description);
               if(part.description != NULL)
                    free(part.description);        /* free memory allocated */
               break;
     case 'p': whatis_part_price(binding_h, part.number, &(part.price));
               printf("price:%10.2f\n", part.price.per_unit);
               break;
     case 'q': whatis_part_quantity(binding_h, part.number, &(part.quantity));
               if(part.quantity.units == ITEM)
                    printf("total items:%ld\n", part.quantity.total.number);
               else if(part.quantity.units == GRAM)
                    printf("total grams:%10.2f\n", part.quantity.total.weight);
               else if(part.quantity.units == KILOGRAM)
                    printf("total kilos:%10.2f\n", part.quantity.total.weight);
               break;
     case 's': whatare_subparts(binding_h, part.number, &subparts);
               for(i = 0; i < subparts->size; i++)
                    printf("%ld ", subparts->numbers[i]);
               printf("\ntotal number of subparts:%ld\n", subparts->size);
               free(subparts);            /* free memory for conformant struct */
               break;
     case 'o': if(num_args < 3) {
                    puts("Not enough arguments");
                    break;
               }
               /* Assume KILOGRAM units and assign quantity input */
               part.quantity.units = KILOGRAM;
               part.quantity.total.weight = atof(quantity);
               result =
                 order_part(binding_h, part.number, &(part.quantity), account);
```

Example D-9: The Explicit Client of the Inventory Application (continued)

```
                if(result > 0) {
                  if(part.quantity.units == ITEM)
                    printf("order:%ld items\n", part.quantity.total.number);
                  else if(part.quantity.units == GRAM)
                    printf("order:%10.2f grams\n", part.quantity.total.weight);
                  else if(part.quantity.units == KILOGRAM)
                    printf("order:%10.2f kilos\n", part.quantity.total.weight);
                }
                else { /* error cases */
                  if(result == -1) puts("Invalid part number");
                  else if(result == -2) puts("Invalid quantity");
                  else if(result == -3) puts("Invalid account number");
                }
                break;
      case 'r':    /* redisplay selection or bad input displays instructions */
      default: puts(instructions);  break;
      case 'e': done = 1;  break;
      } /*end case */
    } /* end while */
} /* end main() */
```

Example D-10: The Makefile for the Implicit Client

```
# FILE NAME: Makefile
# Makefile for the inventory client that uses an ACF and implicit binding
#
# definitions for this make file
#
APPL=inventory
IDLCMD=idl -v
LIBDCE=-ldce -lcma        #OSF/1: DCE libraries
LIBS=$(LIBDCE) -li -ldnet #MIPS ULTRIX: DCE, internationalization & DECnet
CHECK=../../arithmetic     # directory containing check_status.h
CFLAGS=
CC= cc

#
# COMPLETE BUILD of this application.
#
all:  local interface client server

#
# LOCAL BUILD of the implicit client to test locally.
#
local:interface implicit_client.c ../i_procedures.c ../implement_inventory.c
        $(CC) $(CFLAGS) -I../ -I$(CHECK) -DLOCAL -o local_implicit_client.exe \
              implicit_client.c ../i_procedures.c ../implement_inventory.c
#remove object files so they do not interfere with the distributed build
        rm implicit_client.o i_procedures.o implement_inventory.o
```

Example D-10: The Makefile for the Implicit Client (continued)

```
#
# INTERFACE BUILD that uses an ACF for implicit binding.
# Notice this builds only the client stub and the header files.
#
interface:   $(APPL).acf $(APPL).h $(APPL)_cstub.o
$(APPL).h $(APPL)_cstub.o:     ../$(APPL).idl $(APPL).acf
        $(IDLCMD) -I../ -server none ../$(APPL).idl


#
# CLIENT BUILD
#
client:      implicit_client
implicit_client:   interface implicit_client.o \
   do_import_binding.o do_interpret_binding.o
        $(CC) $(CFLAGS) -I../ -o implicit_client.exe implicit_client.o \
             do_import_binding.o do_interpret_binding.o \
                $(APPL)_cstub.o $(LIBS)

do_import_binding.o:    do_import_binding.c
        $(CC) $(CFLAGS) -I../ -I$(CHECK) -c do_import_binding.c

do_interpret_binding.o:  do_interpret_binding.c
        $(CC) $(CFLAGS) -I../ -I$(CHECK) -c do_interpret_binding.c


#
# SERVER BUILD
#
server:
        @echo make server in directory ../


#
# files needed from other directories
#
i_procedures.o:    ../i_procedures.c
        $(CC) $(CFLAGS) -I../ -c ../i_procedures.c

implement_inventory.o:    ../implement_inventory.c
        $(CC) $(CFLAGS) -I../ -c ../implement_inventory.c
```

Example D-11: An ACF File for Implicit Binding

```
/* FILE NAME: inventory.acf (implicit version)*/
/* This Attribute Configuration File is used in conjunction with the     */
/* associated IDL file (inventory.idl) when the IDL compiler is invoked. */
[
implicit_handle(handle_t global_binding_h)  /* implicit binding method  */
]
interface  inventory    /* The interface name must match the idl file.  */
{
}
```

Example D-12: The do_import_binding Procedure

```
/* FILE NAME: do_import_binding.c */
/* Get binding from name service database. */
#include <stdio.h>
#include "inventory.h"
#include "check_status.h"

void do_import_binding(entry_name, binding_h)
char                    entry_name[];      /* entry name to begin search    */
rpc_binding_handle_t *binding_h;         /* a binding handle (rpcbase.h)  */
{
    unsigned32      status;               /* error status (nbase.h)          */
    rpc_ns_handle_t import_context;       /* required to import (rpcbase.h) */
    char            protseq[20];          /* protocol sequence               */

    rpc_ns_binding_import_begin(  /* set context to import binding handles  */
        rpc_c_ns_syntax_default,           /* use default syntax              */
        (unsigned_char_t *)entry_name, /* begin search with this name      */
        inventory_v1_0_c_ifspec,   /* interface specification (inventory.h) */
        NULL,                       /* no optional object UUID required      */
        &import_context,            /* import context obtained               */
        &status
    );
    CHECK_STATUS(status, "Can't begin import:", RESUME);

    while(1) {
        rpc_ns_binding_import_next(                /* import a binding handle  */
            import_context,        /* context from rpc_ns_binding_import_begin */
            binding_h,             /* a binding handle is obtained             */
            &status
        );
        if(status != rpc_s_ok) {
            CHECK_STATUS(status, "Can't import a binding handle:", RESUME);
            break;
        }
```

Example D-12: The do_import_binding Procedure (continued)

```
        /** application-specific selection criteria (by protocol sequence) *  */
        do_interpret_binding(*binding_h ,protseq);
        if(strcmp(protseq, "ncacn_ip_tcp") == 0)  /*select connection protocol*/
           break;
        else {
           rpc_binding_free(          /* free binding information not selected   */
              binding_h,
              &status
           );
           CHECK_STATUS(status, "Can't free binding information:", RESUME);
        }
    } /*end while */

    rpc_ns_binding_import_done(                    /* done with import context   */
        &import_context,          /* obtained from rpc_ns_binding_import_begin */
        &status
    );
    return;
}
```

Example D-13: The do_interpret_binding Procedure

```
/* FILE NAME: do_interpret_binding.c */
/* Interpret binding information and return the protocol sequence. */
#include <stdio.h>
#include <dce/rpc.h>
#include "check_status.h"

void do_interpret_binding(binding, protocol_seq)
rpc_binding_handle_t binding;    /* binding handle to interpret (rpcbase.h) */
char                 *protocol_seq;   /* protocol sequence to obtain         */
{
    unsigned32       status;          /* error status                       */
    unsigned_char_t *string_binding;  /* string of binding info. (lbase.h) */
    unsigned_char_t *protseq;         /* binding component of interest      */

    rpc_binding_to_string_binding(/* convert binding information to string  */
        binding,                          /* the binding handle to convert */
        &string_binding,                  /* the string of binding data    */
        &status
    );
    CHECK_STATUS(status, "Can't get string binding:", RESUME);
```

Example D-13: The do_interpret_binding Procedure (continued)

```
rpc_string_binding_parse(          /* get components of string binding   */
    string_binding,         /* the string of binding data               */
    NULL,                   /* an object UUID string is not obtained     */
    &protseq,               /* a protocol sequence string IS obtained    */
    NULL,                   /* a network address string is not obtained  */
    NULL,                   /* an endpoint string is not obtained        */
    NULL,                   /* a network options string is not obtained  */
    &status
);
CHECK_STATUS(status, "Can't parse string binding:", RESUME);

strcpy(protocol_seq, (char *)protseq);

/* free all strings allocated by other runtime routines              */
rpc_string_free(&string_binding,  &status);
rpc_string_free(&protseq,         &status);
return;
}
```

Example D-14: The Makefile for the Explicit Client

```
# FILE NAME: Makefile
# Makefile for the inventory client that uses an ACF and explicit binding
#
# definitions for this make file
#
APPL=inventory
IDLCMD=idl -v
LIBDCE=-ldce -lcma      #OSF/1: DCE libraries
LIBS=$(LIBDCE) -li -ldnet #MIPS ULTRIX: DCE, internationalization, DECnet
CHECK=../../arithmetic  # directory containing check_status.h
CFLAGS=
CC= cc

#
# COMPLETE BUILD of this application.
#
all:  interface client server


#
# LOCAL BUILD
# No local build is developed for the explicit client because the remote
# procedure implementations for the server have been developed without
# explicit binding.  In order to test this client locally, the remote
# procedure implementations need to have a binding handle as the first
# parameter.
#
```

Example D-14: The Makefile for the Explicit Client (continued)

```
#
# INTERFACE BUILD that uses an ACF for explicit binding.
# Notice this builds only the client stub and the header files.
#
interface:   $(APPL).acf $(APPL).h $(APPL)_cstub.o
$(APPL).h $(APPL)_cstub.o:     ../$(APPL).idl $(APPL).acf
         $(IDLCMD) -I../ -server none ../$(APPL).idl


#
# CLIENT BUILD
#
client:      explicit_client
explicit_client:   interface explicit_client.o \
   do_import_binding.o do_interpret_binding.o
         $(CC) $(CFLAGS) -I../ -o explicit_client.exe explicit_client.o \
              do_import_binding.o do_interpret_binding.o \
                  $(APPL)_cstub.o $(LIBS)


#
# SERVER BUILD
#
server:
         @echo make server in directory ../


#
# files needed from other directories
#
i_procedures.o:    ../i_procedures.c
         $(CC) $(CFLAGS) -I../ -c ../i_procedures.c

implement_inventory.o:    ../implement_inventory.c
         $(CC) $(CFLAGS) -I../ -c ../implement_inventory.c

do_import_binding.o:    ../implicit/do_import_binding.c
         $(CC) $(CFLAGS) -I$(CHECK) -c ../implicit/do_import_binding.c

do_interpret_binding.o:  ../implicit/do_interpret_binding.c
         $(CC) $(CFLAGS) -I$(CHECK) -c ../implicit/do_interpret_binding.c
```

Example D-15: An ACF File for Explicit Binding

```
/* FILE NAME: inventory.acf (explicit version) */
/* This Attribute Configuration File is used in conjunction with the     */
/* associated IDL file (inventory.idl) when the IDL compiler is invoked. */
[
explicit_handle                              /* explicit binding method */
]
interface  inventory     /* The interface name must match the idl file. */
{
}
```

E

The OK Banking Application

The banking application creates, deletes, and performs rudimentary transactions on bank accounts. The client requests a bank account through an object UUID. The two versions of the program, presented in this appendix and Appendix F, illustrate two different ways to use object UUIDs.

The application in this chapter represents a relatively crude access to bank accounts. The UUID is used as an ID for each account. The new techniques shown in this appendix include:

* Creating a UUID

* Manipulating UUID lists

* Exporting UUIDs to the name service and endpoint map

* Importing an interface by UUID

How To Run the Application

To build and start the server, type the following:

```
S> make interface server
S> i_server
```

To build and run the client, type the following:

```
C> make interface client
C> i_client
```

The client displays a menu of operations and you can begin to create and manage accounts.

Application files

Makefile contains descriptions of how the application is compiled (see Example E-1).

banking.idl contains the description of the constants, data types, and procedures for the interface (see Example E-2).

banking.acf customizes how you use an interface. In this application it ensures that communication errors are reported back as variables to the client (see Example E-3).

check_status.h is an expanded version of the CHECK_STATUS macro used in other chapters. In this file, two macros are defined, one for checking communication errors and the other for checking errors pertaining to access to bank accounts (see Example E-4).

svr_support.h contains extra definitions required by the server code (see Example E-5).

ok_svr_main.c contains the initialization for the server, including the preparation and display of the list of bank accounts (see Example E-6).

ok_mgr.c is the implementation of all the remote procedures defined in this interface (see Example E-7).

svr_support.c includes server functions called by the initialization file **ok_svr_main.c** and by the remote procedures in **ok_mgr.c** (see Example E-8).

ok_mgmt_auth.c contains the management authorization function that shuts down the server at the request of the client (see Example E-9).

ok_client.c is the client, which displays a menu of functions and invokes remote procedures on the server. The file includes the *get_id_and_binding* function, which queries the user for a UUID by which to access the bank account (see Example E-10).

ok_import.c contains two functions that choose a server. The client uses *import_interface* to find a server when creating a new account or shutting down servers. For other transactions it uses *import_resource*, called from *get_id_and_binding* (see Example E-11).

Example E-1: The Makefile for the OK Banking Application

```
# FILE NAME: Makefile
#
# Makefile for the banking application
#
# definitions for this make file
#
APPL=banking
```

Example E-1: The Makefile for the OK Banking Application (continued)

```
IDLCMD=idl -v
CFLAGS = -D_SHARED_LIBRARIES -Dalpha -D_REENTRANT -g -w -I.    # DEC Alpha OSF/1
LIBDCE = -ldce -lpthreads -lc_r -lmach -lm              # DEC Alpha OSF/1
CC= cc


#
# COMPLETE BUILD of the application.
#
all:   interface client server


#
# INTERFACE BUILD
#
interface:   $(APPL).h $(APPL)_cstub.o $(APPL)_sstub.o
$(APPL).h $(APPL)_cstub.o $(APPL)_sstub.o: $(APPL).idl
         $(IDLCMD) $(APPL).idl


#
# CLIENT BUILD
#
client:      i_client
i_client:    ok_client.o ok_import.o $(APPL)_cstub.o
         $(CC) $(CFLAGS) -o banking_client ok_client.o ok_import.o \
                 $(APPL)_cstub.o $(LIBDCE)

ok_client.o: ok_client.c
         $(CC) $(CFLAGS) -c ok_client.c

ok_import.o: ok_import.c
         $(CC) $(CFLAGS) -c ok_import.c

#
# SERVER BUILD
#
server:      i_server
i_server:    $(APPL).h ok_svr_main.o ok_mgmt_auth.o \
                 ok_mgr.o svr_support.o \
                 $(APPL)_sstub.o
         $(CC) $(CFLAGS) -o banking_server ok_svr_main.o ok_mgmt_auth.o \
                 ok_mgr.o svr_support.o \
                 $(APPL)_sstub.o $(LIBDCE)

ok_svr_main.o:    ok_svr_main.c
         $(CC) $(CFLAGS) -c ok_svr_main.c

ok_mgmt_auth.o: ok_mgmt_auth.c
         $(CC) $(CFLAGS) -c ok_mgmt_auth.c

ok_mgr.o:    ok_mgr.c
         $(CC) $(CFLAGS) -c ok_mgr.c

svr_support.o:    svr_support.c
         $(CC) $(CFLAGS) -c svr_support.c
```

Example E-2: The IDL File of the OK Banking Application

```
/*
 * File name: banking.idl
 */
[
    uuid (54B40BC1-6E26-11CC-9E76-08002B245A45),
    version (1.0)
]
/*
 * Manages bank accounts
 */
interface banking
{
    const unsigned32 bank_s_ok            = 0;
    const unsigned32 bank_s_not_found     = 1001;
    const unsigned32 bank_s_insuf_funds   = 1002;
    const unsigned32 bank_s_file_open_fail = 1003;
    const unsigned32 bank_s_bug           = 1004;

    /*
     * Name to appear on the account.
     */
    typedef [string, ptr] char *account_name;

    /*
     * Account transaction types.
     */
    typedef enum {
        DEPOSIT,
        WITHDRAWAL,
        BALANCE
    } trans_type;

    uuid_t create_account (
        [in]  handle_t       binding_handle,
        [in]  account_name   name,
        [in]  unsigned32     opening_balance,
        [out] unsigned32     *bank_status
    );

    void delete_account (
        [in]  handle_t       binding_handle,
        [out] unsigned32     *bank_status
    );

    void transaction (
        [in]  handle_t       binding_handle,
        [in]  trans_type     trans_code,
        [in]  unsigned32     amount,
        [out] unsigned32     *balance,
        [out] unsigned32     *bank_status
    );
}
```

Example E-3: The ACF of the OK Banking Application

```
/*
 * File name: banking.acf
 */
interface banking
{
    create_account
    (
        [comm_status, fault_status] dce_status
    );

    delete_account
    (
        [comm_status, fault_status] dce_status
    );

    transaction
    (
        [comm_status, fault_status] dce_status
    );
}
```

Example E-4: Check Error Status Macros

```
/*
 * File name:  check_status.h
 *
 * Check status macros
 */
#include <stdio.h>
#include <dce/dce_error.h>
#define RESUME 0
#define ABORT  1

#define CHECK_DCE_STATUS(input_status, comment, action) \
{ \
    if (input_status != rpc_s_ok) \
    { \
        dce_error_inq_text (input_status, error_string, &error_stat); \
        fprintf (stderr, "%s %s\n", comment, error_string); \
        if (action == ABORT) \
        { \
            exit(1); \
        } \
    } \
}

static int error_stat;
static unsigned char error_string[dce_c_error_string_len];

#define CHECK_BANK_STATUS(input_status, comment, action) \
{ \
    if (input_status != bank_s_ok) \
```

Example E-4: Check Error Status Macros (continued)

```
    { \
        switch (input_status) \
        { \
            case bank_s_not_found: \
                strcpy (error_string, "Account not found\n"); \
                break; \
    \
            case bank_s_bug: \
                strcpy (error_string, "Unexpected error\n"); \
                break; \
    \
            case bank_s_insuf_funds: \
                strcpy (error_string, "Insufficient funds for transaction\n"); \
                break; \
    \
            case bank_s_file_open_fail: \
                strcpy (error_string,  "Unable to open the file\n"); \
                break; \
    \
            default: \
                strcpy (error_string, "Unknown error\n"); \
                break; \
        } \
    \
        fprintf (stderr, "%s %s\n", comment, error_string); \
    \
        if (action == ABORT) \
        { \
            exit(1); \
        } \
    } \
}
```

Example E-5: The svr_support.h File

```
/*
 * File name:  svr_support.h
 *
 * Header file for server support routines.
 */
/*
 * Max namespace entry name size.
 */
#define  STRINGLEN  50
/*
 * Resource map array element
 */
typedef struct
    {
```

Example E-5: The svr_support.h File (continued)

```
        uuid_t    resource_id;          /* Resource ID     */
        char      resource_file[128];   /* Associated file */
        } res_map_element_t;

typedef struct
    {
    int       count;
    res_map_element_t   map_element[1];
    } res_map_list_t;
```

Example E-6: Server Initialization of the OK Banking Application

```
/*
 * File name:  ok_svr_main.c
 *
 * Ok banking server initialization.
 */
#include <stdio.h>
#include <dce/dce_cf.h>         /* DCE configuration file, DCE provided */
#include "banking.h"            /* Application specific, IDL generated  */
#include "check_status.h"       /* Contains macros to check status      */
#include "svr_support.h"        /* Defines obj UUID/res map data type   */

#define bank_c_max_map_size 50       /* Obj UUID/res map size          */

res_map_list_t      *res_map_list;    /* Object UUID/resource map      */
rpc_binding_vector_t *binding_vector;  /* Binding handle list          */
unsigned_char_t  server_entry_name[STRINGLEN];
unsigned_char_t  server_group_name[STRINGLEN];

main ()
{
    uuid_vector_t    *uuid_list;       /* Object UUID list           */
    uuid_vector_t    resource_uuid;    /* Object UUID list           */
    unsigned_char_t  annotation[STRINGLEN];
    unsigned_char_t  *host_name;
    unsigned32       status;
    int              i;
    void             print_uuids();
    boolean32        mgmt_auth_fn();    /* Management operations
                                        * authorization function     */

    /*
     * Register the interface with the RPC runtime library.
     * The two NULL arguments are the default manager type and manager EPV.
     */
    rpc_server_register_if (banking_v1_0_s_ifspec, NULL, NULL, &status);

    CHECK_DCE_STATUS (status, "rpc_server_register_if failed:", ABORT);

    /*
     * Use all available protocol sequences.
```

Example E-6: Server Initialization of the OK Banking Application (continued)

```
    */
    rpc_server_use_all_protseqs (rpc_c_protseq_max_calls_default, &status);

    CHECK_DCE_STATUS (status, "rpc_server_use_all_protseqs failed:", ABORT);

    /*
     * Get the server's binding information.
     */
    rpc_server_inq_bindings (&binding_vector, &status);

    CHECK_DCE_STATUS (status, "rpc_server_inq_bindings failed:", ABORT);

    /*
     * Create the server entry name for export.
     * Make it: <interface-name>_<host-name>.
     */
    dce_cf_get_host_name (&host_name, (unsigned long *) &status);

    CHECK_DCE_STATUS (status, "dce_cf_get_host_name failed:", ABORT);

    /*
     * Since the returned hostname is relative to the cell root
     * (for ex: hosts/hdqrts), we need to extract the leaf name
     * (the host's name) from the returned pathname and use it
     * to create the server entry name.
     */
    sprintf ((char *) server_entry_name, "/.:/banking_%s",
            strrchr (host_name, '/')+1);

    /*
     * Deallocate the returned host name.
     */
    free (host_name);

    /*
     * Create interface group name.
     * Using:  <interface-name>_servers.
     */
    strcpy ((char *) server_group_name, "/.:/banking_servers");

    /*
     * Export binding information to namespace server entry.
     */
    rpc_ns_binding_export (
        rpc_c_ns_syntax_default,    /* Syntax of server entry name.  */
        server_entry_name,          /* Namespace server entry name.  */
        banking_v1_0_s_ifspec,      /* Exporting interface info.     */
        binding_vector,             /* Exporting binding info.       */
        NULL,                       /* Not exporting object UUIDs.   */
        &status
        );

    CHECK_DCE_STATUS (status,
        "Can't export interface.\nrpc_ns_binding_export failed:", ABORT);

    printf (">>> Exported interface to server entry: %s\n\n",
```

Example E-6: Server Initialization of the OK Banking Application (continued)

```
        server_entry_name);
/*
 * Add the server entry to the interface's server group.
 */
rpc_ns_group_mbr_add (
    rpc_c_ns_syntax_default,    /* Syntax of group entry name.   */
    server_group_name,          /* Namespace group entry name.   */
    rpc_c_ns_syntax_default,    /* Syntax of server entry name.  */
    server_entry_name,          /* Namespace server entry name.  */
    &status
    );

CHECK_DCE_STATUS (status,
    "Can't add server to interface group.\nrpc_ns_group_mbr_add failed:",
    ABORT);

printf (">>> Added %s to server group: %s\n\n",
    server_entry_name, server_group_name);

/*
 * Register the binding information and dynamic endpoints in the
 * endpoint map. No objects are registered here.
 */
rpc_ep_register (banking_v1_0_s_ifspec, binding_vector, NULL,
    (unsigned_char_t *) "banking server", &status);

CHECK_DCE_STATUS (status, "rpc_ep_register failed: ", ABORT);

printf (">>> Registered interface in endpoint map\n\n");

/*
 * Allocate an object UUID/resource map for bank_c_max_map_size
 * entries.
 */
res_map_list = (res_map_list_t *) malloc (sizeof(res_map_list_t) +
    (bank_c_max_map_size - 1) * sizeof(res_map_element_t));

/*
 * Get the list of server-managed resources, if any.
 */
read_resources_map ("banking.dat", res_map_list);

/*
 * Only if there are active accounts, should we export resources.
 */
if (res_map_list->count > 0)
{
    /*
     * From the resource map list, gather up the resource IDs and
     * create a UUID vector.
     */
    create_uuid_list (res_map_list, &uuid_list);

    /*
```

Example E-6: Server Initialization of the OK Banking Application (continued)

```
                * Export the UUIDs to the namespace server entry.
                */
               rpc_ns_binding_export (
                   rpc_c_ns_syntax_default,   /* Syntax of server entry name.   */
                   server_entry_name,         /* Namespace server entry name.   */
                   NULL,                      /* Not exporting interface info.  */
                   NULL,                      /* Not exporting binding info.    */
                   uuid_list,                 /* Exporting only object UUIDs.   */
                   &status
                   );

               CHECK_DCE_STATUS (status,
                   "Can't export resource.\nrpc_ns_binding_export failed:", ABORT);

               /*
                * Display the exported UUIDs.
                */
               printf (">>> Exported UUIDs to server entry %s:\n", server_entry_name);

               print_uuids (uuid_list);

               /*
                * Free the UUID vector allocated in create_uuid_list.
                */
               free (uuid_list);
           }

           /*
            * For each resource in the object UUID/resource map...
            */
           for (i = 0; i < res_map_list->count; ++i)
           {
               /*
                * Create an annotation string (that is, a documentation string)
                * using the interface name and the resource name.
                */
               sprintf ((char *) annotation, "banking object: %s",
                   res_map_list->map_element[i].resource_file);

               /*
                * Place the object UUID for the current resource into a UUID
                * list which is one element long.
                */
               resource_uuid.count = 1;
               resource_uuid.uuid[0] = &res_map_list->map_element[i].resource_id;

               /*
                * For this managed resource, add binding information
                * and endpoints to the local endpoint map.
                */
               rpc_ep_register (banking_v1_0_s_ifspec, binding_vector,
                   &resource_uuid, annotation, &status);

               CHECK_DCE_STATUS (status, "rpc_ep_register failed:", ABORT);
```

Example E-6: Server Initialization of the OK Banking Application (continued)

```
    }

    /*
     * NOTE: Don't free bindings since we'll need them for ep-registering
     *       each newly created account.
     */

    /*
     * Register a management authorization function to control client
     * access to rpc-provided management routines.
     */
    rpc_mgmt_set_authorization_fn (&mgmt_auth_fn, &status);

    CHECK_DCE_STATUS(status, "rpc_mgmt_set_authorization_fn failed:", ABORT);

    /*
     * Begin listening for one remote procedure call at a time.
     */
    rpc_server_listen (1, &status);

    CHECK_DCE_STATUS (status, "rpc_server_listen failed:", ABORT);
}
```

Example E-7: Remote Procedures of the OK Banking Application

```
/*
 * File name:  ok_mgr.c
 *
 * Ok banking server manager routines
 */
#include <stdio.h>
#include "banking.h"
#include "check_status.h"
#include "svr_support.h"

extern res_map_list_t       *res_map_list;
extern rpc_binding_vector_t *binding_vector;
extern unsigned_char_t      server_entry_name[STRINGLEN];
extern unsigned_char_t      server_group_name[STRINGLEN];

uuid_t create_account (
    rpc_binding_handle_t  binding_handle,
    account_name          name,
    unsigned32            opening_balance,
    unsigned32            *bank_status,
    unsigned32            *dce_status
    )
{
    uuid_vector_t    uuid_list;
    uuid_t           resource_id;
    char             filename[STRINGLEN];
    unsigned_char_t  annotation[STRINGLEN];
```

Example E-7: Remote Procedures of the OK Banking Application (continued)

```
void            print_uuids ();

/*
 * Create a resource ID for the account.
 */
uuid_create (&resource_id, dce_status);

CHECK_DCE_STATUS (*dce_status, "uuid_create failed:", ABORT);

/*
 * Create a filename from the account owner's name.
 */
sprintf (filename, "%s.dat", name);

/*
 * Create the account itself.
 */
write_account (filename, &resource_id, name, &opening_balance,
    bank_status);

CHECK_BANK_STATUS (*bank_status, "write_account failed:", ABORT);

/*
 * Add an entry for the account to the resource map
 */
add_to_resource_map (res_map_list, resource_id, filename);

/*
 * Write the resource map to disk. If we stop running, we'll know
 * about the new account when we restart.
 */
write_resources_map ("banking.dat" , res_map_list);

/*
 * Create a UUID vector containing the new resource ID.
 */
uuid_list.count = 1;
uuid_list.uuid[0] = &resource_id;

/*
 * Export only the UUID to the namespace server entry.
 */
rpc_ns_binding_export (
    rpc_c_ns_syntax_default,    /* Syntax of server entry name.   */
    server_entry_name,          /* Namespace server entry name.   */
    NULL,                       /* Not exporting interface info.  */
    NULL,                       /* Not exporting binding info.    */
    &uuid_list,                 /* Exporting only object UUIDs.   */
    dce_status
    );

CHECK_DCE_STATUS (*dce_status,
    "Can't export resource.\nrpc_ns_binding_export failed:", ABORT);

/*
 * Display the exported UUID.
```

Example E-7: Remote Procedures of the OK Banking Application (continued)

```
     */
    printf (">>> Exported UUID to server entry %s:\n", server_entry_name);
    print_uuids (&uuid_list);

    /*
     * Register the resource with the endpoint map
     */
    sprintf ((char *) annotation, "banking object: %s", filename);

    rpc_ep_register (banking_v1_0_s_ifspec, binding_vector, &uuid_list,
        annotation, dce_status);

    CHECK_DCE_STATUS (*dce_status, "rpc_ep_register failed: ", ABORT);

    *bank_status = bank_s_ok;

    return (resource_id);
}

void delete_account (
    rpc_binding_handle_t  binding_handle,
    unsigned32            *bank_status,
    unsigned32            *dce_status
    )
{
    uuid_t          resource_id;
    uuid_vector_t   uuid_list;
    char            filename[STRINGLEN];
    unsigned32      status;
    void            print_uuids();

    /*
     * Get the object UUID from the binding handle.
     */
    rpc_binding_inq_object (binding_handle, &resource_id, dce_status);

    CHECK_DCE_STATUS (*dce_status, "rpc_binding_inq_object failed: ", ABORT);

    /*
     * See if we can find this resource.
     */
    resource_to_filename (res_map_list, &resource_id, &filename, bank_status);

    /*
     * If we found the account...
     */
    if (*bank_status == bank_s_ok)
    {
        remove (filename);

        remove_from_resource_map (res_map_list, &resource_id);

        /*
         * Write the resource map to disk. If we stop running, won't think
         * we know about the deleted account when we restart.
         */
```

Example E-7: Remote Procedures of the OK Banking Application (continued)

```
        write_resources_map ("banking.dat" , res_map_list);

        /*
         * Create a UUID vector containing the resource ID to unexport
         */
        uuid_list.count = 1;
        uuid_list.uuid[0] = &resource_id;

        /*
         * Unexport only the uuid_list to namespace entry entry_name.
         */
        rpc_ns_binding_unexport (
            rpc_c_ns_syntax_default,    /* Syntax of server entry name.    */
            server_entry_name,          /* Namespace server entry name.    */
            NULL,                       /* Not unexporting bindings.       */
            &uuid_list,                 /* Unexporting only an object UUID. */
            &status
            );

        CHECK_DCE_STATUS (status,
            "Can't unexport resource.\nrpc_ns_binding_unexport failed:",
            ABORT);

        /*
         * Display the unexported UUIDs.
         */
        printf (">>> Unexported UUID from server entry %s:\n",
            server_entry_name);

        print_uuids (&uuid_list);

        /*
         * Unregister the resource from the endpoint map
         */
        rpc_ep_unregister (banking_v1_0_s_ifspec, binding_vector, &uuid_list,
            dce_status);

        CHECK_DCE_STATUS (*dce_status, "rpc_ep_unregister failed: ", ABORT);

        /*
         * Display the unregistered UUID.
         */
        printf (">>> Unregistered UUID from endpoint map:\n");

        print_uuids (&uuid_list);

        *bank_status = bank_s_ok;
    }
    return;
}

void transaction (
    rpc_binding_handle_t  binding_handle,
    trans_type            trans_code,
    unsigned32            amount,
    unsigned32            *balance,
```

Example E-7: Remote Procedures of the OK Banking Application (continued)

```
unsigned32          *bank_status,
unsigned32          *dce_status
)
{
char               filename[STRINGLEN];
char               name[STRINGLEN];
uuid_t             resource_id;
unsigned32         temp_status;

/*
 * Get the object UUID from the binding handle.
 */
rpc_binding_inq_object (binding_handle, &resource_id, dce_status);

CHECK_DCE_STATUS (*dce_status, "rpc_binding_inq_object failed: ",
    ABORT);

/*
 * Read the savings account info.
 */
read_account (&resource_id, filename, &name, balance, bank_status);

if (*bank_status != bank_s_ok)
{
    return;
}

switch (trans_code)
{
    case DEPOSIT:

        *balance = *balance + amount;
        *bank_status = bank_s_ok;

        break;

    case WITHDRAWAL:

        if (amount <= *balance)
        {
            *balance = *balance - amount;
            *bank_status = bank_s_ok;
        }
        else
        {
            *bank_status = bank_s_insuf_funds;
        }

        break;

    case BALANCE:

        *bank_status = bank_s_ok;

        break;
}
```

Example E-7: Remote Procedures of the OK Banking Application (continued)

```
    write_account (filename, &resource_id, name, balance, &temp_status);
    CHECK_BANK_STATUS (temp_status, "write_account failed: ", ABORT);

    return;
}
```

Example E-8: Supporting Functions for the OK Banking Application

```
/*
 * File name:  svr_support.c
 *
 * Banking server support routines.
 */

#include <stdio.h>
#include <stdlib.h>
#include "banking.h"
#include "check_status.h"
#include "svr_support.h"

extern res_map_list_t      *res_map_list;   /* UUID/resource map      */

void read_resources_map (res_map_file, res_map_list)
char          *res_map_file;
res_map_list_t *res_map_list;
{
    FILE            *res_map;
    unsigned_char_t buffer[80];
    int             i;
    unsigned32      status;

    /*
     * Open the resource map file.
     */
    res_map = fopen (res_map_file, "r");

    /*
     * If the file doesn't exist, we don't currently manage any resources.
     */
    if (res_map == NULL)
    {
        /*
         * Set the resource count to zero.
         */
        res_map_list->count = 0;

        return;
    }

    /*
     * The map file exists, so let's read it.
     */
```

Example E-8: Supporting Functions for the OK Banking Application (continued)

```
    /*
     * Get the number of managed resources.
     */
    fgets ((char *) buffer, 80, res_map);

    res_map_list->count = atoi ((char *) buffer);

    for (i = 0; i < res_map_list->count; ++i)
    {
        /*
         * Get the resource ID stored as a string UUID and the associated
         * resource filename.
         */
        fscanf (res_map, "%s%s", buffer,
            res_map_list->map_element[i].resource_file);

        /*
         * Convert the UUID from string representation to binary
         * representation.
         */
        uuid_from_string (buffer, &res_map_list->map_element[i].resource_id,
            &status);

        CHECK_DCE_STATUS (status, "uuid_from_string failed", ABORT);
    }

    return;
}

void write_resources_map(res_map_file, res_map_list)
char            *res_map_file;
res_map_list_t  *res_map_list;
{
    FILE            *res_map;
    unsigned char   *uuid_string;
    int             i;
    unsigned32      status;

    /*
     * Open the resource map file.
     */
    res_map = fopen (res_map_file, "w");

    /*
     * Record the number of managed resources.
     */
    fprintf (res_map, "%d\n", res_map_list->count);

    for (i = 0; i < res_map_list->count; ++i)
    {
        /*
         * Convert the UUID from string representation to binary representation.
         */
        uuid_to_string (&res_map_list->map_element[i].resource_id,
```

Example E-8: Supporting Functions for the OK Banking Application (continued)

```
                &uuid_string, &status);

        CHECK_DCE_STATUS (status, "uuid_to_string failed", ABORT);

        /*
         * Write the resource id as a string UUID and the associated
         * resource filename.
         */
        fprintf (res_map, "%s %s\n", uuid_string,
            res_map_list->map_element[i].resource_file);

        rpc_string_free (&uuid_string, &status);
        CHECK_DCE_STATUS (status, "rpc_string_free failed", ABORT);
    }

    fclose (res_map);

    return;
}

void add_to_resource_map (res_map_list, uuid, filename)
res_map_list_t   *res_map_list;
uuid_t           uuid;
char             *filename;
{
    int i;

    i = res_map_list->count;

    /*
     * Copy the new resource ID into the next map element
     */
    res_map_list->map_element[i].resource_id = uuid;

    /*
     * Copy the associated filename into the next map element
     */
    strcpy (res_map_list->map_element[i].resource_file, filename);

    ++res_map_list->count;
}

void remove_from_resource_map (res_map_list, uuid)
res_map_list_t   *res_map_list;
uuid_t           *uuid;
{
    int         i,j;
    unsigned32  status;

    for (i = 0; i < res_map_list->count; ++i)
    {
        /*
         * If we find the provided UUID in the resource map...
         */
        if (uuid_equal (&res_map_list->map_element[i].resource_id, uuid,
                &status) == true)
```

Example E-8: Supporting Functions for the OK Banking Application (continued)

```
        {
            /*
             * Remove the entry by moving each element remaining in the map
             * up one entry.
             */
            for (j = i + 1; j < res_map_list->count; ++j)
            {
                res_map_list->map_element[j-1].resource_id =
                    res_map_list->map_element[j].resource_id;

                strcpy (res_map_list->map_element[j-1].resource_file,
                    res_map_list->map_element[j].resource_file);
            }

            --res_map_list->count;

            break;
        }
    }
}

void resource_to_filename (res_map_list, resource_id, filename, status)
res_map_list_t  *res_map_list;
uuid_t          *resource_id;
char            *filename;
unsigned32      *status;
{
    int         i;
    unsigned32  temp_status;
    /*
     * Assume no match found.
     */
    *filename = '\0';
    *status = bank_s_not_found;

    for (i = 0; i < res_map_list->count; ++i)
    {
        /*
         * If we find the provided UUID in the resource map...
         */
        if (uuid_equal (&res_map_list->map_element[i].resource_id, resource_id,
            &temp_status) == true)
        {
            strcpy (filename, res_map_list->map_element[i].resource_file);

            *status = bank_s_ok;

            break;
        }
    }

    return;
}
```

Example E-8: Supporting Functions for the OK Banking Application (continued)

```
read_account (resource_id, filename, name, balance, status)
uuid_t        *resource_id;
char          *filename;
account_name  name;
unsigned32    *balance;
unsigned32    *status;
{
    FILE              *account_fp;
    unsigned_char_t   string_uuid[64];
    uuid_t            account_id;

    /*
     * See if we can find this resource.
     */
    resource_to_filename (res_map_list, resource_id, filename, status);

    /*
     * If we found the account, read it. Otherwise, we'll return with the
     * error status set.
     */
    if (*status == bank_s_ok)
    {
        account_fp = fopen (filename, "r");

        if (account_fp != NULL)
        {
            fscanf (account_fp, "%s%s", string_uuid, name);

            uuid_from_string (string_uuid, &account_id, status);
            CHECK_DCE_STATUS (*status, "uuid_from_string failed: ", ABORT);

            /*
             * If the object UUID in the binding handle (the resource ID)
             * doesn't match the stored account number, we have an unexpected
             * error.
             */
            if (uuid_equal (resource_id, &account_id, status) != true)
            {
                *status = bank_s_bug;
                return;
            }

            fscanf (account_fp, "%d", balance);

            fclose (account_fp);

            *status = bank_s_ok;
        }
        else
        {
            *status = bank_s_file_open_fail;
        }
    }

    return;
```

Example E-8: Supporting Functions for the OK Banking Application (continued)

```
}
write_account (filename, resource_id, name, balance, status)
char         *filename;
uuid_t       *resource_id;
account_name name;
unsigned32   *balance;
unsigned32   *status;
{
    FILE            *account_fp;
    unsigned_char_t *string_uuid;

    /*
     * Convert the UUID to a string for storage in the account file.
     */
    uuid_to_string (resource_id, &string_uuid, status);
    CHECK_DCE_STATUS (*status, "uuid_to_string failed: ", ABORT);

    account_fp = fopen (filename, "w");

    if (account_fp != NULL)
    {
        /*
         * Store the account's resource ID and name in the file
         */
        fprintf (account_fp, "%s %s\n", string_uuid, name);

        /*
         * Store the account balance
         */
        fprintf (account_fp, "%d", *balance);

        fclose (account_fp);

        rpc_string_free (&string_uuid, status);
        CHECK_DCE_STATUS (*status, "rpc_string_free failed:", ABORT);

        *status = bank_s_ok;
    }
    else
    {
        *status = bank_s_file_open_fail;
    }

    return;
}
void create_uuid_list (res_map_list, uuid_list)
res_map_list_t *res_map_list;
uuid_vector_t  **uuid_list;
{
    unsigned32   status;
    int          i;

    /*
```

Example E-8: Supporting Functions for the OK Banking Application (continued)

```
         * Allocate enough memory to hold all of the resource IDs.
         */
        *uuid_list = (uuid_vector_t *) malloc (sizeof(uuid_vector_t) +
            (res_map_list->count - 1) * sizeof(uuid_t *) );

        /*
         * Save the number of UUIDs in the list.
         */
        (*uuid_list)->count = res_map_list->count;

        /*
         * For each element in the map...
         */
        for (i = 0; i < res_map_list->count; ++i)
        {
            /*
             * Place a pointer to the resource ID in the UUID list.
             */
            (*uuid_list)->uuid[i] = &res_map_list->map_element[i].resource_id;
        }
}

void print_uuids (uuid_list)
uuid_vector_t *uuid_list;
{
    int i;
    unsigned_char_t  *string_uuid;
    unsigned32 status;

    for (i=0; i < uuid_list->count; ++i)
    {
        uuid_to_string (uuid_list->uuid[i], &string_uuid, &status);

        CHECK_DCE_STATUS (status, "uuid_to_string failed: ", ABORT);

        printf ("\t%s\n", string_uuid);

        rpc_string_free (&string_uuid, &status);
    }

    printf ("\n");
}
```

Example E-9: Shutdown Procedure for the OK Banking Application

```
/*
 * File name:   ok_mgmt_auth.c
 *
 * OK banking server management authorization function
 */
#include <stdio.h>
#include "banking.h"
#include "check_status.h"
```

Example E-9: Shutdown Procedure for the OK Banking Application (continued)

```
#include "svr_support.h"

extern res_map_list_t        *res_map_list;     /* UUID/resource map    */
extern rpc_binding_vector_t  *binding_vector;   /* binding handle list  */
extern unsigned_char_t        server_entry_name[STRINGLEN];
extern unsigned_char_t        server_group_name[STRINGLEN];

boolean32 mgmt_auth_fn (client_binding, requested_mgmt_operation, status)
rpc_binding_handle_t    client_binding;
unsigned32              requested_mgmt_operation;
unsigned32             *status;
{
    uuid_vector_t    *uuid_list = NULL;
    unsigned_char_t  *string_binding;
    void              print_uuids();

    /*
     * In a more rigorous application, at this point we would
     * perform an authentication check to see if the calling client
     * is who he says he is.
     *
     * For this example, we trust all all clients.
     */

    switch (requested_mgmt_operation)
    {
        case rpc_c_mgmt_stop_server_listen:

            rpc_binding_to_string_binding (client_binding, &string_binding,
                status);

            CHECK_DCE_STATUS (*status,
                "rpc_binding_to_string_binding failed:", ABORT);

            printf (
                ">>> Stop server listening request received from:\n\t%s\n\n",
                string_binding);

            rpc_string_free (&string_binding, status);

            CHECK_DCE_STATUS (*status, "rpc_string_free failed:", ABORT);

            /*
             * In a more rigorous application, at this point we would
             * perform an authorization check to see if the calling client
             * should be allowed to perform this operation.
             *
             * For this example, all clients are allowed to shutdown the
             * server.
             */

            /*
             * Only if there are active accounts, do we need an object UUID
             * vector for unexporting resources.
             */
            if (res_map_list->count > 0)
```

Example E-9: Shutdown Procedure for the OK Banking Application (continued)

```
{
    /*
     * Create a list of resource object UUIDs from the
     * object UUID/resource map
     */
    create_uuid_list (res_map_list, &uuid_list);
}

/*
 * Unexport both the interface and any object UUIDs from the
 * namespace server entry.
 */
rpc_ns_binding_unexport (
    rpc_c_ns_syntax_default,    /* Syntax of server entry name.   */
    server_entry_name,          /* Namespace server entry name.   */
    banking_v1_0_s_ifspec,      /* Unexport bindings for this i/f */
    uuid_list,                  /* Unexport object UUIDs          */
    status
    );

CHECK_DCE_STATUS (*status,
    "Can't unexport.\nrpc_ns_binding_unexport failed:",
    ABORT);

printf (">>> Unexported interface from server entry: %s\n\n",
    server_entry_name);

if (uuid_list != NULL)
{
    /*
     * Display the unexported/unregistered UUIDs.
     */
    printf (">>> Unexported uuids from server entry %s:\n",
        server_entry_name);

    print_uuids (uuid_list);
}

/*
 * Remove the server entry from the interface's server group.
 */
rpc_ns_group_mbr_remove (
    rpc_c_ns_syntax_default,    /* Syntax of group entry name.  */
    server_group_name,          /* Namespace group entry name.  */
    rpc_c_ns_syntax_default,    /* Syntax of server entry name. */
    server_entry_name,          /* Namespace server entry name. */
    status
    );

CHECK_DCE_STATUS (*status,
    "Can't remove server from interface group. \
    \nrpc_ns_group_mbr_remove failed:", ABORT);

printf (">>> Removed %s from server group: %s\n\n",
```

Example E-9: Shutdown Procedure for the OK Banking Application (continued)

```
                server_entry_name, server_group_name);
        if (uuid_list != NULL)
        {
            /*
             * Remove endpoints from local endpoint map for each object.
             */
            rpc_ep_unregister (banking_v1_0_s_ifspec, binding_vector,
                uuid_list, status);

            CHECK_DCE_STATUS (*status, "rpc_ep_unregister failed:", ABORT);

            printf (">>> Unregistered UUIDs from endpoint map:\n");

            print_uuids (uuid_list);

            /*
             * Free the UUID list returned from create_uuid_list.
             */
            free (uuid_list);
        }
        /*
         * Remove endpoints from local endpoint map for the interface
         * itself.
         */
        rpc_ep_unregister (banking_v1_0_s_ifspec, binding_vector, NULL,
            status);

        CHECK_DCE_STATUS (*status, "rpc_ep_unregister failed:", ABORT);

        printf (">>> Unregistered interface from endpoint map\n\n");

        /*
         * Free server binding handles
         */
        rpc_binding_vector_free (&binding_vector, status);

        CHECK_DCE_STATUS (*status, "rpc_binding_vector_free failed:",
            RESUME);

        return (true);

    case rpc_c_mgmt_is_server_listen:

        /*
         * Remember, these requests come from both the banking
         * client as well as the rpcd.
         */
        printf (">>> Request for is server listening received\n\n");

        *status = rpc_s_ok;
        return (true);

    default:
        printf (">>> Unauthorized mgmt op request received\n\n");

        *status = rpc_s_mgmt_op_disallowed;
```

Example E-9: Shutdown Procedure for the OK Banking Application (continued)

```
                return (false);
    }
}
```

Example E-10: A Client File of the OK Banking Application

```c
/*
 * File name:  ok_client.c
 *
 * Ok banking client
 */
#include <stdio.h>
#include "banking.h"
#include "check_status.h"

#define STRINGLEN       80
#define UUID_STRING_LEN 37

unsigned_char_t  server_group_name[STRINGLEN];

main()
{
    int                  selection;
    rpc_binding_handle_t binding_h = NULL;
    uuid_t               account_id;
    unsigned_char_t      *string_account_id;
    unsigned_char_t      name[STRINGLEN];
    unsigned32           amount;
    unsigned32           balance;
    unsigned32           retry_count;
    unsigned32           dce_status;
    unsigned32           bank_status;
    void                 get_id_and_binding();

    /*
     * Create interface group name.
     * Using:  <interface-name>_servers.
     */
    strcpy ((char *) server_group_name, "/.:/banking_servers");

    do
    {
        printf ("1. Open new account\n");
        printf ("2. Deposit\n");
        printf ("3. Withdrawal\n");
        printf ("4. Account balance\n");
        printf ("5. Close account\n");
        printf ("6. Shutdown server\n");
        printf ("7. Exit\n");
        printf ("\nSelection: ");

        scanf ("%d", &selection);
```

Example E-10: A Client File of the OK Banking Application (continued)

```
switch (selection)
{
    case 1:
        /*
         * Get a binding handle to any banking server.
         */
        import_interface ("banking", banking_v1_0_c_ifspec,
            &binding_h, &dce_status);

        CHECK_DCE_STATUS (dce_status, "import_interface:", ABORT);

        printf ("Enter account owner's name: ");
        scanf ("%s", name);

        printf ("Enter opening balance: ");
        scanf ("%d", &amount);

        /*
         * Call remote procedure to create a new account.
         */
        account_id = create_account (binding_h, name, amount,
            &bank_status, &dce_status);

        CHECK_DCE_STATUS (dce_status, "create_account:", ABORT);

        CHECK_BANK_STATUS (bank_status, "create_account:", ABORT);

        /*
         * Set the new account's id into the binding handle in case
         * there are more transactions on this account. In this way
         * we don't need to import by resource for future
         * transactions on this account.
         */
        rpc_binding_set_object (binding_h, &account_id, &dce_status);

        CHECK_DCE_STATUS (dce_status,
            "rpc_binding_set_object failed:", ABORT);

        /*
         * Convert the account's object UUID from binary
         * representation to its string representation.
         */
        uuid_to_string (&account_id, &string_account_id, &dce_status);

        CHECK_DCE_STATUS (dce_status, "uuid_to_string failed:",
            ABORT);

        printf ("Your account's id is: %s\n\n", string_account_id);

        /*
         * Free the rpc runtime allocated string.
         */
        rpc_string_free (&string_account_id, &dce_status);

        CHECK_DCE_STATUS (dce_status, "rpc_string_free failed:",
```

Example E-10: A Client File of the OK Banking Application (continued)

```
                    ABORT);

            break;

        case 2:

            /*
             * Get the id of the account to operate on, and then a
             * binding for the server managing that account.
             */
            get_id_and_binding (&binding_h);

            printf ("Enter amount of deposit: ");
            scanf ("%d", &amount);

            /*
             * Call remote procedure to execute this transaction.
             */
            transaction (binding_h, DEPOSIT, amount, &balance,
                    &bank_status, &dce_status);

            CHECK_DCE_STATUS (dce_status, "transaction:", ABORT);

            CHECK_BANK_STATUS (bank_status, "transaction:", ABORT);

            printf ("Your new balance is: $%d\n\n", balance);

            break;

        case 3:

            /*
             * Get the id of the account to operate on, and then a
             * binding for the server managing that account.
             */
            get_id_and_binding (&binding_h);

            printf ("Enter amount to withdraw: ");
            scanf ("%d", &amount);

            /*
             * Call remote procedure to execute this transaction.
             */
            transaction (binding_h, WITHDRAWAL, amount, &balance,
                    &bank_status, &dce_status);

            CHECK_DCE_STATUS (dce_status, "transaction:", ABORT);

            switch (bank_status)
            {
                case bank_s_ok:

                    printf ("Your new balance is: $%d\n\n", balance);

                    break;

                case bank_s_insuf_funds:

                    CHECK_BANK_STATUS (bank_status, "transaction:",
```

Example E-10: A Client File of the OK Banking Application (continued)

```
                        RESUME);

                printf ("Your current balance is: $%d\n\n", balance);

                break;

            default:

                CHECK_BANK_STATUS (bank_status, "transaction:", ABORT);

                break;
        }

        break;

    case 4:

        /*
         * Get the id of the account to operate on, and then a
         * binding for the server managing that account.
         */
        get_id_and_binding (&binding_h);

        /*
         * Call remote procedure to execute this transaction.
         */
        transaction (binding_h, BALANCE, amount, &balance,
            &bank_status, &dce_status);

        CHECK_DCE_STATUS (dce_status, "transaction:", ABORT);

        CHECK_BANK_STATUS (bank_status, "transaction:", ABORT);

        printf ("Your balance is: $%d\n\n", balance);

        break;

    case 5:

        /*
         * Get the id of the account to operate on, and then a
         * binding for the server managing that account.
         */
        get_id_and_binding (&binding_h);

        /*
         * Call remote procedure to get the account balance before
         * closing the account.
         */
        transaction (binding_h, BALANCE, amount, &balance,
            &bank_status, &dce_status);

        CHECK_DCE_STATUS (dce_status, "transaction:", ABORT);

        CHECK_BANK_STATUS (bank_status, "transaction:", ABORT);

        printf ("Amount due to you is: $%d\n", balance);

        /*
```

Example E-10: A Client File of the OK Banking Application (continued)

```
            * Call remote procedure to close an account.
            */
           delete_account (binding_h, &bank_status, &dce_status);

           CHECK_DCE_STATUS (dce_status, "delete_account:", ABORT);

           CHECK_BANK_STATUS (bank_status, "delete_account:", ABORT);

           printf ("Account closed.\n\n");

           /*
            * Since the account is now closed, remove the object UUID
            * from the binding, so we don't try to access an account
            * the server no longer knows about.
            */
           rpc_binding_set_object (binding_h, NULL, &dce_status);

           CHECK_DCE_STATUS (dce_status, "rpc_binding_set_object failed:",
                  ABORT);

           break;

       case 6:

           /*
            * If we're not already in contact with a particular server,
            * we'll shutdown all available servers.
            */
           if (binding_h == NULL)
           {
               do
               {
                   import_interface ("banking", banking_v1_0_c_ifspec,
                       &binding_h, &dce_status);

                   if (dce_status != rpc_s_no_more_bindings)
                   {
                      CHECK_DCE_STATUS (dce_status,
                          "shutdown import_interface failed:", ABORT);

                      /*
                       * Stop the server from listening for new calls.
                       */
                      rpc_mgmt_stop_server_listening (binding_h,
                      &dce_status);

                      CHECK_DCE_STATUS (dce_status, "shutdown failed:",
                          ABORT);

                      rpc_binding_free (&binding_h, &dce_status);

                      CHECK_DCE_STATUS (dce_status,
                          "rpc_binding_free failed:", ABORT);
                  }
               } while (dce_status == rpc_s_ok);

               printf ("All servers have been shutdown.\n\n");
```

Example E-10: A Client File of the OK Banking Application (continued)

```
                }
                /*
                 * Otherwise, shutdown the one we're dealing with.
                 */
                else
                {
                    /*
                     * Stop the server from listening for new calls.
                     */
                    rpc_mgmt_stop_server_listening (binding_h,
                        &dce_status);

                    CHECK_DCE_STATUS (dce_status, "shutdown failed:", ABORT);

                    printf (
                        "The server for your account has been shutdown.\n\n");

                    /*
                     * Free the binding handle, so that if we try another
                     * transaction we'll first import for another server.
                     */
                    rpc_binding_free (&binding_h, &dce_status);

                    CHECK_DCE_STATUS (dce_status, "rpc_binding_free failed:",
                        ABORT);
                }

                break;

            case 7:

                break;

            default:

                fflush (stdin);
                printf ("Invalid selection. Try again.\n\n");
                break;
        }

    } while (selection != 7);
}

void get_id_and_binding (binding_h)
rpc_binding_handle_t  *binding_h;
{
    uuid_t          account_id;
    unsigned_char_t string_account_id[UUID_STRING_LEN];
    int             retry_count;
    unsigned32      status;

    /*
     * If we don't already have an object UUID (the account ID) in the
     * binding handle, prompt for one until we get a valid UUID and
     * until we find a server for that account.
     */
```

Example E-10: A Client File of the OK Banking Application (continued)

```
if (*binding_h != NULL)
{
    rpc_binding_inq_object (*binding_h, &account_id, &status);

    CHECK_DCE_STATUS (status, "rpc_binding_inq_object failed:", ABORT);
}
else
{
    uuid_create_nil (&account_id, &status);

    CHECK_DCE_STATUS (status, "uuid_create_nil failed:", ABORT);
}

if (uuid_is_nil (&account_id, &status))
{
    retry_count = 0;

    do
    {
        do
        {
            printf ("\nEnter account ID: ");
            scanf ("%s", string_account_id);

            uuid_from_string (string_account_id, &account_id, &status);

            CHECK_DCE_STATUS (status, "uuid_from_string failed:", RESUME);
        } while (status != uuid_s_ok);

        /*
         * Import by resource to get to the server for this
         * account.
         */
        import_resource ("banking", banking_v1_0_c_ifspec,
            &account_id, binding_h, &status);

        CHECK_DCE_STATUS (status,
            "No server for account.\nimport_resource failed", RESUME);

        ++retry_count;

        if (retry_count > 2)
        {
            fprintf (stderr, "Too many bad account ids - bye.\n");

            exit(1);
        }
    } while (status != rpc_s_ok);
}
}
```

Example E-11: Client Import Operations

```
/*
 * File name:  ok_import.c
 *
 * Ok banking client import routines.
 */

#include <stdio.h>
#include <stdlib.h>
#include <dce/rpc.h>
#include "check_status.h"

#define STRINGLEN 50

extern unsigned_char_t        server_group_name[STRINGLEN];

void import_interface (if_name, if_spec, binding_h, status)
unsigned_char_t      *if_name;
rpc_if_handle_t       if_spec;
rpc_binding_handle_t *binding_h;
unsigned32           *status;
{
    rpc_ns_handle_t    import_context;
    unsigned_char_t   *string_binding;
    unsigned32         temp_status;

    /*
     * Import binding information from the namespace server group.
     */
    rpc_ns_binding_import_begin (
        rpc_c_ns_syntax_default,    /* Syntax for server group name. */
        server_group_name,          /* Namespace server group name.  */
        if_spec,                    /* Interface to import           */
        NULL,                       /* Not importing an object UUID.  */
        &import_context,            /* Import context.               */
        status
        );

    CHECK_DCE_STATUS (*status,
        "Can't import by interface\nrpc_ns_binding_import_begin failed", ABORT);

    do
    {
        /*
         * Get a server binding handle.
         */
        rpc_ns_binding_import_next (import_context, binding_h, status);

        if (*status == rpc_s_ok)
        {
            /*
             * Get an endpoint for the binding.
             */
            rpc_ep_resolve_binding (*binding_h, if_spec, status);

            CHECK_DCE_STATUS (*status, "rpc_ep_resolve_binding failed:", ABORT);
```

Example E-11: Client Import Operations (continued)

```
            /*
             * Verify the server is available.
             */
            if (rpc_mgmt_is_server_listening (*binding_h, &temp_status))
            {
                break;
            }
            else
            {
                CHECK_DCE_STATUS (temp_status,
                    "Server not listening \
                    \nrpc_mgmt_is_server_listening failed:", RESUME);

                rpc_binding_to_string_binding (*binding_h, &string_binding,
                    &temp_status);

                CHECK_DCE_STATUS (temp_status,
                    "rpc_binding_to_string_binding failed:", ABORT);

                fprintf (stderr, "Failed binding: %s\n", string_binding);

                rpc_string_free (&string_binding, &temp_status);
                CHECK_DCE_STATUS (temp_status, "rpc_string_free failed:",
                    ABORT);
            }
        }
        else
        {
            if (*status != rpc_s_no_more_bindings)
            {
                CHECK_DCE_STATUS (*status,
                    "Can't import by interface\nrpc_ns_binding_import_next failed:",
                    RESUME);
            }
        }
    } while (*status == rpc_s_ok);

    /*
     * If we have a binding...
     */
    if (*status == rpc_s_ok)
    {
        /*
         * Make sure the returned binding doesn't reference an existing account.
         */
        rpc_binding_set_object (*binding_h, NULL, status);

        CHECK_DCE_STATUS (*status, "rpc_binding_set_object failed:", ABORT);
    }

    return;
}

void import_resource (if_name, if_spec, account_id, binding_h, status)
```

Example E-11: Client Import Operations (continued)

```
unsigned_char_t        *if_name;
rpc_if_handle_t        if_spec;
uuid_t                 *account_id;
rpc_binding_handle_t   *binding_h;
unsigned32             *status;
{
    rpc_ns_handle_t    import_context;
    unsigned_char_t    *string_binding;
    unsigned32         temp_status;

    /*
     * Import binding information from the namespace group entry_name.
     */
    rpc_ns_binding_import_begin (
        rpc_c_ns_syntax_default,    /* Syntax for server group name.   */
        server_group_name,          /* Namespace server group name.    */
        if_spec,                    /* Interface to import             */
        account_id,                 /* Importing for an object UUID.   */
        &import_context,            /* Import context.                 */
        status
        );

    CHECK_DCE_STATUS (*status,
        "Can't import by resource\nrpc_ns_binding_import_begin failed:", ABORT);

    do
    {
        /*
         * Get a server binding handle.
         */
        rpc_ns_binding_import_next (import_context, binding_h, status);

        if (*status == rpc_s_ok)
        {
            /*
             * Verify the server is available.
             */
            if (rpc_mgmt_is_server_listening (*binding_h, &temp_status))
            {
                break;
            }
            else
            {
                CHECK_DCE_STATUS (temp_status,
                    "Server not listening\nrpc_mgmt_is_server_listening failed:",
                    RESUME);

                rpc_binding_to_string_binding (*binding_h, &string_binding,
                    &temp_status);

                CHECK_DCE_STATUS (temp_status,
                    "rpc_binding_to_string_binding failed:", ABORT);

                fprintf (stderr, "Failed binding: %s\n", string_binding);
```

Example E-11: Client Import Operations (continued)

```
                rpc_string_free (&string_binding, &temp_status);
                CHECK_DCE_STATUS (temp_status, "rpc_string_free failed:",
                    ABORT);
            }
        }
        else
        {
            if (*status != rpc_s_no_more_bindings)
            {
                CHECK_DCE_STATUS (*status,
                    "Can't import by resource\nrpc_ns_binding_import_next failed:",
                    RESUME);
            }
        }
    } while (*status == rpc_s_ok);

    return;
}
```

F

The Better Banking Application

This is the advanced version of the banking application shown in the Appendix E. While the version in Appendix E required the client to know the object UUID of each bank account, the version in this appendix associates a name to each account, making requests easier. This appendix demonstrates the following advanced techniques for manipulating object UUIDs:

- Assigning names to resources
- Storing each object UUID in its own group entry

How To Run the Application

To build and start the server, type the following:

```
S> make interface server
S> i_server
```

To build and run the client, type the following:

```
C> make interface client
C> i_client
```

The client displays a menu of operations and you can begin to create and manage accounts.

Application Files

The Better Banking application uses several of the same files as the OK version. See Appendix E for the following files:

- *banking.idl*
- *banking.acf*
- *check_status.h*
- *svr_support.h*
- *svr_support.c*

Makefile contains descriptions of how the application is compiled. (see Example F-1).

btr_svr_main.c contains the initialization for the server, including the preparation and display of the list of bank accounts (see Example F-2).

btr_mgr.c is the implementation of all the remote procedures defined in this interface (see Example F-3).

btr_mgmt_auth.c contains the management authorization function that shuts down the server at the request of the client (see Example F-4).

btr_client.c is the client, which displays a menu of functions and invokes the remote procedures requested by the user on the server. The file includes the *get_name_and_binding* function, which queries the user for a name of a person who has an account (see Example F-5).

btr_import.c contains two functions that choose a server. The client uses *import_interface* to find a server when creating a new account or shutting down servers. For other transactions it uses *import_resource*, called from *get_name_and_binding* (see Example F-6).

Example F-1: The Makefile for the Better Banking Application

```
# FILE NAME: Makefile
# Makefile for the "better" banking application
#
# definitions for this make file
#
APPL=banking
IDLCMD=idl -v
CFLAGS = -D_SHARED_LIBRARIES -Dalpha -D_REENTRANT -g -w -I.    # DEC Alpha OSF/1
LIBDCE = -ldce -lpthreads -lc_r -lmach -lm             # DEC Alpha OSF/1
CC= cc


#
# COMPLETE BUILD of the application.
```

Example F-1: The Makefile for the Better Banking Application (continued)

```
#
all:   interface client server

#
# INTERFACE BUILD
#
interface:   $(APPL).h $(APPL)_cstub.o $(APPL)_sstub.o
$(APPL).h $(APPL)_cstub.o $(APPL)_sstub.o: $(APPL).idl
        $(IDLCMD) $(APPL).idl

#
# CLIENT BUILD
#
client:      i_client
i_client:    btr_client.o btr_import.o $(APPL)_cstub.o
        $(CC) $(CFLAGS) -o banking_client.exe btr_client.o btr_import.o \
                $(APPL)_cstub.o $(LIBDCE)

btr_client.o:     btr_client.c
        $(CC) $(CFLAGS) -c btr_client.c

btr_import.o:     btr_import.c
        $(CC) $(CFLAGS) -c btr_import.c

#
# SERVER BUILD
#
server:      i_server
i_server:    $(APPL).h btr_svr_main.o btr_mgr.o svr_support.o \
                $(APPL)_sstub.o
        $(CC) $(CFLAGS) -o banking_server.exe btr_svr_main.o \
                btr_mgr.o svr_support.o \
                $(APPL)_sstub.o $(LIBDCE)

btr_svr_main.o:   btr_svr_main.c
        $(CC) $(CFLAGS) -c btr_svr_main.c

btr_mgr.o:   btr_mgr.c
        $(CC) $(CFLAGS) -c btr_mgr.c

svr_support.o:    svr_support.c
        $(CC) $(CFLAGS) -c svr_support.c
```

Example F-2: Server Initialization

```
/*
 * File name: btr_svr_main.c
 *
 * Better banking server initialization.
 */
#include <stdio.h>
#include <string.h>
```

Example F-2: Server Initialization (continued)

```
#include <dce/dce_cf.h>        /* DCE configuration file, DCE provided */
#include "banking.h"           /* Application specific, IDL generated  */
#include "check_status.h"      /* Contains macros to check status      */
#include "svr_support.h"       /* Defines obj UUID/res map data type   */

#define bank_c_max_map_size 50     /* Obj UUID/res map size            */

res_map_list_t       *res_map_list;    /* Object UUID/resource map      */
rpc_binding_vector_t *binding_vector;  /* Binding handle list           */
unsigned_char_t   server_entry_name[STRINGLEN];
unsigned_char_t   server_group_name[STRINGLEN];
unsigned_char_t   resource_group_name[STRINGLEN];
unsigned_char_t   *host_name;

main ()
{
    uuid_vector_t    *uuid_list;         /* Object UUID list            */
    uuid_vector_t    resource_uuid;      /* Object UUID list            */
    unsigned_char_t  resource_entry_name[STRINGLEN];
    unsigned_char_t  annotation[STRINGLEN];
    char             resource_name[STRINGLEN];
    unsigned32       status;
    int              i;
    boolean32        mgmt_auth_fn();     /* Management operations
                                          * authorization function      */

    /*
     * Create the server entry name for export.
     * Make it: <interface-name>_<host-name>.
     */
    dce_cf_get_host_name (&host_name, (unsigned long *) &status);

    CHECK_DCE_STATUS (status, "dce_cf_get_host_name failed:", ABORT);

    /*
     * Since the returned hostname is relative to the cell root
     * (for ex: hosts/hdqrts), we need to extract the leaf name
     * (the host's name) from the returned pathname and use it
     * to create the server entry name.
     */
    sprintf ((char *) server_entry_name, "/.:/banking_%s",
            strrchr (host_name, '/')+1);

    /*
     * Deallocate the returned host name.
     */
    free (host_name);

    /*
     * Create interface group name.
     * Using: <interface-name>_servers.
     */
    strcpy ((char *) server_group_name, "/.:/banking_servers");
```

Example F-2: Server Initialization (continued)

```
/*
 * Create resource group name.
 * Using: <interface-name>_resources
 */
strcpy ((char *) resource_group_name, "/.:/banking_resources");

/*
 * Register the interface with the RPC runtime library.
 * The two NULL arguments are the default manager type and manager EPV.
 */
rpc_server_register_if (banking_v1_0_s_ifspec, NULL, NULL, &status);

CHECK_DCE_STATUS (status, "rpc_server_register_if failed:", ABORT);

/*
 * Use all available protocol sequences.
 */
rpc_server_use_all_protseqs (rpc_c_protseq_max_calls_default, &status);

CHECK_DCE_STATUS (status, "rpc_server_use_all_protseqs failed:", ABORT);

/*
 * Get the server's binding information.
 */
rpc_server_inq_bindings (&binding_vector, &status);

CHECK_DCE_STATUS (status, "rpc_server_inq_bindings failed:", ABORT);

/*
 * Export binding information to namespace server entry.
 */
rpc_ns_binding_export (
    rpc_c_ns_syntax_default,     /* Syntax of server entry name.  */
    server_entry_name,           /* Namespace server entry name.  */
    banking_v1_0_s_ifspec,       /* Exporting interface info.     */
    binding_vector,              /* Exporting binding info.       */
    NULL,                        /* Not exporting object UUIDs.   */
    &status
    );

CHECK_DCE_STATUS (status,
    "Can't export interface.\nrpc_ns_binding_export failed:", ABORT);

printf (">>> Exported interface to server entry: %s\n\n",
    server_entry_name);

/*
 * Add the server entry to the interface's server group.
 */
rpc_ns_group_mbr_add (
    rpc_c_ns_syntax_default,     /* Syntax of server group name.  */
    server_group_name,           /* Namespace server group name.  */
    rpc_c_ns_syntax_default,     /* Syntax of server entry name.  */
    server_entry_name,           /* Namespace server entry name.  */
    &status
```

Example F-2: Server Initialization (continued)

```
    );

CHECK_DCE_STATUS (status,
    "Can't add server to interface group.\nrpc_ns_group_mbr_add failed:",
    ABORT);

printf (">>> Added %s to server group: %s\n\n",
    server_entry_name, server_group_name);

/*
 * Register the binding information and dynamic endpoints in the endpoint
 * map. No objects are registered here.
 */
rpc_ep_register (banking_v1_0_s_ifspec, binding_vector, NULL,
    (unsigned_char_t *) "banking server", &status);

CHECK_DCE_STATUS (status, "rpc_ep_register failed: ", ABORT);

printf (">>> Registered interface in endpoint map\n\n");

/*
 * Allocate an object UUID/resource map for bank_c_max_map_size
 * entries.
 */
res_map_list = (res_map_list_t *) malloc (sizeof(res_map_list_t) +
    (bank_c_max_map_size - 1) * sizeof(res_map_element_t));

/*
 * Get the list of server-managed resources, if any.
 */
read_resources_map ("banking.dat", res_map_list);

/*
 * For each resource in the object UUID/resource map...
 */
for (i = 0; i < res_map_list->count; ++i)
{
    /*
     * Place the object UUID for the current resource into a
     * UUID list that is one element long.
     */
    resource_uuid.count = 1;
    resource_uuid.uuid[0] = &res_map_list->map_element[i].resource_id;

    /*
     * Remove ".dat" from the resource filename.
     */
    strcpy (resource_name, res_map_list->map_element[i].resource_file);
    *(strchr(resource_name, '.')) = '\0';

    /*
     * Create resource entry name.
     * Using: <account-name>_savings
     */
    sprintf ((char *) resource_entry_name, "/.:/%s_savings",
```

Example F-2: Server Initialization (continued)

```
                resource_name);
        /*
         * Export the resource's object UUID to namespace resource entry.
         */
        rpc_ns_binding_export (
            rpc_c_ns_syntax_default,    /* Syntax of resource entry name  */
            resource_entry_name,        /* Namespace resource entry name. */
            NULL,                       /* Not exporting interface info.  */
            NULL,                       /* Not exporting binding info.    */
            &resource_uuid,             /* Exporting only an object UUID. */
            &status
            );

        CHECK_DCE_STATUS (status,
            "Can't export resource.\nrpc_ns_binding_export failed:", ABORT);

        /*
         * Display the exported UUIDs.
         */
        printf (">>> Exported UUID to resource entry %s:\n",
            resource_entry_name);

        print_uuids (&resource_uuid);

        /*
         * Add the server entry as a member of the resource entry
         * (which is a group).
         */
        rpc_ns_group_mbr_add (
            rpc_c_ns_syntax_default,    /* Syntax of resource entry name. */
            resource_entry_name,        /* Namespace resource entry name. */
            rpc_c_ns_syntax_default,    /* Syntax of server entry name.   */
            server_entry_name,          /* Namespace server entry name.   */
            &status
            );

        CHECK_DCE_STATUS (status,
            "Can't add server to resource entry. \
            \nrpc_ns_group_mbr_add failed:", ABORT);

        printf (">>> Added %s to resource entry: %s\n\n",
            server_entry_name, resource_entry_name);

        /*
         * Add the resource entry as a member of the resource group.
         */
        rpc_ns_group_mbr_add (
            rpc_c_ns_syntax_default,    /* Syntax of resource group name. */
            resource_group_name,        /* Namespace resource group name. */
            rpc_c_ns_syntax_default,    /* Syntax of resource entry name. */
            resource_entry_name,        /* Namespace resource entry name. */
            &status
            );
```

Example F-2: Server Initialization (continued)

```
        CHECK_DCE_STATUS (status,
            "Can't add resource entry to resource group. \
            \nrpc_ns_group_mbr_add failed:", ABORT);

        printf (">>> Added %s to resource group: %s\n\n",
            resource_entry_name, resource_group_name);
    }
    /*
     * For each resource in the object UUID/resource map...
     */
    for (i = 0; i < res_map_list->count; ++i)
    {
        /*
         * Create an annotation string (that is, a documentation string)
         * using the interface name and the resource name.
         */
        sprintf ((char *) annotation, "banking object: %s",
            res_map_list->map_element[i].resource_file);

        /*
         * Place the object UUID for the current resource into a UUID
         * list which is one element long.
         */
        resource_uuid.count = 1;
        resource_uuid.uuid[0] = &res_map_list->map_element[i].resource_id;

        /*
         * For this managed resource, add binding information and enpoints
         * to the local endpoint map.
         */
        rpc_ep_register (banking_v1_0_s_ifspec, binding_vector,
            &resource_uuid, annotation, &status);

        CHECK_DCE_STATUS (status, "rpc_ep_register failed:", ABORT);

        printf (">>> Registered UUID in endpoint map:\n");

        print_uuids (&resource_uuid);
    }
    /*
     * NOTE: Don't free bindings since we'll need them for ep-registering
     *       each newly created account.
     */

    /*
     * Register a management authorization function to control client
     * access to rpc-provided management routines.
     */
    rpc_mgmt_set_authorization_fn (&mgmt_auth_fn, &status);

    CHECK_DCE_STATUS(status, "rpc_mgmt_set_authorization_fn failed:", ABORT);
    /*
```

Example F-2: Server Initialization (continued)

```
    * Begin listening for one remote procedure call at a time
    */
    rpc_server_listen (1, &status);

    CHECK_DCE_STATUS (status, "rpc_server_listen failed:", ABORT);
}
```

Example F-3: Remote Procedures

```
/*
 * File name:  btr_mgr.c
 *
 * Better banking server manager routines
 */
#include <stdio.h>
#include <string.h>
#include "banking.h"
#include "check_status.h"
#include "svr_support.h"

extern res_map_list_t        *res_map_list;     /* UUID/resource map    */
extern rpc_binding_vector_t  *binding_vector;   /* binding handle list  */
extern unsigned_char_t       server_entry_name[STRINGLEN];
extern unsigned_char_t       server_group_name[STRINGLEN];
extern unsigned_char_t       resource_group_name[STRINGLEN];
extern unsigned_char_t       host_name[STRINGLEN];

uuid_t create_account (
    rpc_binding_handle_t  binding_handle,
    account_name          name,
    unsigned32            opening_balance,
    unsigned32            *bank_status,
    unsigned32            *dce_status
    )
{
    uuid_vector_t    uuid_list;
    uuid_t           resource_id;
    char             filename[STRINGLEN];
    unsigned_char_t  annotation[STRINGLEN];
    unsigned_char_t  resource_entry_name[STRINGLEN];
    void             print_uuids();

    /*
     * Create a resource ID for the account.
     */
    uuid_create (&resource_id, dce_status);

    CHECK_DCE_STATUS (*dce_status, "uuid_create failed:", ABORT);

    /*
     * Create a filename from the account owner's name.
     */
```

Example F-3: Remote Procedures (continued)

```
sprintf (filename, "%s.dat", name);

/*
 * Create the account itself.
 */
write_account (filename, &resource_id, name, &opening_balance,
    bank_status);

CHECK_BANK_STATUS (*bank_status, "write_account failed:", ABORT);

/*
 * Add an entry for the account to the resource map
 */
add_to_resource_map (res_map_list, resource_id, filename);

/*
 * Write the resource map to disk. If we stop running, we'll know
 * about the new account when we restart.
 */
write_resources_map ("banking.dat" , res_map_list);

/*
 * Create a UUID vector containing the new resource ID.
 */
uuid_list.count = 1;
uuid_list.uuid[0] = &resource_id;

/*
 * Create resource entry name.
 * Using:  <account-name>_savings
 */
sprintf ((char *) resource_entry_name, "/.:/%s_savings", name);

/*
 * Export the resource's object UUID to namespace resource entry.
 */
rpc_ns_binding_export (
    rpc_c_ns_syntax_default,     /* Syntax of resource entry name. */
    resource_entry_name,         /* Namespace resource entry name. */
    NULL,                        /* Not exporting interface info.  */
    NULL,                        /* Not exporting binding info.    */
    &uuid_list,                  /* Exporting only an object UUID. */
    dce_status
    );

CHECK_DCE_STATUS (*dce_status,
    "Can't export resource.\nrpc_ns_binding_export failed:", ABORT);

printf (">>> Exported UUID to resource entry %s:\n",
    resource_entry_name);

print_uuids (&uuid_list);

/*
 * Add the server entry as a member of the resource entry.
 */
```

Example F-3: Remote Procedures (continued)

```
rpc_ns_group_mbr_add (
    rpc_c_ns_syntax_default,    /* Syntax of resource entry name. */
    resource_entry_name,        /* Namespace resource entry name. */
    rpc_c_ns_syntax_default,    /* Syntax of server entry name.   */
    server_entry_name,          /* Namespace server entry name.   */
    dce_status
    );

CHECK_DCE_STATUS (*dce_status,
    "Can't add server to resource entry.\nrpc_ns_group_mbr_add failed:",
    ABORT);

printf (">>> Added %s to resource entry: %s\n\n",
    server_entry_name, resource_entry_name);

/*
 * Add the resource entry as a member of the resource group.
 */
rpc_ns_group_mbr_add (
    rpc_c_ns_syntax_default,    /* Syntax of resource group name. */
    resource_group_name,        /* Namespace resource group name. */
    rpc_c_ns_syntax_default,    /* Syntax of resource entry name. */
    resource_entry_name,        /* Namespace resource entry name. */
    dce_status
    );

CHECK_DCE_STATUS (*dce_status,
    "Can't add resource entry to group.\nrpc_ns_group_mbr_add failed:",
    ABORT);

printf (">>> Added %s to resource group: %s\n\n",
    resource_entry_name, resource_group_name);

/*
 * Register the resource with the endpoint map
 */
sprintf ((char *) annotation, "banking object: %s", filename);

rpc_ep_register (banking_v1_0_s_ifspec, binding_vector, &uuid_list,
    annotation, dce_status);

CHECK_DCE_STATUS (*dce_status, "rpc_ep_register failed: ", ABORT);

printf (">>> Registered UUID in endpoint map:\n");

print_uuids (&uuid_list);

*bank_status = bank_s_ok;

return (resource_id);
}

void delete_account (
    rpc_binding_handle_t  binding_handle,
    unsigned32            *bank_status,
    unsigned32            *dce_status
    )
```

Example F-3: Remote Procedures (continued)

```
{
    uuid_t            resource_id;
    uuid_vector_t     uuid_list;
    char              filename[STRINGLEN];
    char              resource_name[STRINGLEN];
    char              resource_entry_name[STRINGLEN];
    rpc_ns_handle_t   inquiry_context;
    void              print_uuids();

    /*
     * Get the object UUID from the binding handle.
     */
    rpc_binding_inq_object (binding_handle, &resource_id, dce_status);

    CHECK_DCE_STATUS (*dce_status, "rpc_binding_inq_object failed: ", ABORT);

    /*
     * See if we can find this resource.
     */
    resource_to_filename (res_map_list, &resource_id, &filename, bank_status);

    /*
     * If we found the account...
     */
    if (*bank_status == bank_s_ok)
    {
        remove (filename);

        remove_from_resource_map (res_map_list, &resource_id);

        /*
         * Write the resource map to disk. If we stop running, won't think
         * we know about the deleted account when we restart.
         */
        write_resources_map ("banking.dat" , res_map_list);

        /*
         * Remove ".dat" from the resource filename.
         */
        strcpy (resource_name, filename);
        *(strchr(resource_name, '.')) = '\0';

        /*
         * Create resource entry name.
         * Using:  <account-name>_savings
         */
        sprintf ((char *) resource_entry_name, "/.:/%s_savings",
            resource_name);

        /*
         * This example assumes that only a single server manages each
         * resource.  If the application supported multiply accessed
         * resources - that is that a resource is available through
         * multiple servers - then at this point, instead of deleting
         * the resource entry, the server would do the following:
```

Example F-3: Remote Procedures (continued)

```
 *
 * - call rpc_ns_group_mbr_remove to remove the server entry from the
 *   resource entry.
 *
 * - call the routines beginning with rpc_ns_group_mbr_inq_ to see if
 *   the resource entry contains any other servers as members.
 *
 * - if the resource entry has no more members, it means the object
 *   is no longer offered by any server. In this case, the server
 *   cleans up the namespace by calling:
 *
 *   . rpc_ns_group_mbr_remove to remove the resource entry from the
 *     resource group
 *
 *   . rpc_ns_mgmt_entry_delete to remove the resource entry
 *     from the namespace
 *
 * - if the resource entry has at least one more member, it means the
 *   object is still offered by another server. In this case, the
 *   server leaves the resource entry alone.
 */

/*
 * Remove the resource entry from the namespace.
 */
rpc_ns_mgmt_entry_delete (
    rpc_c_ns_syntax_default,     /* Syntax of resource entry name. */
    resource_entry_name,         /* Namespace resource entry name. */
    dce_status
    );

CHECK_DCE_STATUS (*dce_status, "rpc_ns_mgmt_entry_delete failed: ",
    ABORT);

printf (">>> Deleted resource entry %s\n\n", resource_entry_name);

/*
 * Remove the resource entry from the resource group.
 */
rpc_ns_group_mbr_remove (
    rpc_c_ns_syntax_default, /* Syntax of resource group name. */
    resource_group_name,     /* Namespace resource group name. */
    rpc_c_ns_syntax_default, /* Syntax of resource entry name. */
    resource_entry_name,     /* Namespace resource entry name. */
    dce_status
    );

CHECK_DCE_STATUS (*dce_status,
    "Can't remove resource entry from resource group. \
    \nrpc_ns_group_mbr_remove failed:", ABORT);

printf (">>> Removed %s from resource group: %s\n\n",
    resource_entry_name, resource_group_name);
```

Example F-3: Remote Procedures (continued)

```
        /*
         * Create a UUID vector containing the resource's object UUID.
         */
        uuid_list.count = 1;
        uuid_list.uuid[0] = &resource_id;

        /*
         * Unregister the resource from the endpoint map
         */
        rpc_ep_unregister (banking_v1_0_s_ifspec, binding_vector, &uuid_list,
            dce_status);

        CHECK_DCE_STATUS (*dce_status, "rpc_ep_unregister failed: ", ABORT);

        printf (">>> Unregistered UUID from endpoint map:\n");

        print_uuids (&uuid_list);

        *bank_status = bank_s_ok;
    }
    return;
}

void transaction (
    rpc_binding_handle_t   binding_handle,
    trans_type             trans_code,
    unsigned32             amount,
    unsigned32             *balance,
    unsigned32             *bank_status,
    unsigned32             *dce_status
    )
{
    char            filename[STRINGLEN];
    char            name[STRINGLEN];
    uuid_t          resource_id;
    unsigned32      temp_status;

    /*
     * Get the object UUID from the binding handle.
     */
    rpc_binding_inq_object (binding_handle, &resource_id, dce_status);

    CHECK_DCE_STATUS (*dce_status, "rpc_binding_inq_object failed: ",
        ABORT);

    /*
     * Read the savings account info.
     */
    read_account (&resource_id, filename, &name, balance, bank_status);

    if (*bank_status != bank_s_ok)
    {
        return;
    }

    switch (trans_code)
```

Example F-3: Remote Procedures (continued)

```
    {
        case DEPOSIT:

            *balance = *balance + amount;
            *bank_status = bank_s_ok;

            break;

        case WITHDRAWAL:

            if (amount <= *balance)
            {
                *balance = *balance - amount;
                *bank_status = bank_s_ok;
            }
            else
            {
                *bank_status = bank_s_insuf_funds;
            }

            break;

        case BALANCE:

            *bank_status = bank_s_ok;

            break;
    }

    write_account (filename, &resource_id, name, balance, &temp_status);
    CHECK_BANK_STATUS (temp_status, "write_account failed: ", ABORT);

    return;
}
```

Example F-4: Shutdown Procedure

```
/* FILE NAME: get_args.c */
#include <stdio.h>

get_args(argc, argv, local_fh, host, remote_name)
int  argc;
char *argv[];
FILE **local_fh;
char host[];
char remote_name[];
{
    char local_name[100];
    char *strcpy();
    void exit();

    switch(argc) {
    case 1:
    case 2: printf("Usage: %s [local_file] host [remote_file]\n", argv[0]);
            puts("Use \"\" for local stdin.");
```

Example F-4: Shutdown Procedure (continued)

```
            exit(0);
            break;
  case 3: strcpy(local_name, argv[1]);  /* use the same file name */
            strcpy(remote_name, local_name);
            strcpy(host, argv[2]);
            break;
  default: strcpy(local_name, argv[1]);
            strcpy(host, argv[2]);
            strcpy(remote_name, argv[3]);
            break;
  }
  if(strlen(local_name) == 0) {
     (*local_fh) = stdin;
     puts("Using stdin.  Type input:");
  }
  else
     if( ( (*local_fh) = fopen(local_name, "r")) == NULL ) {
        puts("Cannot open local file");
        exit(1);
     }
  return;
}
```

Example F-5: A Client File of the Better Banking Application

```
/*
 * File name:  btr_client.c
 *
 * Better banking client
 */

#include <stdio.h>
#include "banking.h"
#include "check_status.h"

#define STRINGLEN 50

unsigned_char_t  server_group_name[STRINGLEN];

main()
{
    int                    selection;
    rpc_binding_handle_t   binding_h = NULL;
    uuid_t                 account_id;
    unsigned_char_t        name[STRINGLEN];
    unsigned32             amount;
    unsigned32             balance;
    unsigned32             retry_count;
    unsigned32             dce_status;
    unsigned32             bank_status;
    void                   get_name_and_binding();
```

Example F-5: A Client File of the Better Banking Application (continued)

```
/*
 * Create interface group name.
 * Using:  <interface-name>_servers.
 */
strcpy ((char *) server_group_name, "/.:/banking_servers");

do
{
    printf ("1. Open new account\n");
    printf ("2. Deposit\n");
    printf ("3. Withdrawal\n");
    printf ("4. Account balance\n");
    printf ("5. Close account\n");
    printf ("6. Shutdown server\n");
    printf ("7. Exit\n");
    printf ("\nSelection: ");

    scanf ("%d", &selection);

    switch (selection)
    {
        case 1:

            /*
             * Get a binding handle to any banking server.
             */
            import_interface ("banking", banking_v1_0_c_ifspec,
                &binding_h, &dce_status);

            CHECK_DCE_STATUS (dce_status, "import_interface:", ABORT);

            printf ("Enter account owner's name: ");
            scanf ("%s", name);

            printf ("Enter opening balance: ");
            scanf ("%d", &amount);

            /*
             * Call remote procedure to create a new account.
             */
            account_id = create_account (binding_h, name, amount,
                &bank_status, &dce_status);

            CHECK_DCE_STATUS (dce_status, "create_account:", ABORT);

            CHECK_BANK_STATUS (bank_status, "create_account:", ABORT);

            /*
             * Set the new account id into the binding handle in case
             * there are more transactions on this account. In this way
             * we don't need to import by resource for future
             * transactions on this account.
             */
            rpc_binding_set_object (binding_h, &account_id, &dce_status);

            CHECK_DCE_STATUS (dce_status,
```

Example F-5: A Client File of the Better Banking Application (continued)

```
                    "rpc_binding_set_object failed:", ABORT);

            printf ("Your account's name is: %s\n\n", name);

            break;

        case 2:

            /*
             * Get the name of the account to operate on, and then a
             * binding for the server managing that account.
             */
            get_name_and_binding (&binding_h);

            printf ("Enter amount of deposit: ");
            scanf ("%d", &amount);

            /*
             * Call remote procedure to execute this transaction.
             */
            transaction (binding_h, DEPOSIT, amount, &balance,
                &bank_status, &dce_status);

            CHECK_DCE_STATUS (dce_status, "transaction:", ABORT);

            CHECK_BANK_STATUS (bank_status, "transaction:", ABORT);

            printf ("Your new balance is: $%d\n\n", balance);

            break;

        case 3:

            /*
             * Get the name of the account to operate on, and then a
             * binding for the server managing that account.
             */
            get_name_and_binding (&binding_h);

            printf ("Enter amount to withdraw: ");
            scanf ("%d", &amount);

            /*
             * Call remote procedure to execute this transaction.
             */
            transaction (binding_h, WITHDRAWAL, amount, &balance,
                &bank_status, &dce_status);

            CHECK_DCE_STATUS (dce_status, "transaction:", ABORT);

            switch (bank_status)
            {
                case bank_s_ok:

                    printf ("Your new balance is: $%d\n\n", balance);

                    break;

                case bank_s_insuf_funds:
```

Example F-5: A Client File of the Better Banking Application (continued)

```
                    CHECK_BANK_STATUS (bank_status, "transaction:",
                        RESUME);

                    printf ("Your current balance is: $%d\n\n", balance);

                    break;

                default:

                    CHECK_BANK_STATUS (bank_status, "transaction:", ABORT);

                    break;
            }

        break;

    case 4:

        /*
         * Get the name of the account to operate on, and then a
         * binding for the server managing that account.
         */
        get_name_and_binding (&binding_h);

        /*
         * Call remote procedure to execute this transaction.
         */
        transaction (binding_h, BALANCE, amount, &balance,
            &bank_status, &dce_status);

        CHECK_DCE_STATUS (dce_status, "transaction:", ABORT);

        CHECK_BANK_STATUS (bank_status, "transaction:", ABORT);

        printf ("Your balance is: $%d\n\n", balance);

        break;

    case 5:

        /*
         * Get the name of the account to operate on, and then a
         * binding for the server managing that account.
         */
        get_name_and_binding (&binding_h);

        /*
         * Call remote procedure to get the account balance before
         * closing the account.
         */
        transaction (binding_h, BALANCE, amount, &balance,
            &bank_status, &dce_status);

        CHECK_DCE_STATUS (dce_status, "transaction:", ABORT);

        CHECK_BANK_STATUS (bank_status, "transaction:", ABORT);

        printf ("Amount due to you is: $%d\n", balance);
```

Example F-5: A Client File of the Better Banking Application (continued)

```
        /*
         * Call remote procedure to close an account.
         */
        delete_account (binding_h, &bank_status, &dce_status);

        CHECK_DCE_STATUS (dce_status, "delete_account:", ABORT);

        CHECK_BANK_STATUS (bank_status, "delete_account:", ABORT);

        printf ("Account closed.\n\n");

        /*
         * Since the account is now closed, remove the object UUID
         * from the binding, so we don't try to access an account
         * the server no longer knows about.
         */
        rpc_binding_set_object (binding_h, NULL, &dce_status);

        CHECK_DCE_STATUS (dce_status, "rpc_binding_set_object failed:",
            ABORT);

        break;

    case 6:

        /*
         * If we're not already in contact with a particular server,
         * we'll shutdown all available servers.
         */
        if (binding_h == NULL)
        {
            do
            {
                import_interface ("banking", banking_v1_0_c_ifspec,
                    &binding_h, &dce_status);

                if (dce_status != rpc_s_no_more_bindings)
                {
                    CHECK_DCE_STATUS (dce_status,
                        "shutdown import_interface failed:", ABORT);

                    /*
                     * Stop the server from listening for new calls.
                     */
                    rpc_mgmt_stop_server_listening (binding_h,
                    &dce_status);

                    CHECK_DCE_STATUS (dce_status, "shutdown failed:",
                        ABORT);

                    rpc_binding_free (&binding_h, &dce_status);

                    CHECK_DCE_STATUS (dce_status,
                        "rpc_binding_free failed:", ABORT);
                }
            } while (dce_status == rpc_s_ok);
```

Example F-5: A Client File of the Better Banking Application (continued)

```
                    printf ("All servers have been shutdown.\n\n");
                }
                /*
                 * Otherwise, shutdown the one we're dealing with.
                 */
                else
                {
                    /*
                     * Stop the server from listening for new calls.
                     */
                    rpc_mgmt_stop_server_listening (binding_h,
                        &dce_status);

                    CHECK_DCE_STATUS (dce_status, "shutdown failed:", ABORT);

                    printf (
                        "The server for your account has been shutdown.\n\n");

                    /*
                     * Free the binding handle, so that if we try another
                     * transaction we'll first import for another server.
                     */
                    rpc_binding_free (&binding_h, &dce_status);

                    CHECK_DCE_STATUS (dce_status, "rpc_binding_free failed:",
                        ABORT);
                }

                break;

            case 7:

                break;

            default:

                fflush (stdin);
                printf ("Invalid selection. Try again.\n\n");
                break;
        }

    } while (selection != 7);
}

void get_name_and_binding (binding_h)
rpc_binding_handle_t  *binding_h;
{
    uuid_t          account_id;
    unsigned_char_t account_name[STRINGLEN];
    int             retry_count;
    unsigned32      status;

    /*
     * If we don't already have an object UUID (the account ID) in the
     * binding handle, prompt for an account name and until we find a
     * server for that account.
```

Example F-5: A Client File of the Better Banking Application (continued)

```
    */
    if (*binding_h != NULL)
    {
        rpc_binding_inq_object (*binding_h, &account_id, &status);

        CHECK_DCE_STATUS (status, "rpc_binding_inq_object failed:", ABORT);
    }
    else
    {
        uuid_create_nil (&account_id, &status);

        CHECK_DCE_STATUS (status, "uuid_create_nil failed:", ABORT);
    }

    if (uuid_is_nil (&account_id, &status))
    {
        retry_count = 0;

        do
        {
            printf ("\nEnter account name: ");
            scanf ("%s", account_name);

            /*
             * Import by resource to get the server for this account.
             */
            import_resource (banking_v1_0_c_ifspec, account_name,
                binding_h, &status);

            CHECK_DCE_STATUS (status,
                "No server for account.\nimport_resource failed", RESUME);

            ++retry_count;

            if (retry_count > 2)
            {
                fprintf (stderr, "Too many bad account names - bye.\n");

                exit(1);
            }
        } while (status != rpc_s_ok);
    }
}
```

Example F-6: Import Operations in the Better Banking Application

```
/*
 * File name:  btr_import.c
 *
 * Better banking client import routines.
 */

#include <stdio.h>
```

Example F-6: Import Operations in the Better Banking Application (continued)

```
#include <stdlib.h>
#include <dce/rpc.h>
#include "check_status.h"
#define STRINGLEN 50

extern unsigned_char_t  server_group_name[STRINGLEN];

void import_interface (if_name, if_spec, binding_h, status)
unsigned_char_t       *if_name;
rpc_if_handle_t        if_spec;
rpc_binding_handle_t  *binding_h;
unsigned32            *status;
{
    rpc_ns_handle_t    import_context;
    unsigned_char_t   *string_binding;
    unsigned32         temp_status;

    /*
     * Import binding information from the namespace server group.
     */
    rpc_ns_binding_import_begin (
        rpc_c_ns_syntax_default,    /* Syntax for server group name.  */
        server_group_name,          /* Namespace server entry name.   */
        if_spec,                    /* Interface to import            */
        NULL,                       /* Not importing an object UUID.   */
        &import_context,            /* Import context.                */
        status
        );

    CHECK_DCE_STATUS (*status,
        "Can't import by interface\nrpc_ns_binding_import_begin failed", ABORT);

    do
    {
        /*
         * Get a server binding handle.
         */
        rpc_ns_binding_import_next (import_context, binding_h, status);

        if (*status == rpc_s_ok)
        {
            /*
             * Get an endpoint for the binding.
             */
            rpc_ep_resolve_binding (*binding_h, if_spec, status);

            CHECK_DCE_STATUS (*status, "rpc_ep_resolve_binding failed:", ABORT);

            /*
             * Verify the server is available.
             */
            if (rpc_mgmt_is_server_listening (*binding_h, &temp_status))
            {
                break;
```

Example F-6: Import Operations in the Better Banking Application (continued)

```
            }
            else
            {
                CHECK_DCE_STATUS (temp_status,
                    "Server not listening\nrpc_mgmt_is_server_listening failed:",
                    RESUME);

                rpc_binding_to_string_binding (*binding_h, &string_binding,
                    &temp_status);

                CHECK_DCE_STATUS (temp_status,
                    "rpc_binding_to_string_binding failed:", ABORT);

                fprintf (stderr, "Failed binding: %s\n", string_binding);

                rpc_string_free (&string_binding, &temp_status);
                CHECK_DCE_STATUS (temp_status, "rpc_string_free failed:",
                    ABORT);
            }
        }
        else
        {
            if (*status != rpc_s_no_more_bindings)
            {
                CHECK_DCE_STATUS (*status,
                    "Can't import by interface\nrpc_ns_binding_import_next failed:",
                    RESUME);
            }
        }
    } while (*status == rpc_s_ok);

    /*
     * If we have a binding...
     */
    if (*status == rpc_s_ok)
    {
        /*
         * Make sure the returned binding doesn't reference an existing account.
         */
        rpc_binding_set_object (*binding_h, NULL, status);

        CHECK_DCE_STATUS (*status, "rpc_binding_set_object failed:", ABORT);
    }

    return;
}

void import_resource (if_spec, account_name, binding_h, status)
rpc_if_handle_t       if_spec;
unsigned_char_t       *account_name;
rpc_binding_handle_t  *binding_h;
unsigned32            *status;
{
    rpc_ns_handle_t     import_context;
```

Example F-6: Import Operations in the Better Banking Application (continued)

```
rpc_ns_handle_t      obj_inq_context;
unsigned_char_t      resource_entry_name[STRINGLEN];
uuid_t               account_id;
unsigned_char_t      *string_binding;
unsigned32           temp_status;

/*
 * Create resource entry name for import.
 * Using:  <account-name>_savings
 */
sprintf ((char *) resource_entry_name, "/.:/%s_savings", account_name);

/*
 * Import binding information from the namespace resource entry.
 */
rpc_ns_binding_import_begin (
    rpc_c_ns_syntax_default,    /* Syntax for resource entry name.  */
    resource_entry_name,        /* Namespace resource entry name.   */
    if_spec,                    /* Interface to import              */
    NULL,                       /* Importing without object UUID.   */
    &import_context,            /* Import context.                  */
    status
    );

CHECK_DCE_STATUS (*status,
    "Can't import by resource\nrpc_ns_binding_import_begin failed:", ABORT);

do
{
    /*
     * Get a server binding handle.
     */
    rpc_ns_binding_import_next (import_context, binding_h, status);

    if (*status == rpc_s_ok)
    {
        /*
         * Get the current resource's object UUID from the resource
         * entry (a group) and place it into the current
         * binding handle.
         */
        rpc_ns_entry_object_inq_begin (
            rpc_c_ns_syntax_default, /* Syntax for resource entry name */
            resource_entry_name,     /* Namespace resource entry name. */
            &obj_inq_context,        /* Inquiry context handle.        */
            status
            );

        CHECK_DCE_STATUS (*status, "rpc_ns_entry_object_inq_begin failed:",
            ABORT);

        /*
         * Get the object UUID.
         */
```

Example F-6: Import Operations in the Better Banking Application (continued)

```
            rpc_ns_entry_object_inq_next (obj_inq_context, &account_id,
                status);

            CHECK_DCE_STATUS (*status, "rpc_ns_entry_object_inq_next failed:",
                ABORT);

            /*
             * End the search.
             */
            rpc_ns_entry_object_inq_done (&obj_inq_context, status);

            CHECK_DCE_STATUS (*status, "rpc_ns_entry_object_inq_done failed:",
                ABORT);

            /*
             * Place the UUID into the binding handle.
             */
            rpc_binding_set_object (*binding_h, &account_id, status);

            CHECK_DCE_STATUS (*status, "rpc_binding_set_object failed:", ABORT);

            /*
             * Verify the server is available.
             */
            if (rpc_mgmt_is_server_listening (*binding_h, &temp_status))
            {
                break;
            }
            else
            {
                CHECK_DCE_STATUS (temp_status,
                    "Server not listening\nrpc_mgmt_is_server_listening failed:",
                    RESUME);

                rpc_binding_to_string_binding (*binding_h, &string_binding,
                    &temp_status);

                CHECK_DCE_STATUS (temp_status,
                    "rpc_binding_to_string_binding failed:", ABORT);

                fprintf (stderr, "Failed binding: %s\n", string_binding);

                rpc_string_free (&string_binding, &temp_status);
                CHECK_DCE_STATUS (temp_status, "rpc_string_free failed:",
                    ABORT);
            }
        }
        else
        {
            if (*status != rpc_s_no_more_bindings)
            {
                CHECK_DCE_STATUS (*status,
                    "Can't import by resource\nrpc_ns_binding_import_next failed:",
                    RESUME);
            }
```

Example F-6: Import Operations in the Better Banking Application (continued)

```
        }
    } while (*status == rpc_s_ok);

    return;
}
```

G

The Grade Server Application

The Grade Server application consists of a server named *grade_server* and a client with the executable filename *get_GPA*. The server stores a fixed database of student names and their Grade Point Averages (GPAs). The *get_GPA* client queries the database.

The only interface defined for the Grade Server is the gpa interface that is called by *get_GPA*. This remote procedure returns the GPA associated with a single student.

The application illustrates the use of authenticated RPC and DCE Security including:

- Annotating a binding for authenticated RPC.

- Determining a server's principal name.

- Setting up a server's login context.

- Creating a thread to manage a server's secret key.

- A sample reference monitor that uses name and group membership for authorization.

How to Run the Application

See Chapters 8 and 9 for the administrative steps you need to perform in order to set up accounts and access rights. To run the server, type the following:

```
S> login grade_server
> make server
> server &
```

To run the client, type the following:

```
C> make client
> dce_login student_1
> get_GPA
```

Application Files

Makefile contains descriptions of how the applicaton is compiled. Some files depend on the header file *check_status.h* from the arithmetic application for the *CHECK_STATUS* macro (see Example G-1).

gpa.idl contains the description of the constants, data types, and procedures for the interface. (see Example G-2).

client.c takes user input specifying the name of the student whose GPA we want. It imports a binding from the name space. It then queries the server specified by the binding or the server's principal name and checks to see if the server is a legitimate Grade Server. If so, it annotates the binding handle for authenticated RPC and calls the *get_GPA* remote procedure to get the data (see Example G-3).

server.c initializes the server with a series of runtime calls prior to servicing remote procedure calls. The server, unlike the other examples in this book, runs authenticated. The server acquires its own login context and establishes itself as a principal. It then creates a separate thread to manage its secret key and registers its principal name with the RPC runtime. In addition, the server performs the normal initialization steps. It registers all available protocol sequences, advertises itself in the name service, and registers its endpoint in the endpoint mapper database (see Example G-4).

gpa_mgr.c, part of the server, is an implementation of the remote procedure defined in *gpa.idl*. In addition, it also implements the reference monitor for the Grade Server. The code will check the authentication parameters, contact the DCE Security registry to see if the client is a member of the teacher group, and then either allow the call to proceed or signal a failure. This module contains an internal routine `lookup_GPA` that actually finds the data (see Example G-5).

Example G-1: The Makefile for the Grade Server Application

```
# Makefile for the get_GPA application.
# IDL compiler
APPL=gpa
IDLCMD = /bin/idl

# libraries for DEC Alpha OSF/1
LIBS = -ldce -lpthreads -lc_r -lmach -lm
```

Example G-1: The Makefile for the Grade Server Application (continued)

```
# CC flags for DEC Alpha OSF/1
CFLAGS = -D_SHARED_LIBRARIES -Dalpha -D_REENTRANT -w

all: interface get_GPA server

#
# INTERFACE BUILD
#
interface: $(APPL).h $(APPL)_cstub.o $(APPL)_sstub.o
$(APPL).h $(APPL)_cstub.o $(APPL)_sstub.o: $(APPL).idl
   $(IDLCMD) $(APPL).idl

#
# CLIENT BUILD
#
get_GPA: client.o $(APPL)_cstub.o
   $(CC) $(CFLAG) -o get_GPA client.o $(APPL)_cstub.o $(LIBS)

#
# SERVER BUILD
#
server: server.o $(APPL)_sstub.o $(APPL)_mgr.o
    $(CC) $(CFLAG) -o server server.o $(APPL)_sstub.o $(APPL)_mgr.o $(LIBS)
```

Example G-2: The IDL File of the Grade Server Application

```
/* FILE NAME: gpa.idl */
/*
**      gpa.idl
*/

/* We use explicit handles so that we can do authenticated RPC. */
[uuid(f657c75c-277f-11cc-88c5-08002b1d3118),
   version(1.0)]
interface gpa
{
    typedef float      gpa_t;
    /*
     * If student_name is NULL, get caller's GPA.
     */
    [idempotent]
    void get_GPA(
      [in]  handle_t    handle,
      [in, string] char *student_name,
      [out] gpa_t       *gpa
      );
}
```

Example G-3: Client File of the Grade Server Application

```
/*
 *    client.c
 *
 *    Client program for get_GPA application.
 */

#include <stdio.h>
#include "gpa.h"
#include "check_status.h"

#include <dce/binding.h> /* binding to registry */
#include <dce/pgo.h>           /* registry i/f */
#include <dce/secidmap.h>      /* translate global name -> princ name */

#endif

/*
 *    main()
 *
 *    Get started, and main loop.
 */

int
main(
    int                       argc,
    char                      *argv[])
{
    rpc_binding_handle_t      binding_handle;
    unsigned32                status;
    rpc_ns_handle_t             import_context;
    unsigned_char_t             *student_name;
    gpa_t                     gpa;
    sec_rgy_handle_t          rgy_handle;
    sec_rgy_name_t            princ_name;
    unsigned_char_t             *server_princ_name;
    boolean32                 is_member;

    /* Get input args. */
    if (argc > 1)
      student_name = (unsigned_char_t *) argv[1];
    else
      student_name = (unsigned_char_t *) "";

    /*
     * Get server binding from the name space.
     */

    rpc_ns_binding_import_begin(rpc_c_ns_syntax_dce,
        "/.:/grade", gpa_v1_0_c_ifspec,
        NULL, &import_context, &status);
    CHECK_STATUS (status, "Import begin failed", ABORT);
    rpc_ns_binding_import_next(import_context,
        &binding_handle, &status);
    CHECK_STATUS (status, "Import next failed", ABORT);
    rpc_ns_binding_import_done(&import_context, &status);
```

Example G-3: Client File of the Grade Server Application (continued)

```
CHECK_STATUS (status, "Import done failed", ABORT);

/*
 * Determine the server's principal name.
 */
rpc_ep_resolve_binding (binding_handle, gpa_v1_0_c_ifspec,
   &status);
CHECK_STATUS (status, "resolve_binding failed", ABORT);

rpc_mgmt_inq_server_princ_name (binding_handle,
      rpc_c_authn_dce_secret, &server_princ_name, &status);
CHECK_STATUS (status, "inq_princ_name failed", ABORT);

/*
 * Find out if the principal name that is returned by the
 * server is a member of the grade_server group.
 */
/* Open a registry site for query */
sec_rgy_site_open_query(NULL, &rgy_handle, &status);
CHECK_STATUS (status, "rgy_site_open failed", ABORT);

   /* Ask the Security registry to translate the global principal
      name into a simple principal name.  */
sec_id_parse_name (rgy_handle, server_princ_name,
   NULL, NULL, princ_name, NULL, &status);
CHECK_STATUS (status, "sec_id_parse_name failed", ABORT);

/* The group membership check. */
is_member = sec_rgy_pgo_is_member (rgy_handle,
   sec_rgy_domain_group, "grade_server",
   princ_name, &status);
CHECK_STATUS (status, "is_member failed", ABORT);

/* We are done with the registry; we can release the
   rgy_handle now. */
sec_rgy_site_close(rgy_handle, &status);
CHECK_STATUS (status, "rgy_site_close failed", ABORT);

/* Make sure that the server is a bona-fide Grade Server. */
if (! is_member )
{
    fprintf (stderr, "got an imposter\n");
    exit(1);
}

/*
 * Annotate our binding handle for authentication.
 */
rpc_binding_set_auth_info(binding_handle,
    server_princ_name, rpc_c_protect_level_default,
    rpc_c_authn_dce_secret, NULL /*default login context*/,
    rpc_c_authz_dce, &status);
CHECK_STATUS (status, "binding_set_auth_info failed", ABORT);

/*
```

Example G-3: Client File of the Grade Server Application (continued)

```
     * Make the actual remote procedure call.
     */
    get_GPA (binding_handle, student_name, &gpa);
    fprintf (stderr, "GPA is: %f\n", gpa);
    exit (0);
}
```

Example G-4: Server Initialization of the Grade Server Application

```
/*
**      server.c
**
**      Server program for Grade Server application.
*/

#include <stdio.h>
#include <pthread.h>
#include "gpa.h"
#include "check_status.h"

#define SERVER_PRINCIPAL_NAME "grade_server_1"
#define KEYTAB "/tmp/grade_server_tab"

void establish_identity();

int
main(
    int                     argc,
    char                    *argv[])
{
    unsigned_char_t               *server_name;
    rpc_binding_vector_t    *bind_vector_p;
    unsigned32              status;
    int                     i;

    /* Register interface with rpc runtime. */
    rpc_server_register_if(gpa_v1_0_s_ifspec, NULL,
        NULL, &status);
    CHECK_STATUS (status,"unable to register i/f",ABORT);

    /* We want to use all supported protocol sequences. */
    rpc_server_use_all_protseqs(rpc_c_protseq_max_reqs_default, &status);
    CHECK_STATUS (status,"use_all_protseqs failed",ABORT);

    /*
     * Establish this server's identity by setting up the
     * appropriate login context.
     */
    establish_identity (&status);
    CHECK_STATUS (status,"Cannot establish server identity",ABORT);

    /*
     * Register authentication info with RPC.
```

Example G-4: Server Initialization of the Grade Server Application (continued)

```
    */
    rpc_server_register_auth_info(SERVER_PRINCIPAL_NAME,
        rpc_c_authn_dce_secret, NULL /*default key retrieval function*/,
        KEYTAB, &status);
    CHECK_STATUS (status,"server_register_auth_info failed",ABORT);

    /*
     * Continue with the normal initialization sequence.
     * Get our bindings...
     */
    rpc_server_inq_bindings(&bind_vector_p, &status);
    CHECK_STATUS (status,"server_inq_bindings failed",ABORT);

    /* Register binding information with the endpoint map. */
    rpc_ep_register(gpa_v1_0_s_ifspec, bind_vector_p,
        NULL,
        (unsigned_char_t *)"GPA server, version 1.0", &status);
    CHECK_STATUS (status,"ep_register failed",ABORT);

    /*
     * Export binding information into the namespace.
     */
    rpc_ns_binding_export(rpc_c_ns_syntax_dce, "/.:/grade",
        gpa_v1_0_s_ifspec, bind_vector_p,
        NULL, &status);
    CHECK_STATUS (status,"export failed",ABORT);

    /* Listen for remote calls. */
    fprintf(stderr, "Server ready.\n");
    rpc_server_listen(rpc_c_listen_max_calls_default, &status);
    CHECK_STATUS (status,"server_listen failed",ABORT);

    /* We don't expect to return from the listen loop. */
    fprintf(stderr, "Unexpected return from rpc_server_listen\n");
    exit(1);
}

/*
 * establish_identity.
 *
 * Internal routine to establish this server as the grade_server_1
 * principal.
 */

#include <dce/sec_login.h>

void establish_identity (o_status)
error_status_t *o_status;
{
    sec_login_handle_t  login_context;
    sec_login_auth_src_t auth_src;
    void                *server_key;
    error_status_t      status;
    boolean32           identity_valid;
```

Example G-4: Server Initialization of the Grade Server Application (continued)

```
boolean32          reset_passwd;
pthread_t          refresh_login_context_thread;
pthread_t          key_mgmt_thread;
void               refresh_login_context_rtn ();
void               key_mgmt_rtn ();

/*
 * Set up the network identity for this server principal.
 * The network credentials obtained are seald and must be
 * unsealed with the server's secret key before they can
 * be used.
 */
sec_login_setup_identity(SERVER_PRINCIPAL_NAME,
                         sec_login_no_flags,
                         &login_context, &status);
CHECK_STATUS (status,"unable to set up identity",ABORT);

/*
 * Retrieve the server's secret key from the private keytab
 * file.
 */
sec_key_mgmt_get_key(rpc_c_authn_dce_secret, KEYTAB,
                     SERVER_PRINCIPAL_NAME,
                     0,  /* return most recent version */
                     &server_key, &status);
CHECK_STATUS (status,"unable to retrive key",ABORT);

/*
 * Unseal the network identity using the server's secret key.
 */
identity_valid = sec_login_validate_identity(login_context,
        server_key, &reset_passwd, &auth_src, &status);

/*
 * Free the secret key as soon as we are done with it.
 */
sec_key_mgmt_free_key (&server_key, &status);
CHECK_STATUS (status,"unable to free key",ABORT);

if (identity_valid)
{
 /*
  * Make sure that the server identity was validated by
  * the network -
  * i.e., the security server, instead of local data.
  */
    if (auth_src != sec_login_auth_src_network)
    {
     fprintf (stderr, "Server has no network credentials\n");
     exit (1);
    }

 /*
  * We make this login context the default for this process.
```

Example G-4: Server Initialization of the Grade Server Application (continued)

```
        */
        sec_login_set_context(login_context, &status);
        CHECK_STATUS (status,"unable to set default context",ABORT);

    /*
     * Start up a thread to refresh the login context when it
     * expires.
     */
    if (( pthread_create (&refresh_login_context_thread,
            pthread_attr_default,
                (pthread_startroutine_t) refresh_login_context_rtn,
                (pthread_addr_t)login_context) ) == -1)
            exit (1);
    /*
     * Start up a thread to manage our secret key.
     */
    if (( pthread_create (&key_mgmt_thread, pthread_attr_default,
                    (pthread_startroutine_t) key_mgmt_rtn,
                    (pthread_addr_t)NULL) ) == -1)
            exit (1);
            *o_status = status;
    }
    else
    {
        error_status_t temp_status;

        CHECK_STATUS (status,"unable to validate network identity",RESUME);

        /* Reclaim the storage */
        sec_login_purge_context (&login_context, &temp_status);
        CHECK_STATUS (temp_status,"unable to purge login context",ABORT);

        *o_status = status;
    return;
    }
}

#include <sys/time.h>
/*
 * A thread to periodically refresh the credentials contained in a
 * login context.
 */

void refresh_login_context_rtn (login_context)
sec_login_handle_t login_context;
{
    struct timeval       current_time;
    struct timezone      tz;
    struct timespec      delay;
    signed32             expiration;
    signed32             delay_time;
    unsigned32           used_kvno;
    boolean32       reset_passwd;
    boolean32       identity_valid;
```

Example G-4: Server Initialization of the Grade Server Application (continued)

```
    void              *server_key;
    sec_login_auth_src_t  auth_src;
    error_status_t        status;

#define MINUTE 60

    fprintf (stderr, "refresh login context thread started up\n");

    while (1)
    {

    /*
     * Wait until the login context is about to expire.
     */

#ifdef BSD
    /* BSD version of gettimeofday has a timezone parameter. */
    gettimeofday (&current_time, &tz);
#else
    gettimeofday (&current_time);
#endif

    sec_login_get_expiration (login_context, &expiration, &status);
    if ((status != rpc_s_ok) && (status != sec_login_s_not_certified))
    {
        fprintf (stderr, "Cannot get login context expiration time\n");
        exit (1);
    }

    delay_time = expiration - current_time.tv_sec - (10*MINUTE);

    if (delay_time > 0)
    {
        delay.tv_sec = delay_time;
        delay.tv_nsec = 0;
        pthread_delay_np (&delay);
    }

    /*
     * Refresh the login context.
     */
    sec_login_refresh_identity (login_context, &status);
    CHECK_STATUS (status, "cannot refresh identity",ABORT);

    /*
     * The refreshed login context still needs to be validated.
     * To do so, first retrieve the server's secret key from the
     * private keytab file.
     */
    sec_key_mgmt_get_key (rpc_c_authn_dce_secret, KEYTAB,
        SERVER_PRINCIPAL_NAME,
        0,    /* return most recent version */
        &server_key, &status);
    CHECK_STATUS (status,"unable to retrieve key",ABORT);

    /*
```

Example G-4: Server Initialization of the Grade Server Application (continued)

```
      * Validate the login context.
      */
     identity_valid = sec_login_validate_identity (login_context,
        server_key, &reset_passwd, &auth_src, &status);

     /*
      * Free the secret key as soon as we are done with it.
      */
     sec_key_mgmt_free_key (&server_key, &status);
     CHECK_STATUS (status,"unable to free key",ABORT);

     if (! identity_valid)
     {
         error_status_t temp_status;

           /* Reclaim the storage */
         sec_login_purge_context (&login_context, &temp_status);
         CHECK_STATUS (temp_status,"unable to purge login context",ABORT);

           CHECK_STATUS (status,"unable to validate network identity",ABORT);

     }

   }

}


/*
 * A thread to periodically change the server's secret key.
 */

void key_mgmt_rtn ()
{
    error_status_t  status;

    fprintf (stderr, "key mgmt thread started up\n");
    while (1)
    {
        sec_key_mgmt_manage_key (rpc_c_authn_dce_secret,
         KEYTAB, SERVER_PRINCIPAL_NAME, &status);
        CHECK_STATUS (status,"key mgmt failure",ABORT);
    }
}
```

Example G-5: Remote Procedure for the Grade Server

```
/*
 *     gpa_mgr.c
 *
 *     Manager routines for the gpa interface.
 */

#include <stdio.h>
```

Example G-5: Remote Procedure for the Grade Server (continued)

```
#include <dce/binding.h> /* binding to registry */
#include <dce/pgo.h>         /* registry i/f */
#include <dce/secidmap.h>    /* translate global name -> princ name */

#include <dce/id_base.h>

#include "gpa.h"
#include "check_status.h"

void lookup_gpa ();           /* forward declaration */

void get_GPA(
    rpc_binding_handle_t handle,
    char               *student_name,
    gpa_t              *gpa)
{
    sec_id_pac_t    *pac;
    unsigned_char_t *server_principal_name;
    sec_rgy_name_t      client_principal_name;
    unsigned32          protection_level;
    unsigned32          authn_svc;
    unsigned32          authz_svc;
    sec_rgy_handle_t    rgy_handle;
    boolean32           is_teacher;
    error_status_t  status;

    /*
     * Check the authentication parameters that the client
     * selected for this call.
     */
    rpc_binding_inq_auth_client (handle, (rpc_authz_handle_t *) &pac,
      &server_principal_name, &protection_level, &authn_svc,
      &authz_svc, &status);
    CHECK_STATUS (status, "inq_auth_client failed", ABORT);

    /*
     * Make sure that the caller has specified the required
     * level of protection, authentication, and authorization.
     */
    if (! ((protection_level == rpc_c_protect_level_pkt_integ)
         &&
         (authn_svc == rpc_c_authn_dce_secret)
       &&
       (authz_svc == rpc_c_authz_dce)
         ))
    {
     *gpa = -1.0;           /* signal failure */
     return;
    }

    /*
     * Establish a binding to the registry interface of the
     * Security Server.
     */
```

Example G-5: Remote Procedure for the Grade Server (continued)

```
sec_rgy_site_open_query(NULL, &rgy_handle, &status);
CHECK_STATUS (status, "rgy_site_open failed", ABORT);

/*
 * Convert the UUID in the PAC into a name.
 */
sec_rgy_pgo_id_to_name (rgy_handle,
              sec_rgy_domain_person,
              &(pac->principal.uuid),
                      client_principal_name,
              &status);
CHECK_STATUS (status, "pgo_id_to_name failed", ABORT);

/*
 * Check to see if the client principal is a member of
 * the teacher group.
 */
is_teacher = sec_rgy_pgo_is_member (rgy_handle,
    sec_rgy_domain_group, "teacher",
    client_principal_name, &status);
CHECK_STATUS (status, "is_member failed", ABORT);
 /*
 * We are done with the Security registry; free the handle
 * now.
 */
sec_rgy_site_close(rgy_handle,&status);
CHECK_STATUS (status, "rgy_site_close failed", ABORT);

/*
 * Security Policy:
 *
 * If you are a teacher, then you can lookup anyone's
 * gpa.
 * else if you are looking up your own gpa, it's ok.
 * else, just return -1.0.
 */
if (is_teacher)
 lookup_gpa (student_name, gpa);
else if ((! strcmp (student_name, client_principal_name)) ||
        (student_name[0] == '\0'))
 lookup_gpa (client_principal_name, gpa);
else
    *gpa = -1.0;
}


/*
 * Internal routine that maintains a fixed table of some
 * student GPA data.
 */
typedef struct {
   char *gpa_name;
```

Example G-5: Remote Procedure for the Grade Server (continued)

```
    gpa_t gpa_value;
    } gpa_entry_t;

gpa_entry_t gpa_table [] = {
    {"Peter", 4.0},
    {"Ruth", 3.8},
    {"Howard", 2.0},
    {"Fran", 2.7},
    {"student_1", 3.2},
    {NULL, -2.0}
};


/*
 * Returns the student's gpa.  If the student is not found,
 * return -2.0.
 */
void lookup_gpa (student_name, gpa)
char *student_name;
gpa_t *gpa;
{
    gpa_entry_t     *gpa_entry_p;

  for (gpa_entry_p = gpa_table;
     gpa_entry_p->gpa_name != NULL;
     gpa_entry_p++) {
       if (! strcmp (student_name, gpa_entry_p->gpa_name)) {
       *gpa = gpa_entry_p->gpa_value;
       return;
     }
   }

   /* Query for student not in our database. */
   *gpa = -2.0;
}
```

H

The Remote_file Application

The *remote_file* client copies ASCII data from the client to the server. The source can be a data file or the standard input of the client. The target on the server system is either a file or the server standard output. The *remote_file* application demonstrates some advanced features of DCE application development including:

- Using a context handle with a context rundown procedure.

- Using the explicit binding method with a primitive binding handle.

- Finding a server using strings of binding information.

How To Run the Application

To run the local test of the application, use an ASCII text file as input and a new data file as output. The host is not relevant for the local test. Type the following:

```
C> make local
C> local_r_client.exe input   host   output
```

To run the server of the distributed application, type the following:

```
S> make server
S> r_server.exe
```

To run the client of the distributed application to transfer ASCII data, use an ASCII text file as input and a new data file on the server host as output. Type the following:

```
C> make client
C> r_client.exe input   host   output
```

Application Files

Makefile contains descriptions of how the application is compiled (see Example H-1).

remote_file.idl contains descriptions of the data types and procedures for the interface (see Example H-2).

r_client.c interprets the user input by calling the application-specific procedure *get_args*. A binding handle representing the information about a client-server relationship is obtained from strings of binding information. The remote procedure *remote_open* is called to open the server target file. A buffer is allocated for a conformant array. The application enters a loop, reading source data and sending the data to the target with a remote procedure call to *remote_send*. Finally, the remote procedure *remote_close* is called to close the target file (see Example H-3).

get_args.c interprets the user input to obtain the name of a local client ASCII file of source data, the server host to use, and the server target file (see Example H-4).

do_string_binding.c contains the *do_string_binding* procedure that shows how to find a server from strings of binding information. A host name or network address is input, and then combined with a generated protocol sequence to create a valid binding handle, which is returned as a parameter (see Example H-5).

context_rundown.c is the implementation of a context rundown procedure. The server stub calls this procedure automatically if communication breaks between a client and the server that is maintaining context for the client. For this application, the context is a file handle of a server data file. This context rundown procedure closes the file (see Example H-6).

r_procedures.c is the implementation of the remote procedures defined in the *remote_file* interface (see Example H-7).

r_server.c initializes the server with a series of runtime calls prior to servicing remote procedure calls. In this application, all available protocol sequences are registered. The server is not advertised in a name service database. The server's dynamic endpoints are added to the server's local endpoint map. A client finds this server by constructing a string binding containing a protocol sequence and the host name or network address (see Example H-8).

Example H-1: The Makefile for the remote_file Application

```
# FILE NAME: Makefile
# Makefile for the remote_file application
#
# definitions for this make file
#
APPL=remote_file
IDLCMD=idl -v
CHECK=../arithmetic        # Directory containing check_status.h
LIBS = -ldce -lpthreads -lc_r -lmach -lm        # DEC Alpha OSF/1
CFLAGS= -D_SHARED_LIBRARIES -Dalpha -D_REENTRANT # DEC Alpha OSF/1
CC= cc


#
# COMPLETE BUILD of the distributed application.
#
all:  local interface client server


#
# LOCAL BUILD of the client application to test locally.
#
local:interface r_client.c get_args.c r_procedures.c
        $(CC) $(CFLAGS) -DLOCAL -o local_r_client.exe \
              r_client.c get_args.c r_procedures.c
# remove object files so they do not interfere with a real build
        rm r_client.o get_args.o r_procedures.o


#
# INTERFACE BUILD
#
interface:  $(APPL).h $(APPL)_cstub.o $(APPL)_sstub.o
$(APPL).h $(APPL)_cstub.o $(APPL)_sstub.o: $(APPL).idl
        $(IDLCMD) $(APPL).idl


#
# CLIENT BUILD
#
client:    r_client
r_client:   $(APPL).h r_client.o get_args.o do_string_binding.o \
   $(APPL)_cstub.o
        $(CC) $(CFLAGS) -o r_client.exe r_client.o \
              get_args.o do_string_binding.o $(APPL)_cstub.o $(LIBS)

do_string_binding.o:    do_string_binding.c
        $(CC) $(CFLAGS) -I$(CHECK) -c do_string_binding.c
```

Example H-1: The Makefile for the remote_file Application (continued)

```
#
# SERVER BUILD
#
server:     r_server
r_server:   $(APPL).h r_server.o r_procedures.o context_rundown.o \
    $(APPL)_sstub.o
        $(CC) $(CFLAGS) -I$(CHECK) -o r_server.exe r_server.o \
            r_procedures.o context_rundown.o $(APPL)_sstub.o $(LIBS)

r_server.o: r_server.c
        $(CC) $(CFLAGS) -I$(CHECK) -c r_server.c
```

Example H-2: The IDL File of the remote_file Application

```
/* FILE NAME: remote_file.idl */
[
uuid(016B2B80-F9B4-11C9-B31A-08002B111685),
version(1.0)
]
interface remote_file          /* file manipulation on a remote system */
{
    typedef [context_handle] void *filehandle;  /* */
    typedef                   byte buffer[];

filehandle remote_open(        /* open for write   */
    [in] handle_t binding_h,   /* explicit primitive binding handle    */
    [in, string] char name[],  /* if name is null, use stdout in server */
    [in, string] char mode[]   /* values can be "r", "w", or "a"       */
);

long remote_send(
    [in] filehandle fh,                         /* */
    [in, max_is(max)] buffer buf,
    [in] long max
);

void remote_close(
    [in,out] filehandle *fh                     /* */
);
}
```

Example H-3: A Client File of the remote_file Application

```
/* FILE NAME: r_client.c */
#include <stdio.h>
#include <string.h>
#include "remote_file.h"
#define MAX 200          /* maximum line length for a file */

main(argc, argv)
int argc;
char *argv[];
{
    FILE        *local_fh;              /* file handle for client file input */
    char        host[100];          /* name or network address of remote host */
    idl_char     remote_name[100];              /* name of remote file */
    rpc_binding_handle_t binding_h;                 /* binding handle */
    filehandle   remote_fh;                     /* context handle */
    buffer      *buf_ptr;               /* buffer pointer for data sent */
    int         size;                   /* size of data buffer */
    void exit();
    char *malloc();

    get_args(argc, argv, &local_fh, host, (char *)remote_name);
#ifndef LOCAL
    if(do_string_binding(host, &binding_h) < 0) {                       /* */
        fprintf(stderr, "Cannot get binding\n");
        exit(1);
    }
#endif
    remote_fh = remote_open(binding_h, remote_name, (idl_char *)"w");   /* */
    if(remote_fh == NULL) {
        fprintf(stderr, "Cannot open remote file\n");
        exit(1);
    }

    /* The buffer data type is a conformant array of bytes; */
    /* memory must be allocated for a conformant array.     */
    buf_ptr = (buffer *)malloc((MAX+1) * sizeof(buffer));

    while( fgets((char *)buf_ptr, MAX, local_fh) != NULL) {
        size = (int)strlen((char *)buf_ptr); /* data sent will not include \0 */
        if( remote_send(remote_fh, (*buf_ptr), size) < 1) {             /* */
            fprintf(stderr, "Cannot write to remote file\n");
            exit(1);
        }
    }
    remote_close(&remote_fh);                                          /* */
}
```

Example H-4: The get_args Procedure

```
/* FILE NAME: get_args.c */
#include <stdio.h>
```

Example H-4: The get_args Procedure (continued)

```
get_args(argc, argv, local_fh, host, remote_name)
int  argc;
char *argv[];
FILE **local_fh;
char host[];
char remote_name[];
{
    char local_name[100];
    char *strcpy();
    void exit();

    switch(argc) {
    case 1:
    case 2: printf("Usage: %s [local_file] host [remote_file]\n", argv[0]);
            puts("Use \"\" for local stdin.");
            exit(0);
            break;
    case 3: strcpy(local_name, argv[1]);  /* use the same file name */
            strcpy(remote_name, local_name);
            strcpy(host, argv[2]);
            break;
    default: strcpy(local_name, argv[1]);
            strcpy(host, argv[2]);
            strcpy(remote_name, argv[3]);
            break;
    }
    if(strlen(local_name) == 0) {
        (*local_fh) = stdin;
        puts("Using stdin.  Type input:");
    }
    else
        if( ( (*local_fh) = fopen(local_name, "r")) == NULL ) {
            puts("Cannot open local file");
            exit(1);
        }
    return;
}
```

Example H-5: The do_string_binding Procedure

```
/* FILE NAME: do_string_binding.c */
/* Find a server binding handle from strings of binding information      */
/* including protocol sequence, host address, and server process endpoint. */
#include <stdio.h>
#include <dce/rpc.h>
#include "check_status.h"              /* contains the CHECK_STATUS macro */

int do_string_binding(host, binding_h) /*return=0 if binding valid, else -1 */
char            host[];        /* server host name or network address input   */
rpc_binding_handle_t *binding_h;     /* binding handle is output (rpcbase.h) */
{
    rpc_protseq_vector_t *protseq_vector;  /* protocol sequence list        */
    unsigned_char_t    *string_binding;   /* string of binding information */
    unsigned32         status;            /* error status                 */
    int                i, result;

    rpc_network_inq_protseqs( /* obtain a list of valid protocol sequences  */
        &protseq_vector,                 /* list of protocol sequences obtained */
        &status
    );
    CHECK_STATUS(status, "Can't get protocol sequences:", ABORT);

    /* loop through protocol sequences until a binding handle is obtained */
    for(i=0; i < protseq_vector->count; i++) {

        rpc_string_binding_compose(  /* make string binding from components  */
            NULL,                          /* no object UUIDs are required    */
            protseq_vector->protseq[i],    /* protocol sequence               */
            (unsigned_char_t *)host,       /* host name or network address    */
            NULL,                          /* no endpoint is required         */
            NULL,                          /* no network options are required */
            &string_binding,               /* the constructed string binding  */
            &status
        );
        CHECK_STATUS(status, "Can't compose a string binding:", RESUME);

        rpc_binding_from_string_binding(/* convert string to binding handle  */
            string_binding,                /* input string binding            */
            binding_h,                     /* binding handle is obtained here */
            &status
        );
        if(status != rpc_s_ok) {
            result = -1;
            CHECK_STATUS(status, "Can't get binding handle from string:", RESUME);
        }
        else
            result = 0;

        rpc_string_free(                   /* free string binding created   */
            &string_binding,
            &status
        );
        CHECK_STATUS(status, "Can't free string binding:", RESUME);
        if(result == 0)  break;                 /* got a valid binding */
```

Example H-5: The do_string_binding Procedure (continued)

```
    }

    rpc_protseq_vector_free(          /* free the list of protocol sequences   */
        &protseq_vector,
        &status
    );
    CHECK_STATUS(status, "Can't free protocol sequence vector:", RESUME);
    return(result);
}
```

Example H-6: The Context Rundown of the remote_file Application

```
/* FILE NAME: context_rundown.c */
#include <stdio.h>
#include "remote_file.h"

void filehandle_rundown(remote_fh)
filehandle remote_fh;                  /* the context handle is passed in  */
{
    fprintf(stderr, "Server executing context rundown\n");
    if( (FILE *)remote_fh != stdout )
        fclose( (FILE *)remote_fh );   /* file is closed if client is gone */
    remote_fh = NULL;                  /* must set context handle to NULL  */
    return;
}
```

Example H-7: Remote Procedures of the remote_file Application

```
/* FILE NAME: r_procedures.c */
#include <stdio.h>
#include <string.h>
#include <unistd.h>
#include "remote_file.h"

filehandle remote_open(binding_h, name, mode)  /* */
rpc_binding_handle_t binding_h;
idl_char              name[];
idl_char              mode[];
{
    FILE *FILEh;

    if(strlen((char *)name) == 0)                        /* no file name given */
        if(strcmp((char *)mode, "r") == 0)
            FILEh = NULL;                          /* cannot read nonexistent file */
        else FILEh = stdout;                              /* use server stdout */

    else if(access((char *)name, F_OK) == 0)              /* file exists */
        if(strcmp((char *)mode, "w") == 0)
            FILEh = NULL;                         /* do not overwrite existing file */
```

Example H-7: Remote Procedures of the remote_file Application (continued)

```
      else FILEh = fopen((char *)name, (char *)mode);   /* open read/append */
   else                                         /* file does not exist */
      if(strcmp((char *)mode, "r") == 0)
          FILEh = NULL;                          /* cannot read nonexistent file */
      else FILEh = fopen((char *)name, (char *)mode);  /* open write/append */

   return( (filehandle)FILEh );       /* cast FILE handle to context handle */
}


idl_long_int remote_send(fh, buf, max)          /* */
filehandle fh;
buffer buf;
idl_long_int max;
{
   /* write data to the file (context), which is cast as a FILE pointer */
   return( fwrite(buf, sizeof(buffer), max, (FILE *)fh) );
}


void remote_close(fh)                           /* */
filehandle *fh;  /* the client stub needs the changed value upon return */
{
   if( (FILE *)(*fh) != stdout )
      fclose( (FILE *)(*fh) );
   (*fh) = NULL;         /* assign NULL to the context handle to free it */
   return;
}
```

Example H-8: Server Initialization of the remote_file Application

```
/* FILE NAME: r_server.c */
#include <stdio.h>
#include "remote_file.h"              /* header created by the idl compiler */
#include "check_status.h"             /* contains the CHECK_STATUS macro     */
main ()
{
   unsigned32            status;        /* error status (nbase.h)         */
   rpc_binding_vector_t  *binding_vector; /* binding handle list (rpcbase.h)*/
```

Example H-8: Server Initialization of the remote_file Application (continued)

```
rpc_server_register_if(        /* register interface with the RPC runtime */
    remote_file_v1_0_s_ifspec, /* handle for interface specification      */
    NULL,
    NULL,
    &status                    /* error status */
);
CHECK_STATUS(status, "Can't register interface\n", ABORT);

rpc_server_use_all_protseqs(           /* establish protocol sequences  */
    rpc_c_protseq_max_reqs_default,    /* queue length for remote calls */
    &status
);
CHECK_STATUS(status, "Can't establish protocol sequences\n", ABORT);

rpc_server_inq_bindings(    /* get set of this server's binding handles */
    &binding_vector,
    &status
);
CHECK_STATUS(status, "Can't get binding handles\n", ABORT);

rpc_ep_register(                      /* add endpoint to local endpoint map  */
    remote_file_v1_0_s_ifspec,        /* handle for interface specification   */
    binding_vector,                   /* vector of server binding handles     */
    NULL,                             /* no object UUIDs to register          */
    (unsigned_char_t *)"remote_file server", /* annotation (not required) */
    &status
);
CHECK_STATUS(status, "Can't add endpoints to local endpoint map:", ABORT);

puts("Listening for remote procedure calls...");
TRY
    rpc_server_listen(                       /* listen for remote calls */
        rpc_c_listen_max_calls_default,      /* number of threads       */
        &status
    );
    CHECK_STATUS(status, "rpc listen failed:", RESUME);
FINALLY
    puts("Removing endpoints from local endpoint map.");
    rpc_ep_unregister(        /* remove endpoints from local endpoint map */
        remote_file_v1_0_s_ifspec,   /* handle for interface specificaiton */
        binding_vector,              /* vector of server binding handles   */
        NULL,                        /* no object UUIDs to unregister      */
        &status
    );
    CHECK_STATUS(status,"Can't remove endpoints from endpoint map:", RESUME);
```

Example H-8: Server Initialization of the remote_file Application (continued)

```
      rpc_binding_vector_free(              /* free set of binding handles */
          &binding_vector,
          &status
      );
      CHECK_STATUS(status, "Can't free binding handles and vector\n", ABORT);
    ENDTRY
}
```

I

The Transfer_data Application

There are two clients for the *transfer_data* application. One sends a binary file of floating-point data from a client to a server. The other receives a binary file of floating-point data from a server. The *transfer_data* application demonstrates the following advanced features of DCE application development:

- Using input and output pipes

- Using the explicit binding method

- Using a customized binding handle and the associated bind and unbind procedures

How To Run the Application

To create a binary file of float data for the application, type the following:

```
C> make utility
C> float_util.exe write datafile
```

To run the local tests of the application, use the binary file of float data as a source file and a new data file as the target file. The host is not relevant for the local test. Type the following:

```
C> make local
C> local_client_send.exe source  host  target
C> local_client_receive.exe target  host  source
```

To run the server for the clients of the distributed application, type the following:

```
S> make server
S> t_server.exe
```

To run the clients of the distributed application, type the following:

```
C> make client
C> client_send.exe source   host   target
C> client_receive.exe target   host   source
```

Application Files

Makefile contains descriptions of how the application is compiled (see Example I-1).

float_util.c contains code that generates and writes a binary file of float data or reads a binary file of float data (see Example I-2).

transfer_data.idl contains the description of the constants, data types, and procedures for the interface (see Example I-3).

client_send.c demonstrates the use of a pipe that is an input parameter. The customized binding handle is initialized; the pipe structure is initialized for an input pipe; and the remote procedure *send_floats* is called to transfer pipe data to the server (see Example I-4).

client_receive.c demonstrates the use of a pipe that is an output parameter. The customized binding handle is initialized; the pipe structure is initialized for an output pipe; and the remote procedure *receive_floats* is called to transfer pipe data from the server to the client (see Example I-5).

binding.c contains the bind and unbind procedures that the client stub calls to obtain and free a binding handle. After the customized binding information is initialized in the client application, the binding is handled entirely by the client stub with these routines (see Example I-6).

send_floats.c contains the implementation of the *send_floats* remote procedure (see Example I-7).

receive_floats.c contains the implementation of the *receive_floats* remote procedure (see Example I-8).

t_server.c initializes the server with a series of runtime calls prior to servicing remote procedure calls. In this application, all protocol sequences available are registered. The server is not advertised in a name service database. Its dynamic endpoints are added to the server's local endpoint map. A client finds this server by constructing a string binding containing a protocol sequence and the host name or network address (see Example I-9).

pipe_state.h contains a structure with client file handle and file name members (see Example I-10).

client_alloc.c contains the *client_alloc* procedure that the client stub calls to allocate a buffer for pipe data (see Example I-11).

in_pull.c contains the *in_pull* procedure that the client stub calls to process input pipe data (see Example I-12).

out_push.c contains the *out_push* procedure that the client stub calls to process output pipe data (see Example I-13).

Example I-1: The Makefile for the transfer_data Application

```
# FILE NAME: Makefile
# Makefile for the customized handle and pipes application
#
# definitions for this make file
#
APPL=transfer_data
IDLCMD=idl -v
CHECK=../arithmetic       # Directory containing check_status.h
LIBS = -ldce -lpthreads -lc_r -lmach -lm        # DEC Alpha OSF/1
CFLAGS= -D_SHARED_LIBRARIES -Dalpha -D_REENTRANT # DEC Alpha OSF/1
CC= cc

#
# COMPLETE BUILD of the application
#
all:  utility local interface client server

#
# BUILD OF UTILITY to create and read files of float data
#
utility:    float_util
float_util: float_util.c
        $(CC) $(CFLAGS) -o float_util.exe float_util.c

#
# LOCAL BUILD of the clients to test locally.
#
local:interface  local_client_send  local_client_receive

local_client_send: client_send.c client_alloc.c in_pull.c \
                send_floats.c
        $(CC) $(CFLAGS) -DLOCAL -I. -o local_client_send.exe \
            client_send.c client_alloc.c in_pull.c send_floats.c
# remove object files so they do not interfere with a real build
        rm client_send.o send_floats.o client_alloc.o in_pull.o

local_client_receive:    client_receive.c client_alloc.c out_push.c \
                receive_floats.c
```

Example I-1: The Makefile for the transfer_data Application (continued)

```
        $(CC) $(CFLAGS) -DLOCAL -I. -o local_client_receive.exe \
            client_receive.c client_alloc.c out_push.c receive_floats.c
# remove object files so they do not interfere with a real build
        rm  client_receive.o receive_floats.o client_alloc.o out_push.o

#
# INTERFACE BUILD
#
interface:  $(APPL).h $(APPL)_cstub.o $(APPL)_sstub.o $(APPL)_saux.o
$(APPL).h $(APPL)_cstub.o $(APPL)_sstub.o $(APPL)_saux.o:      $(APPL).idl
        $(IDLCMD) $(APPL).idl

#
# CLIENT BUILDS
#
client:     client_send  client_receive
client_send: client_send.o client_alloc.o in_pull.o \
            binding.o do_string_binding.o $(APPL)_cstub.o
        $(CC) $(CFLAGS) -I$(CHECK) -o client_send.exe \
            client_send.o client_alloc.o in_pull.o \
            binding.o do_string_binding.o $(APPL)_cstub.o $(LIBS)

client_receive:    client_receive.o client_alloc.o out_push.o \
            binding.o do_string_binding.o $(APPL)_cstub.o
        $(CC) $(CFLAGS) -I$(CHECK) -o client_receive.exe \
            client_receive.o client_alloc.o out_push.o \
            binding.o do_string_binding.o $(APPL)_cstub.o $(LIBS)

#
# module needed by both clients
#
binding.o:  binding.c
        $(CC) $(CFLAGS) -I$(CHECK) -c binding.c

# module needed from remote_file application
do_string_binding.o:     ../remote_file/do_string_binding.c
        $(CC) $(CFLAGS) -I$(CHECK) -c ../remote_file/do_string_binding.c

#
# SERVER BUILD.  Notice the server stub auxiliary file is required.
#
server:     t_server
t_server:   $(APPL).h t_server.o send_floats.o receive_floats.o \
    $(APPL)_sstub.o $(APPL)_saux.o
        $(CC) $(CFLAGS) -I$(CHECK) -o t_server.exe t_server.o \
            send_floats.o receive_floats.o \
            $(APPL)_sstub.o $(APPL)_saux.o $(LIBS)

t_server.o: t_server.c
        $(CC) $(CFLAGS) -I$(CHECK) -c t_server.c
```

Example I-2: The Float File Generating Utility

```
/* FILE NAME: float_util.c */
/* utility to generate or read a file of float data to test pipes */
#include <stdio.h>
#include <string.h>
#include <sys/file.h>
void exit();
char *malloc();

main(argc, argv)
int argc;
char *argv[];
{
    char choice[20], filename[100];

    if(argc == 1)  {
        printf("Usage: %s [write | read] [filename]\n", argv[0]);
        puts("Enter w to create a file, r to read:");
        gets(choice);
    }
    else
        strcpy(choice, argv[1]);
    if(argc > 2)
        strcpy(filename, argv[2]);
    else
        strcpy(filename, "");

    if(choice[0] == 'w')
        write_floats(filename);
    else
        read_floats(filename);
}
write_floats(file)
char file[];
{
    char filename[100];
    int filehand;
    long num, i;
    float *buf, x;

    strcpy(filename, file);
    if(strlen(filename) == 0) {
        puts("enter name of data file to create");
        gets(filename);
    }
    filehand = open(filename, O_CREAT | O_TRUNC | O_WRONLY, 0777);
    if(filehand == 0) {
        fprintf(stderr, "Cannot open file %s for write\n", filename);
        exit(0);
    }
    puts("enter number of data items desired");
    fscanf(stdin, "%ld", &num);
    buf = (float *)malloc(sizeof(float) * num);
    for(i=0, x=1.1; i < num; i++, x+=0.4567) {  /* insert arbitrary numbers */
```

Example I-2: The Float File Generating Utility (continued)

```
        buf[i] = x;
        printf("%f\n", buf[i]);
    }
    write(filehand, (char *)buf, (int)(sizeof(float) * num) );
    close(filehand);
}


read_floats(file)
char file[];
{
    char filename[100];
    int filehand;
    long num, i, total, bytesread, numread;
    float *buf;

    strcpy(filename, file);
    if(strlen(filename) == 0) {
        puts("enter name of data file to read");
        gets(filename);
    }
    filehand = open(filename, O_RDONLY);
    if(filehand == 0) {
        fprintf(stderr, "Cannot open file %s for read", filename);
        exit(0);
    }
    num = 5; total = 0;
    buf = (float *)malloc(sizeof(float) * num);
    while((bytesread =
                read(filehand, (char *)buf, (int)(sizeof(float) * num) )) > 0) {
        numread = bytesread/sizeof(float);
        for(i=0; i < numread; i++)
            printf("%f  ", buf[i]);
        puts("");
        total+=numread;
    }
    printf("Total read: %ld\n", total);
    close(filehand);
}
```

Example I-3: The IDL File of the transfer_data Application

```
/* FILE NAME: transfer_data.idl */
[
uuid(A6876974-F555-11CA-BAE1-08002B245A28),
version(1.0)
]
interface transfer_data    /* data transfer to and from a remote system */
{
    const long NAME_LENGTH = 200;
```

Example I-3: The IDL File of the transfer_data Application (continued)

```
    typedef [handle] struct {         /* a customized handle type */
       char host[NAME_LENGTH+1];
       char filename[NAME_LENGTH+1];
    } file_spec;

    typedef pipe float pipe_type;     /* a pipe data type          */

void send_floats(        /* send pipe of floats to a file on the server */
    [in] file_spec cust_binding_h,    /* customized binding for server */
    [in] pipe_type data               /* input pipe of float data      */
);

void receive_floats(   /* get pipe of floats from a file on the server */
    [in] file_spec cust_binding_h,    /* customized binding for server */
    [out] pipe_type *data             /* output pipe of float data     */
);
}
```

Example I-4: A Client that Uses an Input Pipe

```
/* FILE NAME: client_send.c */
/* Client for customized handle and input pipe test */
#include <stdio.h>
#include "transfer_data.h"
#include "pipe_state.h"     /* definition of state structure for pipe data   */

main(argc, argv)
int argc;
char *argv[];
{
    file_spec   cust_binding_h;         /* customized binding handle  */
    pipe_state state;
    pipe_type  data;                    /* a pipe structure is allocated   */
    char       local_source[100];
               /* procedures in other modules */
    void       client_alloc(), in_pull();
    void       send_floats();

    /* get user input */
    if(argc < 4) {
       printf("USAGE: %s  local_source  host  file\n", argv[0]);
       exit(0);
    }
    /* initialize customized binding handle structure */
    strcpy(local_source, argv[1]);
    strcpy(cust_binding_h.host, argv[2]);
    strcpy(cust_binding_h.filename, argv[3]);

    /* initialize pipe structure */
    state.filehandle = -1;
```

407

Example I-4: A Client that Uses an Input Pipe (continued)

```
    state.filename = local_source;
    data.state = (rpc_ss_pipe_state_t)&state;      /* initialize pipe state    */
    data.alloc = client_alloc;    /* initialize alloc procedure for a pipe  */
    data.pull = in_pull;          /* Initialize pull procedure for input pipe  */

    send_floats(cust_binding_h, data);  /* remote procedure with input pipe    */
}
```

Example I-5: A Client that Uses an Output Pipe

```
/* FILE NAME: client_receive.c */
/* Client for customized handle and output pipe test */
#include <stdio.h>
#include "transfer_data.h"
#include "pipe_state.h"      /* definition of state structure for pipe data   */
main(argc, argv)
int argc;
char *argv[];
{
    file_spec  cust_binding_h;          /* customized binding handle  */
    pipe_state state;
    pipe_type  data;                    /* a pipe structure is allocated   */
    char       local_target[100];
               /* procedures in other modules */
    void       client_alloc(),out_push();
    void       receive_floats();

    /* get user input */
    if(argc < 4) {
       printf("USAGE: %s  local_target  host  file\n", argv[0]);
       exit(0);
    }
    /* initialize customized binding handle structure */
    strcpy(local_target, argv[1]);
    strcpy(cust_binding_h.host, argv[2]);
    strcpy(cust_binding_h.filename, argv[3]);

    /* initialize pipe structure */
    state.filehandle = -1;
    state.filename = local_target;
    data.state = (rpc_ss_pipe_state_t)&state;      /* initialize pipe state    */
    data.alloc = client_alloc;    /* initialize alloc procedure for a pipe  */
    data.push = out_push;       /* Initialize push procedure for output pipe  */

    receive_floats(cust_binding_h, &data);   /* procedure with output pipe    */
}
```

Example I-6: Bind and Unbind Procedures

```
/* FILE NAME: binding.c */
#include "transfer_data.h"    /* header created by the IDL compiler */
#include "check_status.h"     /* contains the CHECK_STATUS macro     */


handle_t file_spec_bind(spec)  /* "bind" procedure for customized handle   */
file_spec spec;
{
   rpc_binding_handle_t binding_h;

   if(do_string_binding(spec.host, &binding_h) < 0) {
      fprintf(stderr, "Cannot get binding\n");
      exit(1);
   }
   return(binding_h);
}

void file_spec_unbind(spec, binding_h) /* "unbind" for customized handle   */
file_spec spec;
handle_t binding_h;
{
   unsigned32 status;  /* error status */

   rpc_binding_free(&binding_h, &status);
   CHECK_STATUS(status, "Can't free binding handle:", RESUME);
   return;
}
```

Example I-7: The send_floats Procedure

```
/* FILE NAME: send_floats.c */
#include <stdio.h>
#include <sys/file.h>
#include "transfer_data.h"
#define MAX_ELEMENTS 1000

void send_floats(c_b_h, in_data) /* copy input data to a server file */
file_spec c_b_h;                 /* customized binding handle        */
pipe_type in_data;
{
   int            file_h;
   idl_short_float buf[MAX_ELEMENTS];       /* pipe data buffer           */
   idl_ulong_int  element_count;            /* number of elements pulled */
```

Example I-7: The send_floats Procedure (continued)

```
/* open local file on server for write */
file_h = open(c_b_h.filename, O_CREAT | O_TRUNC | O_WRONLY, 0777);
if(file_h < 0)      /* If can't open file, need to discard the pipe data */
    file_h = open("/dev/null", O_WRONLY);

while(true) {           /* entire pipe must be processed              */
    (in_data.pull)(     /* pull routine is used for an input pipe      */
        in_data.state,  /* state is controlled by the stub            */
        buf,            /* the buffer to be filled                    */
        MAX_ELEMENTS,   /* maximum number of data elements in buffer  */
        &element_count  /* actual number of elements in the buffer    */
    );
    if(element_count == 0) break;      /* 0 count signals pipe is empty  */
    /****          application specific process of buffer      ****   */
    write(file_h, buf, (sizeof(idl_short_float) * element_count));
}

close(file_h);
return;
}
```

Example I-8: The receive_floats Procedure

```
/* FILE NAME: receive_floats.c */
#include <stdio.h>
#include <sys/file.h>
#include "transfer_data.h"
#define MAX_ELEMENTS  1000

void receive_floats(c_b_h, out_data)   /* copy server file data to a client */
file_spec c_b_h;           /* customized binding handle */
pipe_type *out_data;
{
    int             file_h;
    idl_short_float buf[MAX_ELEMENTS];      /* pipe data buffer           */
    idl_ulong_int   element_count;          /* number of elements pushed */
    int             nbytes;

    /* open local file on server for read */
    file_h = open(c_b_h.filename, O_RDONLY);
    nbytes = sizeof(idl_short_float) * MAX_ELEMENTS;

    if(file_h > 0) {
        while(true) {
            /*****          application specific process of buffer      *****  */
            element_count = read(file_h, buf, nbytes) / sizeof(idl_short_float);
            if(element_count == 0) break;
```

Example I-8: The receive_floats Procedure (continued)

```
            out_data->push(     /* push routine is used for an output pipe   */
                out_data->state, /* the state is controlled by the stub       */
                buf,             /* the buffer of data to send                */
                element_count    /* the number of data elements to send       */
            );
        }
        close(file_h);
    }

    out_data->push(out_data->state, buf, 0);    /* 0 indicates end of pipe   */
    return;
}
```

Example I-9: Server Initialization of the transfer_data Application

```
/* FILE NAME: t_server.c */
#include <stdio.h>
#include "transfer_data.h"              /* header created by the idl compiler */
#include "check_status.h"               /* contains the CHECK_STATUS macro    */
main ()
{
    unsigned32              status;          /* error status (nbase.h)         */
    rpc_binding_vector_t    *binding_vector; /* binding handle list (rpcbase.h)*/

    rpc_server_register_if(         /* register interface with the RPC runtime */
        transfer_data_v1_0_s_ifspec, /* handle to interface specification      */
        NULL,
        NULL,
        &status                     /* error status */
    );
    CHECK_STATUS(status, "Can't register interface\n", ABORT);

    rpc_server_use_all_protseqs(            /* establish protocol sequences   */
        rpc_c_protseq_max_reqs_default,     /* queue length for remote calls */
        &status
    );
    CHECK_STATUS(status, "Can't establish protocol sequences\n", ABORT);

    rpc_server_inq_bindings(        /* get set of this server's binding handles */
        &binding_vector,
        &status
    );
    CHECK_STATUS(status, "Can't get binding handles\n", ABORT);
```

Example I-9: Server Initialization of the transfer_data Application (continued)

```
rpc_ep_register(                    /* add endpoint to local endpoint map */
    transfer_data_v1_0_s_ifspec,   /* handle to interface specification   */
    binding_vector,                /* vector of server binding handles    */
    NULL,                          /* no object UUIDs to register         */
    (unsigned_char_t *)"transfer_data server",        /* annotation */
    &status
);
CHECK_STATUS(status, "Can't add endpoints to local endpoint map:", ABORT);

puts("Listening for remote procedure calls...");
TRY
    rpc_server_listen(                     /* listen for remote calls    */
        rpc_c_listen_max_calls_default,    /* number of threads          */
        &status
    );
    CHECK_STATUS(status, "rpc listen failed:", RESUME);
FINALLY
    puts("Removing endpoints from local endpoint map.");
    rpc_ep_unregister(      /* remove endpoints from local endpoint map */
        transfer_data_v1_0_s_ifspec, /* handle to interface specification */
        binding_vector,              /* vector of server binding handles  */
        NULL,                        /* no object UUIDs to unregister     */
        &status
    );
    CHECK_STATUS(status,"Can't remove endpoints from endpoint map:",RESUME);

    rpc_binding_vector_free(            /* free set of binding handles */
        &binding_vector,
        &status
    );
    CHECK_STATUS(status, "Can't free binding handles and vector\n", ABORT);
ENDTRY
}
```

Example I-10: The pipe_state Structure

```
/* FILE NAME: pipe_state.h */
/* Definition of application-specific state structure of client pipe data.*/
typedef struct pipe_state {
    int  filehandle;         /* handle of client data file */
    char *filename;          /* name of client data file   */
} pipe_state;
```

Example I-11: The client_alloc Procedure

```
/* FILE NAME: client_alloc.c */
#include <stdio.h>
#include "transfer_data.h"
#include "pipe_state.h"
```

Example I-11: The client_alloc Procedure (continued)

```
#define BUFFER_SIZE 2000
idl_short_float client_buffer[BUFFER_SIZE];

void client_alloc(state, bsize, buf, bcount)    /* allocation for a pipe   */
pipe_state        *state;          /* coordinates pipe procedure calls  */
idl_ulong_int     bsize;           /* desired size of buffer in bytes   */
idl_short_float   **buf;           /* allocated buffer                  */
idl_ulong_int     *bcount;         /* allocated buffer size in bytes    */
{
    *buf = client_buffer;
    *bcount = BUFFER_SIZE;
    return;
}
```

Example I-12: The in_pull Procedure

```
/* FILE NAME: in_pull.c */
#include <stdio.h>
#include <sys/file.h>
#include "transfer_data.h"
#include "pipe_state.h"     /* definition of a state structure for pipe data */

void in_pull(state, buf, esize, ecount)/* input pipe uses a pull procedure  */
pipe_state        *state;          /* coordinates pipe procedure calls  */
idl_short_float   *buf;            /* buffer of data pulled             */
idl_ulong_int     esize;           /* maximum element count in buffer   */
idl_ulong_int     *ecount;         /* actual element count in buffer    */

{
    /* for this application, open local source file if not open already */
    if(state->filehandle == -1) {
        state->filehandle = open(state->filename, O_RDONLY);
        if(state->filehandle == -1) {
            fprintf(stderr, "Cannot open file %s for read\n", state->filename);
            exit(0);
        }
    }
    /* process buffer for your application */
    *ecount = read(state->filehandle, buf, (sizeof(float)*esize)) /
                sizeof(float);

    /* To signal the end of data, pull procedure must set the count to 0.   */
    if(*ecount == 0) {       /* end of data reached, do application cleanup  */
        close(state->filehandle);
    }
    return;
}
```

Example I-13: The out_push Procedure

```c
/* FILE NAME: out_push.c */
#include <stdio.h>
#include <sys/file.h>
#include "transfer_data.h"
#include "pipe_state.h"     /* definition of a state structure for pipe data */

void out_push(state, buf, ecount)  /* output pipe needs a push procedure   */
pipe_state      *state;         /* coordinates pipe procedure calls        */
idl_short_float *buf;           /* buffer of data pushed                   */
idl_ulong_int   ecount;         /* number of elements for buffer           */
{
    /* for this application, open local target file if not open already */
    if(state->filehandle == -1) {
        if(ecount <= 0)    /* if first buffer is empty, don't do anything */
            return;
        state->filehandle = open(state->filename,
                                 O_CREAT | O_TRUNC | O_WRONLY, 0777);
        if(state->filehandle == -1) {
            fprintf(stderr, "Cannot open file %s for write\n", state->filename);
            exit(0);
        }
    }
    /* To detect the end of data, push routine must test the count for 0.   */
    if(ecount == 0)                      /* do application specific cleanup */
        close(state->filehandle);
    else                                 /* process buffer for application  */
        write(state->filehandle, buf, (sizeof(float) * ecount));
    return;
}
```

Index

A

access control, 193
  list, 211, 225
  list manager, 225
ACF (Attribute Configuration File),
  automatic binding, 52
  binding handles, 56
  effect on application, 43
  error and exception control, 44
  error parameters, 74-76
  example, 44
  exception handling, 74
  explicit binding, 55-56
  for customizing interface usage,
    43-45
  implicit binding, 53
  purpose of, 43-45
  separating client and server out-
    put, 43
  specifying, 43
ACF attributes, 76, 268-270
  auto_handle, 43
  code, 45
  comm_status, 44
  enable_allocate, 268
  explicit_handle, 44, 56
  fault_status, 44
  heap, 268
  implicit_handle, 44, 53
  in_line, 45, 268
  nocode, 45

out_of_line, 45, 268
represent_as, 268
ACL (Access Control List) manager,
  225
advertising objects, 137-146, 181
  by name only, 138-140
advertising servers, 105-108, 151
  by object, 137-146
aliasing of pointers, 83
allocation memory, context handle,
  242
applications, advanced banking,
  347-373
  arithmetic, 3-24, 275-281;
    (see also arithmetic applica-
    tion.)
  banking, 143-191, 311-347;
    (see also banking application.)
  dryer parts database, 136
  grade server, 194-195, 225,
    375-388;
    (see also grade server applica-
    tion.)
  inventory, 28, 283-310;
    (see also inventory applica-
    tion.)
  producing, 20-22
  remote_file, 235, 389-399;
    (see also remote_file applica-
    tion.)
  running, 22-24
  transfer_data, 246, 401-414

C

About the Authors

John Shirley considers himself a scientist interested in educating himself and others on the use of software tools to analyze and present information. He has developed software and documentation while consulting for companies that include Digital Equipment Corporation, Concurrent Computer Corporation, Inset Systems, The National Association of Securities Dealers (NASDAQ), Tandem Computers, and the Open Software Foundation. John's work has included the development of C programs to demonstrate not only the use of DCE remote procedure calls but also multithreaded programming, an application interface for the GEM graphics environment, and storing scientific data.

John earned a B.A. from Alfred University with a dual major in mathematics and geology, an M.S. in geology from Miami University with a specialty in structural geology, and an M.S. in computer science from Pace University.

Prior to consulting, John's career included six years in the oil industry as a geophysicist and international explorationist. His work included the analysis of seismic data from New Zealand, Australia, Turkey, Norway, the Dominican Republic, Jamaica, and the United States. John also worked as a software engineer developing programs for scientific instrument manufacturers.

John lives in Newtown, Connecticut, where he maintains a consulting business specializing in documenting and demonstrating complex software.

Wei Hu was one of the original designers of DCE. At Digital, Wei was the project leader for the team that worked with HP to deliver DCE RPC to the Open Software Foundation. Wei's team developed the connection-oriented RPC protocols, authenticated RPC, and the name service interfaces to the DCE Cell Directory Service. Wei also worked with the OSF and the other DCE technology providers to integrate this software into DCE.

Prior to DCE, Wei worked on the VAX Security Kernel: a virtual machine operating system designed for the A1 rating (the highest security rating defined by the U.S. government). In addition to working on various aspects of the kernel, Wei invented a new approach for eliminating a class of security flaws that were previously thought intractable; he then led the team that implemented these safeguards.

Before joining Digital, Wei worked for 5 years at Honeywell Information Systems where he experienced first-hand the challenges involved in building heterogeneous distributed applications without the benefits of a DCE. Wei worked on a number of products including electronic mail, distributed calendars, and gateways.

Wei and his wife Irene practice growth through change. Within a six month period, they had a second child, started on this book, changed jobs, and moved across the country. They now live in Palo Alto, California. Wei is currently a Member of the Technical Staff at Silicon Graphics Computer Systems working on a project that will set the standard for the next-generation storage management system.

Wei received his bachelor's and master's degrees in electrical engineering and computer science from the Massachusetts Institute of Technology in Cambridge, Mass. In addition to this book, Wei has published numerous papers in distributed applications and computer security. He also holds four patents based on his work with the VAX Security Kernel and DCE.

David Magid was one of the original members of the Digital team that worked with Hewlett Packard to develop the RPC component of DCE. He wrote the RPC Application Programming Interface specification, designed the RPC Name Service Interface (NSI), and implemented portions of the NSI. With his collegues, David has a patent pending for a DCE namespace usage model.

Prior to working on DCE, David's projects at Digital included a prototype knowledgebase system, a data management system for large VAX design and verification, and an automated memories test system. Before joining Digital, David programmed scientific applications at the Woods Hole Oceanographic Institution.

He received a bachelor's degree with a dual major in geography/mathematics and a master's degree in environmental affairs from Clark University in Worcester, Mass.

David is an avid indoor and outdoor gardener, currently nurturing a new kind of sprout—a daughter, born in July 1993. He is married to a technical writer who's also a wonderful woman and mom. David also enjoys windsurfing and birdwatching and believes that a bad day gardening, windsurfing, or bird-watching is better than a good day at work.

Programming

UNIX, C and MULTI-PLATFORM

Books from O'Reilly & Associates, Inc.

Fall/Winter 1994-95

Fortran/Scientific Computing

Migrating to Fortran 90

By James F. Kerrigan
1st Edition November 1993
389 pages, ISBN 1-56592-049-X

Many Fortran programmers do not know where to start with Fortran 90. What is new about the language? How can it help them? How does a programmer with old habits learn new strategies?

This book is a practical guide to Fortran 90 for the current Fortran programmer. It provides a complete overview of the new features that Fortran 90 has brought to the Fortran standard, with examples and suggestions for use. The book discusses older ways of solving problems—both in FORTRAN 77 and in common tricks or extensions—and contrasts them with the new ways provided by Fortran 90.

The book has a practical focus, with the goal of getting the current Fortran programmer up to speed quickly. Two dozen examples of full programs are interspersed within the text, which includes over 4,000 lines of working code.

Topics include array sections, modules, file handling, allocatable arrays and pointers, and numeric precision. Two dozen examples of full programs are interspersed within the text, which includes over 4,000 lines of working code.

"This is a book that all Fortran programmers eager to take advantage of the excellent feature of Fortran 90 will want to have on their desk."
—*FORTRAN Journal*

High Performance Computing

By Kevin Dowd
1st Edition June 1993
398 pages, ISBN 1-56592-032-5

High Performance Computing makes sense of the newest generation of workstations for application programmers and purchasing managers. It covers everything, from the basics of modern workstation architecture, to structuring benchmarks, to squeezing more performance out of critical applications. It also explains what a good compiler can do—and what you have to do yourself. The book closes with a look at the high-performance future: parallel computers and the more "garden variety" shared memory processors that are appearing on people's desktops.

UNIX for FORTRAN Programmers

By Mike Loukides
1st Edition August 1990
264 pages, ISBN 0-937175-51-X

This handbook lowers the UNIX entry barrier by providing the serious scientific programmer with an introduction to the UNIX operating system and its tools. It familiarizes readers with the most important tools so they can be productive as quickly as possible. Assumes some knowledge of FORTRAN, none of UNIX or C.

C Programming Libraries

POSIX.4

By Bill Gallmeister
1st Edition Fall 1994 (est.)
400 pages (est.), ISBN 1-56592-074-0

A general introduction to real-time programming and real-time issues, this book covers the POSIX.4 standard and how to use it to solve "real-world" problems. If you're at all interested in real-time applications— which include just about everything from telemetry to transation processing—this book is for you. An essential reference.

POSIX Programmer's Guide

By Donald Lewine
1st Edition April 1991
640 pages, ISBN 0-937175-73-0

Most UNIX systems today are POSIX compliant because the Federal government requires it for its purchases. Given the manufacturer's documentation, however, it can be difficult to distinguish system-specific features from those features defined by POSIX. The *POSIX Programmer's Guide*, intended as an explanation of the POSIX standard and as a reference for the POSIX.1 programming library, helps you write more portable programs.

"If you are an intermediate to advanced C programmer and are interested in having your programs compile first time on anything from a Sun to a VMS system to an MSDOS system, then this book must be thoroughly recommended." —*Sun UK User*

Understanding and Using COFF

By Gintaras R. Gircys
1st Edition November 1988
196 pages, ISBN 0-937175-31-5

COFF—Common Object File Format—is the formal definition for the structure of machine code files in the UNIX System V environment. All machine code files are COFF files. This handbook explains COFF data structure and its manipulation.

Using C on the UNIX System

By Dave Curry
1st Edition January 1989
250 pages, ISBN 0-937175-23-4

This is the book for intermediate to experienced C programmers who want to become UNIX system programmers. It explains system calls and special library routines available on the UNIX system. It is impossible to write UNIX utilities of any sophistication without understanding the material in this book.

"A gem of a book.... The author's aim is to provide a guide to system programming, and he succeeds admirably. His balance is steady between System V and BSD-based systems, so readers come away knowing both." —*SUN Expert*

Practical C Programming

By Steve Oualline
2nd Edition January 1993
396 pages, ISBN 1-56592-035-X

C programming is more than just getting the syntax right. Style and debugging also play a tremendous part in creating programs that run well. *Practical C Programming* teaches you not only the mechanics of programming, but also how to create programs that are easy to read, maintain, and debug. There are lots of introductory C books, but this is the Nutshell Handbook®! In this edition, programs conform to ANSI C.

Programming with curses

By John Strang
1st Edition 1986
76 pages, ISBN 0-937175-02-1

Curses is a UNIX library of functions for controlling a terminal's display screen from a C program. This handbook helps you make use of the curses library. Describes the original Berkeley version of curses.

C Programming Tools

Software Portability with imake

By Paul DuBois
1st Edition July 1993
390 pages, ISBN 1-56592-055-4

imake is a utility that works with make to enable code to be compiled and installed on different UNIX machines. imake makes possible the wide portability of the X Window System code and is widely considered an X tool, but it's also useful for any software project that needs to be ported to many UNIX systems.

This Nutshell Handbook®—the only book available on imake—is ideal for X and UNIX programmers who want their software to be portable. The book is divided into two sections. The first section is a general explanation of imake, X configuration files, and how to write and debug an Imakefile. The second section describes how to write configuration files and presents a configuration file architecture that allows development of coexisting sets of configuration files. Several sample sets of configuration files are described and are available free over the Net.

Managing Projects with make

By Andrew Oram & Steve Talbott
2nd Edition October 1991
152 pages, ISBN 0-937175-90-0

make is one of UNIX's greatest contributions to software development, and this book is the clearest description of make ever written. It describes all the basic features of make and provides guidelines on meeting the needs of large, modern projects. Also contains a description of free products that contain major enhancements to make.

"I use make very frequently in my day to day work and thought I knew everything that I needed to know about it. After reading this book I realized that I was wrong! —Rob Henley, Siemens-Nixdorf

"If you can't pick up your system's yp Makefile, read every line, and make sense of it, you need this book." —Root Journal

Checking C Programs with lint

By Ian F. Darwin
1st Edition October 1988
84 pages, ISBN 0-937175-30-7

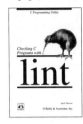

The lint program checker has proven time and again to be one of the best tools for finding portability problems and certain types of coding errors in C programs. lint verifies a program or program segments against standard libraries, checks the code for common portability errors, and tests the programming against some tried and true guidelines. Linting your code is a necessary (though not sufficient) step in writing clean, portable, effective programs. This book introduces you to lint, guides you through running it on your programs, and helps you interpret lint's output.

lex & yacc

By John Levine, Tony Mason & Doug Brown
2nd Edition October 1992
366 pages, ISBN 1-56592-000-7

Shows programmers how to use two UNIX utilities, lex and yacc, in program development. The second edition contains completely revised tutorial sections for novice users and reference sections for advanced users. This edition is twice the size of the first, has an expanded index, and now covers Bison and Flex.

Power Programming with RPC

By John Bloomer
1st Edition February 1992
522 pages, ISBN 0-937175-77-3

RPC, or remote procedure calling, is the ability to distribute the execution of functions on remote computers. Written from a programmer's perspective, this book shows what you can do with RPCs, like Sun RPC, the de facto standard on UNIX systems. It covers related programming topics for Sun and other UNIX systems and teaches through examples.

Guide to Writing DCE Applications

By John Shirley, Wei Hu & David Magid
2nd Edition May 1994
462 pages, ISBN 1-56592-045-7

A hands-on programming guide to OSF's Distributed Computing Environment (DCE) for first-time DCE application programmers. This book is designed to help new DCE users make the transition from conventional, non-distributed applications programming to distributed DCE programming. In addition to basic RPC (remote procedure calls), this edition covers object UUIDs and basic security (authentication and authorization). Also includes practical programming examples.

Distributing Applications Across DCE and Windows NT

By Ward Rosenberry & Jim Teague
1st Edition November 1993
302 pages, ISBN 1-56592-047-3

This book links together two exciting technologies in distributed computing by showing how to develop an application that simultaneously runs on DCE and Microsoft systems through remote procedure calls (RPC). Covers the writing of portable applications and the complete differences between RPC support in the two environments.

Understanding DCE

By Ward Rosenberry, David Kenney & Gerry Fisher
1st Edition October 1992
266 pages, ISBN 1-56592-005-8

A technical and conceptual overview of OSF's Distributed Computing Environment (DCE) for programmers, technical managers, and marketing and sales people. Unlike many O'Reilly & Associates books, Understanding DCE has no hands-on programming elements. Instead, the book focuses on how DCE can be used to accomplish typical programming tasks and provides explanations to help the reader understand all the parts of DCE.

Encyclopedia of Graphics File Formats

By James D. Murray & William vanRyper
1st Edition July 1994
928 pages (CD-ROM included), ISBN 1-56592-058-9

The computer graphics world is a veritable alphabet soup of acronyms; BMP, DXF, EPS, GIF, MPEG, PCX, PIC, RIFF, RTF, TGA, and TIFF are only a few of the many different formats in which graphics images can be stored. *The Encyclopedia of Graphics File Formats* is the definitive work on file formats—the book that will become a classic for graphics programmers and everyone else who deals with the low-level technical details of graphics files. It includes technical information on nearly 100 file formats, as well as chapters on graphics and file format basics, bitmap and vector files, metafiles, scene description, animation and multimedia formats, and file compression methods. Best of all, this book comes with a CD-ROM that collects many hard-to-find resources. We've assembled original vendor file format specification documents, along with test images and code examples, and a variety of software packages for MS-DOS, Windows, OS/2, UNIX, and the Macintosh that will let you convert, view, and manipulate graphics files and images.

Multi-Platform Code Management

By Kevin Jameson
1st Edition August 1994
354 pages (two diskettes included), ISBN 1-56592-059-7

For any programmer or team struggling with builds and maintenance, this book—and its accompanying software (available for fifteen platforms, including MS-DOS and various UNIX systems)—can save dozens of errors and hours of effort. A "one-stop-shopping" solution for code management problems, it shows you how to structure a large project and keep your files and builds under control over many releases and platforms. The building blocks are simple: common-sense strategies, public-domain tools that you can obtain on a variety of systems, and special utilities developed by the author. The book also includes two diskettes that provide a complete system for managing source files and builds.

Understanding Japanese Information Processing

By Ken Lunde
1st Edition September 1993
470 pages, ISBN 1-56592-043-0

Understanding Japanese Information Processing provides detailed information on all aspects of handling Japanese text on computer systems. It brings all of the relevant information together in a single book and covers everything from the origins of modern-day Japanese to the latest information on specific emerging computer encoding standards. Appendices provide additional reference material, such as a code conversion table, character set tables, mapping tables, an extensive list of software sources, a glossary, and more.

"Ken Lunde's book is an essential reference for everyone developing or adapting software for handling Japanese text. It is a goldmine of useful and relevant information on fonts, encoding systems and standards."
—Professor Jim Breen, Monash Univ., Australia

Business

Building a Successful Software Business

By Dave Radin
1st Edition April 1994
394 pages, ISBN 1-56592-064-3

This handbook is for the new software entrepreneur and the old hand alike. If you're thinking of starting a company around a program you've written—and there's no better time than the present—this book will guide you toward success. If you're an old hand in the software industry, it will help you sharpen your skills or will provide a refresher course. It covers the basics of product planning, marketing, customer support, finance, and operations.

"A marvelous guide through the complexities of marketing high-tech products. Its range of topics, and Radin's insights, make the book valuable to the novice marketeer as well as the seasoned veteran. It is the Swiss Army Knife of high-tech marketing."
—Jerry Keane, Universal Analytics Inc.

ORACLE Performance Tuning

By Peter Corrigan & Mark Gurry
1st Edition September 1993
642 pages, ISBN 1-56592-048-1

The ORACLE relational database management system is the most popular database system in use today. Organizations, ranging from government agencies to small businesses, from large financial institutions to universities, use ORACLE on computers as diverse as mainframes, minicomputers, workstations, PCs, and Macintoshes.

ORACLE offers tremendous power and flexibility, but at some cost. Demands for fast response, particularly in online transaction processing systems, make performance a major issue. With more organizations downsizing and adopting client-server and distributed database approaches, performance tuning has become all the more vital.

Whether you're a manager, a designer, a programmer, or an administrator, there's a lot you can do on your own to dramatically increase the performance of your existing ORACLE system. Whether you are running RDBMS Version 6 or Version 7, you may find that this book can save you the cost of a new machine; at the very least, it will save you a lot of headaches.

"This book is one of the best books on ORACLE that I have ever read.... [It] discloses many Oracle Tips that DBA's and Developers have locked in their brains and in their planners.... I recommend this book for any person who works with ORACLE, from managers to developers. In fact, I have to keep [it] under lock and key, because of the popularity of it."
—Mike Gangler

O'Reilly & Associates—
GLOBAL NETWORK NAVIGATOR

The Global Network Navigator (GNN)™ is a unique kind of information service that makes the Internet easy and enjoyable to use. We organize access to the vast information resources of the Internet so that you can find what you want. We also help you understand the Internet and the many ways you can explore it.

In GNN you'll find:

Navigating the Net with GNN

 The *Whole Internet Catalog* contains a descriptive listing of the most useful Net resources and services with live links to those resources.

The *GNN Business Pages* are where you'll learn about companies who have established a presence on the Internet and use its worldwide reach to help educate consumers.

The *Internet Help Desk* helps folks who are new to the Net orient themselves and gets them started on the road to Internet exploration.

News

NetNews is a weekly publication that reports on the news of the Internet, with weekly feature articles that focus on Internet trends and special events. The Sports, Weather, and Comix Pages round out the news.

Special Interest Publications

 Whether you're planning a trip or are just interested in reading about the journeys of others, you'll find that the *Travelers' Center* contains a rich collection of feature articles and ongoing columns about travel. In the *Travelers' Center*, you can link to many helpful and informative travel-related Internet resources.

 The *Personal Finance Center* is the place to go for information about money management and investment on the Internet. Whether you're an old pro at playing the market or are thinking about investing for the first time, you'll read articles and discover Internet resources that will help you to think of the Internet as a personal finance information tool.

All in all, GNN helps you get more value for the time you spend on the Internet.

 The Best of the Web

GNN received "Honorable Mention" for **"Best Overall Site," "Best Entertainment Service,"** and **"Most Important Service Concept."**

The *GNN NetNews* received "Honorable Mention" for **"Best Document Design."**

Subscribe Today

GNN is available over the Internet as a subscription service. To get complete information about subscribing to GNN, send email to **info@gnn.com**. If you have access to a World Wide Web browser such as Mosaic or Lynx, you can use the following URL to register online: http://gnn.com/

If you use a browser that does not support online forms, you can retrieve an email version of the registration form automatically by sending email to **form@gnn.com**. Fill this form out and send it back to us by email, and we will confirm your registration.

O'Reilly on the Net—
ONLINE PROGRAM GUIDE

O'Reilly & Associates offers extensive information through our online resources. If you've got Internet access, we invite you to come and explore our little neck-of-the-woods.

Online Resouce Center

Most comprehensive among our online offerings is the O'Reilly Resource Center. Here, you'll find detailed information and descriptions on all O'Reilly products: titles, prices, tables of contents, indexes, author bios, CD-ROM directory listings, reviews...you can even view images of the products themselves. We also supply helpful ordering information: how to contact us, how to order online, distributors and bookstores around the world, discounts, upgrades, etc. In addition, we provide informative literature in the field, featuring articles, interviews, bibliogrphies, and columns that help you stay informed and abreast.

 The Best of the Web

The *O'Reilly Resource Center* was voted "**Best Commercial Site**" by users participating in "Best of the Web '94."

To access ORA's Online Resource Center:

Point your Web browser (e.g., **mosaic** or **lynx**) to:
`http://gnn.com/ora/`

For the plaintext version, **telnet** or **gopher** to:
`gopher.ora.com`
(telnetters login: `gopher`)

FTP

The example files and programs in many of our books are available electronically via FTP.

To obtain example files and programs from O'Reilly texts:

`ftp` to:
`ftp.uu.net`
`cd published/oreilly`
or
`ftp.ora.com`

Ora-news

An easy way to stay informed of the latest projects and products from O'Reilly & Associates is to subscribe to "ora-news," our electronic news service. Subscribers receive email as soon as the information breaks.

To subscribe to "ora-news":

Send email to:
listproc@online.ora.com

and put the following information on the first line of your message (not in "Subject"):
subscribe ora-news "your name" of "your company"

For example:
subscribe ora-news Jim Dandy of Mighty Fine Enterprises

Email

Many other helpful customer services are provided via email. Here's a few of the most popular and useful.

Useful email addresses

nuts@ora.com
For general questions and information.

bookquestions@ora.com
For technical questions, or corrections, concerning book contents.

order@ora.com
To order books online and for ordering questions.

catalog@ora.com
To receive a free copy of our magazine/catalog, "ora.com" (please include a snailmail address).

Snailmail and phones

O'Reilly & Associates, Inc.
103A Morris Street, Sebastopol, CA 95472
Inquiries: **707-829-0515, 800-998-9938**
Credit card orders: **800-889-8969**
FAX: **707-829-0104**

O'Reilly & Associates—
LISTING OF TITLES

INTERNET

!%@:: A Directory of Electronic Mail
   Addressing & Networks
Connecting to the Internet:
   An O'Reilly Buyer's Guide
Internet In A Box
MH & xmh: E-mail for Users & Programmers
The Mosaic Handbook for Microsoft Windows
The Mosaic Handbook for the Macintosh
The Mosaic Handbook for the
   X Window System
Smileys
The Whole Internet User's Guide & Catalog

SYSTEM ADMINISTRATION

Computer Security Basics
DNS and BIND
Essential System Administration
Linux Network Administrator's Guide
   (Fall 94 est.)
Managing Internet Information Services
   (Fall 94 est.)
Managing NFS and NIS
Managing UUCP and Usenet
sendmail
Practical UNIX Security
PGP: Pretty Good Privacy (Winter 94/95 est.)
System Performance Tuning
TCP/IP Network Administration
termcap & terminfo
X Window System Administrator's Guide:
   Volume 8
X Window System, R6, Companion CD
   (Fall 94 est.)

USING UNIX AND X

BASICS

Learning GNU Emacs
Learning the Korn Shell
Learning the UNIX Operating System
Learning the vi Editor
SCO UNIX in a Nutshell
The USENET Handbook (Winter 94/95 est.)
Using UUCP and Usenet
UNIX in a Nutshell: System V Edition
The X Window System in a Nutshell
X Window System User's Guide: Volume 3
X Window System User's Guide, Motif Ed.:
   Volume 3M
X User Tools (10/94 est.)

ADVANCED

Exploring Expect (Winter 94/95 est.)
The Frame Handbook (10/94 est.)
Making TeX Work
Learning Perl
Programming perl
sed & awk
UNIX Power Tools (with CD-ROM)

PROGRAMMING UNIX, C, AND MULTI-PLATFORM

FORTRAN/SCIENTIFIC COMPUTING

High Performance Computing
Migrating to Fortran 90
UNIX for FORTRAN Programmers

C PROGRAMMING LIBRARIES

Practical C Programming
POSIX Programmer's Guide
POSIX.4: Programming for the Real World
   (Fall 94 est.)
Programming with curses
Understanding and Using COFF
Using C on the UNIX System

C PROGRAMMING TOOLS

Checking C Programs with lint
lex & yacc
Managing Projects with make
Power Programming with RPC
Software Portability with imake

MULTI-PLATFORM PROGRAMMING

Encyclopedia of Graphics File Formats
Distributing Applications Across DCE and
   Windows NT
Guide to Writing DCE Applications
Multi-Platform Code Management
Understanding DCE
Understanding Japanese Information
   Processing
ORACLE Performance Tuning

BERKELEY 4.4 SOFTWARE DISTRIBUTION

4.4BSD System Manager's Manual
4.4BSD User's Reference Manual
4.4BSD User's Supplementary Documents
4.4BSD Programmer's Reference Manual
4.4BSD Programmer's Supplementary
   Documents
4.4BSD-Lite CD Companion
4.4BSD-Lite CD Companion:
   International Version

X PROGRAMMING

Motif Programming Manual: Volume 6A
Motif Reference Manual: Volume 6B
Motif Tools
PEXlib Programming Manual
PEXlib Reference Manual
PHIGS Programming Manual
   (soft or hard cover)
PHIGS Reference Manual
Programmer's Supplement for R6
   (Winter 94/95 est.)
Xlib Programming Manual: Volume 1
Xlib Reference Manual: Volume 2
X Protocol Reference Manual, R5: Vol. 0
X Protocol Reference Manual, R6: Vol. 0
   (11/94 est.)
X Toolkit Intrinsics Programming Manual:
   Volume 4
X Toolkit Intrinsics Programming Manual,
   Motif Edition: Volume 4M
X Toolkit Intrinsics Reference Manual: Vol.5
XView Programming Manual: Volume 7A
XView Reference Manual: Volume 7B

THE X RESOURCE

A QUARTERLY WORKING JOURNAL FOR X PROGRAMMERS

The X Resource: Issues 0 through 12
   (Issue 12 available 10/94)

BUSINESS/CAREER

Building a Successful Software Business
Love Your Job!

TRAVEL

Travelers' Tales Thailand
Travelers' Tales Mexico
Travelers' Tales India (Winter 94/95 est.)

AUDIOTAPES

INTERNET TALK RADIO'S "GEEK OF THE WEEK" INTERVIEWS

The Future of the Internet Protocol, 4 hrs.
Global Network Operations, 2 hours
Mobile IP Networking, 1 hour
Networked Information and
   Online Libraries, 1 hour
Security and Networks, 1 hour
European Networking, 1 hour

NOTABLE SPEECHES OF THE INFORMATION AGE

John Perry Barlow, 1.5 hours

O'Reilly & Associates—
INTERNATIONAL DISTRIBUTORS

Customers outside North America can now order O'Reilly & Associates books through the following distributors. They offer our international customers faster order processing, more bookstores, increased representation at tradeshows worldwide, and the high quality, responsive service our customers have come to expect.

EUROPE, MIDDLE EAST, AND AFRICA
(except Germany, Switzerland, and Austria)

INQUIRIES
International Thomson Publishing Europe
Berkshire House
168-173 High Holborn
London WC1V 7AA
United Kingdom
Telephone: 44-71-497-1422
Fax: 44-71-497-1426
Email: ora.orders@itpuk.co.uk

ORDERS
International Thomson Publishing Services, Ltd.
Cheriton House, North Way
Andover, Hampshire SP10 5BE
United Kingdom
Telephone: 44-264-342-832 (UK orders)
Telephone: 44-264-342-806 (outside UK)
Fax: 44-264-364418 (UK orders)
Fax: 44-264-342761 (outside UK)

GERMANY, SWITZERLAND, AND AUSTRIA
International Thomson Publishing GmbH
O'Reilly-International Thomson Verlag
Attn: Mr. G. Miske
Königswinterer Strasse 418
53227 Bonn
Germany
Telephone: 49-228-970240
Fax: 49-228-441342
Email: gerd@orade.ora.com

ASIA
(except Japan)

INQUIRIES
International Thomson Publishing Asia
221 Henderson Road
#05 10 Henderson Building
Singapore 0315
Telephone: 65-272-6496
Fax: 65-272-6498

ORDERS
Telephone: 65-268-7867
Fax: 65-268-6727

AUSTRALIA
WoodsLane Pty. Ltd.
Unit 8, 101 Darley Street (P.O. Box 935)
Mona Vale NSW 2103
Australia
Telephone: 61-2-979-5944
Fax: 61-2-997-3348
Email: woods@tmx.mhs.oz.au

NEW ZEALAND
WoodsLane New Zealand Ltd.
21 Cooks Street (P.O. Box 575)
Wanganui, New Zealand
Telephone: 64-6-347-6543
Fax: 64-6-345-4840
Email: woods@tmx.mhs.oz.au

THE AMERICAS, JAPAN, AND OCEANIA
O'Reilly & Associates, Inc.
103A Morris Street
Sebastopol, CA 95472 U.S.A.
Telephone: 707-829-0515
Telephone: 800-998-9938 (U.S. & Canada)
Fax: 707-829-0104
Email: order@ora.com